MAKING AND IMPLEMENTING PUBLIC POLIC .

MAKING AND IMPLEMENTING PUBLIC POLICY

KEY CONCEPTS AND ISSUES

CATHERINE BOCHEL AND HUGH BOCHEL

palgrave

First published 2018 by
PALGRAVE

Palgrave in the UK is an imprint of Macmillan Publishers Limited, registered in England, company number 785998, of 4 Crinan Street, London, N1 9XW.

Palgrave® and Macmillan® are registered trademarks in the United States, the United Kingdom, Europe and other countries.

ISBN 978–1–137–48464–2 paperback

This book is printed on paper suitable for recycling and made from fully managed and sustained forest sources. Logging, pulping and manufacturing processes are expected to conform to the environmental regulations of the country of origin.

A catalogue record for this book is available from the British Library.

A catalog record for this book is available from the Library of Congress.

CONTENTS

LIST OF TABLES, FIGURES & BOXES

PREFACE

This book reflects our longstanding teaching and research interests, and perhaps, in particular, a concern with how inequalities in and the exercise of power in policy making and implementation lead to particular policies and outcomes, while others are excluded. It also reflects the very significant developments in studies of public policy over the past two decades, in both empirical and theoretical work, as well as the impact of policy approaches of a variety of governments. We have sought here to describe and apply ideas associated with some of the main contemporary debates over the making and implementation of public policy in order to help explain and understand the policy process using different conceptual frameworks. In particular, we would hope that readers will consider how and to what extent the exercise of power both reflects and contributes to other inequalities in contemporary society.

Although this work is our responsibility, we are grateful to four anonymous reviewers for their comments and suggestions, which helped improve both the contents and the quality of the book. We would also like to recognise the many students who, over the years, have contributed to our thoughts on these topics, and whose work has, at times, helped inform our ideas.

Finally, we are grateful to the editors at Palgrave Macmillan, Helen Caunce, who was involved in the initial development of the book, and subsequently Peter Hooper, as well as Rita Ondarra Capdevila, who also provided significant assistance in the run-up to the book's delivery.

Catherine Bochel and Hugh Bochel
University of Lincoln

ACKNOWLEDGEMENTS

The authors and publishers wish to thank the following for permission to reproduce copyright material:

Coleman, A., Segar, J. and Checkland, K. (2016) 'The Devolution Project in Greater Manchester: Introduction to the Special Issue', *Representation*, 51(4), 377–384, p. 380, reproduced with the permission of Taylor & Francis, on behalf of the McDougall Trust, London;

Crown copyright information is reproduced with the permission of the Controller of HMSO and the Queen's Printer for Scotland;

Freeguard, G., Andrews, E., Devine, D., Munro, R. and Randall, J. (2015) *Whitehall Monitor 2015: The Coalition in 163 charts*, London: Institute for Government, p. 11, reproduced with permission of the Institute for Government;

Gash, T., Magee, I., Rutter, J. and Smith, N. (2010) *Read Before Burning: Arm's Length Government for a New Administration*, London: Institute for Government, p. 22, reproduced with permission of the Institute for Government;

Greener, I. (2013) *Public Management*, Basingstoke: Palgrave Macmillan, p. 69, reproduced with permission of Palgrave Macmillan;

Wilson, D. and Game, C. (2011) *Local Government in the United Kingdom*, Basingstoke: Palgrave Macmillan, p. 338, reproduced with permission of Palgrave Macmillan;

the book contains parliamentary information licensed under the Open Parliament Licence v3.0;

the book contains public sector information licensed under the Open Government Licence v3.0.

Every effort has been made to trace the copyright holders, but if any have been inadvertently overlooked the publishers will be pleased to make the necessary arrangement at the first opportunity.

1

Public Policy and Policy Analysis

This chapter discusses the meanings and scope of public policy and the ways in which the term is used in this book. It considers the development of interest in policy analysis and the uses to which it can be put. The chapter outlines the importance of power and the ways in which it can be exercised. It then considers different approaches to analysing the policy process, including those that consider 'stages' and those grounded in more dynamic perspectives.

The chapter concludes with a brief consideration of important themes and developments under governments since 1979, including the ongoing influence of neo-liberal thinking, changes such as the introduction of the devolved legislatures, and the referendum decision in 2016 to leave the EU, with significant implications for the policy process across all tiers of government.

The study of the making and implementation of public policy is interdisciplinary in nature, drawing upon subjects such as politics, sociology, economics and history, and indeed many others. It is also dynamic and constantly changing, both with respect to the world that we seek to understand, and the concepts, models and methods that we have available to assist us.

While the subject matter covered by this book is wide-ranging, including both theoretical perspectives on and real-world examples of public policy, at its heart might be said to lie a consideration of the exercise of power, and, in particular, who has it (and who does not) and how it is used and applied in the public policy arena. Public policy making is obviously, at least to some extent, about responding to problems. But, equally obviously, public policy responds to problems in many ways, with different aims and different outcomes. The book therefore examines the processes by which public policies are formulated, implemented and evaluated. This includes outlining and applying models of agenda setting and decision making, the variety of actors in the policy process, including politicians, bureaucrats and managers, and considering the operation of different levels of government, including supra-national, central and local government, the tools that they use, and how policies are evaluated and those assessments fed back into policy making. The focus is not simply on who makes decisions, but on a broader concern with the entire policy process. In addition, the book seeks to go slightly beyond the common focus of much of the literature, the 'how' element of Lasswell's (1936/1858) 'who gets what, when, how', to argue that the 'how' significantly influences the 'who', 'what' and 'when', and to explore this in the context of public policy in the United Kingdom in particular, while recognising that both ideas and policies are subject to international, and indeed global, influence.

The book is designed to present a broad approach to the topic, drawing on a wide range of concepts and models that can help us to contextualise, understand, explain and evaluate developments from a perspective that encourages us to consider how power is exercised in contemporary society, and by whom. It also highlights the fundamental point that there are important inter-relationships between many of the ideas and structures discussed in the separate chapters, so that, for example, many of the ideas outlined in the later chapters may be better understood by utilising those from the earlier chapters. The book is also intended to support the analysis of case study material, with the reader applying particular ideas as appropriate to develop their own understanding and interpretation of particular issues. The remainder of this chapter therefore outlines some key debates about the nature of public policy and the study of the topic, as well as developments under governments since 1979, while the subsequent chapters consider concepts, ideas, models and structures in greater depth.

Why look at public policy?

Until the mid-nineteenth century, the role of the state was relatively limited, focused largely on diplomacy and warfare, and the raising of finances with which to pay for them, through borrowing and taxation. However, over time, governments began to be increasingly involved in setting frameworks for developments in the economy, transport and urban planning, and, particularly from the mid-twentieth century, in the direct provision of services, such as education, health care and pensions. Indeed, the post-war period saw a broad acceptance of a greater role for the state in responding to a range of 'problems', although from the 1980s state involvement has been 'rolled back', at least to some extent and in some areas. The effects of public policies continually surround us, not just in terms of services provided by the public sector, but also in setting the framework for and regulating private activities, such as private health care and education, as well as planning, transport and much economic activity, including employment laws and banking, for example. However, in many respects the world appears more complex and uncertain than it once did. Challenges such as global warming, migration, ageing populations and terrorism create problems to which we often expect governments to respond, at a time when the abilities of governments to do so perhaps appear more limited than they once did. Understanding the scope and options for public policy is therefore significant on an individual, state and global basis. However, in order to achieve that, it is helpful to consider in rather more depth what constitutes 'public policy'.

What is policy and what makes it public?

There is no clear consensus on what constitutes 'policy'. It has been described as 'whatever governments choose to do or not to do', and as 'a course of action or inaction rather than specific decisions' (Dye, 1984, p. 1). Birkland (2011) defines a policy 'as a statement by government – at whatever level – of what it intends to do about a public problem' (p. 9), although he recognises that it may also be what a government chooses not to do, while Anderson (1997) suggests that conceptualising policy through an emphasis on actions, rather than intentions, is useful, and that such an approach helps to differentiate between decisions, following which there may be no action, and policy. This suggests that a deliberate decision to do something, or indeed not to do something, is policy, reflecting the arguments of those writers who argue that ideas such as 'non-decisions' or the 'mobilisation of bias' need to be taken more into account (as discussed further in Chapter 3). Others, such as Easton (1953 and 1965) and Jenkins (1978, p. 15), suggest that while policy may sometimes involve one decision, more often 'it involves a course of action or a web of decisions' (see also Hill, 2009, pp. 15–16), and that this encourages us to understand policy making as a dynamic process, and to recognise a government's capacity to act, and the limitations on it, such as resource constraints or the opposition of particular interests.

In terms of what makes something 'public', most commentators emphasise that it involves some sort of specific social issue or problem, rather than a problem facing an individual or even individuals, although clearly something that is experienced by many individuals may become a public problem, and that it involves a response by a public agency. Public policies therefore refer to actions or inactions of public actors, although in many instances other actors are likely to be involved in influencing decision making or implementing policies, a situation that has arguably grown as many governments have sought to shift what had been governmental functions to other bodies. However, contemporary writers generally continue to take a position broadly in line with that of

Howlett *et al.* (2009) that '[g]overnments enjoy a special role in public policy making due to their unique ability to make *authoritative* decisions on behalf of citizens ... Hence, when we talk about public policies we are always talking about initiatives sanctioned by governments' (p. 5). Knoepfel *et al.* (2011) identify eight constituent elements of a public policy that help highlight these factors, seeing it as characterised by:

1. a solution to a public problem – a policy aims to resolve a social problem that is politically acknowledged as public;

2. the existence of target groups that should be able to resolve the problem by changing their behaviour;

3. intentional coherence, with decisions and actions connected in the attempt to resolve the problem;

4. the existence of several decisions and activities, rather than a single or specific decision;

5. an intervention programme, so that the decisions and actions are to some extent concrete and specific;

6. a key role for public actors – in order to be considered as public policy;

7. the existence of formalised measures and a concrete implementation phase, so that this view is normally different from those that see non-decisions as constituting a policy;

8. decisions and activities that impose constraints or incentives.

Governments may decide to introduce policies for a variety of reasons. Peters (2015), for example, suggests that market failure and social failure are important reasons for the public sector intervening in the economy and society, while recognising that different ideological perspectives will give different positions on such issues. There can be a number of types of market failure, such as: public goods that cannot be priced and marketed, for example clean air or national defence, where provision by governments and payment through taxation are likely to be appropriate; a lack of information, especially for buyers, so that markets do not work effectively; monopoly or near monopoly situations, as with many public utilities, where there may be a preference for a regulated market; externalities can also be a problem, with Peters using the example of pollution, where the social costs, such as health problems and lower property values, are not reflected in the price of goods that cause pollution; and, perhaps more ideologically controversial, economic inequality arising from the workings of the market, where high levels of inequality may be seen by some as unacceptable, although others may disagree and even argue that they provide incentives to work and invest. Failures in society, such as crime, poverty and family breakdown, are often highly politicised, and tend to be seen by those on the left as significantly influenced by the poor functioning of markets and a failure of governments to intervene appropriately, while those on the right are more likely to identify the problem as failures of individuals and families, and indeed what they may see as excessive and inappropriate intervention by governments. Similarly, those on the left tend to be much more willing to identify reasons for action, while those on the right tend to argue that the state should intervene only in exceptional circumstances.

Policy making is likely to involve conflict, although it may not necessarily do so, with decisions being made from a number of alternative options, and this involves the exercise of power, which will reflect the power relationships within society. Importantly for this book, and the consideration of inequalities in terms of power and policy outcomes, considerable areas of government activity from the mid-twentieth century have been around social policies, and in that regard it has been argued, for example, that '[s]ocial policy uses political power to supersede, supplement or modify operations of the economic system in order to achieve results which the economic system could not achieve on its own' (Marshall, 1975, p. 15). This quotation highlights that for much of the period from 1945 it was seen by many as appropriate to use political power to intervene in the workings of the market, and to a greater or lesser extent to seek to redistribute wealth (and opportunities) from richer to poorer members of society. However, as discussed elsewhere in this book, such approaches have become much less widely used since the 1980s, although more recently increasing attention has also been paid to the actual or potential distributional outcomes of a wide range of policies, including in relation to transport, the economy, and income and wealth.

Peters (2015) identifies a number of characteristics that can be considered in relation to policy problems, including: the extent to which they fall within or across boundaries (such as functional, geographical and sector); the extent to which they require the creation of public goods, or a balance of public and private goods; scale, with large-scale problems, for example, potentially making coherent decisions difficult; solubility, the extent to which a problem can be ameliorated, or even solved; complexity, in both technical and political senses; certainty and risk, with some problems being fairly predictable, while many have considerable uncertainty, and assessment of the level of risk from particular actions or inactions; difficult (or 'tragic' (Brown, 2007)) choices, where whatever is done in a given situation will be from at least one perspective seen as acting wrongly; and the extent to which problems can be addressed with money, or require other types of response (Peters, 2015).

In recent years, considerable attention has been paid to the idea of 'wicked problems', originally outlined by Rittel and Webber (1973). Although initially applied to planning theory, and to urban and social problems, the concept has become more widely used in relation to complex and stubborn problems. Peters (2015) identifies several criteria that can be used to characterise wicked problems:

1. they are hard to define – it is not easy to say exactly what the problem is;

2. the problems are multi-causal and have many interconnections;

3. they are therefore often unstable, with small changes in one possible cause producing large-scale effects;

4. they have no clear solution, and sometimes not even a set of possible solutions;

5. because the solutions are unclear, any intervention may have unforeseen consequences;

6. they involve multiple actors and are socially complex.

Indeed, some writers have gone further and argued that there are 'super wicked' problems, which have four additional characteristics (Levin *et al.*, 2012; Peters, 2015):

1. time is running out;

2. there is no central authority, or only a weak central authority to manage the problem;

3. the same actors seeking to solve the problem are also contributing to it;

4. the future is discounted rapidly so that contemporary solutions become less valuable.

These ideas around super wicked problems are clearly linked to contemporary issues such as climate change, but would also be applicable to topics such as economic issues and migration, or even so-called 'troubled families' (for example, Hayden and Jenkins, 2014), which produce severe challenges and which lack an entity that can make decisions to solve, or even ameliorate, the problem.

It is also important to be aware that both policies and definitions clearly change over time. For example, national security, while still concerned to some extent with the threat of armed warfare with other nation states, also involves challenges such as cyber threats from both nation states and other groups, and terrorism, while others argue that a much broader definition is necessary to account for other potential risks, such as those arising from environmental change or from economic challenges. Similarly, there may be some periods when policies seek to encourage an activity, while in others they may deter it, as with immigration, for example, which might at some times be promoted to meet perceived needs in the economy, and at others be discouraged, including for political or social reasons.

In addition, policies are not independent of each other. Most 'new' policies involve changes to existing policies, and they will impact upon and be affected by other policies, so that the introduction of a cap on the level of benefits that individuals and families can receive might be expected to have implications for homelessness. Policies are also likely to lead to some individuals or groups making gains, financial or other, while some individuals and groups may lose out. For example, decisions by governments to raise funds by indirect taxes, such as VAT or stamp duty, rather than direct taxes, such as income tax, are often thought to have a proportionately bigger impact upon those with lower incomes, as non-discretionary items tend to make up a larger proportion of their budgets, and even that inequality can affect economic growth, although the evidence on these is not necessarily entirely clear-cut (for example, OECD, 2015; Office for National Statistics, 2016c).

It is perhaps unsurprising that while it is possible to produce definitions of policy, and indeed public policy, as outlined above, the terms continue to be used in a variety of ways, in different contexts and by different groups of users. Levin (1997), for example, drew attention to such differences, including between politicians, who he suggested generally used the term 'to denote a proposal or set of proposals carrying commitment to future action' (p. 20), and academics who 'set out to define "policy" rather than investigate how politicians and officials use the term' (p. 23). Indeed, Hogwood and Gunn (1984) identified 10 uses of 'policy', as:

1. a label for a field of activity – as used, for example, in broad statements about 'economic policy' or 'social policy', as well as applied to more specific areas such as pensions policy, education policy, transport policy, health policy or housing policy;

2. an expression of general purpose or desired state of affairs – such as the statement in Labour's 1997 election manifesto that '[a]n explicit objective of a Labour government will be to raise the trend rate of growth by strengthening our wealth-creating base. We will nurture investment in industry, skills, infrastructure and new technologies. And we will attack long-term unemployment, especially among young people. Our goal will be educational and employment opportunities for all' (Labour Party, 1997, p. 11);

3. specific proposals, so that, for example, in its 2015 manifesto, *Strong Leadership, A Clear Economic Plan, A Brighter, More Secure Future*, the Conservative Party undertook to 'take the family home out of Inheritance Tax for all but the richest by raising the effective threshold for married couples and civil partners to £1 million' (Conservative Party, 2015, p. 65). Other specific proposals may arise out of short-term or *ad hoc* problems or opportunities, such as the pressures on hospital beds that sometimes occur in the winter months, significant natural events, such as large-scale flooding, or acts of terrorism, with governments feeling obliged to respond in some manner;

4. decisions of government – these may frequently be more immediate responses to domestic or international challenges or opportunities, such as the Coalition government's decision to make major changes to the running of the NHS in England through the Health and Social Care Act 2012, which had not been foreshadowed in a general election manifesto;

5. formal authorisation, perhaps reflected in a specific piece of legislation. In the UK, governments can generally be fairly sure about getting formal ratification for legislation through Parliament because of their overall majorities in the House of Commons, and these are widely seen as one form of 'policy'. However, the passage of an Act does not ensure that the activities will then take place. For example, a parliamentary question in 2010 revealed that about 150 sections or schedules of acts passed between 1997 and 2010 had not at that point been implemented (http://www.publications. parliament.uk/pa/ld201011/ldhansrd/text/100614w0003. htm#1006144000778);

6. a programme – a relatively specific sphere of government activity, such as the 'academies programme', designed to encourage schools in England to take academy status, rather than remaining under local authority control, or the programme of the 2015 Conservative government that aimed to increase the supply of affordable housing;

7. output – what government delivers – which may be varied in nature, such as payment of social security benefits, reductions in school class sizes, or increases or cuts in taxation;

8. outcome – what is achieved – the study of which, while the distinction may often be hard to make, involves an assessment of whether the policy is achieving its stated aims, as opposed to a focus on what is actually delivered;

9. a theory or model – as policies involve assumptions about cause and effect. In 1979, in the new Conservative government's first budget, the then Chancellor of the Exchequer, Geoffrey Howe, argued that '[p]ublic expenditure is at the heart of Britain's present economic difficulties' (HM Treasury, 1979, p. 1), with the assumption clearly being that reductions in public expenditure would improve the country's economic performance. Similarly, it may be claimed that being 'tough on crime' through the use of harsher penalties will lead to a reduction in crime, or that reducing the level of social security benefits will increase incentives for people to find work. All of these statements are clearly based on the assumption that if governments do one thing, then another will happen. Yet, in practice, the causal relationships are generally more complex than this, and other factors have a major impact on the success or failure of policy (see, for example, Chapter 8);

10. a process – as policy making and implementation is a continuous process, it cannot easily be analysed through the examination of specific decisions, and the introduction of one policy may itself have implications for others. Those who study public policy need to be aware of this and to take account of the complex and longitudinal nature of the process. Indeed, any given 'policy' may draw upon a variety of motivations, goals and instruments. For example, during its passage through parliament the Academies Act 2010 was related by ministers to improving educational performance in England, giving greater freedom to schools and teachers, and increasing the ability of new organisations to establish new schools. Yet they also emphasised that the Act was permissive (so that schools could convert to academies, but were not required to), and that it was part of a wider group of policies that would help to achieve the desired outcomes. Opponents of the Act would probably identify other motivations and goals behind it. Clearly, in this case, as in many others, seeking to identify what the 'problem' and the proposed 'solution' are is far from straightforward.

From this discussion, an important lesson is, therefore, that rather than attempting to identify one 'true' definition, we should accept that the term 'policy' will be used in a variety of senses which may not be mutually exclusive, and that as students of public policy we need to be aware of those and take them into account in our explorations and analyses. Indeed, much of the discussion in this book reflects different approaches to the understanding and analysis of policy in its different guises, and may itself contribute to and alter our understanding of the concept.

Figure 1.1 A stages model of the policy process

What is the policy process?

In the past, the policy process was frequently depicted as consisting of a number of stages, such as problem definition, formulation, implementation and evaluation (see Figure 1.1 for another stages model). Today, however, it is more likely to be seen as a continual, iterative process, which is unlikely to be ordered in a sequential fashion, while some stages, such as evaluation, may never exist for some policies, and others may be continually considered (Colebatch, 2002), a view that is arguably a more accurate reflection of the realities of contemporary society and politics (for example, Parsons, 1995; Spicker, 2006). Nevertheless, while perhaps unrealistic, stagist approaches to the policy process can help in providing some structure for analysis, and even in encouraging analysts to consider the order in which things should occur. For example, HM Treasury's *The Green Book: Appraisal and Evaluation in Central Government* (2013) notes that '[a]ppraisal and evaluation often form stages of a broad policy cycle that some departments and agencies formalise in the acronym ROAMEF (Rationale, Objectives, Appraisal, Monitoring, Evaluation and Feedback)' (p. 3) (see Figure 1.2). Such approaches are often associated with 'rational'

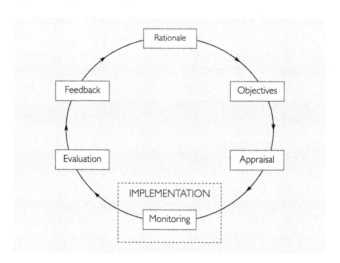

Figure 1.2 HM Treasury's ROAMEF policy cycle

Source: HM Treasury; licensed under the Open Government Licence v.3.0.

approaches to policy making, which assume that a problem will be tackled through a series of cumulative and logical steps in an attempt to identify the best response (Simon, 1945/1957 and 1960; see Chapter 2). However, while useful in providing an analytical framework, the idea of a cycle should not, perhaps, be taken too literally, but instead direct our consideration towards a continuous flow of decisions and actions, which may not always follow the pattern or sequence implied in such descriptions.

Another, more dynamic approach is taken by systems theory (for example, Easton, 1965), which argues that political activity can be analysed in terms of a system containing a number of processes that need to be kept in balance if the system is to survive. According to proponents of this view, we need to look at the environment in which the political system operates, and which contains a number of other systems, including social systems and ecological systems. At its most basic, there are a range of inputs to the political system which are converted into outputs, including policies, which themselves have an impact upon the wider economic, political and social environment, and which may again lead, directly or indirectly, to new inputs. This suggests that policy analysts have to consider the social, economic and political contexts within which problems are tackled and policies emerge.

What is policy analysis?

While it may be possible to trace some elements associated with policy analysis back substantially further, as a recognisable area of activity it arguably emerged in the United States in the 1950s and 1960s, with the development of a culture that saw the government acting as a 'problem-solver' and the use of methods of investigation that aimed to look at problems and develop possible options to solve or reduce them (as reflected, for example, in the discussion of rationalism in Chapter 2, and in other, later, attempts to encourage evidence-informed policy making, as outlined in Chapter 4). This was to some extent linked with a belief that social science could be like 'real' science, and that a knowledge and understanding of society could be used to make it better, with decisions being grounded in 'facts' or 'laws'. Policy analysis therefore began to grow as part of this view.

At roughly the same time, there was also a growth of interest, particularly among political scientists and political sociologists, in the analysis of the policy process, and especially in how problems came onto agendas and in how decisions are made. With the greater attention paid to policy formulation and decision making, ideas such as rational planning and incremental decision making were developed (sometimes as both analytical tools and as normative models), and the scope of study grew to include other areas such as the role and influence of bureaucrats, such as civil servants, and to look further at how power is exercised and by whom, the setting of agendas, the role of the media, and so on. Easton's (1953 and 1965) model of the policy process extended the range of interest even further, by directing analysis towards a consideration of inputs and outputs, while also taking account of the wider environment in which decisions are made.

'Policy analysis' is itself frequently subdivided, for example into 'analysis of policy' and 'analysis for policy'. The former is largely associated with the analysis of policy as an academic discipline, concerned primarily with advancing understanding; the latter is policy analysis as an applied activity, concerned mainly with contributing to responding to problems. However, such a distinction can be misleading, as, for example, academics may have a role in advising politicians and pressure groups, a function that clearly overlaps the two categories. Indeed, the position may be still more complicated. Hogwood and Gunn (1984), for example, identified seven types of policy analysis:

1. *studies of policy content* – where analysts seek to describe and explain the genesis and development of particular policies (this may involve largely descriptive (although often valuable) accounts of policies in areas such as the environment, housing, education, transport or health, etc.). The policy analyst usually investigates a number of issues in order to trace how a particular policy emerged, or how it was implemented and what the results were. Such work is often conducted for academic reasons, although in some cases the results may have some direct or indirect impact on policy makers;

2. *studies of policy process* – where attention is focused on the stages through which issues pass, and attempts are made to assess the influence of different factors on the development of the issue. Whilst such studies show some concern with policy content, the emphasis is on uncovering the various influences on policy formulation. They are often concerned with single issues, but they may also focus on the policy process within an organisation or on the influences on policy within a particular community or society. This would include case studies of the passage of particular pieces of legislation, or the development of particular initiatives;

3. *studies of policy outputs* – which seek to explain why variables such as levels of expenditure or service provision vary between areas. They take policies as dependent variables and attempt to understand them in terms of social, economic, technological and other factors.

Examples of this approach can be found in the literature which seeks to explain national differences in the development of social welfare policies, and why, for example, disability policy in Britain has developed differently from that in the United States. Research of this type can look at who exercises power, who influences decision making and how, how policy proposals change, and to what extent prevailing values and beliefs limit the range of policy possibilities;

4. *evaluation studies (sometimes also referred to as impact studies)* – which for Hogwood and Gunn (1984) mark the borderline between analysis of policy and analysis for policy. These are concerned to analyse the impact policies have on the population. However, such research can sometimes be of a rather basic and uncritical nature, concentrating on the collection of information rather than any real analysis of the goals and outcomes of the policy. On the other hand, it can also be much more important, perhaps highlighting shortcomings with existing policies and providing information on the factors which influence the success and failure of policies, so suggesting a way to 'better' future policies. Even work such as the General Household Survey might fall into this category, as it not only provides detailed survey data, but can also be used to examine the impact of some policies;

5. *information for policy making* – where data are collected and analysed in order to assist policy makers to reach decisions. This might occur when policy makers are considering the introduction of a new policy, or the revision of existing policies. Information may come from reviews carried out within government as part of a regular monitoring process, or it may be provided by academic policy analysts concerned to apply their knowledge to practical problems. It might involve only the provision of useful information, or it may go on to analyse this and to recommend possible options. However, the emphasis is clearly on the contribution to policy making;

6. *process advocacy* – which is a variant of analysis for policy in which analysts seek to improve the nature of policy-making systems. Process advocacy is manifested in attempts to improve the machinery of government through the reallocation of functions and tasks, and in efforts to enhance the basis for policy choices through the development of planning systems and new approaches to option appraisal. It generally aims to work towards 'better' policy making, for example through taking a more 'rational' or 'evidence-based' approach. The emphasis is likely to be on the efficacy of different approaches, methods and procedures for the making of policy;

7. *policy advocacy* – where the analyst is involved in pressing specific options and ideas in the policy process, either individually or in association with others, for example through a pressure group. Hogwood and Gunn (1984) note that this can take two principal forms: a) the analyst as a political actor, supporting or lobbying for a particular policy, for example those who work in pressure groups who examine policies but have particular values which clearly influence the way in which they interpret research; b) the political actor as analyst, who again brings a particular perspective to their interpretation. Both of these roles are clearly controversial as their objectivity as analysts and as consumers of analysis can be questioned, but both also reflect the role of values in the public policy process and the difficulty of achieving objectivity.

Hogwood and Gunn characterised the first three of these as 'policy studies' (knowledge *of* policy and the policy process) and the latter three as 'policy analysis' (knowledge *in* the policy process), with evaluation falling into both categories. Howlett *et al.* (2009) identify a number of strands within the 'policy studies' literature, including: classifying different types of political regime and seeking to identify insights into the policies they adopt; attempting to identify causal variables, or 'policy determinants'; and analyses of 'policy content', linked to the idea that the nature of a problem and the policies devised to address it often determine how it will be dealt with by the political system, so that ultimately 'policy determines politics' (Lowi, 1972), rather than the other way round. Knoepfel *et al.* (2011) distinguish between three major currents within policy analysis: approaches based on theories of the state, drawing upon, for example, pluralist, Marxist and neo-corporatist or neo-institutionalist ideas; those that seek to explain the ways in which public action, through the state and public authorities, works, and are concerned to understand the complexity of decision making, including through the application of perspectives such as bounded rationality, incrementalism and systems theory; and work that focuses upon evaluation of the effects of public action, including the provision of evidence for policy. Finally, John (2012) focuses on five broad approaches that he suggests help to 'explain why policies differ between different policy sectors and countries, and why some policies are stable and others change' (p. 12): institutional approaches, which see political organisations structuring public decisions and outcomes; groups and network approaches, with associations and informal relationships shaping decisions and outcomes; exogenous approaches, which see factors external to the political system as determining the decisions of political actors and affecting policy outputs and outcomes; rational actor approaches, sometimes called 'rational choice', which see the preferences and bargaining of actors as explaining decisions and outcomes; and ideas-based approaches, which see ideas about solutions to problems as circulating and gaining influence in the policy process. This book, while drawing, in places, upon all of these, does not, however, follow any of them, emphasising instead that these and other ideas constitute a set of tools for analysis which can help in understanding the reality of the policy process.

Policy, administration and management

As Knoepfel *et al.* (2011) note, 'professional management of public administrations and the resources at their disposal (particularly with respect to personnel, finance and organisation) is essential' (p. xi), a prerequisite of quality public service. It is not surprising, therefore, that there are considerable bodies of literature that deal with the administration and management of public policy and the public sector. However, any attempt to clearly distinguish between public policy and the administration of policies is likely to experience a number of difficulties. 'Administration' is not necessarily any easier to define than 'public' or 'policy'. While at one time administration was widely viewed as the way in which policy was implemented after it had been made, Greenwood and Wilson (1989), among many others, have argued that such a distinction does not stand up to close scrutiny, and that 'all policy decisions are to some extent predicated upon considerations about implementation' (p. 3), as governments must inevitably consider the means of implementation before introducing policies. At the same time, administrative decisions also require implementation, and themselves often take the form of a policy decision. They also point out that it is simplistic to assume that politicians determine policy while officials implement those decisions. Indeed, politicians can frequently be seen to be involved in the implementation of policies at central and local levels (see also Chapters 5 and 6), while it is equally clear that officials can have significant influence on policy, through their expert advice to politicians at the formulation stage and their ability to influence the implementation of policies (see, for example, the discussion of bureaucracies in Chapter 2).

Similarly, there is continuing debate over whether management in the public sector is distinct from that in the private sector (for example, Boyne, 2002), and these views can be descriptive, normative, or both (Pollitt, 2016a). One perspective has sought to differentiate between 'management' and 'administration', suggesting that management is an approach to organisational decision making that has traditionally been associated with the private sector through attempts to achieve organisational goals with the most efficient use of resources, emphases that were perhaps not always present in the administrative systems of much of the public sector. In contrast, the term 'public administration' was traditionally used of public sector provision, with the emphasis on public officials implementing policies that had been determined by political decision makers within a framework of law, with the efficient use of resources often being only of secondary importance. Farnham and Horton (1996) suggested that the dominance of an administrative, rather than managerial system in the public sector was partly due to the historical emergence and growth of the public services as administrative bodies to support policy makers and legislators (for example, Hughes, 2012). Civil servants, in particular, did not regard themselves as managers, but as policy advisers to ministers and as guarding the public interest. Greener (2013), building on Dunsire (1999), suggests that there are five principles underlying public administration as an ideal type, although these may not always be transferable in practice, and may be goals rather than expectations: public provision leads to more equitable and reliable services than commercial or private provision; the state should not only plan for and finance a service, but also deliver it; there should be uniformity of provision grounded on fairness; there should be a hierarchical chain of command; and there should be accountability through democratic means.

Others argue that while there may be similarities, and indeed the transfer of ideas between public and private sectors, there are significant differences between them. Hughes (2012) highlights a number of these. One is the ability of the public sector to be coercive, for example by forcing people to pay taxes. Another is the forms of accountability of the two sectors, with the management of private companies being accountable to the board and shareholders, while public sector accountabilities include to the political leadership and elected representatives, and through them to the public. He also notes the difficulty of measuring outputs (and hence efficiency) in the public sector, which he argues is possible, although it is likely to be less precise and meaningful than for the private sector.

An alternative view has been that 'management' and 'administration' describe very similar activities, with the former being used in association with the private sector and the latter with the public sector, with the implication that many of the basic practices and activities are transferable between organisations in different sectors. Pollitt (2016a), for example, is one of those who suggest that there are no significant differences between the academic study of public management and public administration.

However, and importantly for large public sector bureaucracies, from the 1980s there has been the emergence and development of a 'new public management' (NPM) that draws on ideas around self-interest and the free market, 'public choice' approaches to bureaucracy, and views that the state has become too large and distorts individuals' ability to exercise freedom and choice, and that combines elements of what might be seen as traditional public administration and the more instrumental approach of business management. Hood (1991) identified seven key features of the new public management:

1. a focus on management, with accountability requiring the clear assignment of responsibility for action;

2. the use of explicit standards and measures of performance, including clear goals and targets;

3. emphasis on output controls, with resource allocation and rewards linked to measured performance;

4. the disaggregation of public bureaucracies into agencies with the use of contract arrangements;

5. the use of greater competition and contracting out;

6. a move towards private sector management practices, including greater flexibility in terms of staff contracts and rewards;

7. an emphasis on discipline and parsimony in the use of resources, including cutting direct costs.

These characteristics have been strongly encouraged by central government in the UK from the 1980s, and have been reflected in bodies such as the NHS, quangos and local government. Clarke *et al.* (2002) noted that from the 1980s managerialism 'tended to subordinate other principles of judgement to the managerial calculus of economy and efficiency' (p. 10), an approach that arguably ran from the Conservative years through those of the Labour governments, and into the Conservative-Liberal Democrat Coalition and the following Conservative governments. These developments served to further blur any distinction between public administration and public management.

However, some have continued to argue that there are, and should be, significant differences. For example, to some extent reflecting Dunsire's (1999) characterisation of 'traditional' public administration during the post-war years, Ranson and Stewart (1994) have argued that public organisations are created to serve the needs of society as a whole, within a statutory framework that imposes legal obligations, and where there is a concern to identify needs rather than demand, and to serve rather than to accumulate profit. Pollitt (2016a), however, suggests that while it is quite possible to find examples that would appear to fit *a priori* assumptions, such as private sector efficiency and public sector inefficiency, or public caring and private sector callousness, and that there may well be differences between the two sectors, there is also a significant degree of variation within each sector, while in addition 'hybrid' and 'arm's-length' organisations, often associated with developments such as contracting out and partnerships, as discussed in Chapter 4, have become more common.

In opposing the spread of the new public management, some on the left have sought to argue for alternative approaches, including the idea of the 'relational state' (for example, Cooke and Muir, 2012). This perspective accepts that the new public management delivered improvements in some areas, but argues that it also introduced a number of damaging approaches, including the development of a 'tick-box' culture in response to command and control techniques, that its core tenets have been increasingly rejected by the private sector, that it has not increased public trust and confidence in public services, and that it has neglected the importance of human relationships. As a result, there is seen to be a need to change the way in which government interacts with civil society and citizens, with an emphasis on relationships, although commentators differ significantly in how they see the form and extent of the relationships between state organisations and citizens, and in the degree to which public services should be provided by non-state bodies. Others have argued for a New Public Governance (for example, Osborne, 2010; Morgan and Cook, 2014), which Morgan and Cook suggest emphasises three trust- and legitimacy-building characteristics that NPM ignores or undervalues: it is value-centred, seeing the goal of government as being to promote the common good (Moore's (1995) 'public value') and going beyond concerns with efficiency, effectiveness and responsiveness to include objectives such as satisfaction, outcomes, trust and legitimacy; it seeks to create government processes that facilitate the creation of implementable agreements among stakeholders; and it sees the achievement of the public good as arising from a co-production process involving public, private and non-profit sectors.

Public administration is, however, also intrinsically political in nature, being determined by values, and with the performance of public services being evaluated through the ballot box at both local and national levels. Public organisations are therefore accountable to the electorate in a way in which private organisations are not. In addition, the goals of public organisations are often complex and vague, and can be conflicting or even unattainable. There are a number of reasons for this, but in part it arises from governments' need to build broad bases of support; the fact that goals can change significantly over time, and even within the lifespan of one parliament; the difficulty of assessing the extent of success or failure to achieve objectives in many areas of public policy; and the potential for governments to present different perspectives on their actions as required during political debate (Pollitt, 1990).

The divisions of responsibilities between public organisations add another level of complexity. For example, responsibility for various aspects of care for vulnerable adults in England can be located in the Department of Health, the Department for Work and Pensions, and the Department for Communities and Local Government, while the Treasury maintains an obvious interest through its oversight of public expenditure. In addition, policies and goals may be set at one level of government and implemented at another, with education being one example (although it also illustrates how the public sector can be subject to change, with the spread of academy schools reducing the role of local government and enhancing that of schools, multi-academy trusts and the Department for Education), while providers of services may come from public, private or third sectors.

On broadly similar lines, Farnham and Horton (1996) highlight significant differences in the goals and accountabilities of the two sectors. In the public sector, politicians are responsible for setting goals; the success or failure of those goals is often not easily reduced to a notion of 'profit' and 'loss', and public sector organisations cannot go bankrupt, as they do not rely on the market for revenue.

At the same time, it can be argued that the absence of market discipline can lead to waste, inefficiency and a failure to respond to customers' wants, and that management in public bodies can be significantly diluted compared with that in some private organisations. Hughes (2012), too, argues that the accountability structures in the public sector make managers' jobs different from those in the private sector. The variety of pressures and controls and the complicated interface with the political process create an 'ambiguous accountability' for much of the public sector, with the need for political accountability in terms of following decisions and policies, at the same time as being accountable to the users of public services. Flynn contrasts this with the clear ultimate accountability to shareholders in the private sector. Given these differing interpretations, it is perhaps unsurprising that Greener (2013) identifies five 'contradictions' in public management as it has developed (Table 1.1).

However, Bovaird and Loeffler (2016a) suggest that public management is 'an approach that uses managerial techniques (often originating in the private sector) to increase the value for money achieved by public services' (p. 5), and that it covers both public sector organisations and public *service* organisations, whether in public, private or voluntary sectors. They also link it to the concept of 'public governance', how an

Table 1.1 Contradictions in public management

Contradictions	Description
Both managers and professionals believe that they should be in charge of public services	Public management implies that it is managers in charge of public services, when those managers often depend on highly trained professionals who do not wish to be managed
Public services must both be democratically accountable to citizens and also achieve good results for individual users	Public services have to manage resources for the benefit of the population as a whole, as well as for individual users who may want very different things
Public services must be run according to public values, but also according to market values	Public services are often associated with distinctively public values, including collectivity and solidarity, but at the same time must work within individualistic market frameworks requiring them to adopt market values
Public services must be efficient, yet also deliver strong customer service	Public services often achieve efficiency by organising around professional schedules, but have to demonstrate customer service by organising around user schedules
Public managers are appointed by contradictory means (election and selection)	Public managers may have very different duties if elected or selected, creating very different lines of accountability

Source: Greener, I. (2013) *Public Management*, Basingstoke: Palgrave, p. 69.

organisation works with its partners and networks to influence the outcomes of public policies. They suggest that while the differences between public management and public administration have often been exaggerated, behaviour in the public domain may have become closer to the image of the public manager and less that of the public administrator, a view broadly shared by Hughes (2012), who notes the much more widespread use of the title 'manager' than in the past, and suggests that this may be a better description of the work now done.

Who are policy analysts?

From the 1980s, there has been a growth of employment for 'policy analysts'. The nature of such work can vary widely, reflecting the various types of policy analysis discussed above. Some will be working on the provision of information to inform policy making, some on evaluation, and others on the study of outputs or outcomes. Policy analysts can be found in a variety of settings, including a significant number of academics in universities, researchers and others in independent research organisations and think tanks, and researchers and policy analysts employed in different tiers of government and in many other public bodies. In addition, they may also be found in voluntary organisations and pressure groups, which may be seeking to monitor and influence policy, the political parties, and among freelance consultants and lobbyists. They are very likely to be involved in activities and areas that are closely related to the coverage of this book, including fields such as health, transport, the environment, the economy and planning, while some will be more focused on the policy process, including how to make and implement policy more effectively. They have a range of concerns (Parsons, 1995) including:

➤ 'problems' and the relationship of public policy to these;

➤ the content of public policies;

➤ what decision makers and policy makers do and do not do, and the inputs and processes in a policy area;

➤ the consequences of policy in terms of outputs and outcomes.

Howlett *et al.* (2009) suggest that policy analysts working for governments and for groups directly affected by public policies tend to focus on policy evaluation, including the impact on their client organisation, while those in think tanks and research institutes are likely to have more autonomy, although, given their interest in the 'practical' side of policy, they are still likely to concentrate on outcomes or the instruments and techniques that generate those outcomes. Academics may have the greatest independence, although they too are likely to work within a particular ideological framework, and they are the most likely to consider theoretical and methodological issues, and to consider the entire policy process.

Understanding change over time

Change and stability are arguably central to the study of public policy, and indeed to politics more generally, whether they stem from a desire to change the world or to maintain it as it is. Of course, this raises questions about how we might measure policy change. Hall (1993) suggested that there are three components of policy outputs: policy paradigms, the overarching goals that guide a policy; policy instruments, the means used to achieve these goals (see Chapter 2); and the precise settings or calibrations of these instruments. He described the latter as first-order changes, when it is only the calibration of policy instruments that is adjusted, generally implying only minor change in policies; second-order change is when policy goals remain unaffected but the type of instrument being used to achieve those goals is changed, as happens when one instrument is replaced by another; and the most fundamental change, third-order, is associated with changes to policy paradigms. Policy paradigms provide a basis for much of the policy agenda, reflecting a broad consensus on problems and solutions (Heffernan, 2002), and are generally stable, changing only periodically, as with the breakdown of the Keynesian economic paradigm during the 1970s and the shift to monetarist and neo-liberal approaches.

From a rather different perspective, Hay (2002) suggests that there are three broad analytical strategies for considering the process of political change over time. The *synchronic* approach is where the object of analysis is effectively frozen in time, so that it might be possible, for example, to describe the UK state on 3 May 1979 in a way that might be generalisable to the post-war period more generally, but no matter how good our descriptive and analytical skills, it will not tell us anything about the process or extent of change. *Comparative statics* is effectively a variant, whereby synchronic analyses from different moments in time, such as 3 May 1979, 1 May 1997, 6 May 2010 and 8 June 2017, are compared. However, again this tells us little or nothing about the process or pace of change, or the reasons for it. In contrast, *diachronic* analysis is an approach that emphasises the process of change over time, so that there is 'a desire to trace and chart the complex interaction of causal processes to produce structural and behavioural change – whether continuous or discontinuous, incremental or punctuating, evolutionary or revolutionary' (Hay, 2002, p. 149). Clearly, while in many respects likely to be preferable, diachronic analysis is likely to be laborious and time-consuming, while synchronic snapshots provide a relatively simple tool, albeit limited.

Hay also identifies three models that can help in understanding the nature and extent of change: revolutionary change, evolutionary change, and punctuated equilibrium, while, drawing on John (2012), the advocacy coalition framework and policy streams and windows may be added to those.

Revolutionary change

This conception sees social and political change as occurring unevenly over time, with an alternation between lengthy periods of stasis and short moments of major transformation. Although it clearly fits well with the Marxist idea of historical materialism, it can also sit easily with other theoretical perspectives. Hay (2002) suggests that while some view a punctuated and revolutionary conception of political change as part of a universal human condition, it would not be implausible to suggest that non-democratic political systems, where there may be few pressure release valves, may be more likely to exhibit a punctuated political development than systems which are more participatory and democratic and more able to respond constructively to discontent (Hay, 2002).

Evolutionary change

Ideas of evolutionary change might be expected to emphasise continuous, incremental, yet directional processes, and it is certainly the case that in the past evolutionary perspectives have indeed posited gradual yet directional change, with the mechanisms of change being linked to adaptation and selection rather than the mobilisation of protest and the build-up of pressure on the state apparatus. However, importantly, it regards all of the elements of the political system as constantly interacting with each other, as with Kingdon's 'primeval soup' (see below and Chapter 2). John (2012) suggests that the various elements compete or cooperate in contexts that may be very different, but that there is evolutionary change in the sense that some potential policies develop while others do not, so that '[t]here is a chance conjunction of events that makes it successful. It is an idea that works' (p. 165). He goes on to argue that the evolutionary approach helps to explain the variety of ideas and interests that compete within the institutional, cultural, group-based and socio-economic environments, with implementation strategies also being part of the selection process.

Among the attractions of evolutionary theory in public policy is that it does not see an automatic process by which some ideas and interests are favoured and others are not; it also does not imply stability, but can just as easily be seen as associated with instability, as with Baumgartner and Jones' punctuated equilibrium approach; and its supporters argue that it can map out causal mechanisms. However, it might also be argued that it perhaps describes what happens, rather than providing a testable model with clear causal mechanisms and identification of the selection mechanisms, and how these are related to the selection of policies, given that it can be argued that, in reality, policy making is often skewed to certain powerful groups.

Punctuated equilibrium

In recent years, the idea of 'punctuated equilibrium' has been taken up by a number of analysts. It is associated with the view that there is both stability and change in political systems. Arguably originating with the work of Baumgartner and Jones (1993) in the US, in comparative public policy these ideas have often been associated with perspectives that emphasise 'critical junctures' (Collier and Collier, 1991), 'crises' (Hay, 1999), or 'critical institutional events' (Baumgartner and Jones, 1993).

The idea of punctuated equilibrium is used to refer to periods of relative stability that are interrupted by rapid and intense periods of significant change. Institutions and the influence of powerful groups can mean that particular policies remain in place for considerable periods of time, with only incremental change, yet in the right conditions agendas can change rapidly and the rules of decision making can institutionalise new policies and outputs into the policy process. For liberal democratic states this might be seen as recognising their ability to respond to demands for societal change, but also that at times they may have moments of crisis when that ability is compromised and the pace of change can be rapid (Hay, 2002). Institutions are important, as they include certain participants in the policy process and exclude others, and help ensure that problems are defined in a particular manner (John, 2012). However, interests and networks are also important in determining agendas and the definition of problems, while policy entrepreneurs play crucial roles, with some seeking to maintain the existing partial equilibrium while others seek to have the political system adopt different policy solutions. Ideas provide the building blocks for agendas. John and Jennings (2010), for example, use the content of the King's or Queen's Speech from 1940 to 2005 to consider the nature of post-war British politics and policy making, and conclude that there are dramatic and disproportionate changes in political attention in Britain, as in other political systems, with long periods of stability and incrementalism being interrupted by sudden increases or decreases in the attention of the executive to particular topics, giving rise to agenda change.

This model reflects aspects of both the revolutionary and evolutionary approaches, so that for considerable periods of time change may be limited and incremental, punctuated, at times, by much more rapid change, when, for example, political regimes are changed or governing paradigms replaced, with one example of that being widely seen as the late 1970s and 1980s, when the Keynesian period was replaced by a neo-liberal paradigm in many Western states. It can, however, be criticised for being largely descriptive, and for potentially underplaying the ability of elites to shape preferences and overstating the bottom-up influences on policy (see Chapters 2 and 3).

Policy streams and policy windows

Kingdon (1984, 1995 and 2014) sees policy selection as emerging from the continual interplay of three streams or processes: problems, policies and politics. Problems require attention, policies are proposals for change, and the political process (including elections and public opinion) influences how opinion formers define public problems and assess possible solutions (see also Chapter 2). For Kingdon, however, policy formation is as much a result of luck as of intention. When there is a policy window, for example, as a result of a new policy problem or a change of government, then there is an opportunity for change. Windows may only be open briefly, while the involvement of different decision makers may also be intermittent, so that some opportunities may be missed. The policy streams approach is valuable for its attention to how ideas emerge (or not), and for its emphasis on the dynamic framework within which policies are adopted. It suggests that while policies and problems may be floating in a primeval soup, political factors are important in influencing agendas.

The advocacy coalition framework

The advocacy coalition framework (ACF), again discussed in greater depth in Chapter 2 in relation to its utility in relation to understanding policy making, is also useful in examining change. As with many other network accounts, it sees policy making as a continuous process, but seeks to present a much broader picture of it. An advocacy coalition is a group of organisations and individuals with the same ideas and interests, arguing against other coalitions in the same policy sector. Sabatier and his colleagues (Jenkins-Smith et al., 2014) argue that policy change needs to be analysed over a decade or more, as the ACF assumes that beliefs are broadly stable unless disrupted by a major crisis. Major, rapid changes in the outside world can disrupt stable patterns of interests, change relationships between actors and lead to policy change. However, the ACF takes little account of institutional constraints, nor of human agency, although this is to some extent because it takes the view that ideas and interests socialise individuals into particular patterns of behaviour. It also draws heavily on the United States, with its federal system and relatively open policy system, and its application to other states, while potentially useful, should be treated with a degree of caution.

Directions and dimensions of policy change

While change is perhaps often associated with a new policy or programme, or the development of an existing one, it is important to recognise that it can also, potentially, involve the reduction or even the removal of one. Knill and Tosun (2012) suggest that it is important to consider the *density* of policy – the extent to which a given policy area is covered by governmental activities – and its *intensity* – the level of intervention. They argue that changes in policy density can be assessed by the number of policy targets and the number of policy instruments that are applied in a given field, while the intensity might be measured by the settings of the policy instruments used. However, although helpful in directing attention at the need to assess the extent and nature of policy change, such measures have to be treated with caution, as they might reflect, for example, a government keen to be seen to be responding to a problem in the short term, while paying less attention to longer-term needs. At the same time the implementation and efficacy of the policy response is clearly also important.

Themes and developments from the 1980s

The approaches and emphases in policy making, implementation and evaluation vary significantly over time. Indeed, one of the key arguments of this book is that such changes can themselves have implications for the nature of policies that are developed and thus for policy outcomes. It is therefore worth drawing out some of the main themes that have developed from the 1980s onwards. While these are not necessarily 'party political', and indeed they clearly frequently reflect the ideas discussed in the preceding section and some of the themes from Chapter 4, it is arguable that they can to some extent be linked to broader political preferences, and they are therefore outlined below in relation to the changes in administration since 1979.

In the period prior to that there were a number of developments intended to improve the quality of policy making, including through more rational (Simon, 1945/1957 and 1960) decision making with regard to public expenditure, such as the Public Expenditure Survey Committee, established in 1961, the Programme Analysis and Review Committee, set up in 1970, and a growth in the use of planning units within government departments, as well as attempts to improve collaboration between departments, such as the Joint Approach to Social Policy (Challis et al., 1988). In 1968, the Fulton Committee argued that the civil service was largely the product of a nineteenth-century philosophy which was inadequate to meet the needs of the twentieth century. Its report was followed by a series of reforms, including the creation of a civil service college to provide training for civil servants (later becoming the National School of Government, before closing in 2012, when some of its functions were taken on by Civil Service Learning), and the creation in the Cabinet Office of the Central Policy Review Staff in 1971, with the intention that it define government strategy and provide a framework for the formulation of government policies, followed by the Policy Unit in 1975, to provide advice specifically for the Prime Minister.

From the 1980s, new intellectual challenges, perhaps particularly those associated with the New Right and rational choice theory (see Chapter 3), have had an impact not just on how we understand and analyse public policy, but also on the mechanisms and processes of policy making and implementation and the practical outcomes of government policies and practices. Rational choice theorists have tended to take the view that the 'best' outcomes are achieved through the maximum use of market forces and the minimum intervention by governments. In addition, principal-agent theory has been used by some to suggest that because the interests of principals (the public, through politicians and public managers) are diffuse, and there is no influence from a profit motive or the workings of the market, then contracting out much of the public sector may help to ensure accountability. These ideas were put forward strongly in the 1980s and 1990s by New Right thinkers and a variety of right-wing think tanks, such as the Adam Smith Institute, the Institute of Economic Affairs and the Social Affairs Unit, and have been built on since then by many, particularly on the right.

These developments can be seen as having had three main impacts: they have led to new policies and new types of policies; they have challenged some of the once fundamental assumptions about the forms of public policies and how they should be administered and delivered; and they have led to major changes in the administration and management of public policy. For example, the ideas that bureaucrats attempt to maximise their budgets – so that there is a constant pressure from within many public organisations for growth – and that this counteracts aims such as efficiency, and the preference for market or market-type mechanisms, have led to such changes as the creation of 'agencies' and the use of contracting, quasi-markets and other attempts to stimulate competition, as discussed elsewhere in this book (see Chapters 4 and 7).

In addition, of course, the analysis of public policy has been informed by developments within the subjects that relate to it, such as organisation theory, which emphasises actors and decision-making processes within organisations, and the emergence of the new institutionalism, with a focus on rules, norms and patterns of behaviour, punctuated equilibrium theory, with its concern to explain long periods of stability followed by short but intense change, and the advocacy coalition framework, which seeks to understand the policy process by focusing on actors promoting their beliefs, all of which are covered in the remainder of this book (see, for example, Chapters 3 and 4).

Conservative governments, 1979–1997

As noted above, the concern of this section is not with particular policy developments under the Conservatives, or even with changes in broad policy areas. Rather, it seeks to draw out some of the main themes that can be seen as having underpinned and derived from the Conservatives' years in government, some of which continue to be highly influential. The 1980s and 1990s saw significant changes in government and in public policies, many of which were designed to reduce the role of the state and to give individuals greater power over and responsibility for their own lives. While, after almost two decades, public policy and the public sector remained important factors in everybody's lives, there had nevertheless been major changes. These included a blurring of distinctions between public and private sectors, with privatisation of formerly public utilities and their regulation by independent offices such as Ofcom and Ofwat, the transfer of many residential homes and domiciliary care services to the private sector, and the greater involvement of the private sector in the NHS; the increased use of quasi-governmental organisations and the creation of 'next step' agencies, in many respects based upon the view that there is a reasonably clear divide between policy made by ministers and the implementation and management of those policies; and greater acceptance of the role of markets in providing a wide range of goods and services. In addition, there was the growth in influence of neo-liberal ideas, including theories about rational choice and the growth of bureaucracies, such as the civil service, together with the rise of the new public management. Some of these were clearly related to the Conservatives' ideological imperatives, including the preference for the market, so that market forces were introduced to many areas of the public sector, while the Conservatives also argued that real accountability comes through the power of the consumer to move from one provider to another, rather than the traditional concern with accountability to the public through elected representatives. This period also saw a new emphasis on the use of audit and inspection bodies, including for local authorities, the NHS, social care, schools and universities.

The period also saw two other changes. The long period of one-party dominance raised some perhaps inevitable questions about ethics, accountability and morality, with the rise of non-elected public bodies and the powers of patronage and appointment available to others. And despite the hostility of many Conservatives to both, the rise of nationalism (in Scotland, Wales and Northern Ireland) and of European integration were features of the period, although the former only became a significant influence on policy following Labour's return to power in 1997.

Labour governments, 1997–2010

Under New Labour, considerable attention was paid to the policy process, underpinned in large part by the wider emphasis on the 'modernisation' of public services (Cabinet Office, 1999; Newman, 2001). There were a number of developments intended to improve policy making, reflected in the Cabinet Office Strategic Policy Making Team's (1999) report, which set out a 'descriptive' model of policy making based on three themes (vision, effectiveness and continuous improvement) and nine core 'competencies' (looking forward, looking outward, being innovative and creative, using evidence, being inclusive, thinking in a joined-up way, evaluating, reviewing, and learning lessons (see Bochel and Duncan, 2007). Reflecting these aspirations, in 2001, the Centre for Management and Policy Studies produced *Better Policy Making* (Bullock *et al.*, 2001), and the National Audit Office *Modern Policy Making* (NAO, 2001), while the idea of policy making as a skill was taken up by the Professional Skills for Government programme, covering all government departments and agencies. Many of the initiatives of this period were based upon a broadly rational approach to policy making, and implied that 'good' policy making would produce 'better' policies and outcomes.

At the same time, New Labour arguably took on many of the Conservatives' ideas, maintaining and extending the use of performance measurement and inspection, often together with a greater emphasis on targets for public services and attempts to make more decisive judgements over 'quality', including by describing some organisations as 'failing'. As with the Conservatives, there continued to be a significant emphasis on the role of users, in particular as consumers of services, with attempts to promote user choice, such as parental choice of schools, including through the provision of information such as performance indicators and league tables. And, like the Conservatives, Labour also made extensive use of arm's-length organisations, increasing the power and responsibilities of many of those bodies.

There were, however, some areas where Labour's approach did differ from that of the Conservatives, including through a greater emphasis on collaboration and partnership between organisations as a means of improving service delivery (Burnham and Horton, 2013), rather than the primary commitment to competition and the market. This itself reflected the fragmentation of service provision that had occurred as a result of the Conservatives' policies, but was in part also due to a view that the policy process is dynamic and requires governments to respond to problems in a more joined-up fashion, and in part a belief that many policy problems need more holistic and comprehensive responses.

In many respects linked to this there was considerable emphasis, at least rhetorically, on evidence-based policy making, including, for example, the greater use of analysis and modelling, as well as some use of policy pilots before full implementation. Such approaches have been criticised for being highly positivist in nature, for making assumptions about the links between measurement and policy success or failure (what works is largely what can be measured), and for ignoring questions around social construction and social control. In addition, the Labour governments, as with others, could certainly be criticised for their selection of 'evidence' in some cases. Nevertheless, the use of evidence in policy making, albeit recognising the contestability of such notions, did come much more to the fore during this period.

With the development of information and communication technology, which appeared to fit well with Labour's 'modernisation' agenda, e-government was identified as an area that could alter the relationship between citizens and government, including by providing online access to services 24 hours a day, seven days a week. However, while Labour sought to make all government services available electronically, progress was not as smooth or as rapid as the government had hoped (see Chapter 4).

There were also other changes under Labour that had an impact on the policy process, not least with regard to the roles of different tiers of government, with the establishment of devolved legislatures in Scotland, Wales and Northern Ireland, acceptance of the social chapter of the Maastricht Treaty, and the passage of the Human Rights Act, the latter two of which arguably extended the power of European institutions in relation to the UK (see Chapter 6).

Finally, it is important to note the financial crisis that began in 2007 and 2008, when what Greener (2013) describes as a 'combination of reckless borrowing, careless lending, the upside-down pyramid of financial assets being built on the property market, and investors not really knowing much about the financial assets they were buying' (p. 10) led to a series of financial assets becoming worthless, governments bailing out banks with taxpayers' money, and cuts in public expenditure as governments then sought to repay the debts they had incurred as a result, which, together with a new reluctance on the part of banks to lend, in turn contributed to a further economic slowdown. In the UK, the response of the Labour government was largely to maintain public spending initially, with the intention of providing a stimulus to the economy, although cuts were planned for the future; however, following the 2010 general election the approach was to change significantly.

Coalition and Conservative governments, 2010 onwards

While the beginnings of 'austerity' can be seen towards the end of the Labour government, it was under the Conservative-Liberal Democrat Coalition that it became most central to public policy, with the emphasis on lowering the deficit by reducing public expenditure, rather than through increasing taxes, having major implications for policy making and implementation (for example, Bochel, 2016), while, despite rhetoric about 'rebalancing' the economy, banks and the financial sector in general were seen as part of the solution, as wealth creators (Greener, 2013). As a result, it is hard to disagree with Flynn's view at the time that '[i]t is difficult to distinguish the Coalition's policies that are designed to reduce the deficit and those that represent a thoroughly different view of the role, scale, functions and organising principles of the public sector' (2012, p. 41). Indeed, the use of commissioning, including the greater use of payment by results, was central to much of the Coalition's reform agenda for the public sector, underpinned by the idea that it would create efficiencies and increase productivity. It was accompanied by other NPM/neo-liberal influenced ideas, drawing strongly on a belief that the public sector could learn from the private sector, with, for example, new providers being able to enter the education and health sectors, while some local authorities, such as Barnet and Suffolk, put forward radical proposals to outsource all but a handful of services.

The Coalition government also made much, at least rhetorically, of 'localism', implying that local authorities and communities would be given the responsibility for responding to problems, although critics pointed out that they were rarely given the resources to do so, resulting in a further rolling back of the state (Clarke and Cochrane, 2013; Featherstone et al., 2012). Similarly, David Cameron's idea of the 'Big Society', with a greater role for community groups and voluntary organisations, failed to gain much adhesion, despite a number of re-launches, although it was arguably reflected in the continued shift away from government providing services towards a more diverse range of providers and individual citizens being required to take greater responsibility for their own well-being. Of course, the very existence of a coalition government for the first time since 1945 itself raised a number of questions, including in relation to collective ministerial responsibility and how manifesto commitments might be seen by the House of Lords (House of Lords Select Committee on the Constitution, 2014).

Perhaps unsurprisingly, after the Conservatives' victory at the 2015 general election, there was considerable continuity with the approaches taken under the Coalition government. However, one area where there was a significant change was in relation to different tiers of government (discussed in more detail in Chapter 6), perhaps the most notable of which was the holding in June 2016 of a referendum on the United Kingdom's membership of the European Union, which resulted in a vote to leave, the departure of David Cameron, his replacement by Theresa May as Prime Minister and the 2017 general election. In addition, following the referendum on independence for Scotland in 2014, the new government extended the idea of devolution to some of England's regions, particularly building upon the Coalition's proposals for the creation of a 'Northern powerhouse' and the introduction of an elected mayor for Greater Manchester, with substantial powers over transport, housing, health and social care, planning and policing. Devolution agreements were subsequently signed with a number of areas of England, although under May's premiership this appeared to come lower down the government's agenda. Critics also noted that there was no devolution of control over the levels of spending (or for that matter the power to raise income), so that such arrangements might simply devolve the blame for decisions made by central government. In addition, the call by Nicola Sturgeon, Scotland's First Minister, initially in early 2017, and repeated during that year's general election campaign, for a second referendum on independence for Scotland highlighted the ongoing salience of this issue, perhaps particularly in the face of the Conservatives' policies at Westminster. However, the failure of the Conservatives to secure a majority at that election, their consequent need to reach an agreement with the Democratic Unionist Party in order to govern, the Labour Party's relative success in fighting an election campaign based upon an end to austerity and in mobilising younger voters, and the SNP losing seats in Scotland, raised further questions about the relative instability and future direction of politics in the UK.

Many of the developments noted above have much in common with what some have seen as a 'post-bureaucratic' age, with more localised public services, hybrid organisational forms, and a belief that communities are able to organise themselves, including through greater use of information and data, with post-bureaucratic organisations supposed to be faster, more efficient, more flexible, more committed and more outward-looking (Salaman, 2005). However, it can also be argued that the 'post-bureaucratic' age is simply one of different forms of bureaucracy and different mixes of policy instruments (see Chapter 2) (Lodge and Wegrich, 2012a).

Conclusion

This chapter has sought to outline some of the main ideas that can be seen as underpinning the study of public policy and the policy process. It is clear that on much of the terminology there are significant differences between writers, and that some use different phrases to describe the same or similar phenomena, while equally, very different approaches may tell us different things about particular topics. We therefore need to at least have an understanding of the different ways in which concepts such as 'policy', 'administration' and 'management' are used and applied, and how 'public' can be understood. In addition, the entire policy process is not only concerned with but itself impacts upon policies and programmes that do or do not emerge and the ways in which they are implemented, and consequently on outcomes. We also need to be aware that the subject of public policy is itself constantly evolving, and that the tools and methods with which we analyse policy, and the theoretical perspectives that underpin our understanding, are also contestable and changing, and that in some cases these in turn can impact upon policies, as with the adoption of new public management ideas by consecutive governments. Finally, from the 1980s, many of the developments in public policy can perhaps be summed up in the widespread use of the term 'governance', rather than 'government', with the implication, although not universally accepted, that we have shifted away from a position where governments had the ability to control and shape policy and society to one where governments operate in a complex, fragmented and decentralised environment, and have less capacity to bring about change through their own policies and actions.

While taking a sceptical approach to stagist approaches to the policy process, it is recognised here that attempts to identify stages such as formulation, implementation and evaluation can be helpful both for analysts and for those working within the policy process, for example in considering how particular policy decisions are made, or why some policies work less well than others. Indeed, as with many books, parts of this book draw upon the identification and analysis of particular stages, not least as a means of structuring discussion, although it is important to be aware that the policy process does not necessarily actually reflect those stages.

The remainder of this book sets out to provide material to assist our knowledge and understanding of the policy process, using both theoretical concepts and frameworks and reference to the real world. Of course, the application of different models and theories will often lead to different insights, but they may well be complementary, and they are certainly likely to provide additional ways of understanding how decisions are made and implemented. Chapters 2 and 3 introduce a variety of models and perspectives that can help provide an understanding of the policy process and the exercise of power. Chapter 4 highlights a number of important trends in policy making and implementation, while Chapters 5, 6 and 7 look in more depth at some of the structural factors and institutions that are important in the policy process in the United Kingdom. Finally, Chapter 8 considers the development and use of policy evaluation and Chapter 9 offers some conclusions.

Further reading

Although published more than 20 years ago, a thorough view of a wide range of concepts associated with the policy process is provided by:

Parsons, W. (1995) *Public Policy: An Introduction to the Theory and Practice of Policy Analysis*, Aldershot: Edward Elgar.

Other useful works on policy analysis include:

Hill, M. (2013) *The Public Policy Process*, Harlow: Pearson.
Hogwood, B. and Gunn, L. (1984) *Policy Analysis for the Real World*, Oxford: Oxford University Press (older, but valuable).
John, P. (2012) *Analyzing Public Policy*, Abingdon: Routledge.

For assessment of evidence on how governments choose to implement policies, which also considers how to improve policy outcomes, try:

John, P. (2011) *Making Policy Work*, Abingdon: Routledge.

A comprehensive discussion of a number of theoretical approaches can be found in:

Sabatier, P. A. and Weible, C. M. (eds) (2014) *Theories of the Policy Process*, Boulder: Westview Press.

Good overviews on public administration and management include:

Bovaird, T. and Loeffler, E. (eds) (2016) *Public Management and Governance*, London: Routledge.
Greener, I. (2013) *Public Management*, Basingstoke: Palgrave Macmillan.
Hughes, O. E. (2012) *Public Management and Administration*, Basingstoke: Palgrave Macmillan.
Pollitt, C. (2016) *Advanced Introduction to Public Management and Administration*, Cheltenham: Edward Elgar.

2

Perspectives on Policy Making

This chapter is concerned with exploring why a variety of models and theories can help us understand and explain different elements of the policy process. It outlines a number of models, such as rational and incremental decision making and models of bureaucratic influence, and illustrates how they can inform our understanding of the making and implementation of policies. The chapter also emphasises the impact that implementation can have on the outcomes of public policies. Theoretical perspectives, such as top-down approaches, and the problems of implementation are discussed, together with the variety of factors that can affect the implementation of policies. The chapter also considers issues around policy instruments, and how they might reflect existing power distributions, as well as the potential impacts of particular choices of instrument.

While the preceding chapter highlighted some of the complexity and variety, and hence some of the challenges, associated with studying the policy process, this chapter moves on to consider a range of theoretical perspectives that can inform our understanding of the making and implementation of policy, and through that give us a greater appreciation of the forces that can exert an influence over the shaping of policies. It draws upon contributions from a variety of fields, including public policy, public administration, economics, sociology and social policy, to illustrate the value of the production of models, concepts and categorisations designed to help further our understanding of the policy process, or parts of it, and of exploring different disciplinary areas in doing this.

As made clear in Chapter 1, for the purpose of analysis the making of policy in its broadest sense is often conceived of as a series of stages. However, while that approach has its uses, and indeed is used to some extent as a framework for discussion in this book, if taken at face value it can project a somewhat misleading picture of the development of policies. Policy making is rarely a simple, straightforward process. Policies evolve over time and according to the needs of the population, the state of the national economy, the world economy, the ideology and priorities of the government in power, and many other factors. It is a complex process, so that Lindblom and Woodhouse (1993) argue that '[d]eliberate, orderly steps … are not an accurate portrayal of how the policy process actually works. Policy-making is, instead, a complex inter-active process without beginning or end' (p. 11).

Furthermore, a whole range of actors, not limited to elected representatives such as local councillors or MPs, is involved in aspects of the policy process, including in agenda setting, formulation, implementation, evaluation and feedback. In addition, the view that politicians make policies and that officials implement them has arguably always been misleading, and by the mid-1980s it was quite clearly possible to argue that '[p]oliticians do not necessarily cease to try to intervene in the policy process once the law-making process has ended' (Hill and Bramley, 1986, p. 139), while since then there has been considerable evidence that such intervention has increased at both local and central government levels. Similarly, while in the past local government might often have seen itself as making policy within a broad statutory framework established by central government, new representative bodies now exist with the creation of the devolved legislatures in Northern Ireland, Scotland and Wales, which have had an impact on the policy process in their own jurisdictions and also in the United Kingdom as a whole, and have arguably led to further diversification not only of the processes by which policies are made, but also of policies themselves, while at the supra-national level the EU and other organisations both create their own policies and to some extent limit the freedom of action for nation states.

Some writers have produced models or formulated typologies that are designed to enable analysis of these complex processes, and which can often make them simpler to understand. The notion of 'stages' in the policy process, as noted in Chapter 1, is one example of that, and has tended to be part of the perceptions of both academics and practitioners, although with little agreement over what they might be. Lasswell (1936/1958), for example, argued for seven stages of decision making: intelligence, promotion, prescription, invocation, application, termination and appraisal; Hogwood and Gunn (1984) identified nine stages: issue search and agenda setting, issue filtration, issue definition, forecasting, objectives and priorities, options analysis, policy implementation, monitoring and evaluation, and policy succession and termination; Burch and Wood (1990) proposed three stages: initiation, formulation and implementation; while Knoepfel *et al.* (2011) use four stages: agenda setting, programming of the intervention, implementation and evaluation.

Even in the form of the more dynamic 'policy cycle', such approaches have, of course, been widely criticised as simplistic and as not representing the realities of policy making and implementation. Any such divisions between stages are inevitably somewhat arbitrary as there is likely to be overlap between them, actors and tiers of government involved, while the notion of structural discontinuities suggested by stages is likely to be misleading as policy making continues even when implementation is underway. Jenkins-Smith and Sabatier (1993), for example, have argued that a stagist approach is problematic as: there is no causal explanation of how policy moves from one stage to another; it cannot be tested on an empirical basis; it is descriptively inaccurate; it characterises policy making as essentially top-down and fails to take account of many actors; the idea of a policy cycle does not reflect the real world of policy making, which involves different tiers of government and interacting cycles; and it does not enable an integrated view of the analysis of the policy process and the analysis that is used in the policy process.

However, despite the criticisms, stagist models do provide one means of mapping the policy process and reducing its complexity to a form that is more amenable to analysis and understanding, which is why they remain widely used, including in books seeking to explain the policy process. While not driven by a stagist approach, this book does draw upon it in places in order to provide a map, or a model, that helps us to make sense of the complexity of activities, ideas and analytical tools associated with policy making and implementation, while remaining aware of its limitations, and of the dangers that can arise in seeking to impose the idea of stages on more complex and fluid processes.

Why do we use models of policy making?

As discussed in relation to the idea of stages in the policy process above, models can be useful as tools for analysis that help us understand what is going on, including how power is distributed and the role of different actors. By applying different models, we can, for example, gain an understanding of the role of different groups, their power relative to one another, the motivations behind the development of policies, and so on. Models and theoretical perspectives such as those set out in the remainder of this chapter therefore provide tools that we can use to analyse the ways in which decisions have been made. However, we should recognise that many politicians and policy makers are themselves concerned to improve the quality of policy making and implementation, as seen in the discussion of some of the developments under the Labour governments from 1997 to 2010 in Chapter 1. While they rarely set out to follow the processes suggested in these models, they may, from time to time, draw on the academic literature in order to try to improve the quality of decision making and the implementation and evaluation of policies.

Agenda setting

As noted above, the portrayal of the setting of agendas, or 'problem definition', as the first 'stage' in the policy process may not always match reality, as some issues may not reach the agenda of governments (see, for example, the discussion of the three dimensions of power in Chapter 3), some policies will emerge as unintended consequences of other actions, and in some instances attempts to implement one policy will create problems which may need new policy responses. However, the question of how issues emerge onto policy makers' agendas is clearly important in understanding the public policy process, and arguably also reflects the distribution and exercise of power in contemporary society.

As discussed in Chapter 1, some accounts suggest that policy is made and implemented in response to a perceived problem, and that to be considered as on the agenda an issue must usually be seen to require the attention of policy makers. These might be general topics, such as rising crime rates or growing obesity within the population, or specific issues, such as a shortage of affordable housing or a lack of GPs in rural areas. However, this is a rather simplistic and unrealistic view, with, for example, Cobb and Elder (1972) identifying two types of agenda: systemic, consisting of issues that are seen by members of the political community as worthy of attention, and as appropriate matters for the exercise of government authority; and institutional, the problems or issues that policy makers see as appropriate for serious and active attention. While reaching the institutional agenda does not guarantee that there will be action, the chances of it are significantly higher than if an issue is only on the systemic agenda, as it is the former that is effectively the agenda for action.

Kingdon (1984, 1995 and 2014), drawing on the development of health and transport policy in the United States, has suggested that agenda setting can be seen as comprising three largely independent streams of activity – problems, proposals and policies, and politics – and that when these converge there is a 'policy window' that permits some issues to reach the governmental agenda. The problem stream consists of those problems or issues with which policy makers become concerned; the proposals or policies stream is composed of policy communities, with a wide range of ideas being developed, for example by pressure groups, civil servants or local government officers, and academics, some of which are taken seriously while others are discarded; and the politics stream includes elements such as changes in public opinion, elections and other changes in government, and pressure group or media campaigns. For Kingdon, the 'garbage can' model (see the discussion of alternatives to rational and incremental approaches later in this chapter) and his own metaphor of 'primeval soup' are useful ways of portraying the policy environment, with the associated notions of constant change and shapelessness and only some issues emerging and being developed. He argues that policy entrepreneurs play a major role at an open policy window, linking solutions to problems and redrafting proposals to make them more acceptable. Kingdon suggests that policy windows open because of a compelling problem or as a result of developments in the political stream, and when this occurs the policy entrepreneurs have the opportunity to push an alternative policy from the policy stream. If all three streams come together, then a topic has a good chance of reaching the top of the decision-making agenda. If there is no such coincidence, then the policy window slips by and it is necessary to wait for another time when conditions are appropriate. In his later work, Kingdon (2014) links such ideas with punctuated equilibrium, with issue development proceeding in jumps and step-changes following periods of more gradual evolution.

However, Anderson (1997) suggests that Kingdon's view, while useful, over-emphasises the role of timing and luck in agenda setting, and that it is necessary to be aware of the range of other factors, such as the role of political parties and pressure groups, political leadership and parts of government (see Chapter 5), as well as the role of the news media in shaping opinions and helping structure policy agendas. Majone (1989) and Baumgartner and Jones (1993 and 2009) have also argued that policy options may be limited by existing institutional arrangements and the exclusion of certain ideas and interests, a perspective reinforced by the discussion of the three dimensions of power below. Harrison et al. (2002) deploy broadly similar arguments and use the case of the growth of 'scientific-bureaucratic medicine' (drawing on large-scale research and translating the output into 'clinical guidelines') in the USA and the UK in the 1990s to suggest support for Kingdon's emphasis on the centrality of ideas in shaping the policy agenda, but note that the convergence found would not be expected given his stress on chance and contingency at the level of individual governments. Similarly, Hill (2009) notes that Kingdon's work draws only on the United States, and that his ideas may not be entirely generalisable to other countries, highlighting, for example, the looser programmatic bonds within US political parties compared with those in the United Kingdom. He also criticises Kingdon's acceptance of the role of the media as simply messengers, rather than shaping the message.

One of the most influential pieces of work on the role of the media in setting agendas has been that of Downs (1972) (see Box 2.1). This sees there being a 'cycle of attention' for issues. Although developed by

---

Box 2.1 Downs' issue attention cycle

Five stages:

1. *the pre-problem stage* – the problem exists, and may be recognised by experts and groups in the field, but there is little public interest;

2. *alarmed discovery and euphoric enthusiasm* – often the result of a crisis or catastrophic event, such as a child abuse or health service scandal. The public is alerted and there is enthusiasm for dealing with the problem, including demands for government action;

3. *realising the cost of significant progress* – the public and policy makers become aware of the costs of tackling the problem;

4. *gradual decline of public interest* – having realised the cost of solutions, people become discouraged, bored or refuse to contemplate the problem anymore. This process is assisted by the emergence of new issues which drive out the old;

5. *the post-problem stage* – the issue has lost its position on the agenda and receives only spasmodic attention, although it may remain in a better position than at stage 1.

Source: Adapted from Downs, A. (1972) 'Up and down with ecology: the issue attention cycle', *Public Interest*, 28, 38–50.

Downs in relation to environmental policy, it has generally been seen as having wider applicability, and, in particular, helping understanding of why issues may come to prominence and appear to fall off the agenda from time to time.

In the United Kingdom, in addition to the environment, it is possible to identify a variety of other subjects that can regularly recur on the policy agenda, such as knife crime, binge drinking, child abuse and national educational performance. It is therefore worth considering what ideas such as those of Downs might tell us about the variations in levels of attention to such issues.

Rationalism and incrementalism

Moving on from the setting of agendas, perhaps the two best known models of the policy-making process are rationalism and incrementalism. Although they are sometimes seen as representing different ends of a spectrum, such a view is rather simplistic as they make different assumptions about the nature of policy making and the possibilities of change. In addition, rationalism is generally portrayed as an ideal state of affairs, and incrementalism as aiming to show the world as it actually is. In that sense, therefore, the debate about their relative merits can be rather misleading, and both can assist in adding to our understanding of policy making.

The rational model

This approach is usually traced back to Herbert Simon's book *Administrative Behaviour*, first published in 1945 and revised in 1957, in which he put forward a strong argument that rationality should be a goal in decision making. He suggested that 'rational' decision making in organisations can be seen as being a choice between alternatives that will help achieve previously selected goals that will reflect the values of the decision maker, and that in order to achieve this there should be a comprehensive analysis of the alternatives and their likely consequences prior to the decision being made.

While there are a number of weaknesses with this approach, some of which are discussed below, Simon argues that it is because of the limits to human rationality (for example, he notes that knowledge, particularly of consequences, is always fragmentary) that it is necessary to attempt to improve decision making in organisations, so that when there are a variety of possible ways of meeting a particular goal, the decision maker chooses that which is most likely to achieve the desired outcome. Decision makers should therefore attempt to identify the desired objectives, or ends, and the different means of reaching these using the 'means-end rational model':

> identifying the goal;

> listing all of the alternative strategies;

> assessing the consequences of each of these strategies, including their costs and benefits;

> choosing the preferred strategy in order to achieve the desired outcome.

The rational model assumes that a given problem will be tackled by following cumulative and logical steps in the search for the best response. However, in setting out this model, Simon recognised that it is rarely possible to separate facts and values, and that values will often affect both the aims of policies and the chosen means of achieving them. While it is therefore inevitably an idealised view of decision making, it is one which Simon suggests should lead to greater achievement of desired ends.

In the second edition of *Administrative Behaviour* (1957) and a series of other works, Simon recognised that people's decisions are inevitably constrained by a variety of factors, including those that arise from the organisational and psychological context within which they are made, such as attitudes, culture and experience, and he termed this 'bounded rationality' (Simon, 1957, p. xxiv). These limits mean that decision makers are not choosing alternatives from a full range of possibilities, but nevertheless a form of rational decision making can still be applied within the restrictions that exist to produce an outcome that is satisfactory.

In later work (1960 and 1965), Simon extended his argument to link his ideas about the rationalisation of decision making with the then emerging use of computers, by suggesting that while organisations do not work entirely rationally, new techniques and technology could improve this. For example, he suggested that decision making could be made better by improving approaches to what he calls 'programmed' decisions, those routine, standardised decisions which he argued might benefit from techniques such as the application of computerisation (including simulations), set procedures and mathematical approaches. Overall, therefore, while recognising the many factors that work against it, Simon put forward a case that rationality should be a goal in decision making.

Yet, despite attempts by Simon and others to respond to some of the weaknesses of the rational approach, a number of criticisms remain. Perhaps one of the most obvious problems is that while it may be possible to set out processes in a model as a series of logical steps that it is necessary to go through in order to achieve the desired outcome, in practice the reality is normally far more complex. For example, the formulation and development of any policy, whether it be for criminal justice, education, housing, immigration, transport, social care or nuclear power, rarely proceeds in such an orderly fashion. Rather, policy making is a complex process which can involve many different actors, from different tiers of government (elected representatives, ministers and officials), quasi-governmental bodies, pressure groups, the media, political parties, and private and not-for-profit sector organisations. All of these groups will have their own values and agendas, as well as resources. And the relative power of these groups in relation to each other, which itself will vary over time and from issue to issue, will inevitably affect the processes of policy development. There are, therefore, many push and pull factors which constantly work for and against each other.

The recognition that there are different values and objectives raises the question of whose should be used in the decision-making process? Within any organisation, whether it be the Prison Service, a local authority, a housing association, a university or a hospital trust, there are a variety of individuals and groups, some of whom may have values and objectives that vary from those set by the organisation itself, and who may have a degree of discretion in the implementation of 'policy'. Within the NHS, for example, managers may be concerned with their perception of the most efficient use of resources, or meeting targets set by government, while health professionals may see their primary goal as being to provide good-quality care. While these aims do not necessarily conflict, there is certainly the potential for them to do so. Lipsky (1974 and 1980) uses the term 'street-level bureaucrats' to describe those who actually implement the policy goals set by management, and points out that these people frequently have discretion in the way in which they interpret and implement policies. As a result, policies may be adapted or reworked by street-level bureaucrats during the implementation process in order to make them workable in practice, for those both delivering and receiving them (see the further discussion later in this chapter).

Overall, the rational approach is often seen as utopian; in the real world, decisions are rarely as clear-cut and systematic in terms of evaluation as this model implies. However, despite the shortcomings, it should not be assumed that this approach has not had a significant influence. The idea of rational decision making has actively influenced a whole range of attempts to improve the quality of the policy-making system, perhaps particularly in the UK and the USA. In the UK, for example, during the 1960s and 1970s initiatives such as that designed to improve planning on public expenditure, overseen by the Public Expenditure Survey Committee (PESC), the spread of planning units within government departments, and the Joint Approach to Social Policy, designed to improve collaboration between government departments (Challis et al., 1988), recognised many of Simon's criticisms of policy making in their attempts to move towards a better system. Similarly, under the Labour governments of 1997 to 2010 there were a range of initiatives that reflected a broadly 'rational' approach to decision making, including in relation to the use of evidence, 'joining up' government, 'learning lessons' and improving evaluation (see Bochel and Duncan (2007) for a fuller discussion of policy making under Labour). In relation to specific policies, examples included the use of commissions, such as the Low Pay Commission and the Royal Commission on Long Term Care for the Elderly, both of which involved the setting up of a committee of experts to look into the issue, consider the options and make recommendations, although in the latter instance the government chose not to implement its recommendations (however, the Scottish government did follow them, at least to a degree). Under the Coalition government,

What Works Centres were established to guide decision making on £200 billion of public spending in areas such as crime, ageing, early intervention and local economic growth (Cabinet Office, 2013). Like its predecessor, the Coalition established a commission to look at how to pay for care for older people, and again chose not to implement all of its recommendations. The rational approach also links with policy transfer, as with the Coalition government's use of models of free schools and charter schools from countries such as Sweden and the United States in helping justify the introduction of free schools in the Academies Act 2010 (see Chapter 4). However, it is worth noting that the concept of rationality adopted by policy makers in government has tended to be based on an intuitive and 'common sense' view of rationality, perhaps more similar to bounded rationality than the more refined concept as initially devised by Simon. Nevertheless, the rational model remains a useful tool with which to analyse the actions and decisions of policy makers, while the literature analysing decision making may also have value to decision makers concerned with trying to improve the quality of policy making.

The incremental model

One of the main critiques of the rational model came from Charles Lindblom, initially in his article 'The science of muddling through' (1959), and subsequently in a variety of sometimes rather different forms. One of his main targets was the suggestion that rational approaches and techniques could replace the need for political argument and consensus. Lindblom argues, instead, that 'muddling through' is an important part of decision making. He also points out that the pure rational model is rarely, if ever, achieved in the real world, and that policy makers are generally more concerned about coping with problems rather than solving them. While sharing Simon's view that the choices available to policy makers are restricted by a variety of factors, Lindblom believes that rather than seeking to achieve rational decisions, we should be more aware of the strengths of 'non-comprehensive analysis'. His preference is, therefore, for an 'incremental' approach to policy making, both as a model for how policies should be made, and as a better description of how they are actually made. The incremental model emphasises the extent to which policy makers tend to stick with the known, the accepted, the familiar and the manageable. It avoids the global, fundamental and wide-ranging analysis sought by proponents of the rational view (Box 2.2).

Box 2.2 Characteristics of incremental policy making

Burch and Wood (1990) identify five central characteristics of incrementalism:

1. policy making is restricted – policy makers do not wander far from the status quo, they keep to the familiar, with new policies or responses to problems differing only marginally from existing policies;

2. means rather than objectives determine policy;

3. incremental strategies are remedial – they deal with problems as they arise and there is little looking ahead, as, for policy makers, the status quo is largely satisfactory until it cannot be maintained;

4. incrementalism is reconstructive and serial – policy makers realise that problems change over time and solutions will raise new problems, meaning that policy making becomes a never-ending activity;

5. incrementalism is fragmentary – the involvement of different groups of people and different institutions in policy making varies with issues and across time.

Source: Adapted from Burch, M. and Wood, B. (1990) *Public Policy in Britain*, Oxford: Blackwell.

In *The Intelligence of Democracy* (1965) and other work, Lindblom developed his argument further, introducing the idea of 'partisan mutual adjustment' to reflect the processes of negotiation, bargaining and concession between decision makers that takes place in pluralist societies, and arguing that 'understanding a social problem is not always necessary for its amelioration' (Lindblom, 1979, p. 525). From this perspective, the adjustments and compromises of decision making also help to develop consensus and coordination, although it can be argued that at the same time such discussion and compromise are likely to eat into radical proposals as different actors realise that they need the support of others, so that aspirations are checked and small steps result. However, as Harrison *et al.* (1990) point out in their discussion of health policy, incrementalism does not necessarily equate with conservatism or slow change, as if there are frequent small steps over a fairly short period of time, the degree of policy change can be substantial. If that is the case, then at some stage the nature of such policies might have to be reconsidered.

As a prescriptive view, Lindblom argues that the dominant style of decision making in government is incremental, and that there are good reasons for policy makers adopting such a strategy. For example, policy making is made manageable by successive limited comparisons with the status quo, thus limiting the number of alternatives considered and the consequences of policies. Disagreements over objectives can be avoided as objectives are seldom considered; the information and intellectual skills for decision making are more likely to be available; and, for most actors, focusing on the familiar is more comfortable than assessing the unknown. Even where radical change is required, taking 'many smaller steps in a relatively short period ... is often – but not always – both more politically feasible and more prudent analytically than leaping well beyond the limits of understanding' (Lindblom and Woodhouse, 1993, pp. 27–28).

One of the main weaknesses of Lindblom's early discussion of incrementalism lay in his optimistic pluralism. Like the influential pluralist writer Dahl (see the explorations of pluralism and the three dimensions of power in Chapter 3), he came to recognise that power is skewed in favour of certain groups, and in particular in favour of big business. Indeed, he sought to respond to this by arguing that one of the roles of planners in the policy-making process is to give a voice to those who are less able to access and influence decision making. He also argued that in a stable society there exists a set of unifying beliefs which favour and to some extent emanate from dominant social groups, and which are communicated to the population through mechanisms such as education, churches and the media (1977). These limit the scope of partisan mutual adjustment to only some policy areas, while others, such as the distribution of wealth, or the existence of private enterprise, are not included on the agenda.

Other criticisms of incremental approaches have included that they can be a force for conservatism and a barrier to innovation. For example, by taking the status quo as a starting position, incrementalism may ignore problems such as how fair and equal the distribution of resources actually is. Similarly, its emphasis on remedial and short-term change can be seen as risking ignoring fundamental issues and perhaps the need for radical change.

While much policy making is certainly incremental, in the sense that it involves relatively small changes in response to particular problems, as an evaluative tool, one of the problems of incrementalism is the difficulty of making a clear distinction between incremental and radical change. For example, was the encouragement of academy schools by the Coalition and Conservative governments from 2010 and 2015 respectively incremental, or not? The Labour governments of 1997–2010 had enabled the establishment of academies, although they had been focused on 'turning round' 'failing' schools, whereas the intention under the Coalition and the Conservatives was essentially to make academies the norm, especially for secondaries, and the scale of academisation consequently far exceeded that under Labour.

Alternative models

A number of commentators have been critical of both the rational and the incremental views of policy making. As noted earlier, they have sometimes been treated as two models at either end of a spectrum, but that is not really the case. For example, Simon (1960) recognises that decision makers examine the options until something satisfactory (and usually less than the optimum) is discovered. If nothing satisfactory is found, the level of aspiration will be reduced until eventually what is desired matches what is available in policy terms. Such an approach can be seen as not dissimilar to Lindblom's incrementalism, where means rather than objectives are seen to be determining policy.

Another criticism is that the rational model tends to overemphasise significant changes in policy while the incremental model suggests that any change is difficult to achieve. If we take Simon and Lindblom as at either end of a spectrum (although noting the artificiality of doing so, as discussed above), then other views can be located as more central relative to them, with the two best known alternatives perhaps being Etzioni's (1967) 'mixed-scanning' and Dror's (1964) 'optimal model'.

Etzioni criticised the rationalistic approach for being both unrealistic and undesirable, but saw flaws in incrementalism, particularly with regard to how to deal with 'large' or 'fundamental' decisions, such as a declaration of war or those that may have a significant long-term impact on a state's budgets. He drew upon weather observation and the forecasting techniques of the time to produce a mixed-scanning approach. His analogy was that a rationalistic approach would require an exhaustive, detailed survey of weather conditions as often as possible, resulting in a great deal of detailed information that would be expensive to analyse and which would reduce the capacity of decision makers to respond. On the other hand, an incremental approach would tend to focus on areas where there had been particular weather patterns in the past, and might neglect to observe developments in unexpected areas. His strategy therefore draws upon elements of both approaches, with a broad overview of all parts of the sky, together with an examination of those areas identified from the broad picture as potentially requiring more in-depth attention. Etzioni argues that '[w]hile mixed-scanning might miss areas in which only a detailed camera could reveal trouble, it is less likely than incrementalism to miss obvious trouble spots in unfamiliar areas' (1967, p. 389). Applied to policy making, mixed-scanning implies that from time to time a broad scanning should be undertaken to check for distant but 'obvious' dangers or problems, while allowing the generally incrementalist nature of most decision making to continue. In Etzioni's opinion this would allow more detailed consideration to be given where fundamental decisions are required.

Dror (1964), too, criticises both rationalism, for its failure to reflect the reality of decision making, and incrementalism, for its conservatism and support for the status quo. He therefore proposed a 'normative optimum model', which aimed to increase the level of rationality in decision making but which recognised the extra-rational processes that are significant in policy making, including values, intuitive judgement and creative invention of new alternatives. He produced an 18-phase model, from the processing of values to communication and feedback, which operates at the two levels of rationality and extra-rationality (1989), designed to encourage decision makers to use rational analysis but also to think creatively, to draw on holistic impressions and to use their intuition.

Dror and Etzioni each set out to produce models that were both descriptive of the reality of policy making and prescriptive, in that they argue that policy making would be improved through the use of these approaches. However, while seeking to tackle the limitations of the rational and incremental models, they too have their weaknesses, so that Parsons (1995) notes, for example, that Dror has 'very little regard for the public in policy making' (p. 296), relegating them to a marginal evaluative role, while Ham and Hill (1984) questioned both the significance of Etzioni's 'fundamental' decisions, and how to distinguish between fundamental and incremental decisions.

Taking a different approach, Cohen *et al.* (1972) argued that decision making is 'organised anarchy' (p. 1), as a result of problematic preferences, with inconsistent goals being common in organisations, unclear technologies (the processes by which an organisation operates), and fluid and inconsistent participation by actors in the process. They therefore presented a 'garbage can' model, whereby decision making can be considered as a garbage can into which different kinds of problems and solutions are dumped by participants as they are generated. The mix of garbage in a particular can depends on the mix of cans available, the labels on the cans, what garbage is being produced and the speed with which garbage is being collected and removed from the scene. From this perspective, decision making is not sequential or hierarchical, but is messy, and the identification of problems and solutions will depend on the time, availability of resources and organisational preferences. Cohen *et al.* identify four streams that consistently appear in public policy processes:

1. *choices* – with an entry time at which each choice is activated for decision and a decision structure involving participants who are eligible to participate in making that choice;

2. *problems* – each having an entry time at which the problem becomes visible, an energy requirement to resolve a choice to which the problem is attached, and a structure with a list of choices to which the problem has access;

3. *rate of flow of solutions* – where, because of variations in the stream of solutions or the efficiency of search procedures within organisations, different energies are required to solve the same problem at different times;

4. *energy from participants* – so that in each time period each participant can provide a specified amount of potential energy.

They argue that while the garbage can process does not resolve problems well, 'it does enable choices to be made and problems resolved, even when the organization is plagued with goal ambiguity and conflict, with poorly understood problems that wander in and out of the system, with a variable environment, and with decision makers who may have other things on their minds' (p. 16).

While these, and other models, can all be criticised for not reflecting how policy making actually happens, or for being idealistic in relation to how they suggest that it should happen, they do serve to help us understand different ways in which policy can be conceived of being made, and, in most instances, also seek to suggest how those processes can be improved.

The advocacy coalition framework

The advocacy coalition framework (ACF) draws significantly on literature on the ways in which knowledge is used by policy makers as a way of understanding policy change. The ACF sees the policy subsystem as the most useful unit of analysis for understanding policy change, with such subsystems normally involving actors from all levels of government as well as other public and private organisations and individuals (its genesis and development is explained in Jenkins-Smith *et al.*, 2014).

It sees policy change over time arising from four sets of processes: the interaction and negotiations between competing advocacy coalitions ('actors from a variety of public and private institutions at all levels of government who share a basic set of beliefs (policy goals plus causal and other perceptions) and who seek to manipulate the rules, budgets and personnel of governmental institutions in order to achieve these goals over time' (Jenkins-Smith and Sabatier, 1993, p. 5)) within a policy subsystem; changes external to the subsystem, such as socio-economic conditions, regime change and output from other subsystems that provides opportunities and obstacles to the competing coalitions; developments that occur within the territorial and/or topic boundaries of the subsystem, with some types of event, such as crises, policy failures and fiascos, being likely to influence beliefs and focus attention on particular governmental programmes, with advocacy coalitions then engaging in debates over the causes, severity and policy implications; and policy change arising from 'policy-oriented learning' (p. 5), although, because of resistance to changing core beliefs, this is seen as generally limited to minor policy change, and while it 'can also facilitate major policy change ... this result is more likely in conjunction with an external or internal shock' (Sabatier and Jenkins-Smith, 2014, p. 203).

Within the policy subsystem it is assumed that a large and diverse range of actors can be aggregated into a number of advocacy coalitions composed of those who share a set of normal and causative beliefs and who often act together, although not everyone in a policy system will necessarily belong to an advocacy coalition. The ACF argues that in most subsystems, while there may be hundreds of actors, the number of politically significant advocacy coalitions will be quite small (Jenkins-Smith *et al.*, 2014), and Sabatier (1993) suggests that in most cases there will be two to four important coalitions, although in quiescent subsystems there might only be one. The coalitions are seen as relatively stable over time. Conflicting strategies from different coalitions are normally mediated by a separate set of actors, 'policy brokers', whose main concern is to find a compromise that will reduce intense conflict. The end result is one or more governmental programmes which will in turn lead to outputs.

The ACF has a particular interest in policy-oriented learning, including emphasising internal feedback, perceptions about external dynamics, and changing knowledge of problem parameters and the factors that affect them. However, changes to system dynamics can alter the composition and resources of various coalitions, and in turn public policy within a subsystem; changes to personnel are another source of potential change.

The focus on the analysis of policy change means that stable external factors have to be distinguished from more dynamic ones. The relatively stable parameters significantly constrain the options available to subsystem actors, for while changing them is not impossible, it is seen as very difficult, requiring concerted effort by an advocacy coalition for at least a decade, and often several decades. Changes to public policy within a subsystem are therefore more likely to arise from dynamic system events, such as large-scale socio-economic change, crises or disasters.

The ACF has been subject to a number of criticisms over the years, including because: it draws heavily on the United States and that may limit its generalisability to other (perhaps especially non-pluralist) political systems; it is not sufficiently clear about the role of ideas or self-interest in the policy process; it could also be clearer about how coalitions are formed and maintained; and it does not account adequately for the place of public opinion in policy making. In response, its supporters have sought to develop the framework, so that it has evolved significantly over time (for example, Jenkins-Smith *et al.*, 2014).

A number of other approaches have also drawn on ideas of policy learning, from Heclo's (1974) 'political learning', through Hall's (1993) 'social learning' and ideas of lesson-drawing (Rose, 1991), to Meseguer's (2005 and 2009) concepts of 'rational learning' and 'Bayesian learning', which see governments as rational actors looking for policies that work well abroad, and which she contrasts with policy emulation.

The power of bureaucracies

Bureaucracies are an important part of the machinery of government and can play a very significant role in the policy process. They have been the object of considerable academic interest to students of the policy process from Weber onwards. The reliance on and part played by bureaucracies within different forms and levels of government are discussed in greater detail in Chapters 5 and 6, and to some extent also in Chapters 4 and 7. Here, the concern is with a variety of perspectives that can encourage thought about and lead to an appreciation of the role and power of bureaucracies and the ways in which they can influence the policy process.

Terms such as 'bureaucracy', 'bureaucratic' and 'bureaucrat' are frequently used in a critical or pejorative sense, yet it is perhaps impossible to conceive of a modern society without such organisations. Much of the writing on bureaucracy has built upon the work of Weber, which has had great influence on the study of these entities. Weber saw the basis for the work of bureaucracies as rational-legal authority, and depicted them as working like a machine within which officials are selected for their posts by merit on the basis of clearly established procedures, with clear career and promotion paths, and as having a strictly hierarchical structure (Gerth and Mills, 1970). Similarly, the tasks that the organisation undertook were seen as being based upon clearly established rules and regulations.

The meaning of the term 'bureaucracy' has evolved considerably, but generally it contains connotations of both government by a bureau of officials and the structure of large modern organisations. Finer (1997) provided a succinct summary of the characteristics of bureaucracy: 'it is hierarchical; permanently in function; specialised into its various fields; educationally and/or vocationally qualified; paid and full-time; rule governed' (p. 64). Brown (1971) gave a rather fuller description:

> The members of a bureaucracy are career officials, who are selected, controlled and as far as possible promoted according to impersonal rules. They occupy positions in which they carry out prescribed functions. The authority which

they exercise (on behalf of the head of the organisation) belongs to their office, not to themselves. They are expected to work impersonally, regardless of their own feelings. Senior positions are filled by promotion. The security of a salary and a life career protects them from any personal consequences of their decisions, so long as they have been taken in accordance with the rules.

(p. 125)

While some elements of this may now hold less true, in particular the security and permanence of the job in many circumstances, the other characteristics remain a useful guide.

Although from the 1980s successive governments have made attempts to reduce and transform the traditional public sector bureaucracies, they remain important, and even a brief consideration of the agencies responsible for the making and implementation of public policy in the United Kingdom makes it obvious that bureaucracies play a significant role. The civil service is probably the best known example of a 'bureaucracy', and the roles of government departments such as the Department of Health, the Department for Transport and the Department for Work and Pensions, along with their equivalents in the devolved administrations, are immediately apparent. Many other 'bureaucratic' organisations staffed by public sector employees are also directly involved in the public policy process, such as where local government remains a provider of housing, and the National Health Service. In addition, the size and structure of some large private and not-for-profit organisations mean that they too can have bureaucratic characteristics.

Perspectives on bureaucracies

A number of perspectives have been developed that can help us to understand the role and influence of bureaucracies in the policy process in its broadest sense. This section draws heavily on writing on the civil service, in part because it is perhaps the most obvious and powerful bureaucracy, and in part as it has been the focus of the greatest amount of literature. However, many of the perspectives and critiques are applicable to other bureaucratic organisations involved with policy making and implementation, including local and devolved governments, and the NHS and other welfare bureaucracies.

The public administration model

As outlined briefly in Chapter 1, the traditional public administration, or Whitehall, model was based upon the view that it is elected politicians who make policy while bureaucrats provide policy advice and implement decisions. The bureaucracy was generally seen as working on a hierarchical basis in the public interest (Hughes, 2012). Arguably this was not only the traditional model put forward in textbooks, but also the dominant view held by ministers and civil servants. A similar view would have held, for example, in relation to local government, where elected politicians would be seen as making policy that would then have been implemented by officers.

However, from the 1970s, both the accuracy and utility of this model were increasingly questioned, and a number of alternative, more 'realistic' views were put forward on how far decision-making power lies in the hands of civil servants. In particular, there were criticisms centred on the perceived neutrality of civil servants and the advice that they give to ministers, and the argument (discussed in Chapter 1) that there is actually significant overlap between policy and administration, and that it is not possible or appropriate to draw a firm distinction between them.

The liberal-bureaucratic model

This model, sometimes referred to as the 'new public administration model', builds upon the view that while the ideal may be that politicians control bureaucrats, the reality is that there are a number of factors that can shift power away from elected politicians towards permanent officials (Theakston, 1995). These include the permanence and experience of bureaucrats and their ability to control advice and information passed to politicians, as well as the significant workloads of ministers and the fact that many may not be experts in the area of work of their departments (see, for example, Burnham and Pyper, 2008).

The power-bloc model

This perspective is based upon the continuing reality that senior civil servants are drawn largely from elite and privileged sections of society, with many, for example, having public school and Oxbridge backgrounds, and the view that this introduces an inherently conservative bias, as they use their skills and knowledge to continue to promote the ideals and interests of the sections of society from which they are drawn, which can result in only minimal change taking place. This position was initially associated with the political left, linking to some extent with Marxist arguments (for example, Miliband, 1969), while a number of former Labour ministers from the 1960s and 1970s, such as Benn (for example, 1988) and Crossman (1975, 1976 and 1977), claimed that civil servants obstructed their attempts to introduce more radical policy change. However, some ministers from the Thatcher governments (perhaps influenced by the ideas of Niskanen and others, discussed below) also claimed that the civil service tried to block some of those governments' more radical policies.

Public choice models

Some of the most powerful critiques of bureaucracies have come from those who draw upon public choice (also called rational choice) approaches, which influenced many areas of the political agenda from the 1970s and 1980s (broadly aligned with the New Right ideas of the time), as reflected in a number of places in this book. They are frequently associated with the work of Downs, Niskanen and Tullock.

In *Inside Bureaucracy* (1967), Downs recognised that bureaucracies are necessary to perform some functions that cannot be undertaken by market-oriented organisations (he uses examples such as traffic regulations and clean air). However, he asserts that officials act either partly or solely in their own self-interest, although their motivations may vary significantly, including, for example, to increase their power, income, prestige, security or their desire to serve their interpretation of the public interest. While motivations may vary, bureaucrats and bureaus are likely to maximise their self-interest by growing bigger, and consequently they require strong supervision and control.

Taking a different starting point in terms of motivation, Niskanen (1971) argued, based on economic theory (the idea that individuals make rational choices of maximising benefits over costs), that bureaucrats shape bureaus on the basis of their self-interest. He suggested that, while in the private sector profit maximisation is the motivating factor, the public sector is not concerned with profit maximisation and instead bureaucrats maximise the budget of their bureau in order to gain power, income, status and job security.

Tullock (1976), too, suggests that bureaucrats' welfare (in terms of security, pay, size of offices and so on) increases with a rising agency budget, that they seek to maximise their personal welfare by expanding that budget, and that this is only possible because allocation of resources happens in a different way from the market. As a result, rather than seeking to be profit maximisers, as assumed to be the case in the private sector, bureaucrats in government departments are argued to typically over-supply up to twice the level that would be produced by private firms under competitive market conditions (Perlman, 1976).

These views were reinforced during the 1970s and 1980s by arguments from the New Right that political control over the bureaucracy is often ineffective, and accusations that the civil service supported interventionist government and high levels of public expenditure.

Critics have noted, however, that these ideas are very difficult to test, and that empirical research has not provided clear evidence to support the theory of budget maximisation (Lewin, 1991), while the reduction in the size of the civil service and the increase in marketisation in the UK and many other countries in the 1980s and again in the period of 'austerity' following the financial crisis of 2008–10 also appear not to support such arguments.

Principal-agent models rest on the idea that relationships can be reduced to contractual terms, with the principal buying something from the agent. However, unlike in ideal market models, they assume that the agent has specialised knowledge and some degree of decision-making authority that the principal does not, and there is therefore an incentive for the agent to sell more services, or to sell them at a higher price, than are actually needed. The challenge for the principal, therefore, is to ensure that the agents will have sufficient incentive to comply with their wishes. When applied to the private sector, accountability is assumed to be from management to shareholders, while there are also other incentives to perform, such as competition, or the threat of takeover or bankruptcy. These ideas have been applied to bureaucracies in a way that tends to support NPM approaches, as the possibility of being able to contract out functions in a market-like fashion would be seen as a good thing (for example, Hughes, 2012). However, it can be argued that such approaches neglect ideas such as the values that may be present in a bureaucracy, together with relationships based upon trust, while at the same time not taking account of the potential for coercion in bureaucracies (for example, Meier and Hill, 2005).

Finally, Dunleavy (1986 and 1991), broadly a critic of these ideas, sought to develop an alternative model of bureaucratic behaviour based on public choice theory. He argued that in public service systems pay and conditions are often relatively fixed, and that bureaucrats' perceived welfare is also linked to the type of work that they do and the status of their organisation, so that their behaviour may be better characterised by their attempts to shape their organisation in a different way: 'Maximising a bureau's conformity to an ideal, high status organizational pattern ... provides a powerful explanation of a wide range of observed administrative behaviour' (Dunleavy, 1991, p. 205). Indeed, Dunleavy suggests that this might help explain the lack of resistance in Whitehall to developments associated with privatisation and shrinking budgets in the 1980s, such as hiving off and contracting out, as in some circumstances these provided senior officials with the opportunity to serve their best interests by radically transforming the character and status of their organisation to fit the direction taken by politicians, and to some extent the perceived strengths of the private sector, rather than by attempting to preserve budgets and staffing levels, for example by hiving off routine operational tasks to arm's-length agencies, while retaining a significant policy role close to the centre of power.

The bureaucratic coordination model

This approach draws upon the idea that elected policy makers overseeing large organisations, such as government departments or other substantial bodies, are unlikely to be able to be in complete control of all that goes on within their area of responsibility. For example, given that there are large numbers of civil servants in each department and only three or four ministers (see Chapter 5), no minister, no matter how well organised they are, is likely to be able to have complete oversight of everything that their department is doing. This would arguably be likely to apply to those in similar positions in devolved and local government. As a result, bureaucrats tend to play a major role in the coordination that is necessary for the smooth running of government, while elected politicians may sometimes be relegated to more of a backseat role. At central government level, in particular, this might suggest that whichever political party is in office, politicians will never be able to exercise total control over detailed policy making and implementation, and will to some extent have to rely on the bureaucracy.

While each of these perspectives may have strengths and weaknesses, taken together they encourage us to consider a number of wider issues, including the importance of ministers providing a clear policy lead; how to get individuals to act together for the common good; the size and shape of government and its internal structures; and how we can ensure that service deliverers are held accountable. One obvious development, discussed further in Chapter 5, has been the growth, for example under the Labour governments of 1997–2010, of the Prime Minister's Office, and in other departments the wider use of special advisers – political appointees – arguably used at least in part to counter the influence of civil servants, a pattern followed by ministers in the Coalition and Conservative governments that followed.

Street-level bureaucrats

A rather different perspective on the importance of bureaucrats is that often associated with the work of Lipsky (1976, 1980 and 2010), who developed a model to explain the behaviour of what he termed 'street-level bureaucrats': those who work in bureaucracies at local level and (a) interact constantly with citizens in the course of their jobs; (b) have a significant degree of independence in their work, including discretion in making decisions; and (c) have the potential for a fairly significant impact on the citizens with whom they deal. Lipsky argues that, at street level:

> ... public policy is not best understood as made in legislatures or top-floor suites of high ranking administrators, because in important ways it is actually made in the crowded offices and daily encounters of street level workers.
>
> (1980, p. xii)

The power of street-level bureaucrats can be seen in a number of different ways:

> ➤ *control of clients* – through the ability to differentiate, for example between those seen as deserving and undeserving, to withhold information from clients, and to perpetuate or delay service delivery. Such activities may help to limit client demand, and while the services can always be presented as in the best interests of clients, they may often run in the interests of bureaucracy;

> ➤ *control of their own activities* – through the ability to modify their own activities and perceptions of their jobs and clients, and also to modify their objectives to match their ability to perform;

> ➤ *power over their own agency* – as street-level bureaucrats carry out much of the difficult rationing at client level, it is often convenient for organisations to permit this discretion to continue as the exercise of street-level bureaucrats' discretion can be functional to the organisation.

Lipsky argued that the reality of policy making at that level is that it is more concerned with the development of practices that enable officials to cope with the pressures that they are under than with the achievement of public service ideals. This situation arises because the nature of the work is such that the demands upon those who work in these services are often so great that they can become unmanageable. Street-level bureaucrats often come into service with high expectations about what they can achieve for their clients, but the pressures of the job lead them to develop methods that process their clients in a largely routine manner and to adjust their work habits to lower expectations of themselves and those who use their services. For example, if resources do not allow them to work with children on an individual basis, teachers might develop techniques such as encouraging children to read in groups and to help one another, or teaching them on a mass basis. Similarly, social workers who are unable to visit all of their clients on a regular basis may introduce systems of prioritisation, only seeing those deemed in greatest need frequently. Yet, at the same time, street-level bureaucrats, such as lecturers, teachers and social workers, are sometimes seen to have a significant degree of freedom and autonomy, as well as power over the users of services. For example, they exercise discretion in a situation where demand for resources exceeds supply by deciding which services a consumer may or may not receive; they also have considerable autonomy from the agency which employs them because the existence of pressures such as large classes and huge caseloads, together with inadequate resources, means that instead of dealing with consumers on a one-to-one basis, they must deal with them on a mass basis. Lipsky also observes that these features can be further enhanced by the fact that such jobs frequently have ambiguous or even conflicting goals, and that it is difficult to measure their performance.

The exercise of discretion is a key feature of Lipsky's model. It is a source of power, whether it be for housing officials making decisions about who gets housing, and if so whether it be a flat in a tower block, a room in shared accommodation, or a house, police who decide which offences to record and which to turn a blind eye to, or health care workers deciding who will or will not receive treatment. As noted above, the exercise of discretion is often related to the rationing of resources, but for many public sector agencies there may potentially be no limit to the demand for free services, and changes in the level of resourcing will not necessarily result in significant changes for individual workers.

Hupe *et al.* (2015) note that within the scholarly writing on street-level bureaucracy there is considerable diversity, highlighting horizontal, vertical and discursive diversity. Horizontal diversity is concerned with the type of work that can (or cannot) be regarded as street-level bureaucracy; vertical diversity refers to the question of whether it is only street-level bureaucrats that exercise discretion, or also their managers, and indeed other actors, which they suggest 'leaves us with a blurred view of the location of the street' (p. 16); and discursive diversity is when different terms are used to describe essentially the same phenomenon.

In a work edited by Brodkin and Marston (2013), the focus is on street-level organisations and workfare, including active labour market policies. In it, Brodkin (2013a) highlights that not only can street-level organisations mediate policy through their practices, but they can also mediate politics 'by structuring the possibilities for advancing claims on the state, asserting rights, and pursuing redress' (p. 24), and that contested political projects can be advanced indirectly using administrative means, including administrative reform, in addition to more overtly political means. In the conclusions, she goes on to argue that in relation to workfare-type policies, both in Europe and the United States, street-level organisations mediate the policy experiences of those who are the targets of such policies, including whether they will have access to services that might help them in the labour market, and that, for example, governance and managerial practices are 'shifting street-level practices away from social support and investment and towards greater social regulation' (Brodkin, 2013b, p. 280).

There are potentially important implications for public policy that arise from these arguments. For example, McDonald (2002) applied the concept of street-level bureaucracy to GPs in the National Health Service, noting that such an approach might be more appropriate than the frequent references to the 'power of the medical profession', as the degree of cohesion and uniformity of belief and action associated with the latter may be inadequate at the micro level. She pointed out that the professional status of GPs is such as to justify relatively weak forms of top-down control, and that as a result they are able to adopt 'implicit rationing to cope with service demands' (p. 134) and that this can conflict with attempts to introduce more 'rational' and systematic managerial techniques within the NHS. However, more recently, Harrison has suggested that the emphasis on evidence-based medicine and the introduction of quasi-markets (the latter primarily in England) in the NHS may be leading to the development of a medically qualified administrative elite that is likely to further undermine the professional discretion of doctors. In contrast, Ellis (2015) argues that reforms to social care in England, including greater personalisation, appear to create the possibility for street-level behaviour, although while, at times, social workers may exercise a 'paternalistic authority as professionals' (p. 201) at the point of implementation, the formalisation of decision making over the past four decades has encouraged a broad conformity with bureaucratic rules.

One area where it can perhaps be argued that discretion has been increasingly limited is in relation to social assistance, with discretionary payments having been virtually eliminated following reforms to the social security system in the 1980s and the replacement of individual judgements by computerised systems (Walker, 2015).

Implementation

At its most simplistic, 'implementation' is the process of putting policies into practice. For example, central government might create and implement a state pension scheme, or it may formulate planning policies which local authorities might then be expected to implement in their areas. Such a view fits well with the traditional top-down model that sees neutral bureaucracies implementing policies determined by elected politicians, so that the original thinking around theories of implementation '... evolved from a starting point in which the translation of policy into action was seen as being, under normal circumstances, an unproblematical process so long as bureaucracies were clearly subservient to their political masters' (Hill, 1997b, p. 213). However, as discussed in Chapter 1 and above, this view arguably bears little resemblance to the realities of implementation in contemporary society, and in practice both the number of actors and their roles in policy making and implementation are far more complicated, as are interpretations of how successful (or unsuccessful) policies might be (see Chapter 8).

Instead, there is a strong argument that implementation should be seen as part of the complex and dynamic policy process, rather than as a distinct component of it. It is sometimes suggested that implementation starts only when a policy or programme has been formally ratified, but such a chronological separation from other elements of the policy process can be misleading, since, for example, some policies do not need formal ratification, but simply emerge from statements of intent or practices in the field. Such a separation also implies that once implementation starts there is no more policy making, whereas in reality the processes are inseparable since policy making is a never-ending process. In addition, it is possible to seek to explain the nature of implementation by referring to how policy is made (for example, Boswell and Rodriguez, 2016).

Top-down approaches

One of the first works to make a significant impact on the until-then widely accepted distinction between policy making and implementation was Pressman and Wildavsky's (1973) *Implementation*, an examination of the implementation of economic development in Oakland, California, from which the authors became aware that the problems of policy implementation were rarely considered. They argued that each stage that a decision passes through (including the number of agencies involved in delivering it) reduces the chances of it being carried out according to the original wishes of the sponsor. As a result, policies are quite likely to fail. This work was effectively grounded in a 'top-down' approach to policy making, arguing that successful implementation requires a top-down system of control and that policy makers should only promise what they are actually able to deliver.

Subsequently, British writers such as Hood (1976), Gunn (1978) and Hogwood and Gunn (1984) expanded upon this with examinations of what would be necessary to achieve 'perfect' implementation. In addition, in many policy areas, and in particular those requiring the participation of a wide variety of organisations, such as social care (which can involve agencies from public, private and not-for-profit sectors, including those responsible for social care, health and housing) or an integrated transport system, the problems of inter-agency collaboration have often been cited as contributing to difficulties with implementation, thus apparently encouraging the need for a top-down approach. Hogwood and Gunn identified 10 preconditions that they argued would have to be satisfied for perfect implementation:

1. that circumstances external to the implementing agency do not impose crippling constraints;

2. that adequate time and sufficient resources are made available to the programme;

3. that not only are there no constraints in terms of overall resources but also that, at each stage in the implementation process, the required combination of resources is actually available;

4. that the policy to be implemented is based upon a valid theory of cause and effect;

5. that the relationship between cause and effect is direct and that there are few, if any, intervening links;

6. that there is a single implementing agency which need not depend upon other agencies for success or, if other agencies must be involved, that the dependency relationships are minimal in number and importance;

7. that there is complete understanding of, and agreement upon, the objectives to be achieved; and that these conditions persist throughout the implementation process;

8. that in moving towards agreed objectives it is possible to specify, in complete detail and perfect sequence, the tasks to be performed by each participant;

9. that there is perfect communication among, and coordination of, the various elements involved in the programme;

10. that those in authority can demand and obtain perfect obedience.

(Hogwood and Gunn, 1984, pp. 199–206)

This list illustrates clearly why this is called the top-down approach, with the central purpose being to provide advice to those at the top on how to minimise implementation problems, and 'policy' being seen as belonging to policy makers at the 'top'. Hogwood and Gunn recognise that these preconditions are unlikely ever to be achieved in practice, but they retain 'a measure of sympathy with the top-down view, if only on the grounds that "those seeking to put policy into effect" are usually elected while "those upon whom action depends" are not' (p. 207), citing the case of civil servants and health service employees as examples of the latter, and suggest that in some circumstances it can indeed be attractive, such as a Home Secretary attempting to reduce racism within the police force, rather than accepting the persistence of racist attitudes and actions at 'street level'. Top-down models of implementation came to be associated with managerialist approaches to the achievement of policy objectives that became dominant in much of the public sector from the 1990s, so that Parsons (1995) was able to include such ideas as 'operational management', 'corporate management' and 'personnel management' in his exploration of implementation.

It is possible to identify a number of criticisms of top-down models (Matland, 1995). For example, the emphasis tends to be on formal decisions and tends to downplay broader public objectives. Similarly, much public policy does not have clear and unambiguous goals, it may not take the form of an explicit programme or set of actions, and indeed, as noted in Chapter 1, it may not always be clear that something is or is not 'policy', and therefore its implementation cannot be reduced to a purely administrative process. But perhaps the most important criticism of the top-down approach is its failure to take into account the variety and importance of other actors involved in implementing policies, as considered below.

Bottom-up approaches

Such perspectives owe their prominence to those who have '... particularly discovered a "bottom/up" perspective – effective implementation was more likely to be a function of street-level adjustment than of perfect policy design' (Dunsire, 1999, p. 372). This criticism of top-down approaches makes many of the same points as Lipsky's consideration of street-level bureaucrats outlined earlier in this chapter. Critics argue that control over people is not the best way of achieving successful implementation, and that it is necessary to take account of the exercise of discretion in the implementation of policy, with professionals, such as doctors, police officers, social workers and teachers, all playing a part in controlling and delivering the services for which they are responsible, so that the actual outcomes of policy may be very different from those intended by policy makers. In addition, supporters of a bottom-up approach argue that the reality is,

> [n]ot of imperfect control, but of action as a continuous process of interaction with a *changing and changeable policy*, a *complex interaction structure*, an *outside world which must interfere* with implementation because government action impinges upon it, and implementing actors who are *inherently difficult to control*.
>
> (Hill, 1997b, p. 139)

A different approach is taken by Hull and Hjern (1987), who sought to identify the variety of actors involved in implementation (in this case, the growth of small businesses) and to map the relations between them, which might also require looking at several policies that affect the same problem (Winter, 2006). They suggest that, in practice, implementation structures are often less hierarchical and are cross-organisational, with collaboration working across formal borders at the operational level.

Matland (1995) identifies both a normative and a methodological criticism of bottom-up approaches. The normative one is that in a democratic system policy control should be exercised by those whose power derives from their position as elected representatives, and that simply because local service deliverers may have flexibility does not mean that it should be the basis for designing policy. The methodological criticism is that even if there are local differences in policy implementation, centrally determined policy sets the borders for actions and will substantially impact on policy outcomes, even if implementation is not 'perfect'.

Thus, while the top-down approach emphasises the creation of implementation deficiency, the bottom-up view stresses the continual re-creation of policy. This latter viewpoint has led some to suggest that there is a need not just for forward mapping, but also for 'backward mapping' (Elmore, 1980), from the problems and choices facing individuals to the policies required to change those things. Elmore criticises the dominant top-down perspective, 'forward mapping', for its 'implicit and unquestioned assumption that policymakers control the organizational, political and technological processes that affect implementation' (p. 603). He suggests that backward mapping, starting at the lowest level of the implementation process and working up level by level, is valuable, looking at the ability to affect the behaviour that is the target of the policy and the resources that would be needed to have that effect, and argues that this would produce policy objectives which would be achievable.

A policy continuum?

Others have tried to draw upon both top-down and bottom-up perspectives to '... consider implementation as a policy/action continuum in which an interactive and negotiative process is taking place over time between those seeking to put policy into effect and those upon whom action depends' (Barrett and Fudge, 1981, p. 25).

It is apparent that whilst the top-down approach reflects the view that it is a policy elite (however that may be defined) that 'makes' policy, the bottom-up perspective is perhaps more realistic in recognising that at each level of government there is a variety of often interacting policies that those at local level are affected by and seek to use in the pursuit of their own goals; it also recognises and reinforces the view of 'policy making' as a continually developing continuum. As Hill and Hupe (2002) note, from the mid-1980s there have been increasing attempts to produce 'synthesised' or other alternative approaches to implementation, and indeed it is arguable that the use and application of any model in researching policy implementation should depend upon the subject and its context. The advocacy coalition framework, as discussed earlier in this chapter, emphasises that policy makers can learn from their mistakes, especially over the long term, and that as a result successful implementation can happen over a 10–20-year period, although Winter (2006) suggests that their focus may move away from implementation towards policy change.

Matland (1995) argues that the degrees of conflict and ambiguity associated with a policy are likely to affect its implementation, so that traditional top-down models generally present an accurate description of the implementation process when policy is clear and there are low levels of conflict over it, while bottom-up models may be more useful when policy is ambiguous and conflict is low. Where there is a high degree of conflict and little ambiguity, and there is likely to be a highly politicised atmosphere, top-down models may be helpful; and where there is significant conflict and an ambiguous policy, both approaches are likely to be relevant. Sausman *et al.* (2016) suggest that, as policy is implemented, meaning is negotiated by both central and local actors, so that there is adaptation to account for local circumstances and at the same time such adaptations can also reshape the policy context.

Winter (2003 and 2006) highlights that it may be wrong to place the entire blame for a policy not succeeding on implementation, as the connections between policy formulation, policy design and policy implementation are important, and '[t]he roots of implementation problems can often be found in the prior policy formulation process' (2006, p. 155), so that there may be ambiguous goals and invalid assumptions about causal links between goals and means, while in some instances policies may be largely or entirely symbolic, without offering the means to achieve their objectives.

Policy instruments

The final topic covered in this chapter considers the instruments that are available to governments in the formulation and implementation of policies. As noted in the discussion of implementation above, Pressman and Wildavsky (1973) considered issues of policy failure, which they suggested are not caused only by poor implementation, but also by the poor choice of policy instruments. Different mixes of instruments are not necessarily equally effective in achieving a given policy objective, and Winter (2006) argues that the

> ... effects of instruments on implementation are often driven by the context, including the political context. Consequently, designing good policies is not a simple, technocratic process like selecting the best type of materials for building a bridge [and] ... the chosen instruments may affect the overall implementation structure and process, as certain instruments tend to favor the formation of particular implementation structures.
>
> (p. 155)

Policy instruments are therefore clearly linked with the formulation of policies, as, when considering policy options, attention is paid not only to what to do, but also to how to do it. Most policy goals could, in theory, probably be accomplished using different instruments, so that a goal of providing health care to a population could be met through state provision, delivered by the private market, or could be left to be achieved by individuals and families. Similarly, one route to improving health would be to treat people who are unwell or who have accidents, while preventing people from becoming ill or reducing the likelihood of accidents would be another. Perhaps unsurprisingly, given the complexity of many issues and the challenges of identifying causes and effects, in most cases policy makers are likely to use a variety of tools when they seek to achieve particular ends.

Lowi (1972) identified four types of public policy, which can effectively be related to types of policy instrument: distributive policies are those that affect the ways in which governments use public funds to assist particular social groups; redistributive policies involve the reallocation of costs and benefits between different groups; regulatory policies are concerned with managing citizens' behaviour, rather than financial resources; and constitutive policies affect the way that other policies are made, for example through the creation or rearrangement of institutions.

There have been many other attempts to produce taxonomies of policy instruments, but that developed by Christopher Hood, known as NATO, has been influential. Hood argued that all policy tools derive from four broad categories of governing resource, so that governments address problems through: the use of the information that they possess as key policy actors ('Nodality' – being at the centre of a network); their legal powers ('Authority' – the power to demand, forbid, guarantee or adjudicate); their financial resources ('Treasure'); or the formal organisations available to them ('Organisation'). Governments might, for example, choose to make certain information available, or not, may choose to finance different activities, could use their coercive powers to force other actors to undertake particular activities, or might simply undertake those activities themselves. Much of the early work on policy instruments was heavily influenced by economics approaches, focusing on *substantive* instruments, tools that more or less directly affect the type, quantity or price of goods or services, while later on more attention came to be paid to *procedural* instruments, those that might affect other parts of the policy process other than simply economic or social behaviour. Howlett (for example, 2000 and 2011) has suggested a number of potential amendments to Hood's typology to take account of the differences between substantive (designed to directly or indirectly affect the behaviour of those involved) and procedural (intended to affect the behaviour of actors involved in policy implementation) instruments and tools.

The variety of instruments that might fall under each of the NATO headings is substantial. For example, nodality-based instruments could range from public information campaigns through attempts to influence the preferences and behaviour of the public or particular groups, and would also include commissions and inquiries, as well as benchmarking and performance indicators, as frequently used for schools, hospitals and other public services. Authority-based instruments would include regulations that require people and organisations to comply with particular rules, whether in relation to criminal behaviour, markets, such as the new regulatory mechanisms that have frequently been introduced following privatisation and marketisation of former public services, or social concerns, such as sales of alcohol or attempts to tackle discrimination, or to governments also allowing some groups to regulate themselves, as with doctors and lawyers, and much press activity, which should, in theory, be cheaper for governments, but which might risk being less effective. Government funding, in terms of paying the full or partial cost of services such as schools or public transport, or using tax incentives to direct people towards a particular action, is clearly a treasure-based instrument, as are financial disincentives, such as taxes and user charges, which may both raise money for governments and seek to encourage or discourage particular behaviour, as with higher taxes on alcohol or tobacco. Finally, there is a plethora of organisation-based instruments, ranging from direct provision by the public sector, as with defence, social security and the state pension, public enterprises, which were widely used in the post-war period, although most were privatised in the 1980s and 1990s, arm's-length bodies (see Chapter 7), and encouraging community, voluntary or informal provision. In addition, as there is no ideal way of organising government structures, governments sometimes seek to respond to particular problems by reorganisation, as, for example, happened in 2007, when the Home Office was split up, with some of its functions going to the Ministry of Justice, and in 2016, when the new Prime Minister Theresa May closed the Department for Energy and Climate Change and created a Department for Exiting the European Union, or with the introduction of devolution and the creation of new elected legislatures for Northern Ireland, Scotland and Wales in 1998 and 1999 (see Chapter 6).

Of course, a variety of alternative conceptualisations has also been developed, with John (2011), for example, identifying six sets of resources that governments can use to influence policy outcomes:

Top-down

Law and regulation

Public spending and taxation

Internal to the state

Bureaucracy and public management

Institutions

Non-standard

Information, persuasion and deliberation

Networks and governance.

The formulation of a policy therefore requires decisions about its aims, then the selection of policy instruments to address the particular issue, taking into account their technical and political feasibility. The selection of instruments will therefore depend on the context of the problem, who conducts the analysis, how it is conducted, and their fit with the general values and goals of a government, so that questions associated with efficiency, effectiveness, equity, legitimacy and political support may affect the choices in any given situation. Howlett *et al.* (2009) suggest that where there are both new actors and new ideas, there is the potential for change to policy goals themselves, but where there are new actors and old ideas, the most likely result is a change in policy instruments, and where there are old actors and old ideas, changes are likely to be at the more micro level of instrument components, rather than in the nature of the instruments themselves.

Lodge and Wegrich (2012a) argue that three key developments have been shaping the environment for the choice of policy instruments: internationalisation and Europeanisation, including the presence of global norms in terms of tool choices, concerns about major corporations relocating production to other states, and the constraints of supranational law; electoral politics, with increasingly volatile domestic electorates and the rise of 'anti-tax coalitions' and attempts by governments to avoid risk and manage blame; and technological change, so that governments have access to unprecedented amounts of data, and are potentially able to automate administrative activities, although at the same time the public also has greater access to a variety of information while technology has also made it possible for concerns to be voiced rapidly, such as through social media.

Howlett (2011) notes that others have suggested that the perceived shift from government to governance and the emphasis on networks have led to changes in the instruments used, including greater consultation and changes in regulatory activities to stress compliance more than enforcement. However, he argues that, while there have been changes in how governments function, 'the scope, significance and causes of these changes remain contentious' (p. 5). This view is broadly reflected by Wurzel *et al.* (2013), who argue that within Europe, while there has been a significant growth in the adoption and use of new environmental policy instruments, which are said to reflect a greater emphasis on cost effectiveness and to allow stakeholders more involvement in the formulation of their goals, as well as greater flexibility in achieving them, regulation has remained the dominant policy instrument (they note also that this reinforces the continued importance of the state), and that while there have been some differences in approach between states, 'the overarching trend has been one of smarter regulations and more complex policy instrument mixes including the hybridisation of different types of environmental policy instruments', including both 'old' government tools and 'new' modes of governance (p. 217). They also suggest that while there is some evidence of policy transfer, the policy instruments that emerge in each jurisdiction strongly reflect domestic legal and political contexts.

In addition, not only is the choice of instrument a potentially political issue, but instruments are not neutral and the choice will therefore partially structure the process and its results, so that Lascoumes and Le Galés (2007) have argued that it is important to examine the interests of those implicated in the choice of instruments and that '[t]he most powerful actors will be induced to support the adoption of certain instruments rather than others' (p. 9). They suggest, for example, that as part of a broad typology, legislative and regulatory instruments might be associated with a 'social guardian' state drawing on conceptions of a general interest, while *de facto* and *de jure* standards and best practice instruments might be more associated with a less interventionist and more competition- and market-oriented state that emphasises the role of civil society.

Conclusion

As this chapter has made clear, there are many different approaches that can be used to help us understand agenda setting, policy making and policy implementation. It is necessary to understand the ways in which ideas emerge and develop, and how they may reach or be prevented from reaching the agendas of policy makers, as well as how and when decisions are made and implemented. Both rational and incremental models have strengths and weaknesses as normative models, and while incrementalism arguably more often provides a more accurate picture of what happens in real-world policy making, the idea of rationalism continues to exert considerable appeal. Both approaches can, of course, be useful for analytical purposes. The advocacy coalition framework, too, is of interest, not least because of its emphasis on the ways in which knowledge is used by policy makers as a way of understanding policy change over longer periods of time.

Despite, and in some respects because of, changes from the 1980s, bureaucracies continue to play a significant role, and therefore remain of interest in studying the making and implementation of public policy, even if some of their forms have changed and some functions have been devolved to other organisations. Similarly, as the chapter makes clear, while in some policy areas there have been developments that might be expected to reduce the discretion available to front-line workers, the nature of many public service occupations is such that some elements of street-level bureaucracy can be identified, and the insights of Lipsky and others can therefore prove valuable.

Finally, from the 1980s, while governments have frequently used the rhetoric of devolution of power and decision making in public policy, there have been many examples of the use of top-down approaches in policy implementation, not least through the greater use of tools such as performance measures and targets, as discussed in Chapter 8. As a result, the use of a variety of models can again make a significant contribution to understanding this part of the policy process.

Further reading

Discussion of the advocacy coalition framework and a number of other approaches can be found in:

Sabatier, P. A. and Weible, C. M. (eds) (2014) *Theories of the Policy Process*, Boulder: Westview Press.

Also covering much of the range of this chapter are:

Parsons, W. (1995) *Public Policy: An Introduction to the Theory and Practice of Policy Analysis*, Aldershot: Edward Elgar.
Cairney, P. (2012) *Understanding Public Policy*, Basingstoke: Palgrave Macmillan.

A thorough overview of this topic is provided by:

Hupe, P., Hill, M. and Buffat, A. (eds) (2016) *Understanding Street-Level Bureaucracy*, Bristol: Policy Press.

For a focus on the design of policies and the instruments that can be used to pursue them, see:

Howlett, M. (2011) *Designing Public Policies: Principles and Instruments*, Abingdon: Routledge.

3

Power and Policy

This chapter discusses a number of what might loosely be termed 'theories of power' that can contribute to the analysis and explanation of the making and implementation of public policy in the UK. These include a variety of different interpretations of how widely power is dispersed and shared, from pluralist to elite theory approaches, the role of the state and how power is exercised. A knowledge of these perspectives is valuable, as the sources of power are likely to be perceived differently depending upon the theory adduced.

While Chapter 1 outlined a variety of approaches that can help us understand policy change, and Chapter 2 considered a variety of perspectives that can be used to analyse and interpret the policy agenda, decision making and implementation, this chapter builds upon those by considering a number of approaches that are important in explaining the exercise of power, and, given the focus on public policy, the role of the state and state institutions in particular. The state can, for present purposes, be defined in terms of the institutions of which it is composed, and in terms of the functions that it performs. For example, Chapters 5, 6 and 7 are concerned largely with the public policy process in different parts of the state. In the United Kingdom, state institutions include representative bodies, such as the Westminster Parliament, the devolved legislatures in Northern Ireland, Scotland and Wales, and local government, executive bodies such as government departments and some quangos, and judicial bodies, such as the courts. In addition, in recent years it has been possible to identify a growth in European (notably, but not only, arising from the European Union, prior to the 2016 referendum on leaving the EU) and international influences, with the UK being bound by international obligations across a number of areas of policy and forms of activity, as discussed further in Chapter 6.

State institutions perform a wide variety of functions. Historically, the most important were the maintenance of law and order and peace (or war), the protection of property rights and the system of justice. From the nineteenth century, the state increasingly became involved in other areas of activity, such as the management of the economy and the provision of a wide range of services, including the welfare state, traditionally seen as primarily concerned with education, employment, health, housing, social care and social security. There was, broadly speaking, a continuous growth in state activity in these areas until the 1980s, although, particularly since then, the extent of the state's role has been of significant political contention, and there has been a series of initiatives aimed at altering the balance of responsibilities between public, private and third sectors and between individuals and the state. The management of the economy, including taxation, law and order and defence have continued to be important areas of state activity, together with the welfare state, while more recently areas such as the environment have become important.

Perspectives on the exercise of power by and within the state can be presented in a variety of ways, as is clearly demonstrated by a brief consideration of the contents of many textbooks dealing with public policy. Here, the emphasis is on providing overviews of some of the main viewpoints that can contribute to our understanding of the exercise of power in the public policy process, including how that can reflect and reinforce economic, political and social inequalities. As with much of this book, the primary emphasis is on the utility of those perspectives for analysis and increasing our understanding of public policy; in other words, they are to some extent empirical, attempting to explain the nature of public policy decisions and implementation. However, many of these ideas are also seen by some as ideal models, normative views of how the world should be, towards which societies can work for a better future. In both instances, they are also generally highly political and contestable concepts, and it is important to bear these issues in mind when considering some of these ideas and their discussion both in this book and in the wider literature.

Pluralism

Pluralism is the theory that has generally been dominant in studies of British politics and policy making. The central feature of pluralist theory is its contention that in Western industrialised societies, such as Britain, power is widely distributed among different groups. This plurality of power-centres makes available a multiplicity of channels of influence, so that in the long term any legitimate interest can be represented at the political level and no one group is dominant in the decision-making process. There is, however, considerable debate within pluralism over the role of the state and government institutions. Some pluralist writers have emphasised the even-handedness and the basic 'public interest' orientation of administrative agencies, while others have argued that they are only one set of pressure groups among many, or that they are not as neutral as sometimes implied; for some, this has involved an acceptance of criticisms that early pluralist writings often failed to take account of the constraints on decision making imposed by the capitalist economy.

As noted in Chapter 2, pluralist theory owes much to the work of Robert Dahl in the United States during the 1950s and his view that, in relation to the issues that he defined as 'key', no one person or group was dominant and there was no consistent pattern of success or failure (Dahl, 1961). This work is widely seen as underpinning subsequent pluralist analyses of decision making, and to some extent as providing a normative view that supports the operation of liberal democracy. However, over time Dahl's views developed further, reflecting the views of others who suggested that it was possible to have many groups operating in particular policy areas without implying that policy making was fair or representative (McFarland, 2007), and by the 1980s he had arrived at a position that might more accurately be equated with 'neo-pluralism' (for example, Dahl, 1985 and 1986), with business groups, in particular, seen as likely to have more power than others.

As discussed further in Chapter 5, interest groups (also referred to as pressure groups) are arguably of key importance to the pluralist approach, particularly in states such as the United Kingdom where there is a diverse range of groups seeking to influence many areas of public policy, varying from small *ad hoc* groups, such as those that might oppose local school or hospital closures or new roads or developments, through organisations such as Child Poverty Action Group, Greenpeace and the Howard League for Penal Reform, to large bodies such as the National Farmers' Union, the Confederation of British Industry or the Trades Union Congress. It is also worth noting the existence of social movements, which are less formally constituted than interest groups and which tend to pursue non-institutionalised coordinated actions to achieve their goals and to be keen to preserve their autonomy. The suffragettes in the United Kingdom and the civil rights movement in the United States are two notable examples of such movements, while more recently movements of disabled people, the environmental movement and anti-capitalist movements have come to prominence.

In the UK, interest in pluralism and the activity of pressure groups grew rapidly during the 1960s as governments, academics and the public became increasingly aware of the existence of a wide range of groups. For example, as they attempted to manage the economy, both Conservative and Labour governments found it necessary to bargain with organised groups, in particular employers' organisations and trade unions, seeking their advice and cooperation. Similarly, the development of the state and the spreading of its activities, particularly the welfare state, stimulated action not only by workers, including a wide variety of professional groups, such as the British Medical Association and the British Association of Social Workers, but also by groups seeking to represent users of services, such as patients and social housing tenants. The 1960s and 1970s saw a growth in pressure groups involved with welfare issues from what might be termed a 'consumer' or 'user' orientation, with the emergence of what Whiteley and Winyard (1984) called the 'new poverty lobby', including organisations such as Child Poverty Action Group, the Disablement Income Group (which campaigned for adequate social security support for disabled people) and Shelter. As other issues, such as the environment, came to prominence, pressure group activity in those areas also increased. This period arguably saw the heyday of pressure group influence in public policy in the UK, so that by the late 1970s Richardson and Jordan (1979) contended that policies in Britain were being developed in negotiations between government agencies and pressure groups organised into policy communities. According to them, pressure groups were able to influence public policy from issues emerging on to the agenda through to implementation. It was also possible to identify issues where they had real impact, acting both inside and outside the formal state organisation, as with the introduction of Child Benefit (Field, 1982) and the creation of a duty on local authorities to house homeless people through the Housing (Homeless Persons) Act 1977 (Raynsford, 1986). More recently, there has been a growth in professional lobbying, reflecting that which had developed earlier in the United States. This is significantly different, as it involves firms that are paid to lobby government and that claim particular expertise in terms of their ability to do so. While this is discussed further in Chapter 5, it is worth noting here that, despite efforts by government and some lobbyists to increase transparency, these activities perhaps inevitably raise questions about the nature of lobbying and the ability of some well-resourced interests to seek privileged access and potentially greater influence, perhaps at the expense of others.

The election of the first Thatcher government in 1979 marked a significant change in pressure group politics in the UK. As a conviction politician, Thatcher was not easily amenable to open discussion with or persuasion by groups, even those such as the Confederation of British Industry (CBI), with which she might have been expected to share some common beliefs, and many were excluded from some elements of policy formulation (for example, Baggott, 1995). Indeed, the approach of the Thatcher governments could be confrontational, as with a number of professional groups, such as doctors and teachers, local government organisations and the churches. Rather than pressure groups, Thatcher sought and received ideas and advice from a newly-influential set of bodies, right-wing think tanks, such as the Adam Smith Institute, the Institute of Economic Affairs and the Social Affairs Unit. To take the example of education policy in England, Trowler (1998) argued that between 1979 and 1987 there was a decline in its pluralistic nature, highlighting that, during the design of the National Curriculum in the 1980s, education professionals were not only not consulted about the reforms but were largely excluded from the policy-making arena, while right-wing think tanks played a more central role. However, there remained a number of areas where pressure groups did successfully influence government, such as with the disability lobby with regard to the Disabled Persons' (Services, Consultation and Representation) Act 1986 (Bochel, 1992) and the sophisticated and coordinated approach of the child care lobby during the passage of the Children Act in 1988–89 (Parton, 1991).

The election of the Labour government in 1997 saw a shift back towards a more consultative manner of government, with numerous consultation papers being issued and a greater use of enquiries and commissions, in line with the apparent desire for more evidence-informed and inclusive policy making, which held out the prospect of some input from pressure groups, particularly on issues where the government was less committed to a particular policy direction. However, some among the trade unions felt that Labour, seeking to be a pro-business government, did not include the unions fully in consultations (Ludlam, 2004) and this was reflected in its public sector reform agenda and its failure to relax the constraints on strike action introduced under the Conservatives. At the same time, there was considerable use of ideas that emerged from centre-left think tanks such as Demos and the IPPR (Institute for Public Policy Research). With the formation of the Conservative–Liberal Democrat government in 2010, despite the commitment to voluntarism and a significant role for non-state providers, there was a decline in the number of government consultations and arguably in the ability of many pressure groups to have an influence on policy making, a situation that continued under the Conservative majority government from 2015–2017. Indeed, there was something of a view that business interests continued to be privileged compared with consumer interests, for example with the publication of the government's childhood obesity action plan in August 2016, which relied on voluntary action by the food and drink industry, rather than restrictions on the advertising and marketing of junk food (https://www.theguardian.com/society/2016/sep/13/jamie-oliver-theresa-may-obesity-strategy-uk).

Over time, there has also been a Europeanisation of interest group representation, with some groups deciding to direct at least parts of their activities towards EU institutions, and particularly the European Commission, as discussed further in Chapter 7, although, with progress towards the United Kingdom leaving the EU being worked through from 2016, such activity might be expected to diminish in many policy areas.

Critiques of pluralism

As a theory of power, pluralism arguably has a general level of acceptance among society and among policy makers, in that it can be seen as representing many of the ways in which decision making works. In addition, it can be argued that pressure groups: are a valuable resource that allows citizens to mobilise with others who hold similar views so that their opinions can be communicated to government and others; can help with the dispersal of power downwards and to counterbalance the powers of central institutions; allow a greater degree of participation in the political system; and provide an outlet for citizens with grievances.

However, the idea of pluralism can be criticised in a number of ways. Firstly, the basic premise that power is widely distributed and that over time many interests may be heard can clearly be questioned. Indeed, analysts of poverty and responses to it have long argued that poor people are poor simply because they are powerless (for example, Miliband, 1974; Townsend, 1979) and that in times of economic stress it is frequently spending on and support for poorer groups that is hit, as with the Coalition government from 2010 to 2015, with its emphasis on reducing the deficit through cuts in public expenditure, including social security benefits (for example, Bochel and Powell, 2016; Lupton *et al.*, 2016).

Other critiques of Dahl's original position, which are also relevant to pluralism more generally, have emerged from more sophisticated theories of power, as discussed later in this chapter. Lukes, for example (1974 and 2005), pointed out that a number of writers see political systems that are apparently open as containing mechanisms that serve to exclude the influence of legitimate interests. The exclusion of issues from agendas, the manipulation of voting procedures, the involvement of more powerful groups or networks, the choice of community representatives for consultation and the operation of secrecy in political affairs can all serve to slant power upwards, while public policies can also be seen as being produced within particular economic, ideological and political constraints, so that within the UK policies can clearly operate more to the benefit of some sections of society than others. From this perspective, the notion of all groups and interests being able to access power is clearly erroneous.

Similarly, critics might argue that in many respects pressure groups can be undemocratic as: resources and channels of influence open to groups are severely skewed and, as a result, some, such as the poor, are largely excluded from power; much of the influence of 'insider' groups is exerted informally and in a manner that may not easily be observed; in some areas of policy a 'corporatist' bias (see below) may operate, reinforcing the influence of major interests, excluding others and reducing the influence of elected representatives; the views put forward by pressure groups may not necessarily be representative of the interests that they claim to represent, or even of their members; and, by their nature, pressure groups have sectional or partial interests, rather than representing the interests of the country as a whole.

Finally, while pluralists may view the existence of a wide variety of groups and organisations competing to influence the state as constituting a pluralism of power, Marxist and public choice theories, as discussed later in this chapter, provide very different insights. For Marxists, pluralist democracy is itself a façade, disguising the state's support for capitalism, and the most powerful groups will inevitably represent the interests of business (for example, Jordan, 1985). In addition, most members of elite groups will accept the dominant values. As a result, pressure group activity is likely to be largely concerned with managing inequality, rather than with achieving genuine openness and democracy. From a public choice perspective, pressure groups are seen as damaging to democracy as they are concerned with their own, rather than society's, interests. In addition, their attempts to influence decision making mean that the executive and the legislature are forced to respond to their demands and therefore cannot represent the interests of all. This view suggests that, in protecting their sectional interests, pressure groups therefore damage economic growth and encourage higher public expenditure, while their demands can lead to 'democratic overload'.

Neo-pluralism

In response to some of these criticisms, variations of pluralism have emerged, perhaps the most important of which is usually termed 'neo-pluralism'. This view recognises that power and resources are not evenly distributed and that decision making is not, therefore, equally open to all (McFarland, 2007). In particular, big business is seen as occupying a particularly privileged position as it controls wealth, employment and expertise, and as able to often veto public policies which it sees as threatening to its interests. The state is also seen as important, with a recognition that as it has grown it has acquired interests of its own and a large and powerful bureaucratic apparatus. At the same time, neo-pluralists also recognise that there has been a decline in the relative influence of representative political institutions, such as Parliament, the political parties and local government. Supporters of this perspective therefore argue that it gives a more realistic reflection of the contemporary situation than does pure pluralism. However, Howlett *et al.* (2009) suggest that the approach still does not sufficiently take into account international pressures, such as those arising from economic interdependence, or the role of ideology in influencing politics and public policy.

Corporatism

Corporatist theory differs from pluralist approaches in that groups are not necessarily free-forming, voluntary or competitive, but rather depend on the state for recognition and for their role in influencing policy making. It emphasises policy being shaped by the interactions between the state and groups recognised and mediated by the state, and through a more cooperative rather than competitive process. Although the heyday, if indeed there was one, of these ideas in the United Kingdom came in the 1970s, it is worth considering them briefly here, not least as they potentially offer different insights, while the 'dual state thesis', though arguably of limited relevance today, is nevertheless noted (Box 3.1) as it highlights

---

Box 3.1   The dual state thesis

Although arguably of little relevance today, the 'dualistic' theoretical approach developed by Cawson and Saunders (1983) and Saunders (1984) is of interest for the way that it draws upon the different ideas of pluralism and corporatism, two theories that have often been seen as incompatible, in seeking to make sense of what the authors saw in the British state of the time.

Focusing for current purposes on the 'functional' dimension, Saunders (and Cawson and Saunders) argued that at the central government level power had shifted away from elected representatives (the House of Commons) into a relatively exclusive 'corporate' sector, including many arm's-length bodies (see Chapter 7), whose members were not directly elected, but were appointed from representatives of particular interests, such as business, professional organisations and trade unions. They suggested that this contributed to a 'corporate bias' that reflected central government's desire to insulate itself from the pressures of competing interests and to direct its policies to the needs and demands of particular (often private sector) interests which had direct access to government both formally, through the range of quasi and non-governmental organisations, and informally, for example through links between the Treasury, the Bank of England and City-based financial institutions. They also argued that the scale and organisation of local government meant that it had remained more accessible to a wider range of interests, including through competition between different 'consumption sectors'. Consequently, they suggested that there was a division between a more democratic or pluralistic sector of politics and a more closed and exclusive corporatist sector, which to a considerable extent was reflected in the division between local and central government. Such arguments appeared to lose much of their force from the 1990s, in part as a result of the powers and expenditure of local government being increasingly constrained by central government, although many of the criticisms of quasi-governmental organisations outlined in Chapter 7 echo Cawson and Saunders' concerns over a corporate bias towards business, albeit that neo-pluralism might equally serve as an explanation for such a situation.

the way that different perspectives can sometimes usefully be combined in analysing policy making.

Corporatism, as a body of theory, focuses on major interest groups, particularly those which command resources that are essential for economic activity. The key to their influence over government is seen as lying in their organisational power and their ability to tap strong solidaristic loyalties among those that they represent, rather than in particular electoral strengths. For example, business associations and trade unions, along with some professional organisations, are often organised into single, hierarchical organisations. In some cases these organisations can develop a special bargaining position with government, and their close and permanent 'insider' relationship with state agencies can create a 'corporate bias' in policy making, which relegates other interests to a secondary position. In return for this, the leaderships of corporate groups not only represent their members to government, but also control their members for the government. The groups' leaderships themselves are often integrated into government functions, including through appointments to the boards of, or other involvement with, quasi-governmental agencies. With a corporatist model there is therefore no longer freewheeling interest group activity, as with pluralism, or open access for any group to influence policy.

The high point of a corporatist approach in practice in the United Kingdom is usually seen as the 'social contract' of 1975–78, under which the Labour government gave trade union and business leaders a voice in many domestic policy issues, in exchange for their delivering their members' compliance with government wage norms. This agreement lent support to arguments at the time that corporatism was becoming an important part of British political life, with some seeing evidence for such a development not only in central government (Middlemass, 1979; Schmitter and Lehmbruch, 1979) but also in local government (Newton, 1976; Saunders, 1979). However, during the 1980s, under the more ideologically-led and right-wing Conservative governments, corporatist bodies fell from favour and were gradually abandoned, while not only was trade union opposition to government policies ignored, but significant parts of the business community also felt that government was not listening to their calls for changes to some elements of economic policy, so that by the 1990s it would have been hard to argue that there was significant evidence for corporatist decision making in central government.

Like pluralism, corporatism can be criticised for its view of the role of the state, with many writers having seen the state as moving from a position of supporting capital accumulation to directing that process. Although viewed as constrained by major economic interests, the state is often seen as autonomous as a result of its control of legal, organisational and other resources, and is therefore able to act in the interests of capital, labour or other groups. However, as noted above, other perspectives, most notably, perhaps, Marxists, would argue that the state is not a neutral body but instead acts in the interests of capital.

As a normative model, corporatism in the UK was damaged not only because the 'social contract' was short-lived, but also because it was widely perceived as a failure. As a result, it has arguably been more use as a descriptive model of one form of political arrangement in countries that are or have been organised along corporatist lines, such as Austria and Sweden, and tells us much less about policy making in states such as the United Kingdom or the United States.

Yet, there remain potentially important implications for the study of the policy process from corporatist ideas. For example, Cawson (1982) suggested that they could help in focusing attention on the recipro-cal relationships between the state and organised interests in society in relation to the formulation and execution of public policy, while Grant (1995) pointed out that in encouraging a reconsideration of pluralist the-ory it contributed to the development of new ideas such as policy com-munities (discussed in the following section). It is also worth noting that while traditional approaches to corporatism focused on the economy, certain policy sectors may, at times, exhibit some of the characteristics of corporatism. For example, until at least the food scares of the 1990s, the relationship between the then Ministry of Agriculture, Fisheries and Food (MAFF) and the National Farmers' Union was such that the NFU had a significant input into policy making on agriculture and farming, whilst it also gave the Ministry specialised information, advice and support, as well as representing its position to farmers. Many consumer groups and others in turn felt excluded from the policy-making process, for example over environmental and food safety issues, as a result of this close rela-tionship. However, eventually, following a series of concerns including salmonella and BSE that highlighted the shortcomings arising from such arrangements, the Labour government passed many of the functions of the MAFF on to a new Department for Environment, Food and Rural Affairs (DEFRA) and created an independent Food Standards Agency to reflect the interests of consumers. Indeed, it might be argued that in areas such as alcohol policy, the relationship between the industry and the government, including the Portman Group acting as a conduit between the two (Hawkins and Holden, 2014), also has corporate characteristics. It is therefore worth considering the close relationships that can develop between government (of whatever tier) and powerful interests, and the type of arrangements that may occur in such cases. In addition, in such cases power may be located outside Parliament and other representative institutions, and decisions can be made in negotiations between the executive and powerful interest groups, potentially with little attention to the interests of consumers and with minimal democratic scrutiny.

Three dimensions of power

Building on the discussion of pluralism above, and reflecting the potential importance of agendas in policy making as discussed in Chapter 2, is the debate over the three dimensions of power (see Box 3.2). As noted above, early pluralist accounts of democracy, such as those of Dahl (1961), tended to assume that power was widely distributed within society, with the policy-making process being driven by public demands and pressure. In his study of New Haven, in the United States, Dahl set out to ask *Who Governs?* (1961), an elite or ruling class, or something more complicated? He examined what he described as 'key' decisions in three areas: nomination for political office, education policy, and urban redevelopment. He claimed that no one group won out consistently in these areas of decision making, and that therefore there could not be a ruling elite. He argued that in the United States power was widely distributed and the political system worked in a way that meant that the policy process was largely driven by public opinion and public demands. Dahl's view of power was that power is exercised if person A gets person B to do something that they would not otherwise do, and therefore for public policy the powerful are those who can influence decision making. Hay (2002) notes four attributes of such a definition: power is

---

Box 3.2   Three different views of the exercise of power

1. *Dahl* – power is getting someone else to do something that they would not normally do – 'A has power over B to the extent that he [or she] can get B to do something that B would not otherwise do' (1957, pp. 202–03);

2. *Bachrach and Baratz* – 'Power is also exercised when A devotes his [or her] energies to creating or reinforcing social and political values and institutional practices that limit the scope of the political process to public consideration of only those issues which are comparatively innocuous to A' (1970, p. 7);

3. *Lukes* – power is exercised not only when preferences are prevented from having an impact on policy outcomes but also when preferences are moulded through socialisation, so that 'A exercises power over B when A affects B in a manner which is contrary to B's interests' (1974, p. 34).

understood in terms of its *effects* and if there is no effect there is no power relation; power is an attribute of *individuals* and is exercised in their relations with other individuals – it is *behavioural*; power is associated with *domination* or *power over*; and power is unproductive (or zero-sum), so that some gain only to the extent that others lose out. From this perspective it is possible to identify when power is exercised, and it can be measured by examining patterns of influence in decision making, as Dahl sought to do.

Dahl's 'one-dimensional' view can be criticised in a number of ways. For example, it implies that the exercise of power can only be analysed where there are conflicting preferences, and focuses on the analysis of 'concrete key decisions', with the assumption that the powerful are those who get their own way in those instances. However, this is a simplistic view and, for example, does not take into account that demands may be carefully prepared to avoid opposition, or who decides what is a 'key' issue. One of the most powerful critiques of Dahl and the pluralist view was put forward by Bachrach and Baratz (1963 and 1970), who argued that such an approach failed to take into account the extent to which power could be exercised through the exclusion of issues and problems from the policy-making agenda. They therefore highlighted the concept of the 'mobilisation of bias', drawing on the work of Schattschneider, who suggested that 'all forms of political organization have a bias in favor of the exploitation of some kinds of conflict and the suppression of others because *organization is the mobilization of bias*. Some issues are organized into politics while others are organized out' (Schattschneider, 1960, p. 71). They also introduced 'non-decisions' into the debate, as

> ... the practice of limiting the scope of actual decision making to 'safe' issues by manipulating the dominant community values, myths, and political institutions and procedures,
>
> (Bachrach and Baratz, 1963, p. 632)

arguing that,

> [w]hen the dominant values, the accepted rules of the game, the existing power relations among groups, and the instruments of force, singly or in combination, effectively prevent certain grievances from developing into full-fledged issues which call for decisions, it can be said that a nondecision-making situation exists.
>
> (Bachrach and Baratz, 1963, p. 641)

In such a situation, the need for a decision never arises, since the 'existence of the "mobilization of bias" ... is sufficient to prevent a latent issue from becoming a question for a decision' (Bachrach and Baratz, 1963, p. 641).

This approach suggests that rather than simply influencing decisions once an agenda has been set, those with power can keep issues off the agendas that they control, with non-decisions being 'a decision that results in the suppression or thwarting of a latent or manifest challenge to the values or interests of the decision-maker' (Bachrach and Baratz, 1970, p. 4). Consequently, Bachrach and Baratz argued that it is necessary to look not only at formal decision-making arenas, but also at where agenda setting might occur behind the scenes, and that while a non-decision is not observable, 'a latent issue is discernible and so is the mobilisation of bias. Thus, it can be said that the *nondecision-making process* (the impact of the mobilization of bias upon a latent issue), in distinction to a nondecision, is indeed subject to observation and analysis' (Bachrach and Baratz, 1963, p. 641). They suggest, therefore, that it is possible to identify examples of non-decision making.

In applying their ideas, Bachrach and Baratz examined race relations in Baltimore in the 1960s. They argued that the pluralist position failed to appreciate the extent to which those with power were able to exclude issues and problems from the policy agenda, and that due to non-decisions by political leaders in the white community, the black population was unable to generate a politics of conflict. The city's decision-making machinery was inaccessible to many black people, so that there was effectively a closed political system.

Jenkins suggested that it may be possible to identify non-decisions through, for example, attempts to localise conflicts and control demands, labelling demands in a way that eliminates them from the system or routinises them by directing them towards committees or enquiries, or threats of sanctions (Jenkins, 1982, p. 322), while Moran (2011, p. 375) set out three strategies to help in identifying non-decisions, involving looking across individual policy areas and comparing across countries and time. In terms of particular policy areas, Parsons (1995) suggests, for example, that in the early stages of development of social movements it is relatively easy for decision makers to ignore such issues if they choose, giving the example of 'women's issues', while Saggar (1991) showed how the issue of 'race' was excluded from local politics in two London boroughs in the 1960s and 1970s, arguing that radical policy proposals were not heard because they were threats to the existing policy framework; disability or gay rights issues or environmental issues would perhaps be equally relevant examples.

This 'two-dimensional' perspective clearly criticises the one-dimensional view's preoccupation with observable decisions. It suggests that in order to analyse the distribution of power within a society or community it is necessary to focus not simply on what gets discussed, but also on 'non-decisions' and the 'mobilisation of bias', which may not involve deliberate fixing by identifiable individuals, but is rather the systematically discriminatory impact of working within particular institutions or following particular rules of procedure (for example, the socially discriminatory consequences of selection procedures for higher education). It therefore shifts the focus to the question of who systematically gains and who loses from the operation of an institution's rules.

Lukes (1974) took the argument a stage further by describing three dimensions of power: firstly, that which can be identified in relation to decisions; secondly, that which is manifested in non-decisions; and thirdly, that which involves the shaping of people's attitudes and preferences such that they do not recognise their real interests, so that no visible conflict may occur at all, and that the most powerful groups in society are effectively able to impose a set of values or beliefs on others. As a result, for example, some issues may not be recognised as problems, but may instead simply be assumed to be natural or inevitable. Some would argue that such a view helps explain not only why issues such as poverty, inequality and the redistribution of wealth are rarely seen as significant policy issues, but also why poorer sections of society generally accept their relatively low incomes, even at a time when the rich are getting richer and inequality is growing, as the dominant ideology depicts wealth as arising from hard work, risk-taking and success, while inequality is seen as natural and even desirable.

This third dimensional view not only clearly reflects the idea of the mobilisation of bias (and so denies that the study of the exercise of power should be restricted to the deliberate action of individuals), it also rejects the centrality of conflict in the analysis of power. This involves the examination of claims such as those of false consciousness, and requires the separation of people's real interests from their expressed preferences. However, there are again methodological challenges, such as how to identify 'real interests' and how to analyse the exercise of power not only where there is apparently no observable conflict but also where beliefs are shaped by a system that ensures that its beliefs, myths and values dominate. It also suggests that some people (presumably often academics (Hay, 2002) are in a position to be able to judge the genuine interests of others.

The use of power through means such as socialisation and the manipulation of preferences may be observed, albeit that it is likely to be difficult, although it should also be possible to identify it from an examination of economic, political and social relations. However, the application of Lukes' conceptualisation of power has been limited (Shapiro, 2006; Hathaway, 2016). Lukes highlights one study as being at least on the border between the second and third dimensions in its approach. In *The Un-Politics of Air Pollution*, Crenson (1971) studied the failure of US cities to tackle air pollution as quickly as might have been expected. He argued that since no one wishes to breathe polluted air, if some cities were not active in addressing the issue whilst others were, there would be a strong empirical case for non-decision making. Crenson looked at the steel-producing towns of East Chicago and Gary (in Indiana) and pointed out that whilst East Chicago tackled the problem quickly, introducing controls in 1949, Gary did not, introducing controls only in 1962. He suggests that this was because Gary was dominated by one major polluter, US Steel. The company did not make any threats, but its reputation influenced not only what decisions were taken, but also those that were not taken. When this analysis was extended to 52 other US cities, Crenson concluded that where they were dominated by one major polluter, clean air was unlikely to emerge as an issue on the policy agenda. From this perspective, power may therefore be exercised as much in ensuring inaction as in taking action. Indeed, Crenson argued that merely the reputation for having power, as in the case of US Steel in Gary, may be sufficient to prevent some topics from becoming issues. Crenson also extended his analysis to suggest that there is a greater order and rationality to issues than may at first be apparent. For example, concerns about air pollution might apparently lead to the issue of government reforms to tackle the issue. However, if there is a commitment to maintaining employment or economic growth, the agenda is likely to be framed in a fashion that will play down the environmental costs. He also posits the view that power can be exercised at an 'ideological' level through the promotion of particular perceptions of social issues and conflicts, and that the issues on a political agenda may be linked to 'an ideological vision of the political system' (p. 173), rather than to each other. Lukes (1974) builds further upon this when he argues that power is exercised through the control of ideas, such as through the mass media and the processes of socialisation.

Another notable attempt to examine the third face of power empirically was made by Gaventa (1980), who studied power and quiescence in Appalachian mining communities. However, the challenges associated with identifying 'real interests' and the implication that a researcher can identify them while the subjects being studied cannot remain problematic, particularly when moving away from policies (such as pollution) where the harms may be reasonably easily assessed. Hay (2002) suggests that one way forward is not to accept the third dimension, but to see two uses of power: 'conduct shaping', manifest in actions such as persuasion and coercion; and 'context shaping', which sees power relations in structures, institutions and organisations being shaped in such a way as to affect the parameters of future action. Hill (2009) points out that Hay's suggestion fits with the way in which writers such as Gaventa (1980) have shown that power can be exercised through social myths, language and symbols, and argues that power reinforces power and powerlessness reinforces powerlessness.

In 2005, Lukes published a second edition of his book, which contained the original chapters but added others that both qualified his original arguments and sought to respond to some criticisms of them and to recognise the work of writers such as Foucault (for example, 1977). In particular, he suggested that in the original he fell into the same trap as others in focusing on the *exercise* of power and equating power with *domination* or 'power over', neglecting the many ways in which power over others can be positive, productive, transformative and compatible with dignity, such as through parenting or teaching. He also addressed the question of the extent to which structures possess power, recognising that actors within structures exercise power by deciding whether or not to tackle a problem. In doing these things, he continues to defend the third dimension, including by arguing that '[i]t would be simplistic to suppose that "willing" and "unwilling" compliance to domination are mutually exclusive' (p. 150), as individuals can both consent to power and still resent the mode of its exercise.

More recently, Gaventa and others have developed a framework for understanding power, the 'powercube' (www.powercube.net), which reformulates the three faces of power as *forms* of power: visible, operating conspicuously, with the focus being on decisions, who makes them and in whose interests; hidden, where manipulation occurs behind the scenes; and invisible, which moves beyond the consideration of actions to the importance of ideas and the discourses that support the powerful, and which may not be limited to intentional acts (see also Hathaway, 2016). Hathaway suggests that using this conceptualisation may allow more empirical application of Lukes' ideas. While there would still be significant challenges with its operationalisation, a regime evolution approach could consider both the forms of power and how ideas and discourses serve to empower some actors, and measure the extent to which an actor realises their interests not simply in political outputs, but also in societal outcomes.

As Hay (2002) notes, the debate over the three faces of power can be portrayed as one between 'a definition of power so narrow, even banal, as to be uninteresting, yet which is easy to operationalise in political analysis and, on the other, a more subtle and complex conception of power yet one which is almost impossible to measure and quantify' (p. 169), and one which draws almost entirely on Anglophone ideas, particularly from the United Kingdom and the United States. However, other writers, perhaps most notably Foucault and Habermas, reflect a more continental European intellectual tradition (see, for example, Nik-Meyer and Villadsen, 2013), less concerned with methodological considerations, and their arguments are therefore more philosophical in nature, focusing on the extent to which power is ubiquitous and the possibility of liberation from power, and highlighting the importance of language and communication. Their ideas suggest that we need to consider the role of rationality and reason in relation to public policy and policy analysis and recognise the contexts and conditions within which policy is made or constructed.

Habermas, in his consideration of 'communicative rationality' (1984a, 1984b), sees reason as context specific, that communication through language necessarily involves the raising of 'validity claims' (he suggests three validity dimensions: normative rightness, theoretical truth, and expressive or subjective truthfulness) that can only be resolved through discussion, and that solidarity and collective decisions are built through the development of shared understandings. Social and political arrangements that inhibit unconstrained discussion would be free from domination, with all participants being equal, and we therefore have to consider all speech-acts by taking a position with regard to their validity claims and how existing arrangements limit such discussion.

Foucault (for example, 1977) links the development of the state with the growth of scientific knowledge, so that together they are seen as oppressing individuals. He emphasises the body as a site for power relations, highlighting society's reaction to crime and the ways in which incarceration and physical repression have changed over time, and the development of disciplinary 'power-knowledge' regimes with institutionalised regimentation and surveillance. Foucault claims that 'power produces knowledge' (p. 217), that there is no power relation without a correlative constitution of a field of knowledge, nor any knowledge that does not presuppose and constitute power relations. For him, the development of disciplines such as architecture and criminology and the knowledge claims that they advance actually reflect the regime of power-knowledge in the carceral institutions of modern society. For Foucault, power is ubiquitous, exercised at many levels in society and by many people, and, given that we are all socialised, even 'normalised', within a carceral regime, our own judgements may be the product of that normalisation. And if power is indeed ubiquitous, then there can be no liberation from it, as implied by writers such as Habermas and Lukes, and 'the best that we can hope for is to change the manner in which power is displayed' (Hay, 2002, p. 192).

Of course, ideology and politics play an important role in influencing what are perceived as problems and the most appropriate policy responses to them. Even identifying when something becomes a 'problem' can be challenging, as with immigration, when some employers may perceive the availability of workers willing to work hard for relatively low pay as a positive, while others may feel that they are losing the opportunity to work because of migrants, or that immigration holds down levels of pay. Clearly, it is possible to draw on the work of writers such as Bachrach and Baratz and Lukes to argue that certain issues, such as poverty and inequality, and potential policy responses, such as the greater use of the tax and benefits system to redistribute from richer to poorer elements of society, rarely reach the policy agenda, as, given the dominant ideology within a capitalist society, inequalities are seen as inevitable, and even desirable, and reducing them would damage the interests of powerful groups, including wealthy individuals and the business community. From this perspective, there is probably no decision taken not to pursue policies that might damage such interests; they are not even considered in the first place. Similarly, the public at large may generally accept the position as inevitable. Indeed, the Labour governments of Blair and Brown, which did to some extent redistribute, particularly to working families with children, sought to do so largely by stealth, and chose not to publicise it to any significant degree. In contrast, the decision, following the financial crisis, by the Coalition and Conservative governments to reduce the deficit primarily through cuts in public expenditure, including reducing benefits for many of the poorer members of society, rather than through tax increases, was presented as a necessary approach that was aimed at 'skivers', in contrast to 'strivers' and 'hard-working families'.

Policy communities and policy networks

One of the responses to debates over the applicability of pluralist ideas came in the form of the idea of policy communities and policy networks, an area of analysis that developed rapidly from the 1980s, although the terms have been utilised in a variety of sometimes rather different senses. The importance of these ideas lies in the view that in most areas of policy making there is a variety of government departments or agencies, advisory bodies and pressure groups with interests in the area, as well as other bodies or individuals that may be affected by the policies or issues, with Grant (2000) suggesting that in the UK policy communities are generally organised around government departments and their networks of client groups. Some argue that policy 'communities' involve organisations that are linked to each other by resource dependencies, and that they are therefore normally smaller, with more frequent and high-quality interaction between members, and more stable, integrated and consensual groupings, with restricted memberships (Judge, 2005), while policy or issue 'networks', on the other hand, have larger and fluctuating numbers of members encompassing a broader range of interests, have more unequal power relationships, have less constant and intensive contacts and, while there may be general agreement on policy, also contain a degree of conflict.

Rhodes (1997) suggested that there may be a continuum from 'policy communities', through professional, inter-governmental and producer networks, to 'issue networks'. However, for many purposes the two can be used interchangeably, and a policy network can be seen as comprising those likely to be involved with or affected by decisions in a particular policy area, as with Ball's work on education, discussed below.

Rhodes also usefully summarises some of the key ideas of the policy networks approach, explaining that it

> ... emphasizes the need to disaggregate policy analysis and stresses that relationships between groups and government vary between policy areas. At the same time it recognizes that most policy areas involve few interests in policy making. Continuity of both outcomes and groups characterizes policy making in many policy areas.
>
> (Rhodes, 1997, p. 32)

Of course, policy outcomes inevitably feed back into the policy community, and thus will affect future policies and outcomes. In some cases, government bodies may encourage the development of policy communities as that may facilitate regular communication and the implementation of policy. However, the existence of a policy community or network does not necessarily mean that there is consensus or an absence of conflict, as the emphasis is not so much on those aspects, but rather on the shared framework within which decisions are made and policies implemented. Indeed, Klijn and Koppenjan (2015) are clear that networks are often not places where there is harmony and consensus, and that there can be differences over values, while resources, and especially knowledge, can be dispersed across many actors, so that sharp conflicts can arise, decision making can be time consuming and cooperation can be hard to achieve. Operating within networks involves taking account of the potential benefits and costs. They suggest that the management of networks is therefore focused on handling complexity by facilitating interaction and coproduction amongst the parties involved, for example by encouraging mutual learning, creating institutional links between actors, seeking to reduce knowledge conflicts and asymmetries, coordinating research efforts, guaranteeing independence through agreements about boundaries and the division of roles and promoting trust between parties. Kisby (2007) takes a rather different view, suggesting that in order to explain why a policy is developed in the first place, it is necessary to examine the programmatic beliefs (that provide guidelines for practical activity and therefore provide the ideational framework within which programmes of action are formulated (Berman, 1988)) of members of a network.

Ball has undertaken considerable work on networks and governance in the field of education (for example, Ball, 2008, 2009; Ball and Junemann,

2012). Drawing on interviews with senior figures in the education services industry and Internet searches, he sought to trace some of the relationships between participants in new policy communities in education, linking business, business philanthropy, quangos and non-governmental organisations and government bodies. He notes that these were not 'political' networks in any traditional sense, but that they were a policy device that facilitated experimentation and *ad hoc* development by the state, and also that some previous or potential participants in education networks were excluded, such as trade unions (Ball, 2008). Ball and Junemann (2012) also highlight organisations such as ARK, Teach First and the New Schools Network as examples of new actors that were endorsed and/or funded by the 2010 Coalition government in relation to the development of networks that formed an alternative infrastructure of policy and provision in education in England, and state that these were not simply networks but forms of network governance concerned not only about who does what, but also with changing the forms, purposes and values of public service.

As Ball's work perhaps helps illustrate, there can be dangers in the existence of policy communities, so that, as Grant (1995) points out, while 'the idea of policy communities clearly provides a good fit with the available empirical evidence on how decisions are made in British government ... [it] does raise some worrying problems for normative democratic theory' (p. 37). Weale (2011) also notes that under 'new modes of governance' decision-making 'escapes direct control by democratically elected representatives' (p. 60) and that they therefore raise questions of political legitimacy. Some of these concerns are similar to those raised by corporatism and neo-pluralism, with issues around access and openness to policy networks, including the possibility that they may come to consist of 'insider' groups and that some interests might be excluded from the policy-making process. Richards and Smith (2002) note that for much of the post-war period there was a closed policy community around health policy, centred on the Ministry of Health (later the Department of Health), the British Medical Association and the royal colleges representing hospital consultants, and that as a result it was hard for other groups, such as patients or nurses, to have any say in the development of policy, an example broadly similar to that of agriculture and food policy noted in the discussion of corporatism above. Associated with this is the further danger that such exclusive processes may actually damage the quality of decision making, becoming more concerned with avoiding conflict and maintaining existing relationships than with tackling policy problems.

There are also significant criticisms of the network approach as a theoretical perspective. Dowding (1995), for example, has argued that it is not so much the networks that explain policy change or stability, but the resources and bargaining strategies used by the actors within them. In addition, it can be difficult to tell where the boundaries of a network might lie, particularly away from the more stable policy community end of the spectrum, reflecting Kassim's (1994) criticism that networks are too flexible a concept to apply usefully. Another significant challenge is that associated with explaining the exercise of power, for although many network accounts tend to suggest that policy is developed in a consensual manner, as policy making generally involves conflict, bargaining and winners and losers, it is important to understand how these might occur within networks. John suggests that these criticisms mean that more recently the idea has been used in more limited ways, for example to explore the more fragmented patterns of government that have followed from the new public management, or to understand the cultures and practices of government departments (John, 2012), although it is clear that it continues to exert significant appeal for many analysts.

Network approaches can also be seen as having links with the advocacy coalition framework of Sabatier and his colleagues (for example, Jenkins-Smith *et al.*, 2014), which, as discussed in Chapters 1 and 2, sees those with particular beliefs and values being potentially involved in advocacy coalitions, which are subsystems of actors from a variety of organisations who are actively concerned over particular issues or problems and who regularly seek to influence public policy in that area, engaging in coordinated activities with others in pursuit of their policy goals.

Institutional approaches

Like pluralism, institutional approaches were seen for some time as something of a 'traditional' perspective, emphasising the centrality of institutions in understanding the exercise of power, in contrast to policy network approaches, for example. Conventionally, in political science this was grounded in descriptions of institutions such as Parliament, the courts, political parties and the executive, and to some extent the formal relationships between them. This was frequently associated with attempts at comparison across countries as a means of seeking to describe and measure the differences in the role of particular institutions, such as the legislature or the courts. Unsurprisingly, among the main criticisms of institutionalism was its emphasis on a highly historical and legalistic approach to the study of politics, and a consequent failure to recognise and account for policy or power that occurs or is exercised outside these formal institutions. Together with the reliance upon a rather descriptive, formalistic methodological approach, a fairly static view of the policy process and an emphasis on the state without taking account of the society within which it operates, including the role of voters and pressure groups, this meant that it was widely seen as not well suited to the study of public policy. However, in part as a response to these criticisms, the study of institutions developed in new directions across a variety of disciplines.

In the field of economics, the relationship between institutions and individuals' preferences has been a key area of debate, and in particular the extent to which institutions are created by individuals who are seeking to maximise their own utility, and/or the extent and means by which institutions shape individuals' preferences. In organisation theory, the concern has been with the ways in which particular organisational forms become 'institutionalised' and respond to the culture and values of their wider environment. And from a 'sociological institutionalist' perspective (for example, DiMaggio and Powell, 1983), it might be argued that there has been more of an emphasis on the process by which institutions emerge and develop, and therefore on change. Knill and Tosun (2012) also highlight 'historical institutionalism', which is concerned with how institutions change over time (see also Pierson, 2004; Pollitt, 2008), as well as 'rational choice institutionalism', with a focus on how institutions affect the strategies of actors pursuing their interests, while other variants can also be identified (see, for example, Lowndes, 2010).

Lowndes and Roberts (2013), while recognising that differences remain between the different strands of institutionalism, suggest that over the past two decades there has been a process of convergence and consolidation around: interests in both formal and informal institutions and three different forms of constraint – rules, practices and narratives; stability and desta-bilisation, in terms of the processes by which institutions become stabilised and what may drive change; how power is used and why some actors have greater power than others, even when procedures and arrangements may seem broadly neutral; recognition that institutions are 'messy and differ-entiated' (p. 43) in terms of the activities that they cover and the modes through which they affect political behaviour, the functions that they ful-fil and the power resources that they impart to different individuals and groups; the notion that institutions can determine, or at least influence, certain outcomes, but that contingent effects arise from the wider context and the interplay with other institutions and actors; and an interest in agency, recognising that actors must have some reflective and strategic capacities.

New (or neo-)institutionalism, therefore, recognises that institutions and actors influence each other. While some critics have suggested that there is little new about this 'new institutionalism', supporters argue that it differs from the original in recognising the importance of taking account of not only formal institutions and practices, but also less formal networks and relationships (see Peters, 1999). Colomer (2001), for example, has argued that political institutions (defined as the rules of the game, and in particular, who can vote, how votes are counted and what is voted for) shape the strategies of actors, and that these, in turn, produce collective outcomes that can themselves only be explained in terms of the information, opportunities, incentives and constraints provided by institutions and the consequent strategies adopted by both citizens and leaders.

Immergut (1990) and Tsebelis (1995 and 2002) have pointed out that institutions confer a veto power on certain actors who are able to block policy or legislative proposals, and that they therefore have considerable bargaining power in a political system, with institutional players being those that are established by the constitution, such as the executive and the legislature, while partisan veto players, political parties, in parliamentary and perhaps potential systems, operate within institutional players, and that these veto players play a part in shaping policy (for example, Ha, 2008).

Ostrom's institutional analysis and development framework (IAD) (for example, Ostrom *et al.*, 2014) explores what happens with regard to 'common pool resources' (or public goods) such as parks or policing. It builds on rational choice theory and the assumption that because people are boundedly rational (Simon 1945/1957) they come together to make choices within 'institutions' through the use of 'rules' (the 'logic of constitutional choice'). But Ostrom argues that the study of institutions and rules is not straightforward, noting, for example: that 'institution' refers to many different types of entity, including both organisations and the rules that structure interactions within and across organisations; that, while the buildings within which organised entities are located are visible, the institutions themselves are invisible; that, given the multiple languages used across disciplines, a coherent institutional framework is needed to allow for the expression and comparison of diverse theories applied to particular puzzles and problem settings; that decisions about rules at any one level are usually made within a structure of rules at a different level, so that institutional studies need to encompass multiple units of analysis; and that at any one level of analysis, combinations of rules, attributes of the world and communities of individuals involved are combined in a configural rather than an additive manner (Ostrom, 1990).

For Ostrom, the 'action arena' is a social space influenced by the physical world, the attributes of a community and the rules that structure individual and group behaviour, and within that arena the action situation contains those who participate in making decisions (individuals or groups), their positions on what they would like to happen, the outcomes that they would like to happen (or worry will happen), the connection between what is done and what will happen, the nature and extent to which the participants can shape outcomes, the adequacy of the information available to actors and the rational weighting of costs and benefits resulting from outcomes. The activities of the participants in the action situation, and the outcomes, are influenced by a variety of factors including efficiency, equity, accountability, conformance to general morality (following the rules) and adaptability. Ostrom *et al.* (2014) use the IAD to suggest that under proper conditions people can form institutions to successfully manage common resources, so that, for example, they are not overexploited, while, if there is a lack of 'collective-choice arenas' (p. 274), open-access, common-pool resources potentially face overuse and even destruction.

While, as highlighted above, there may, inevitably, be challenges associated with defining what is (or is not) an institution, for the study of public policy the institutional approach directs us towards an examination of the formal organisations, rules and procedures of government and organisations, informal norms that are implicit but shared, and how they vary over time, as well as how they shape behaviour and confer or limit power (for example, Lowndes and Roberts, 2013). This extends beyond political structures to other forms of 'institution', including the media, quasi-governmental bodies and supranational organisations such as the European Commission and the World Health Organization. It focuses on regularised patterns of behaviour, and these 'which we often call rules or structures ... can affect decision-making and the content of public policy' (Anderson, 1997, p. 32). As much of the discussion in Chapter 2 makes clear, rules and structures are often not neutral in the impact that they have and frequently favour certain policy options or particular sections of society to the disadvantage of others. They may also give incentives to particular forms of behaviour. The institutional approach therefore remains relevant, for not only do institutional structures, arrangements and relationships set the context for policy making, but they themselves must also be considered as part of the dynamic in the study of policy.

Institutional rules themselves change over time, and these too have been explained differently. For example, particularly from a rational choice perspective, it has been suggested that institutions survive for as long as they produce more benefits for the interested individual groups than do alternatives, although there are likely to be costs associated with change, and this can help explain the stability of institutions and incremental rather than radical reform. 'Path dependency', an idea closely associated with historical institutionalism (Pierson, 2000; Greener, 2005), encapsulates these ideas, with Myles and Pierson (2001) demonstrating how countries' pensions systems have been affected by path-dependent processes based on policy decisions in the past (policy legacies), although the approach has been criticised for appearing too deterministic and for failing to recognise sufficiently that change does happen. Others have argued that change can be explained by inconsistencies between different institutional rules, or between institutions and others, as with new demands from particular social groups, for example for political representation. A third suggestion is that change occurs when there are ideological paradigm changes, as with Keynesianism being 'superseded' by monetarism in many parts of the world in the 1980s (for example, Hall, 1986 and 1993). And finally, some suggest that there is institutional change when there are external shocks to a system, such as globalisation or global warming (see also the discussion of change over time in Chapter 1).

Elite theory

In contrast to the pluralist approach, elite perspectives on policy making contend that power is concentrated in the hands of a few groups of individuals and that the processes of decision making will therefore work to the advantage of those elites. The 'classical' elite theorists, Mosca (1896[1939]), Pareto (1935) and Michels (1915), argued that the concentration of power and the existence of elites are necessary and inevitable features of all societies, although Pareto, drawing on Machiavelli, saw a process of circulation among different types of elite – 'foxes', who seek to govern through consent and who do not resort to the use of force, and 'lions', who are prepared to use force to win or achieve their position – while Mosca saw the transfer of power between elites as occurring when the political formula that maintains the position of an elite fails and a new intellectual force takes over. Michels (1915) propounded the 'iron law of oligarchy', which suggests that over time elites in organisations will develop their own interests and goals, which will be distinct from those of the membership. However, it is worth noting that these three were writing at a time when many were still opposed to newly emerging democracy, and to socialism in particular, and when there were fears of the disorganised masses and demands for democracy and equality. They can also be criticised for a failure to test their ideas in any significant empirical manner.

In modern society elites can gain power from a variety of sources: holding formal office, as in government or business; wealth; or technical knowledge and expertise. From a Marxist perspective (discussed further in the next section), political power is determined by its relationship with the means of production, so that in a capitalist state economic power is concentrated in the hands of the small group who own the means of production (the bourgeoisie) and the state functions to create the conditions that will ensure the production of profit, capital accumulation and class domination. The state does that because: the power of capital constrains the exercise of power; there are shared social backgrounds and values among the bourgeoisie and the state elite; and the bourgeoisie can exercise influence through networks, personal contacts and lobbying. From a Weberian perspective, power is acquired through the development of large organisations and bureaucracies that administer the functions of government (notably the civil service). While bureaucracies may provide an effective and efficient means of administration, at the same time they can be seen as concentrating power in the hands of unelected and unaccountable officials. For some, power is expressed through the control and transmission of ideas, so that rather than public demands being transmitted into public policies, elites respond to public concerns through symbolic actions that are intended to reassure, rather than dealing substantively with the problem (Edelman, 1977).

Some writers have attempted to bring together the notions of democracy and elites. Schumpeter (1974) argued that in a democracy elitism is legitimised by the political market, which is made up of the competing parties and rival elites, while Lowell Field and Higley (1980) similarly suggested that elites require support from non-elites, for which they must compete. As noted above, some theorists have argued that social change in the modern state means that the position of elites is related to the development of large-scale organisations in many areas of life, and that there are therefore different kinds of elite, with Bottomore (1966), for example, suggesting that elite power can arise from a variety of sources including formal office (such as Parliament), wealth, and knowledge and technical expertise. It has therefore been argued that the existence of elites is not necessarily incompatible with pluralist democracy, with its many competing interests, as competition between elites protects democratic government. In addition, the fact that different elites may operate in different areas of society (including economic, political and social arenas) has been seen by some as protection against domination by one group.

Other writers, such as Miliband (1969), have pointed out that while there may be several elites, they have similar backgrounds and exercise power in the interests of a dominant class. However, whilst an important perspective, this makes the assumption that shared background implies a shared consensus of values, yet simply because a person originates from a particular social class it does not inevitably follow that they will adopt policies that are designed to promote the interests of that class.

For elite theorists, the fact that policies are made by these elite groups skews policy making. It can be argued that they focus on policies which benefit them and their position. For example, they might tend to use different services, and in particular those from the private sector, rather than the public sector, whether it be education, health, housing or pensions, so that services used by the masses are neglected; or they may focus on policies that they think are best for non-elites, but of which most of them will have little or no experience.

It is perhaps worth asking to what extent the agendas of those in authority do or do not concur with the priorities of the population in general? In addition, by their very status as leaders, elites can influence the attitudes and behaviour of citizens. They are not passive recipients of pressure from individuals and groups; indeed, they are often responsible for placing issues on the agenda. A good deal of public participation is reactive, responding to decisions or proposals from those in authority. In this way, matters may assume an importance in the minds of citizens which they might not have been aware of but for elite intervention. The acts or decisions of leaders frequently make news in their own right, and such publicity, sometimes fostered by elites themselves, can generate support. In a democratic society, the mobilising role of groups is therefore an essential feature of the process of agenda setting.

One of the major problems for elite theorists, however, is the need to demonstrate that elites do inevitably rule in democratic societies. For example, Birch (1993), one of the leading critics of such a view, has argued that in order to show that elite rule occurs in reality, it would be necessary to show that at least one of the following is the case:

1. access to political office is restricted to a small and cohesive group whose members share common interests and values that are not shared by the majority of the people;

2. office holders are unresponsive to the views and interests of the public, rather drawing on their own views and interests, and avoid public accountability either because mechanisms of accountability are inadequate, or because they use other means to circumvent accountability;

3. office holders regularly take decisions on behalf of a small class or group with a non-political power base whose interests are different from those of the majority.

Birch suggests that none of the classical elite theorists was able to produce sufficient evidence of any of these to show that there was any inevitability about elite rule. From a different perspective, Scott (2001) identifies a number of specialised elites within a modern state (legislative, government or executive, administrative, judicial, local state, military and policy and para-police) and suggests that to draw firm conclusions it would be necessary to look empirically at the extent to which these overlap to form a single elite with a policy and programme (perhaps drawing on Meisel's (1958) 'three Cs' – cohesion, consciousness and conspiracy).

Another weakness of the classical elite theorists lay in their negative and pessimistic assumptions about the possibilities for democracy. They believed that the public would be unable and unwilling to exercise power and that an undemocratic elite would therefore inevitably emerge. They did not consider that the people would develop greater political understanding as society developed and that it might be appropriate for responsibility for decisions to be taken by a few, so long as the mass retained ultimate control.

In terms of the exercise of power in public policy, elite theory directs us to look in a number of directions. It may be the case that in most organisations there is a tendency over time for power to slide towards a few people, whether through their energy, expertise, availability, or merely their willingness to take on either tasks or decision making, and for elites to avoid control by the remainder of the organisation. Issues for consideration may therefore include who the elite (or elites) are in society, whence they draw their power, and how powerful different elites may be in relation to each other. Do they have common interests and do they regularly make decisions that support those interests? And, ultimately, do such elites have control, or are they dependent upon public support which may be withdrawn?

Finally, particularly in the context of the growth in wealth of the top 10 per cent (Office for National Statistics, 2015b) and indeed the top 1 per cent of the population in recent years, including following the financial crisis (see Figure 3.3), it may be worth returning to Scott's (1991) analysis

Great Britain, July 2012 to June 2014

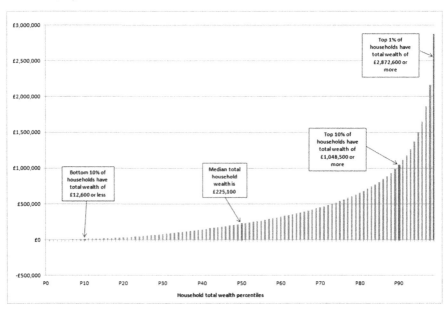

Figure 3.1   Distribution of total household wealth, percentile points

Source: Office for National Statistics (2015b) licensed under the Open Government Licence v.3.0.

of the United Kingdom, in which he saw privileged groups exercising power that came from class, status and politics and argued that 'Britain is ruled by a capitalist class whose economic dominance is sustained by the operations of the state and whose members are disproportionately represented in the power elite which rules the state apparatus. That is to say, Britain does have a ruling class' (pp. 151–52).

Marxist perspectives

The Marxist concept of the state is distinctive in that the state is seen as the product of the historical struggle between classes and as an institutional superstructure resting on the economic base. In 1884, Engels described the state as the instrument by which

> ... the most powerful, economically dominant class ... by its means becomes also the politically dominant class and so acquires new means of holding down and exploiting the oppressed class.
>
> (Engels, 1981, p. 231)

For Marxists, therefore, the state is not a politically neutral apparatus, but instead represents and operates in the interests of the dominant class and the private ownership of capital. Its legitimacy and authority are irrelevant and only exist in the minds of the ruling class and the false consciousness of those unaware of its true nature. Once the class struggle has been resolved, following the proletarian revolution and the emergence of a classless society, the state will wither away.

Neo-Marxists, such as Gramsci and Althusser, explained the persistence of the state in capitalist society through its ability to elicit consent from members of society, as well as the threat of force. Gramsci (1971) argued that the bourgeoisie maintained its dominance in Western societies by securing passive acquiescence, including by making concessions to the working class and accepting compromises that did not fundamentally undermine its position and therefore that of the state. Althusser (1971) stressed the importance of ideology and the ability of the bourgeois state to secure the acceptance of its values through relatively autonomous ideological state apparatuses such as the education system, the Church and trade unions, rather than through oppressive state power such as the police and the armed forces, although the latter were seen by him as part of the core of the state, together with the executive, the legislature and the judiciary, and coercion therefore remained in reserve.

Miliband (1969) distinguished between the government and the state, arguing that the government is the most visible, although not the most important, part of the state. He points out that the state also includes the bureaucracy, the police, the judiciary, local and regional authorities, economic institutions (such as the Bank of England), national, regional and local representative institutions and even some elements of civil society. Winning control of the government through elections is therefore no guarantee of winning control of the state. He also suggests that the state does have a significant degree of autonomy, which helps it operate in the interests of the dominant class but makes it appear neutral, and, like Gramsci, he points out that it can make concessions to subordinate classes that help preserve the position of the ruling class. For Miliband, the state's key function is to defend the interests of the dominant class, and it does so for three main reasons: the occupancy of key state positions (with people being drawn from the dominant class and having similar socio-economic characteristics, and therefore similar economic and social values); the political power of business interests (for example through the funding of political parties, the media, and through their ability to influence the economy and economic policies); and the constraints of a capitalist system (so that, for example, business interests are often equated with the national interest, while the capitalist system is portrayed as the only viable one). Miliband argues that in countries like Britain, therefore, the power of capitalism and the capitalist state rests not on their repressive capacities, but on a variety of subtler and more deep-seated influences.

A different approach is taken by Poulantzas (1973), who regards the characteristics of the ruling class as irrelevant and instead emphasises understanding the state as a social relation, although he too argues that the state is able to develop some autonomy, while remaining a far from neutral actor. Indeed, he sees the state's role as not to eliminate class struggle, but to regulate it, keeping it within manageable proportions and therefore preventing any direct challenge to capitalism. In order to do that, it requires some autonomy from the ruling class.

It is also possible to consider the functions of the state in capitalist society. The main function can be portrayed as assisting the process of capital accumulation, creating the conditions in which capitalists are able to promote production for profit; in addition, it is responsible for maintaining order and control within society. From a structuralist, or functionalist, perspective, it can be argued that broad changes in the structure of the economy can lead to policy shifts, and indeed changes in the exercise of power. While rational or incremental change, interest group bargaining and indeed policy networks may exist, they operate within the interests of the economic order, so that, for example, the provision of physical resources such as roads and industrial sites as well as services such as education, health and housing to groups in the working population is not concerned with reducing inequality, but rather perpetuating the interests of capitalism by preparing people for their roles in the workforce. State provision can also be seen as reducing the cost of labour power to capital. Maintaining order and control is carried out through repressive mechanisms such as the police, but also through systems such as education, and even through forms of social control such as the provision of benefits.

Marxist theories therefore hold two rather different views of the relationship between the state and the different classes. One is that the state is merely a tool of the economically dominant class, the bourgeoisie, who not only own the bulk of wealth, but also form an elite in terms of class origin, education, lifestyle and values. While there may be occasional divisions of interest between different sections of the ruling class, the common interest in preserving and strengthening capitalism dominates. From this perspective, the UK is a 'capitalist' democracy rather than a 'liberal' democracy, as economics takes precedence over politics. The working of the political system is determined by the economic system, rather than vice versa. Inequalities of income and wealth arise from capitalism and the state does not challenge this. 'Rights' such as civil and political rights cannot be seen truly as rights, while there are enormous inequalities in wealth and life chances. Even apparently radical reforms such as the growth of the franchise, or the creation of devolved assemblies, do not affect the power of the ruling class; nor do they significantly improve the position of the poor. Elections and Parliament serve primarily to legitimise capitalist democracy and to contain pressures from below; similarly, while policy making might, for example, involve rational planning and pressure group activity, it nevertheless reflects the interests of the wider economic order, capitalism. Marxists would argue, for example, that when in government the Labour Party has done little to weaken capitalism, but has sought merely to win some concessions for the working class. Regardless of which party is in power, the state is inherently biased in favour of capitalism and against the working class.

The second Marxist (or neo-Marxist) perspective is that which proposes the relative autonomy of the state (Jessop, 2007). There are different approaches here: firstly, there are those, such as Gramsci (1971), who focus on class domination through ideological, cultural and political means, as well as coercion; and secondly, there are some modern Marxists who see politicians effectively as managers of the state (Block, 1987), whose main aim is to further their self-interest rather than the interests of capital, although Block is not clear whether reforms by state managers will always work for capital.

There are a number of potential criticisms of Marxist approaches. For example, while in the UK there is substantial evidence that political elites come disproportionately from a propertied and privileged group who share significant economic, educational, cultural and social experiences, and that this may create bias, including favouring the capitalist system, it is also possible to argue that over time most citizens benefit from capitalism and that the ruling class may not rule solely in its own interests.

It is also apparent that democratic governments spend large sums of money on social and environmental programmes that are funded in part by taxes from industry and the financial sector. Marxists generally respond that such programmes help to legitimise the capitalist system and are therefore in the long-term interests of capitalism. In addition, some, such as education, may help to ensure that capitalism has a suitable supply of appropriately skilled labour, while income maintenance payments may help to maintain social order. However, it is also possible to argue that capital has made some concession to labour interests and that the working class can therefore negotiate benefits from capitalism in the form of state welfare. Yet Marxists also see these gains as largely or entirely illusory and acting only to preserve the power of the capitalist ruling class.

Marxist notions of 'false consciousness', that the thoughts and wishes of the working class are simply reflections of the ideology of the ruling class, can in turn be criticised for their outlook on society, with the suggestion that people, and in particular the working class, do not recognise what their real interests are, appearing both elitist and dismissive of the working class.

Finally, it can be argued (for example, John, 2012) that deterministic approaches, such as Marxism, are unable to explain the complexity and variety of public policy, whether it be between countries or different tiers of government, or in terms of the social and political goals of policies. While ideas of the relative autonomy of the state may help respond to such criticisms, some suggest that in becoming more realistic the approach may lose its Marxist focus (Amenta and Skocpol, 1989; Skocpol, 1992), moving closer towards neo-pluralism or new institutionalism. Indeed, Skocpol (1979, 1985) takes a non-Marxist structural perspective, arguing that social revolutions need to be analysed by recognising that while groups and movements are inevitably part of revolutions, the success of revolutions depends on socio-economic conditions and the international environment; in this she sees the state as having its own interests and the potential to act autonomously from society.

Rational choice theories

Rational choice (sometimes called public choice, with the terms widely being used interchangeably, including within this book) approaches are rather different from the pluralist, corporatist and Marxist analyses discussed above. Rather, they can be seen as drawing upon some aspects of the institutionalist approach, combining accounts of how institutions can operate with more behaviouralist accounts. These ideas have had significant implications, both for the study of public policy and in setting the political and public policy agenda since the late 1970s, not least because they have widely been seen as hostile to the state and much of what it does (Hindmoor, 2006).

A key feature of rational choice theory is its assumption of the self-interested rationality of individuals, with actors seeking to fulfil their preferences. In turn, political outcomes are seen as being the product of the aggregated actions of individuals. It draws upon economic theory and techniques to analyse political processes. While some, notably the work of Downs (for example, 1957), is written from a pluralist context, much rational choice writing has been associated with the views of what became widely known as the New Right (for example, Niskanen, 1973; Olsen, 1968; Tullock, 1976; Buchanan, 1986), often associated with some of the approaches of the Thatcher governments, and to varying extents their successors, in the UK. The application of some of these ideas to bureaucracies was outlined briefly in Chapter 2.

Tullock (1976), for example, argues that, in order to win elections, politicians are forced to 'bribe' voters by offering benefits to different groups to attract their votes. It is in the interests of an elector to vote for the party offering the best package of policies for themselves, as the cost of the proposals will be spread across all taxpayers, not just those who share the characteristics of their group. The voter therefore does not pay the full price of the benefit that they receive, but across the political system as a whole the result is excessive promises. Tullock also examines the power of bureaucracies in the decision-making process and argues that one of the principal characteristics of the modern state has been that bureaucracies have been serving their own rather than the public interest (see also Chapter 2). For Tullock, the existence and operation of pressure groups also create problems, as such groups are seen as diverting resources to their own self-interested ends (1976, 1988). As with voting, this happens because the cost to individuals of a benefit is low when it is spread across the whole community and the net cost of organising to resist a programme is relatively much higher than the net cost of organising to support it. As a result, the political system becomes disproportionately skewed towards increasing public expenditure.

Like Tullock, Niskanen begins with the assumption that bureaucrats maximise their self-interest. He views government agencies as types of business and applies theories that attempt to model the behaviour of firms to state bureaucracies, conceptualising government agencies as seeking to maximise their budgets and size, in the same way as private companies (see also the discussion of the bureaucratic over-supply model in Chapter 2). However, while business people are assumed to seek to maximise their profits and will therefore not produce additional output for which the benefit to consumers (and hence the market price) is less than the costs of production, Niskanen (1973) argues that it is only through increasing their budgets that bureaucrats can maximise their self-interest and personal welfare, and that they do this through supplying outputs to the legislature in return for a budget. Unlike a firm operating in the market, government agencies do not have to reveal the cost of a unit of output at different levels of production, and the legislature may therefore find it hard to ascertain the benefits of an agency's activities. Also, unlike in a market situation, bureaucrats have a monopoly of information about the costs and benefits of what they are doing, and this enables them to maximise their interests while making it harder for governments to maintain control. Rational officials therefore seek to maximise their welfare by expanding their agencies' budgets, leading to oversupply. Building upon such arguments, rational choice theorists have frequently claimed that political control over state bureaucracies is ineffective and that, in attempting to achieve their self-interest, bureaucrats are diverting resources that could be better used in other ways.

This approach can be used to support the view that society should merely lay down a basic set of general rights and that individuals should be allowed to operate freely with no other constraints (a negative view of freedom), and is often linked to ideologies and policies that favour small government and the market provision of goods and services. It also supports the view that in a two-party political system, where voters are forced to choose between what may be polarised alternatives, there may be excessive promises by politicians and inadequate control by citizens. Rational choice theory also appears to provide a powerful view for explaining how bureaucrats might be primarily motivated by their own self-interest and be unresponsive to other demands; and, when applied to government departments within any tier of government, it may help to explain what is sometimes seen as a constant struggle for bigger shares of public expenditure.

Many criticisms have focused on rational choice theory being simplistic and unrealistic, although there is nothing that prevents it being modified to take account of more complex circumstances, and indeed simplicity may allow for the identification and exploration of ideas that might otherwise be missed. A further criticism of rational choice perspectives is that they are based upon the assumption of self-interested behaviour, and that they do not recognise that in many instances, such as in relation to family and friends, social norms tend not to support such behaviour.

It is here perhaps that some of the accusations of a lack of fit with the real world can be appropriate. For example, where bureaucracies are concerned, rational choice theory assumes not only that bureaucrats are motivated primarily by self-interest, but also that those self-interests are best served by bigger departments and bigger budgets, and this, as Parsons (1995) has pointed out, is somewhat simplistic. The evidence from many countries, including the UK, also shows that during the 1980s and 1990s, and again following the financial crisis of 2008, the number of civil servants fell while markets and/or market techniques were introduced into many public sector bureaucracies. To this can be added the argument that where empirical evidence may exist that supports the ideas of writers such as Niskanen, Tullock and others, it originates largely from the United States and may not easily or appropriately be transferred to different cultural, political and social contexts, such as those that exist in the UK. In addition, public choice ideas do not simply try to explain the world; they also seek to change it, as indeed they have done, and some find the emphasis on purely self-interested actions, rather than altruism and public interest, both unattractive and inappropriate.

Critics have also sought to draw upon rational choice theory to produce alternative outcomes. In addition to Ostrom, whose work is also discussed in this chapter, who has demonstrated the possibility of non-market solutions to collective action problems, Dunleavy (1985 and 1991) illustrated that it was possible to produce an alternative model for bureaucratic behaviour (see the discussion of bureau shaping in Chapter 2). In analysing the large-scale privatisations that took place during the 1980s, Dunleavy points out that the relationships between types of bureaucrat and the differences in power were much more complex than writers such as Niskanen suggested. In particular, he argued that self-interest does not have to be expressed in terms of departmental size or budgets and that senior civil servants were more concerned with 'shaping' their departments and budgets so that they could advance their interests in a similar way to politicians and private business. As a result, senior civil servants did not resist privatisation as it was in their class interests, although the cost was job losses and poorer working conditions for those lower down the civil service ladder. He concluded that collective action strategies for maximising welfare were only used by bureaucrats when other strategies had failed.

Game theory

Game theory examines the choices that actors make when faced with a particular set of 'payoffs' in a strategic decision-making environment and the need to anticipate the choices that might be made by other actors. In the simplest version, the assumptions are made that all players are instrumentally rational, that all know that the other players are rational, that all understand the rules of the game and the payoff from each choice and that everyone would make the same choice in the same circumstances. Other games may introduce greater degrees of uncertainty or vary the assumptions, such as the motivations of the actors. The aim is to identify points of equilibrium where actors will make a choice and stick with it.

The best-known example of a game is the prisoner's dilemma. In it, two prisoners are accused of the same crime, arrested, kept in separate cells and questioned. The prisoners are offered three options: if they both remain silent they will each receive a mild punishment; if one confesses but the other does not the former will be released while the latter will receive a severe punishment; and if they both confess they will each receive a heavy punishment. The game predicts that they will not be able to choose the outcome that benefits them both (remaining silent) as they do not trust each other, and that therefore both will confess as they fear that the other will confess first and they will consequently receive a sterner punishment. The game thus suggests that people will not cooperate in their own best interests as they are concerned that others will take advantage of them. So, from this perspective, even where people may face a collective problem and might all benefit from action, they will not necessarily cooperate.

Given that problems that are likely to require collective action occur at every level, from very local areas to international politics, such as in relation to climate change, this would suggest that tackling such problems is likely to be difficult, as with over-fishing, where it may be that actors will continue to fish as they are concerned that even if they stop, others will continue. However, game theory suggests that the possibilities for collective action depend on the nature of the public good, and where there are clear benefits, such as in providing sanitation or controlling air pollution, introducing policies is not difficult. Of course, in the real world, 'games' are rarely one-off, and it can be argued that policy makers learn to take account of benefits over time, rather than simply in one particular instance, while some theorists, such as Ostrom (1990), whose institutional analysis and development framework was discussed earlier in this chapter, argue that individuals may often be motivated to cooperate with each other.

Conclusion

Clearly, as this and the preceding chapters make clear, the concept of power is complex and multi-faceted and can be analysed from a variety of different positions, each of which can add to our understanding of the exercise of power and the policy process. In addition, these varied positions can be used to raise questions about how and why the world is as it is, and in some cases can also be used in a normative sense, as a description of how the world should be. There are also other analyses, not discussed here, such as those that focus on disability, gender and 'race', that often highlight, in particular, the ways in which policy and the state assume that people should lead their lives and the power relations that shape them (see, for example, Williams, 1989; Lister, 2003; Bloch and Solomos, 2010; Craig *et al.*, 2012; Roulstone and Prideaux, 2012).

The ideas discussed in this chapter encourage us to focus on a variety of phenomena, from how decisions are made, through the ways in which policy aims are set out and policies implemented, to a consideration of the economic, political and social institutions that shape the way in which we see the world, and which might also limit the scope of governments' consideration of social problems and their responses to them.

Further reading

These works are useful for their coverage of many of the issues discussed in this chapter:

Cairney, P. (2012) *Understanding Public Policy*, Basingstoke: Palgrave Macmillan.

John, P. (2012) *Analyzing Public Policy*, London: Routledge.

On the three dimensions of power, see:

Lukes, S. (2005) *Power: A Radical View*, Basingstoke: Palgrave Macmillan.

For in-depth coverage of institutions and institutionalism, see:

Lowndes, V. and Roberts, M. (2013) *Why Institutions Matter*, Basingstoke: Palgrave Macmillan.

4

Key Trends and Influences in Policy Making

This chapter discusses a variety of trends in policy making and implementation, both national and international. Many of these, such as a growing emphasis on the use of technology, marketisation and contracting, and attempts to encourage citizen participation, along with the growth of supra-national organisations, are likely to be very familiar, while others, such as policy transfer and the increasing fragmentation of many areas of public service delivery, have arguably become much more common over time. The chapter seeks to explore and explain their relevance for understanding the contemporary policy process.

The first three chapters of this book have introduced a range of models and theories that can help us understand the ways in which policies are made and implemented, and some of the influences upon policy making. This chapter moves on to consider a variety of trends that have been significant in recent years. Inevitably, this is highly selective and concise, in that without the pressures of space it would be possible to identify many more areas of development that might be included, and to provide much more discussion of them. In relation to the first point, for example, Pollitt (2016a) identifies a number of 'megatrends' that he suggests will continue to have an impact: fiscal austerity, which he suggests will have significant implications for public sectors and their staff, which might include a smaller and ageing workforce, potentially with inappropriate skills and disillusionment, together with demands for greater innovation 'to do more with less'; technological change (and some aspects of 'e-government' are discussed below), which has affected and will continue to affect the public sector in a variety of ways, with changing technologies affecting the tasks that public officials carry out, and with implications for recruitment and training of staff, as well as the ways in which citizens interact with public authorities; the ageing population in much of the developed world, which has implications for public spending, particularly on pensions, health care and social care in terms of volume and affordability; and climate change, which will require changes such as to building regulations, energy generation and transmission, transport systems, agriculture, and potentially immigration and security. He also highlights that such megatrends are not independent of each other. As a positive example of interaction he suggests that technological innovation may help respond to both demographic change and climate change, for example by providing some health care remotely. On the other hand, he notes that there are negative interactions between austerity and both demographic and climate change, with long-term investment programmes being casualties of public sector cuts.

The 'key trends' discussed here are generally of a lesser order than Pollitt's megatrends, and it would be possible to identify others, such as the use of regulation, audit and inspection (see Chapter 8), attempts to 'join up' or integrate government services, the emphasis on risk and crisis management, and 'agencification' (see Chapter 7), but these are chosen because they have had, and continue to have, a significant impact on the making and implementation of public policy, and it is possible to identify many ways in which these trends are reflected in or interact with the issues discussed throughout this book.

Evidence-based policy making

The idea that policies should be based on evidence, or perhaps at least informed by evidence to some extent, appears obvious. It certainly fits well with rational approaches to policy making as discussed in Chapter 2. However, the explanations of how policy change comes about that were considered in Chapter 1 highlight how complex and messy the policy process is, and that problems, solutions and political opportunities may not align easily, while most of this book also makes clear that there are many different interests and pressures involved in making and implementing policy. Yet, despite these challenges, there is a long history of seeking to use good-quality information to underpin policy decisions. Indeed, such approaches can be seen as linked, to greater or lesser extents, with a number of the other topics covered in this chapter, including policy transfer, elements of e-government, and some of the pressures for greater public participation and engagement, as well as evaluation, as discussed in Chapter 8.

What is evidence-based policy making?

While the discussion above highlights that governments, and their critics, understandably like to claim that 'the evidence' supports their policy positions and decisions, with policies based upon objective assessments of that evidence, most commentators recognise that the linkage is far from straightforward, and that what counts as evidence is varied.

'Evidence-based' policy has been contrasted with 'opinion-based' or 'value-based' policy, which draws upon either the selective use of evidence or the often untested views of influential individuals or groups (see, for example, Davies, 2004), although, as discussed below, the divide is perhaps not as stark as those terms might appear to suggest. In addition, 'and practice' is often added to the phrase, reflecting both the proponents' views of the ideas' potential roles, and also that some elements of the 'evidence base' draw strongly on studies of the effectiveness of interventions, particularly in areas of health and social care (see, for example, Nutley *et al.*, 2007). Boaz and Nutley (2016) identify four main uses of evidence to promote improvement in policy making, programme development and service delivery:

1. to design and develop public policy (option appraisal);

2. to assess the impact of policy interventions (evaluation);

3. to improve policy implementation (ongoing evaluation or monitoring);

4. to identify tomorrow's issues (evidence-based innovation).

It is also worth noting that there is a variety of critiques of evidence-based policy, as outlined in the next section. While some interpretations of evidence-based policy have drawn strongly on the use of systematic reviews in medicine, which seek to synthesise and summarise the findings of existing research, and often reflect quantitative and positivist approaches, others have argued for a much broader approach, drawing upon a wider range of types of research and forms of data. Head (2008) has suggested that there are three types of evidence relevant to modern states: scientific knowledge, based upon the systematic analysis of conditions and trends and seeking to identify the causal relationships between them; policy management knowledge, reflecting the experience of and knowledge gained by professionals and organisations from the implementation of policies and programmes; and political knowledge, held by political parties, politicians, organised interests and the media, which recognises the importance of agenda setting, building coalitions of support, and the need to determine priorities. He argues that scientific knowledge alone is not sufficient to underpin evidence-based policy formulation, and that it must be complemented by the other two forms. Weiss (1979) developed a typology of the roles of research that drew on empirical work on how policy makers use

---

Box 4.1   Seven different meanings of research use

1. *The knowledge-driven model* – Basic research identifies something that may be relevant for public policy; applied research tests those findings and assesses them; research-based technologies are developed for implementation; and then implementation occurs.

2. *The problem-solving model* – A problem exists and a decision about how to respond has to be made; research helps generate a solution which can then be implemented.

3. *The interactive model* – Policy makers actively seek knowledge from a variety of sources, including researchers. Unlike the first two 'meanings' this is not a straight line model but sees the relationship between research and policy as messy and dynamic, with interactions between many types of people in the policy process.

4. *The political model* – Where political opinions have been firmly formed, whether for ideological or other reasons, research is unlikely to have a direct influence. However, research may still be used, politically, to provide support for particular positions or to critique others.

5. *The tactical model* – Research is used for purposes that are not related to the substance of the research, as when policy makers may fund or conduct research to avoid taking action or to deflect criticism.

6. *The enlightenment model* – Rather than the findings of a single study, or even of a body of related work, research can have a gradual influence on public policy. Ideas, concepts and theoretical perspectives seep into the policy-making process through a wide variety of channels, including the media and interest groups. Over time, research can therefore both shape the ways that problems and possible solutions are framed, and redefine the policy agenda.

7. *Research as part of the intellectual enterprise of society* – Like policy, research can be seen as responding to the changing currents of thoughts and priorities of society. Wider social concerns may, for example, mean that funds are made available for research on a topic, and researchers are thereby drawn to study it. Research may, in turn, contribute to the thinking of policy makers.

Source: Adapted from Weiss (1979).

---

research, which is useful in thinking about how research can influence public policy (Box 4.1).

Weiss, and others, suggest that it is rare that approaches such as those of the first two models are actually used in policy making, and that more strategic approaches to research use, as reflected in the political and tactical models, are more common. The tactical, enlightenment and intellectual models also encourage us to recognise that the impact and use of research may be much more long term, complex and indirect, and that it interacts with other forms and sources of knowledge in the policy arena (Nutley *et al.*, 2007).

The idea of evidence-based policy was strongly promoted by the Labour governments from 1997, in particular following the publication of the White Paper *Modernising Government* (Cabinet Office, 1999), with their 'what matters is what works' mantra (Davies *et al.*, 2000), seeking to high-light a shift away from what was portrayed as the dominance of ideology during the Thatcher years (and indeed previous Labour governments) towards the greater use of evidence to inform policy making, including as a way to make better policies. The move also reflected an increase in the number of groups and organisations, such as pressure groups and pro-fessional organisations, trying to exert influence on government policy, and using evidence as a way to do this, and a growing distrust among the public towards professionals, responsible for service delivery, who had hitherto largely been seen as experts. It could also be seen as linked with the increased use of audit and inspection in public services (for example, Dorey, 2014). The idea gained significant traction and there was a range of initiatives that were designed to encourage the greater use of evidence (see, for example, Bochel and Duncan, 2007), including in local government (see, for example, Box 4.2). Labour also made more extensive use of pilot schemes, for example trialling a project in a particular area before imple-menting it nationally (as with 'Sarah's law', allowing parents to check if a convicted paedophile lives in their locality (Kemshall *et al.*, 2010)), although these are not unproblematic, as governments might be unwill-ing to defer a policy to allow testing, and even where testing highlights problems, there may be a reluctance to cease or even significantly modify a programme. In addition, even under Labour, at times the relationships between evidence and policy were problematic, as with drugs policy in 2009, when Professor David Nutt was forced to resign as a government scientific adviser on the misuse of drugs after he claimed in a paper that alcohol and tobacco were more harmful than many illegal drugs, and towards the end of the government, while there were still considerable claims about the use of evidence in policy making, they were often more tempered, and many of the early advocates of the idea had taken more critical, or perhaps more realistic, positions, reflecting the continued influ-ence of values and politics, rather than policy being led by 'evidence'.

The Coalition government (2010–2015) continued to pay lip-service to the use of evidence in policy (for example, HM Treasury, 2011), although the idea was arguably even more problematic than it had been under Labour. There was certainly a variety of initiatives that appeared to work

---

Box 4.2   Evidence-based policy in local government: the Leicestershire Family Insight Review

The exercise included:

➤ ethnographic research with individual families;

➤ workshops with members of other families and practitioners;

➤ journey maps for families setting out their experience of services;

➤ a review of the evidence base on family intervention models.

Partners mapped and profiled 1,300 families using government criteria on complex needs. They then developed a new Family Model, with partners committing resources and agreeing a joint evaluation framework. The model focused on risk triggers and life events, and drew on findings of the customer journey mapping exercise to identify the best points at which to offer services. The research highlighted the need for a flexible approach in understanding the issues for families with complex needs, the importance of understanding the variety of existing services and their contributions in supporting change, and the benefits of sharing service data at the individual level in collecting objective data to evidence the financial impacts of and on services.

Source: http://socialvaluecommissioning.org/2016/10/20/supporting-leicestershire-families/ (accessed 8 November 2016).

---

in that broad direction, such as the creation of the Office for Budget Responsibility and the Educational Endowment Foundation, and the establishment of What Works Centres in 2013 to provide evidence to help guide decision making on public spending in areas such as local economic growth, crime, ageing and early intervention (Cabinet Office, 2013). There were also attempts to make better use of the data collected by government with a move towards Open Government Data (OGD), although this may have been driven as much by seeking to make services more accountable and efficient through consumer pressures as by enabling organisations to interrogate the data in order to improve services and perhaps devise new or innovative policy solutions. On the other hand, a number of commentators offered views broadly in line with those of the Liberal Democrat MP Norman Baker, who resigned as a Home Office Minister in 2014, saying that 'in the Home Office [where Theresa May, who became Prime Minister in July 2016, was Home Secretary], the goodwill to work collegiately to take forward rational evidence-based policy has been in somewhat short supply' (http://www.libdems.org.uk/norman_baker_resigns_as_home_office_minister, accessed 4 October 2016) (see also, for example, Exley and Ball, 2011, on education; Fenwick and Elcock, 2014, on elected mayors; Gibb, 2015, on the 'bedroom tax'; Nicholls and Greenaway, 2015, on alcohol policy; Williams, 2015), albeit sometimes recognising the impact of a variety of other influences on policy. With the referendum on EU membership and its aftermath, including a new Prime Minister and significant changes to the Cabinet, the extent of the use of evidence in policy by the Conservative governments elected in 2015 and 2017 was somewhat unclear, although some found it possible to suggest that many of the claims of both sides during the referendum campaign lacked an evidence base, while critics of the government's rhetoric on immigration were able to point to a lack of clear evidence (for example, http://www.bbc.co.uk/news/uk-34456622, accessed 24 June 2017), and others suggested that in fields such as housing, policy was not driven by evidence, including the extension of the right to buy housing association homes (Hetherington, 2015), and that in education evidence on social mobility did not support the proposed policy of allowing grammar schools to expand (https://www.theguardian.com/education/2016/aug/07/senior-tories-likely-to-resist-theresa-mays-grammar-schools-agenda, accessed 24 June 2017), while the extension of the programme of badger culling in an attempt to reduce TB in cattle was also seen as problematic in terms of evidence (https://www.theguardian.com/environment/2016/aug/30/badger-cull-areas-more-than-triple-under-new-government-licences, accessed 24 June 2017).

Critiques of evidence-based policy making

Although the idea of evidence-based policy, as with rational approaches more broadly, may have considerable appeal, it is also important to recognise that there are many constraints and other pressures, as highlighted throughout this book. The use of evidence is inherently political in nature, and those issues which are excluded from the political agenda may be just as important as those which are included (see, for example, Bachrach and Baratz, 1963; see also Chapter 2). Governments are constantly expected to solve, or at least respond to, problems, and may not have either the time or the resources available to gather evidence or introduce what might be the 'best' policies, and therefore have to make decisions based on partial information and using resources that may be relatively easily accessible. The use of evidence for policy making is further compounded by organisational issues. Organisations have different information needs, and their evidence use may vary according to the function of the organisation, such as policy development or service delivery (Head, 2016), as well as with the commitment of managers to using it. In addition, in many policy areas evidence does not necessarily all point in one direction, while assumptions about causality may not always appear in practice, so that policy makers have to assess the credibility of different sources of evidence against their own views, including of how those affected by a policy will act, and their interpretation of what the public might think. They also need to consider how a new or changed policy might impact upon or be affected by other extant policies. The contested nature of evidence has led some, such as Head (2016), to suggest that there has been a move towards the more modest 'evidence-informed' rather than evidence-based policy.

Bannister and O'Sullivan (2014) note that policy development and the role of evidence and knowledge within it are always context dependent, and that evidence and knowledge can take fundamentally different forms, with the extent to which one form is favoured over another again being context dependent. They examine the development, and to some extent the divergence, of antisocial behaviour policy in England and Scotland from 1997, and argue that while in Scotland policy may have developed somewhat differently, in both countries *epistemic* knowledge, based on 'investigation of the nature and foundations of ASB, its incidence or the social costs, benefits and overall value of different approaches to the problem' (p. 87), has been no more important than *phronetic* (subjective, centred on what matters to individuals and groups within society) or *techne* (practical, relating to what works in particular situations, and the knowledge of practitioners and others involved in the implementation of policy) knowledge, and indeed that across the policy cycle 'in both England/Wales and Scotland, *phronetic* evidence has been accorded by far the greatest primacy' (p. 86), playing a constant role in reaffirming and reinforcing policy makers' perceptions of voters' concerns, so that in this area 'policy making has responded strongly to a democratic imperative, but in doing so may not necessarily have served it to best effect' (p. 87). On broadly similar lines, following research on the Department for Work and Pensions, Ingold and Monaghan (2016) found that '[o]fficials were concerned about how particular methodologies would be perceived by key decision-makers, suggesting that it is the evidence which maps onto dominant ideology, electioneering and "playing to the gallery" which is most effectively translated into policy' (p. 182).

'Realist' perspectives have, perhaps unsurprisingly, emphasised the difference between more rationalist models of the policy-making process and what happens in practice, with Pawson and Tilley (1997) and Pawson (2002), for example, arguing that successful outcomes emerge not simply from a policy or programme, but from the underlying policy mechanisms and the ways in which they interact with the context. As a result, they suggest that it is necessary to test theories about which combinations of mechanisms and contexts might produce the desired outcomes. In addition, rather than looking at 'what works', a more appropriate question is 'what works for whom in what circumstances' (Pawson, 2002, p. 342).

Given these challenges to evidence-based policy making, after a decade of New Labour, Sanderson (2009) argued that there appeared to be sufficient doubts and criticisms to provide grounds for questioning the validity of the concept. He highlights, for example, whether the term evidence-based policy making was used in a 'positive' mode (seeking to describe the current position), or a 'normative' mode (seeking to show how things might change for the better), and that there are dangers in conflating description and prescription, as a normative concept risks legitimising the status quo and potentially undermining the role of vision and ideals in guiding human affairs. More fundamentally, he points out that in recent years our understanding of processes of change has advanced significantly through the adoption and application of dynamic, non-linear concepts and models, and that in such a world, where change, inequality and disequilibrium are the norm, rather than stability and equilibrium as assumed in traditional mechanistic models, the implications are that we are limited in our capacity to predict, plan and control the behaviour of social systems. He notes that for a number of authors, dealing with these 'new realities' has meant a fundamental shift in the role of government from 'command and control' regulatory strategies to interactive governance, including the greater involvement of and reliance on non-state actors. However, he argues that rather than either rejecting or relying on particular forms of evidence, an enhanced capacity for experimentation and learning is important, allowing the testing of policy hypotheses, recognising the validity of the experiences of practitioners and of informed public opinion, and recognising that policy making is not simply a technical exercise drawing on evidence and expertise, but a process within which many concerns should be addressed and legitimate voices heard before coming to a reasonable decision.

Policy transfer

In recent years, both policy makers and policy analysts have paid significant attention to policy learning and policy transfer. As Cairney (2012) notes, the use of those terms, while providing some indicator of the areas being considered, is somewhat vague, and there is also a number of other expressions used to describe areas that are more or less strongly related to policy transfer and learning, such as the ideas of lesson drawing and policy convergence and policy diffusion. Policy transfer, the focus of this section, is, perhaps inevitably, difficult to define in a way that separates it clearly from other activities, but it is essentially concerned with the transfer of arrangements, ideas, institutions or policies from one political system to another (for example, Dolowitz and Marsh, 1996 and 2000; Dolowitz, 2000). Rose (1991) sees lesson drawing as concerned with the question of '[u]nder what circumstances and to what extent would a programme now in effect elsewhere also work here?' (p. 4), see also Rose (1993 and 2005). He notes that while the literature on policy diffusion highlights the ways in which some states often lead while others may more frequently follow, and the processes and patterns associated with this (Walker, 1969; Berry and Berry, 2014), that on policy convergence considers whether it is possible to identify a move, over time, towards policy similarities across different states, and if so, whether the processes that might underpin such a development can also be identified (Bennett, 1991; Holzinger and Knill, 2005). Some critics, such as James and Lodge (2003), have suggested that because policy transfer is difficult to disentangle from other forms of policy making, it may be that alternative theories are more useful, particularly in seeking to assess the impact of learning and policy making on policy outcomes. However, the ideas clearly raise questions about the activities of policy makers, including governments' attempts to learn from other countries, and the variety of influences upon policy making, and are therefore worthy of consideration here.

The stimulus for policy transfer is frequently dissatisfaction with existing programmes or policies and a consequent desire to do something new. This may be especially true for new governments that want to make their mark and show themselves as doing something distinctive from the previous administration. For example, when Labour were elected in 1997 they introduced a number of significant policies that were arguably based in part on policy transfer, including giving the Bank of England control of interest rates, which reflected the role of central banks in other countries, such as Germany, which were seen as having helped create low inflation and economic stability, and the New Deal programmes for unemployed people, which could be argued to have been adopted from policies pursued in the United States. When the Coalition government came to power in 2010 it justified the expansion of academies and the introduction of free schools in part as building on Labour's changes to school-age education, but also as reflecting the perceived successes of free schools in Sweden and charter schools in Canada and the United States. Similarly, the same government and its Conservative successor sought to examine possible lessons from countries such as China and Singapore in relation to approaches to teaching and learning (Forestier and Crossley, 2015), including by inviting 68 maths teachers from Shanghai to England for three weeks in 2015 to demonstrate how they worked (https://www.gov.uk/government/speeches/shanghai-maths-teaching-exchange-opening-ceremony, accessed 24 June 2017). However, it is important to consider the motivations for transfer as they are likely to impact on what information is sought and how it is used (Dolowitz and Marsh, 2012).

The idea of policy transfer can be seen as having links with rational approaches to policy making (see Chapter 2), particularly in relation to attempts to improve the quality of decision making through detailed consideration of the policy options. The fact that problems rarely occur in one jurisdiction alone is likely to encourage policy makers to look elsewhere for possible responses. However, it can also at times be seen as reflecting incrementalist approaches, perhaps particularly where policy responses are seeking to respond to and cope with problems, rather than as setting out to solve them. Dolowitz and Marsh (1996) identified two main types of transfer: voluntary, where policy makers freely choose to adopt policies or practices from another place or time; and coercive, which in turn may be direct, when one entity is forced by another to adopt a particular policy or practice, or indirect, when the transfers arise as a result of externalities, developments such as technological change, economic pressures or a broad international consensus. One frequently used example of coercive policy transfer is when bodies such as the International Monetary Fund and the World Bank have persuaded governments, particularly in developing countries, to follow policies of privatisation and market liberalisation, using their powers as lenders to exert influence, including through attaching conditions to loans ('conditionalities') (for example, Stiglitz, 2001). However, 'coercive' transfer would also apply to occasions when the United Kingdom is obliged to abide by rulings such as those from the European Court of Human Rights.

Policy transfer can also be seen as being manifest at either internal or external levels. Internal policy transfer is when the process involves searching for policies or programmes locally or internally, as when local authorities look to see what other councils are doing, for example in managing customer care services or establishing e-petition systems. When initiatives are particularly successful they tend to attract attention from other organisations working in that field, who are interested to see how a scheme works and whether it could be transferred successfully to another location. Examples of such transfers are fairly common, and indeed governments and other organisations frequently seek to highlight such examples to encourage others to follow, as with child care schemes and crime prevention programmes. External policy transfer takes place across countries, with governments looking to see what has worked in other states so that they can draw upon those experiences in dealing with problems at home. However, it is important to recognise that it is likely to be necessary to adapt a policy for it to be likely to work successfully in the new country, for example to take account of different cultural, economic or social contexts.

Some countries have been identified as particularly attractive in terms of borrowing, such as Sweden, as a result of its long social-democratic leanings, and Germany for effective control of inflation and its success in maintaining its manufacturing industries. The Anglophone countries, the UK, the USA, Australia, Canada, Ireland and New Zealand, have also sometimes been seen as sharing ideas, such as privatisation and the new public management in the 1980s and 1990s (for example, Hood, 1991), perhaps not least because there were some common ideological leanings across governments during that period, while Hobbs and Hamerton (2014) discuss perceptions of 'American expansionism' into the UK's penal policies.

The growth of international institutions and actors has arguably contributed not just to coercive forms of transfer, with states required to abide by the rules set down by the European Union, the United Nations and international treaties, but also to the spread of 'policy entrepreneurs' (actors, either individuals or organisations) who promote particular policies, international policy communities, and the rise of multinational and transnational corporations (Bennet, 1991; Dolowitz and Marsh, 1996). For example, Jordan *et al.* (2003) identify a number of roles that international organisations can play in policy transfer:

➢ by bringing member states and their key actors together, they can facilitate policy transfer 'passively';

➢ they can create conditions to 'actively' facilitate policy transfer;

➢ they may harmonise policies across their member states (as with the creation of the Single European Market in the EU);

➢ individual member states can act by themselves to affect other states' policies, thereby leading to policy convergence;

➢ international organisations may also have a role in 'negative integration', such as when removing trade barriers between countries, as with the WTO and the EU. Such moves can have consequences, including creating more competition between states, which may then lead some to create their own regulations to impose on other states.

Of course, not all policy transfer is equal, and the type and extent of borrowing and lending can vary significantly. As Cairney (2012) notes, a decision not to emulate a policy might be made very quickly, while a decision to borrow and implement the arrangements, including the aims and institutions, for a major policy change could take decades to complete. Rose (1993) identifies five main categories on a continuum from complete duplication or copying of policy, through adaptation, hybridisation (combining elements from two different jurisdictions) and synthesis (combining elements from more than two jurisdictions), to simply using a policy or programme as inspiration to develop a new approach. In addition, Cairney (2012) suggests that a sixth category might be when the information gathered is used to support a decision that has already effectively been made. In summarising research into zero-tolerance policing (supposedly imported from the USA into Britain and Australia), 'workfare' (supposedly imported from the USA into Britain), the development of regulatory agencies (a trend which started in the USA and Britain and was adopted by many countries) and enterprise zones (which started in Hong Kong, and were imported into Britain and then the USA), Page and Mark-Lawson (2007) conclude that while each case may initially appear to be 'wholesale policy learning' (duplication or copying), on closer inspection all turn out to constitute only very loose and not very detailed emulation and/or a transfer of attitudes or symbols (see also Dorey (2014) on welfare to work and zero-tolerance policing), closer to the adaptation and inspiration ends of Rose's spectrum.

Similarly, there is a range of factors that might be expected to increase (or reduce) the likelihood of successful transfer, such as the extent of similarities between the importer and the exporter, the level of resources available, the degree of simplicity or complexity and of cause and effect, the potential impact(s) on the target population, and whether a policy is dependent upon particular organisational forms that might be difficult to replicate (see, for example, Rose, 1991 and 1993; Dolowitz, 2000). Many of these can be seen as related to issues of implementation more generally, as discussed in Chapter 3. The UK has long had a shortage of organ donors, and it has sometimes been suggested that this could be reduced by replacing the existing 'opt in' system with an 'opt out' system as used in several European states (indeed, such a system was introduced in Wales from 2015), but it is not necessarily the case that increased levels of consent will automatically lead to an increase in the number of donations and transplants, as other mechanisms would be likely to be necessary, including infrastructure such as more intensive care beds to keep the donor on life support until the transplant can be carried out, and the provision of adequate information for public awareness for those opting out. Sharman (2010) gives the example of states seeking to develop tax blacklists in response to the use of tax havens, where attempts to 'cut and paste' blacklists from other states reproduced existing errors, but also added additional ones, while the original lists were becoming more obsolete over time. He labels this 'dysfunctional policy transfer'.

On broadly similar lines, Dolowitz's classic study of the Child Support Agency highlights both the reasons for attempting a particular transfer, but also the problems that emerged from what was arguably too simplistic an approach (Box 4.3).

Box 4.3 The Child Support Agency – transfer from the USA

Why look to the USA?

➤ The Thatcher government perceived the US Child Support Enforcement System (and in particular that of Wisconsin) as well developed and successful in reducing single-parent dependence on welfare benefits and instilling a sense of parental responsibility.

➤ There were similar problems in the UK and the US with child-support enforcement systems.

➤ The Thatcher government shared the Reagan administration's New Right ideological perspective.

➤ The Conservatives viewed the US CSES as successful in reducing the public sector borrowing requirement, one of the government's aims for the UK.

What was transferred?
Dolowitz identifies a number of aspects including:

➤ the requirement on the Child Support Agency to establish a formula for maintenance obligations;

➤ the obligations on the CSA to undertake periodic review and adjustment of child support awards;

➤ the guarantee of a minimum 'protected level' of exempt income for the non-custodial parent;

➤ the ability of administrators to reduce benefits for any parent refusing to cooperate in identifying the 'liable' parent unless they could prove 'good cause' for not helping.

Problems associated with the transfer included:

➤ a lack of attention to how the CSES operated across a range of US states and selectivity in the interpretation of information that the government did have;

➤ that some of the more successful elements of the US system were not transferred;

> ➤ insufficient attention to the social, political and cultural differences between the US and the UK, for example over attitudes to single parents, the ability of women to enter the labour market and the importance of work;
>
> ➤ the imposition of the CSA over the pre-existing system for granting and collecting child-support maintenance, even where the couple had come to an equitable agreement within the courts, compounded by the initial failure of the formula to take account of property or capital settlements;
>
> ➤ the emphasis on the reduction of PSBR, which changed the target group to those who could make the biggest contribution and to 'soft' targets rather than non-payers, reducing legitimacy in the eyes of the public; in the US, wider coverage, rather than revenue generation, had been the goal.
>
> *Source*: Adapted from Dolowitz (2000).

While an understanding of policy transfer can therefore be a valuable tool in helping to analyse the policy process, it is important to be aware of the reasons for transfer, including whether it is voluntary or coercive, the extent of transfer, and the extent to which the range of factors that might work for or against successful transfer is taken into account. Similarly, those who seek to undertake policy transfer need to be aware not only of the potential benefits, but also of the challenges that can be associated with it.

E-government

E-government has been defined in a number of different ways, but can be understood as referring to the use of information and communication technology, including the Internet and private intranets, interactive television, mobile phones and social networks, to deliver public services. It has often been seen as having the potential to do that in a more efficient, cost-effective and customer-centred fashion than traditional forms of delivery, perhaps not least as it began to develop at the same time as large-scale public sector reform in many states (Hughes, 2012).

The National Audit Office (2011a) has identified five main areas of use of ICT in government: online services, such as for filing tax returns, applying for passports or booking medical appointments; business intelligence systems, with the automation of the collation, analysis and presentation of financial information, management information and other measures of organisational performance; business systems, ranging from simple database applications to large transactional systems, such as those for tax collection and benefits payments; back office systems, including for human resources, facilities management and procurement; and infrastructure, in terms of the essential tools of the working environment – computers, printers, telephones, servers, software applications and so on. Another, widely recognised form of classification reflects four different levels of communication:

1. *information* – with departments and agencies providing information about themselves and their work, but without the capacity for further interaction;

2. *interaction* – when sites enable two-way communication, for example allowing citizens to change information about themselves, but largely rely on low-level technologies such as email;

3. *transaction* – when it is possible to complete a task or transaction online, such as filling in a tax return or renewing a driving licence;

4. *transformation* – when government services are provided online in an integrated fashion, replacing the traditional forms of communication and interaction, and enabling citizens to understand the particular structures of government (for example, Hughes, 2012).

Bellamy (2009) has outlined four processes of transition in the use of ICT in public sector organisations, which to some extent reflect the different ideas discussed above. First, the use of technology advanced from using it to support a business strategy to using it to shape strategy, or even the organisation, as with the use of personal computers and networks, which allowed organisational deconcentration without the loss of managerial control, while software developments allowed some tasks that had previously required significant experience and skills to be performed by more junior staff. Second, there was a move away from function-based ICT systems that largely replicated existing bureaucratic roles towards a vision of more joined-up working, both horizontally across departments, and vertically, from the first enquiry to the delivery of a service, although in practice this has often been hard to realise. Third is the electronic networking of back-office systems in order to make it easier for individuals or organisations to obtain a public service or fulfil a public duty. And fourth is the move from collecting data to manipulating data to produce additional knowledge, although ethical issues have served to limit some ambitions in this area.

Under Labour, Coalition and Conservative governments, it is possible to identify developments in most of these areas, although they have perhaps not achieved the degree of transformation that some of their advocates, including Tony Blair and David Cameron, had wished. Building on a Green Paper published under the Major government, *government.direct* (Cabinet Office, 1996), the Labour government's white paper on government reform, *Modernising Government* (Cabinet Office, 1999), confirmed that the use of ICT was central to the government's plans, promising that all government services would be available electronically by 2008, a target that was subsequently moved forward to 2005. While there was some real progress, although the Blair government claimed to have met that target, in reality the bulk of government websites at that time provided information, and perhaps limited levels of interaction, while many services did not offer significant levels of transaction. Under the Coalition government, progress continued to be made, and in October 2012 GOV.UK was established, further consolidating central government websites, and incorporating content that had previously been on separate departmental and arm's-length body websites. In some respects, therefore, there has been clear progress, for example, in terms of the number of people visiting GOV.UK and the variety of activities offered (Figures 4.1 and 4.2).

In addition, the way that people interact with government has been changing quite rapidly. In April 2013, 73 per cent of visits to GOV.UK were made from a desktop computer, with 18 per cent from a mobile phone and 10 per cent from tablets, but by April 2017 mobile access had increased to 42 per cent and desktop access had fallen to 48 per cent, with 10 per cent from tablets.

However, many transactional services are still to be made available online, and perhaps as a result savings have been relatively small (something over £100 million in each of 2013/14 and 2014/15 (Freeguard *et al.*, 2015)). E-government is also seen by some as having significant implications for both politics and government, including through online voting – the use of social media as a channel of communication between

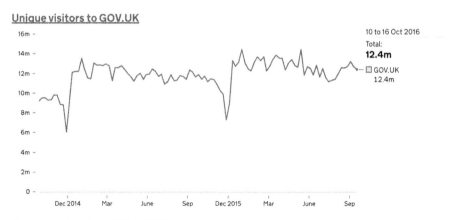

Figure 4.1   Use of GOV.UK

Source: Activity on GOV.UK: web traffic (https://www.gov.uk/performance/site-activity, accessed 18 October 2016) (reproduced under the Open Government Licence v.3.0).

Top content

Most pageviews in past 7 days

1 Check your State Pension age
2 Find a job with Universal Jobmatch
3 Tax your vehicle
4 Get information about a company
5 Check if you need a UK visa
6 Check if a vehicle is taxed
7 Check how much Income Tax you paid last year
8 Tell DVLA you've sold, transferred or bought a vehicle
9 Calculate holiday entitlement
10 View or share your driving licence information

Trending content

Largest percentage increase in pageviews week-on-week

1 National Minimum Wage and Living Wage calculator for workers
2 Your State Pension
3 Automatic external defibrillator (AED) LIFEPAK CR Plus and LI...
4 Collision between the stern trawler Karen and a dived Royal Na...
5 Thailand travel advice
6 Field Safety Notices - 10 - 14 October 2016 Medical safety alert
7 Drink-drive rehabilitation courses
8 IEIM404700 - International Exchange of Information Manual - ...
9 AAIB investigation to Boeing 747-436, G-CIVX Air Accidents In...
10 Schedule 14 decisions

Top policies

Most pageviews in past 7 days

1 Criminal justice reform
2 Immigration and borders
3 Obesity and healthy eating
4 Childcare and early education
5 Building regulation
6 Cyber security
7 Research and innovation in health and social care
8 Children's health
9 Dementia
10 Exports and inward investment

Top announcements

Most pageviews in past 7 days

1 Statement: the status of EU nationals in the UK
2 Faulty defibrillator warning
3 The Small Business, Enterprise and Employment Act is here
4 Funding support for EU students
5 The Government accepts minimum wage rate recommendations
6 Driving licence counterpart abolished: changes you need to kn...
7 The Queen and Duke of Edinburgh Receive Long Service and G...
8 Hiring a vehicle
9 MHRA statement on products containing Cannabidiol (CBD)
10 Flag-flying from UK government buildings for the death of the ...

Figure 4.2   Example of activity on GOV.UK

Source: Activity on GOV.UK: web traffic (https://www.gov.uk/performance/site-activity, accessed 16 June 2016) (reproduced under the Open Government Licence v.3.0).

citizens and their elected representatives and between citizens and the providers of services, with some arguing that well-designed systems could both enable people to 'reach in' to the political system (for example, Bochel and Bochel, 2016), while others note the potential for more direct forms of democracy. On the other hand, some highlight the dangers of populism and the risk of disenfranchising those who do not use electronic resources as inputs (for example, Hughes, 2012), while there are also significant questions over how such initiatives sit with the tradition and mechanisms of representative democracy.

Challenges for e-government

The development of e-government has not always gone as smoothly as its supporters have anticipated (for example, National Audit Office, 2017). There have arguably been several main issues. First, there have frequently been problems with the design and implementation, so that while making information available to citizens has been relatively straightforward, achieving the degree of interactivity that some have aspired to has been problematic. Second, while the number of people accessing the Internet continues to increase (87.9 per cent of adults in the UK had used the

Internet in the first three months of 2016), 10.2 per cent of the population, more than 5 million people, had never used it, and usage remains unequal, with only 38.7 per cent of those aged 75 and over being recent users while 25 per cent of disabled adults had never used the Internet (Office for National Statistics, 2016b). Clearly, there are still significant parts of society that risk being left behind if they are unable or unwilling to access services online. Given that government has to reach all citizens, including through offering equal availability, there therefore still need to be mechanisms for interacting using traditional, probably paper-based, processes.

The greater use of ICT has been accompanied by concerns around ethical issues. Bellamy and Campbell (2016) highlight privacy and data protection, perhaps underpinned by the idea of consent of the data 'subject' and data not being used for purposes that are incompatible with the reasons that they were collected, which might apply to both the mining and the sharing of data. For example, Disclosure and Barring Service (an arm's-length body (see Chapter 7) associated with the Home Office) checks details from the Police National Computer and criminal intelligence records of local police forces, while health research increasingly draws upon the linking of anonymised data from patient records (Bellamy and Campbell, 2016). There have also been attempts to encourage service delivery bodies to share more personal information about users and offenders, including in many partnerships. However, some organisations have been unwilling to provide detailed information on their clients to other organisations, while at the same time inquiries into agency failures, including around child sex abuse, have frequently highlighted shortcomings in information sharing as a significant contributory factor.

Perhaps one of the most obvious examples of the impact of concerns about the increasing collection and use of data was with regard to the Labour government's proposals for a national identity register and card, which met stiff opposition, and were ultimately dropped by the Coalition government. Indeed, in 2008 the Home Affairs Committee raised questions about surveillance, and asked the government to 'adopt a principle of data minimisation', collecting 'only what is essential, to be stored only for as long as is necessary' (p. 5).

Open data

Government agencies inevitably collect large amounts of data about citizens, usually for transactional purposes, and it is often argued that better use could be made of this 'administrative data' (although the ethical and privacy concerns outlined above remain pertinent), for example in terms of the more efficient use of resources through the targeting of interventions on the basis of analysis of the data, and recent governments have sought to exploit 'big data' (see, for example, Dunleavy (2016) on 'big data' and policy learning). The EU has also made a commitment to make data available (see http://data.europa.eu/eurodp/en/data) with the claim that administrative datasets offer the potential for supporting economic growth (European Commission, 2011).

Under both Tony Blair and Gordon Brown there were steps towards making more open use of government data, and, on taking office, the Coalition government sought to make increased use of open data, with David Cameron saying that there should be 'a presumption in favour of transparency', and that departments should publish underlying data in a standardised format so that it could be used by third parties (Cameron, 2010). However, while the main portal for government data, data.gov. uk, makes available very significant quantities of data, five years later the Institute for Government concluded that '... this basic principle – far short of more developed standards such as those supported by the Open Data Institute – is not being applied', and that there were inconsistencies in the quality of data provided and what was and was not included, while budget documentation sources' frequently changing baselines were making comparison over time difficult (Freeguard *et al.*, 2015, p. 15). The collection and release of data is also in many respects clearly political, with, for example, Freeguard *et al.* also noting that, despite the government's desire to use data to enhance transparency, there is no collection of data on the performance of companies contracted by government to provide public services.

Competition through markets, or partnership?

One of the key developments in many areas of public policy since the 1980s has been the increasing use of markets, or market-type mechanisms. However, in some policy areas, particularly under the Labour governments of 1997–2010, there has also been an emphasis on the development of 'partnerships', while others have argued for the greater involvement of users and citizens in other ways, including the co-production of services. This section outlines these developments and some of the key arguments about the advantages and disadvantages of these differing approaches.

Marketisation

From the 1980s, marketisation, in a variety of forms, has been a key feature of public policy in the UK, and indeed in many other states, including Australia and New Zealand, and a number of European countries, including those in Scandinavia, although not always to equal extents (for example, Pollitt, van Thiel and Homburg, 2007). Advocates of market approaches claim a number of advantages over planned allocation systems, including that markets allow consumers to choose between competing suppliers and to combine different packages of goods and services that suit them, rather than the suppliers; they transmit information about what those who are in a position to pay for a service want, swiftly and effectively; and they are a spur to efficiency, with competition taking place on price, quality, or a combination of the two. In addition, markets can provide a powerful force for political legitimation, with market outcomes being seen as the result of impersonal forces, so that it becomes pointless for losers to protest about market allocations. The Conservative government elected in 1979 believed that the public sector was inherently inefficient, and that marketisation, where possible, and reorganisation along private sector business lines, where not, would improve performance, and would also help to hold down public expenditure. It is not surprising, therefore, that the period from 1979 to 1997 saw the introduction of a range of market mechanisms to public services, as discussed further below.

On the other hand, it is also possible to identify a number of broad problems with markets. One of these is market failure, including that some public goods cannot be charged for, particularly on an individual basis, such as clean air, or defence; some can be seen as vital social goods, such as public health measures; and there are difficulties with externalities, such as the developments of monopolies and imperfect competition (a school or hospital may have a geographic monopoly, etc.). For some market goods the true costs of production are not included in the selling price, with pollution being an obvious example, as health problems and the impact on property values or business are not reflected in the price paid by consumers, and that requires governments either to regulate the price to take such costs into account, or to find some other means of tackling the resulting problems. Information failure is also a problem for many areas of public policy, where there are likely to be limits to consumer knowledge, including in relation to how much of a service might be needed, at what quality and price, and future need (as with the challenge of encouraging younger people to save for pensions that they do not perceive as of immediate salience to them), while providers may not want to take on people who they know are a bad risk, resulting in 'cream skimming'. There can also be uncertainty over who the 'users' are (service users, taxpayers or all citizens, for example, or other organisations with which there are important interactions?) and free-rider problems, when there is investment in a service which may then be used by the public without full payment, as with street lighting, where it might be possible to charge local residents but not the rest of the public who may also benefit from it, and where some people consume more than their fair share of resources, or do not make their fair contribution, so that the only way to provide such goods is through governments and public funding. Finally, it is frequently argued that one of the consequences of marketisation has been a fragmentation of public organisations and public services (for example, Massey and Pyper, 2005; Greener, 2013), and this in turn has led to questions of regulation and accountability, as discussed later in this chapter.

While a number of states, including Australia, New Zealand and the United Kingdom, have been viewed as the most prominent users of markets (and indeed new public management reforms more generally – see Chapter 1), many others, such as France, Germany, the Netherlands and Sweden, have adopted such reforms, although not to the same extent (Pollitt, 2007). Pollitt and Bouckaert (2004) have suggested that many continental European states have followed a neo-Weberian model of reform which retains a greater emphasis on the role of the state in responding to many problems, and sees representative democracy and public service as central to the state, but which has also sought to use a variety of mechanisms to listen to the wishes of citizens and to professionalise public services.

Privatisation

From the 1980s the term 'privatisation' has been widely used, but it is not necessarily easy to define. At one time it was widely seen as involving the transfer of something from the public to the private sector, as with the selling-off of the public utilities (gas, water (although not in Northern Ireland or Scotland as a result of significant opposition), telecommunications) and nationalised industries, and the sale of council houses under the Conservative governments. Under the Labour governments, while the term was rarely used, with 'public private partnership' (PPP) (discussed in a subsequent section) frequently being preferred, part of air traffic control (NATS) was sold, although the government remained the largest shareholder in the new company, while the defence technology company Quinetiq, and British Nuclear Fuel were also sold. The Coalition government sold off the Horserace Totaliser Board (Tote) and the Royal Mail (see House of Commons Library, 2014). However, it has not only been the UK government that has created such pressures. In Wales, following the collapse of a private water company in 2001, a not-for-profit company took over providing the region's water supplies. Contracting with public bodies purchasing goods and services from other bodies has been subject to directives of the European Union, notably Directive 2014/24 on public procurement, which sets out rules for public procurement, including the role of competition, the advertising of contracts and the procurement procedures to be followed (Crown Commercial Service, 2015). In Scotland, ferry services, particularly on the west coast, were affected by EU regulations requiring subsidised ferry services to be open to competition, so that in 2006 the state-owned company Caledonian MacBrayne was split into two, one, CMAL, owning the harbours and ships, and the other, CalMac Ferries, leasing them, and winning the tender to operate the services, and doing so again in 2016. The devolved administrations have, however, in general been much less willing to embrace both marketisation and privatisation than have their Westminster equivalents.

It is also possible to argue that there are other forms of privatisation, including introducing an element of private provision within a publicly financed service, as has happened with the NHS, particularly in England; outsourcing services to private bodies, as with the growth of privately run prisons in England; or even introducing an element of private funding (charging for sight tests, or providing equipment or books for schools). The switch from public funding of the bulk of higher education to what is effectively private funding through tuition fees, most notably in England but also in Northern Ireland and Wales, can also be viewed as a form of privatisation. There have also been attempts to stimulate competition through the removal of regulatory controls, as happened with bus routes in 1985 (other than in London).

In contrast, it is still possible to identify a few examples of nationalisation. In rail, the Labour government replaced the network operator Railtrack with Network Rail, a company whose debts are guaranteed by the state and which has a large appointed board, and from 2009 to 2015, following the withdrawal of a private operator, the East Coast rail franchise was also run by a public sector body. Perhaps most notably, during the crisis in the financial sector in 2008, the Labour government took over two former building societies (Northern Rock and Bradford & Bingley) and bought 80 per cent of Royal Bank of Scotland and 40 per cent of HBOS-Lloyds TSB, albeit with the clear emphasis that these were only temporary 'nationalisations'.

Contracting

In line with attempts to use markets to secure competition and value for money, contracting is widely utilised by government to procure goods and services from external providers, estimated at £187 billion per year in 2013 (Figure 4.3), with £84 billion from local government, £50 billion

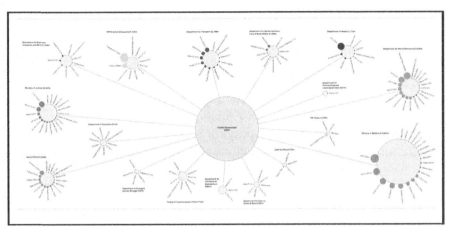

Figure 4.3   Estimated central government expenditure with third parties, showing strategic suppliers

Source: National Audit Office (2013c) *Managing Government Suppliers*, London: The Stationery Office, p. 8 (National Audit Office copyright).

from the NHS, £40 billion from central government and £13 billion from 'devolved and independent bodies' (National Audit Office, 2013c).

The Coalition government displayed considerable enthusiasm for contracting, including through the commissioning of public services (Buckingham and Rees, 2016). However, during the 2010–15 Parliament there also were a number of controversies around outsourcing, including security for the London Olympics by G4S, provision of out-of-hours GP services in Cornwall by Serco, work capability assessments by Atos, and electronic tagging of criminals by G4S and Serco, with the last involving the over-billing of government by those companies. In 2013, the National Audit Office raised three questions over contracting, focusing on four providers, Atos, Capita, G4S and Serco (National Audit Office, 2013d): is there sufficient competition in contracted-out public services; can we see whether contractors' profits reflect a fair return; and how can we know whether contractors are delivering? The following year the NAO suggested that the government was moving in the right direction in responding to the challenges of contracting, but that there was still much work to be done across a variety of areas including planning and governance, understanding risk and managing performance (National Audit Office, 2014c).

On similar lines, the Public Accounts Committee's (PAC) 2014 report *Contracting Our Public Services to the Private Sector* estimated that around half of the £187 billion the government spent on goods and services with third parties each year was on contracting out services (while much of that money is spent on the private sector, a significant sum (£11 billion in 2011/12) goes to the third sector). It argued that the '[g]overnment is clearly failing to manage performance across the board, and to achieve the best for citizens out of the contracts into which they have entered' (p. 3), and that a much more professional approach was required, while contractors needed to demonstrate high ethical standards and to be more transparent about their performance and costs. It highlighted the poor performance of G4S in supplying security guards for the London Olympics, Capita's failure to deliver court translation services, issues with Atos's work capability assessments, misreporting of out-of-hours GP services by Serco, and the overcharging by G4S and Serco for electronic tagging contracts. The report noted that SMEs are currently excluded from the contracting process, and that the innovation that might come from a wider range of suppliers was therefore not available to the government, so that there has been the evolution of 'privately-owned public monopolies' (p. 3). The PAC highlighted five areas for improvement:

1. *transparency* – with greater visibility to government, parliament and the public about supplier performance, costs, revenues and profits;

2. *contract management and delivery* – with central government's management of contracts having too often been weak;

3. *competition* – as there is not enough effective competition in the market for government business;

4. *capability* – as government does not currently have the expertise to extract the greatest value from contracting to private providers;

5. *public service standards* – as contractors have not consistently demonstrated the high ethical standards expected in the conduct of government business.

Quasi-markets

During the 1980s and 1990s the Conservative governments used 'quasi-markets' in some areas where privatisation and full competition either were not possible or were not politically acceptable, as with allowing parental choice of schools and patients greater choice of health care providers, using performance measures and league tables in attempts to inform users. However, choice between providers was generally fairly limited, and in many cases it was purchasers (commissioning agencies) rather than users who made the choice, while the information available on which to base choices was often both limited and complex. Labour did little to reverse many of these quasi-market reforms, for example retaining commissioning and introducing payment by results in the NHS, and continuing to emphasise parental choice in school-age education, although at the same time it frequently put greater emphasis on partnership and cooperation rather than outright competition than had its predecessors (see, for example, Institute for Government, 2012). The Coalition government and its Conservative successor made significant changes, for example in education, with the spread of the academies programme and the growth of 'free schools', and attempts to improve the quality of information available to parents on school performance, and in the NHS, with further attempts to strengthen competition and choice.

Partnership

While continuing to use marketisation, and even privatisation in some areas, the Labour governments of 1997 to 2010 also made much of the idea of 'partnership' across public–private and third sectors as an alternative to both marketisation and the bureaucratic state (Burnham and Horton, 2013). Some of the early initiatives were based upon areas that were seen as suffering from persistent complex problems, such as Education Action Zones and Health Action Zones, although these were generally incorporated into or overtaken by other initiatives, such as reforms of the NHS and the creation of Local Strategic Partnerships, bringing together representatives of different sectors to address local problems. This approach was based upon the view that partnerships can respond to problems in a way that single organisations are unlikely to be able to, as they can share expertise, resources and risk-taking, fill gaps in services, and encourage learning from other organisations; they are seen by some as offering ways to deal with 'wicked problems' (Bovaird and Klijn, 2016). Baggott (2011) notes that the Labour governments sought to strengthen partnership working between the NHS and local government, for example in attempting to reduce health inequalities, as with the Sure Start programme, which sought to improve the health and well-being of pre-school children in deprived areas, including by drawing strongly on a multi-agency approach. While central government was a source of many partnerships, the idea has also been used quite extensively by Scottish and Welsh governments. In Scotland, for example, Community Planning Partnerships (CPPs) were given a statutory basis in 2003, with local authorities having the duty to initiate and maintain community planning, and other public bodies, such as health boards and the police, having a duty to participate, although a wide range of other organisations can also be involved. A report by Audit Scotland in 2013 suggested, however, that while there were many examples of community planning making a difference for specific communities and groups, overall it was not clear that they were contributing to delivering improved outcomes across Scotland, and that there needed to be a renewed focus on community planning both locally and nationally, including in relation to budget setting and business planning by the CPP partners (Audit Scotland, 2013).

There are also potential problems or challenges associated with partnerships, including that: there can be fragmentation of structures and processes; there can be a blurring of responsibilities and accountabilities; politicians may fear losing control over decisions; there may be risks of a shift away from a public service ethos; not all participants are equally powerful, so that powerful actors, frequently public sector bodies, may be able to block actions or keep items off the agenda; and third sector bodies may fear losing their independence and ability to speak critically if they are drawn into a particular decision-making or service-providing role (see, for example, Bovaird and Klijn, 2016). In many cases, it is also worth noting that collaborative arrangements are introduced in a top-down fashion, and overlaid on existing hierarchical boundaries, rather than replacing them, so that the opportunities for the development of trust and new ways of working across organisations may be more limited than might sometimes be intended.

Partnerships received considerably less emphasis under the Coalition and then Conservative governments, although the former did replace the Regional Development Agencies with Local Enterprise Partnerships involving businesses and local authorities, intended to help develop local priorities, including economic growth and job creation.

Public–private partnerships

The United Kingdom was one of the originators of public–private partnerships in the sense that the term is used to describe private sector companies financing, building and maintaining public facilities for a long period of time, with a public authority paying to use it. This means that private finance is used rather than public borrowing, and in theory it should gain advantages from competition and the principal-agent split (see Chapter 2). The Private Finance Initiative (PFI) was introduced by the Conservative government in 1992 (Treasury Committee, 2011) and has been used by governments since then. One of the key characteristics of PFI is that it transfers risk, in theory, to the party most able to minimise it, so that the private contractor takes the risk in terms of design, costs and maintenance, while the public sector risks the obligation to pay for 30 years for facilities such as hospitals and schools that may not fit future policy requirements, or to pay the high costs of terminating such contracts (Treasury Committee, 2011). Table 4.1 illustrates the broad benefits and disadvantages of PFI. The National Audit Office (2011b) concluded that most PFI projects were delivering the services that had been expected, but that the government had not demonstrated that PFI provided better, or worse, value for money than

Table 4.1 The use of public–private partnerships

Potential benefits include ...	Potential disadvantages include ...
Encouraging the allocation of risks to those most able to manage them, achieving overall cost efficiencies and greater certainty of success	Higher cost of finance, which has increased since the credit crisis
Delivery of an asset which might be difficult to finance conventionally	Prospect of delivering an asset using private finance may discourage a challenging approach to evaluating whether this route is value for money
Potential to do things that would be difficult using conventional routes, e.g. encouraging the development of a new private sector industry	Reduced contract flexibility – the bank loans used to finance construction require a long payback period, resulting in long service contracts which may be difficult to change
Delivery to time and price – the private sector is not paid until the asset has been delivered, which encourages timely delivery as PFI construction contracts are fixed price contracts with financial consequences for contractors if delivered late	Public sector liability for the inherent risk transfer but also for the ultimate risk
Finance conduct checking procedures, known as due diligence, carried out by banks before the contract is signed, reducing the risk of post-contract problems	Inherent complicatedness of private finance, which can add to timescales and reliance on advisers
Encouraging ongoing maintenance by constructing assets with more efficient and transparent whole-life costs (many conventionally funded projects fail to consider whole-life costs)	High termination costs reflecting long service contracts
Encouraging innovation and good design through the use of output specifications in design and construction, and increased productivity and quality in delivery	Increased commercial risks due to long contract periods and the high monetary values of contracts
Incentivising performance by specifying service levels and applying penalties to contractors if they fail to deliver	
Fewer contractual errors through use of standardised contracts	

Source: Treasury Committee (2011) (p. 5), adapted from National Audit Office (2011b) *Lessons from PFI and Other Projects*, Figure 1.

other forms of procurement. The Treasury Committee suggested that PFI 'is only likely to be suitable where the risks associated with future demand and usage of the asset can be efficiently transferred to the private sector' (p. 3). However, it is important to be aware that, despite the attention paid to it, PFI accounts for only around 10 per cent of public investment, with most major projects being procured, funded and delivered by conventional means (Burnham and Horton, 2013).

There are, of course, other forms of public–private partnerships, with shared ownership being another, of which National Air Traffic Services (NATS) and Network Rail are perhaps the best known. In addition, in Scotland, 'non-profit distributing', effectively a variant of PFI, has been used by SNP governments, with the creation of 'special purpose vehicle' companies intended to allow greater transparency and to enable excess profits to be returned to the public sector, although the perceived advantages have been questioned by some (Hellowell and Pollock, 2009).

Co-production

Co-production is based upon the involvement of citizens, users and others in producing as well as consuming public services (for example, Loeffler, 2016). It has been used to refer to initiatives from very minimal levels of involvement, such as recycling household waste, to much more extensive activities, such as supplementing or even replacing the activities of professionals. Its proponents argue that when there is 'an equal and reciprocal relationship between professionals, people using services, their families and neighbours ... both services and neighbourhoods become far more effective agents of change' (Boyle and Harris, 2009, p. 11). Co-production can sometimes be seen as taking place from the design of services to their delivery and monitoring, although Boyle and Harris suggest that it is only where services are both co-planned and co-delivered by users and communities and professionals that there can be 'full co-production' (p. 16). In this respect, co-production can be seen as linked to the more 'bottom-up' approaches to policy making outlined in Chapter 2, in terms of recognising both the interests of service users and the role of street-level bureaucrats. As Loeffler (2016) notes, in many respects the normative concept of social production has long been a key part of the 'social model' of disability, which, rather than seeing the 'loss' and 'problems' of disabled people reflected in the 'medical model', emphasises the resources that people have and that they can use in improving their own well-being, and which has seen co-production as the means of achieving the delivery of services.

Partnership or marketisation?

Returning to the question at the start of this section, which can be phrased in either order, it is apparent that both market and partnership approaches can have significant strengths and weaknesses, and that supporters and critics of each can emphasise different aspects of these to greater and lesser extents. For example, while there are strong arguments from some quarters that markets, and the choice that they can provide to the users of public services, can bring benefits, there are also significant questions about the extent to which they are appropriate in at least some areas of provision. These include some of those issues noted at the start of this discussion, such as market failure and information failure, while for many areas of public policy it is not clear who the 'users' are, and marketisation has frequently been seen as being associated with fragmentation, and has consequently raised questions of regulation, as discussed below. Indeed, a review established by the Coalition government to look at the barriers to choice faced by disadvantaged people, particularly in accessing public services (Boyle, 2013), found that, 'despite the rhetoric of choice and the rights that users of services have been given, the culture of services ... sometimes gets in the way, especially for disadvantaged groups' (p. 71) and that the choice agenda had been too focused on competition and not focused enough on what choices people actually want (see also Gash *et al.*, 2013).

Similarly, partnerships can be seen to have the potential to draw expertise and resources from across a range of providers and sectors, and to help address problems in a way that might be difficult for individual organisations. However, they too can be problematic, for example in relation to the distribution of power within partnerships and in potentially blurring lines of accountability. Finally, it is worth returning to the point made in Chapter 2 in relation to the choice of policy instruments, in that both decisions made about which instruments to use, and indeed the instruments themselves, are frequently political, and not neutral, and that actors are likely to have preferences for particular approaches for those reasons, as much as for concerns about efficacy.

Participation and engagement

A desire to enable greater engagement with or participation by citizens has been a feature that has been apparent in many areas of public policy over the last four decades. There are a number of reasons for this. At the level of individual users of services there has been a move away from the idea that professionals have known what was best for their clients, to perspectives that have recognised the desirability of individuals having greater control over decisions that affect them, reflected in a shift in terminology to typically view them as 'customers' of agencies. Indeed, ideas from the right, such as an emphasis on individual freedom and choice, and from the left, such as the concept of individuals having social rights, have reinforced these developments. The growth of the consumer movement and the spread of consumerism more generally have also reinforced these shifts. In addition, there has been greater recognition that many voices, particularly the poor and those with fewer resources (for example, Lister, 1990), or those who are less 'media savvy' (Alaszewski and Brown, 2012), can be excluded from the policy process, while in a separate but to some extent related argument it has been suggested that more inclusive policy making can lead to better policy (Cabinet Office Strategic Policy Making Team, 1999; Bochel and Evans, 2007). Finally, the widespread availability of information and communication technology is seen as having made it possible for citizens to interact easily with each other and with governments, and as making more new opportunities for more collaborative and transformative forms of communication (see the discussion of e-government earlier in this chapter).

Approaches to participation

It is possible to identify two quite different approaches to participation: 'consumerist' and 'democratic'. The consumerist view is linked with notions of choice and the role of the market, and from the 1980s has been associated with the spread of neo-liberal ideas underpinned by rational choice theories, including their analysis of the motivations and operations of bureaucracies (see Chapters 2 and 3). From this perspective, participation is therefore overlaid with the language of consumerism and the concerns of the market, while challenging the perceived dominance of bureaucrats and professionals and the idea of a broader public interest. It has as its basis the idea of individuals buying goods and services rather than making collective provision, and gives priority to the wants and needs of the consumer and the commodification of their needs so that they can be met through the market.

The democratic view is grounded in people's roles as citizens and taxpayers, and the rights and responsibilities relating to them. It has often been associated with a view that public services are provided as part of the state's commitment to enable its citizens to participate in social and public life. It is underpinned by a belief that participation is a key element in ensuring a healthy democracy and society, and that the full range of interests in society should be represented in the decision-making process.

Richardson (1983) identified an important distinction between direct and indirect participation, the former being when people come face to face with decision makers, while indirect participation covers other attempts to influence the policy process, such as through pressure group or political party activities. Lupton *et al.* (1998) usefully add 'mediated' representation, when citizens' views are represented by others, as with 'elected representation, professional representation or advocacy, provider representation within managed markets and statistical representation' (p. 52).

Reflecting on the arguments in Chapter 3, the concept of power, how it is exercised and the limitations on it are clearly important in any consideration of the impact of participation. Perhaps the best known models are Hirschman's (1970) conceptualisation of involvement through 'exit', 'voice' and 'loyalty', and Arnstein's (1969) ladder of citizen participation (Box 4.4). Hirschman saw individuals exercising control within a market system not as citizens using their voice through complaints and consultation mechanisms, but as consumers who are able to exit by moving to another supplier, assuming that there is an accessible alternative. However, he recognised that factors such as convenience and commitment to a product (loyalty) could ensure that consumers continue to use it even if they are not completely satisfied. At the same time, these activities are all inter-related, so that consumers who are vulnerable and have limited access to alternatives may be unwilling to express discontent, while providers may be more likely to listen to consumers if there is a realistic danger that they may lose them. Arnstein identified a variety of different types of public participation, and recognised that they can be subject to other influences on the exercise of power, and these affect the presentation of the 'ladder' in terms of who has power and the extent

---

Box 4.4 Arnstein's ladder of citizen participation

8	Citizen control	}	
7	Delegated power	}	Degrees of citizen power
6	Partnership	}	
5	Placation	}	
4	Consultation	}	Degrees of tokenism
3	Informing	}	
2	Therapy	}	Degrees of non-participation
1	Manipulation	}	

Source: Adapted from S. Arnstein (1969) 'A ladder of citizen participation', *Journal of the American Institute of Planners*, 35(4), 217.

of influence involved. The lower rungs of the ladder are those forms of 'participation' that she argues may give a feeling of involvement, but with few possibilities for real influence, while towards the top of the ladder are those that she suggests give the public 'decision-making clout' (p. 217) and which bring with them some commitment to the continuity of such processes and the integration of participants' views into the wider decision-making process.

However, while useful, this typology can be criticised for being over-simplistic, not least as many citizens do not want to be continuously and actively engaged, and different intensities of engagement, such as the provision of information, consultation, participation and co-production (Loeffler, 2016), may be appropriate at different times. Others, such as Simmonds and Brennan (2013), argue that since choice generally remains more limited in the public sector than in the private sector, and as public service users have little power of exit, it is particularly important that they are given voice, suggesting that complaints provide opportunities to demonstrate customer care, identify areas for improvement, help identify operational 'blind spots', where organisations may be missing a particular issue, and can help drive innovation in a 'relational' model of public services (see Cooke and Muir, 2012).

Developments in citizen participation and engagement

As noted elsewhere, under the Thatcher and Major governments there were attempts to make services more responsive to users and more accountable to them through market mechanisms, linked with changes such as the importation of private sector techniques into public management, as seen in the introduction of the Citizen's Charter in 1991, which sought to set out the level of service provision that could be expected and the Charter Mark for organisations that could show that they were delivering quality public services (Public Administration Committee, 2008) and the involvement of parents on school governing bodies.

Under the Labour governments, the importance of participation was repeatedly emphasised, perhaps not least because of the awareness of falling levels of electoral participation and apparent disillusionment and disengagement among significant proportions of the population, and a desire to foster an active civil society (Giddens, 2008), also seen in attempts at 'democratic renewal' (Labour Party, 1997; Newman, 2001). This included arguments for a greater public say in key decisions affecting the services provided by local authorities (Department of the Environment, Transport and the Regions, 1998) and involvement in the development of communities and neighbourhoods (for example,

Home Office, 2004), and in policy making more generally, with the view that this would produce better outcomes (for example, Cabinet Office Strategic Policy Making Team, 1999; Cabinet Office, 2002). Labour also took on some of the Conservatives' market-based approaches, using and publicising performance measures for a variety of public services including hospitals and schools, developing the Charter Mark before creating the Customer Excellence Scheme. In addition, it began introducing Public Service Guarantees, setting out citizens' entitlements to minimum standards of public service provision. In addition to central government (Cabinet Office, 1999), local authorities and the devolved administrations also broadly sought to develop a range of mechanisms for public engagement, so that by the end of the 1990s many different techniques were being used by public sector bodies (for example, Rao, 2000; Scottish Executive Central Research Unit, 2000).

Reflecting some of the Labour government's emphasis on participation and inclusion, the Coalition government introduced the idea of 'open policy making' in 2012 as part of its plan for civil service reform, including the idea of engaging the public and experts from beyond Westminster in debates about policy and in the policy-making process, seeing citizens as partners in identifying problems, developing new thinking and proposing solutions. It argued that this was a new departure from more traditional approaches to involving the public, which have tended to occur once the government has already decided upon a course of action. The Public Administration Committee (2013), however, emphasised that while open policy making had potential, ultimate responsibility and accountability for leadership in policy making must remain with ministers and senior civil servants, including effective strategic thinking. The PAC also noted the risks of disappointment and scepticism associated with participative initiatives, and argued that ministers must allow sufficient time for engagement beyond Westminster, to manage citizens' expectations and provide feedback on the results of engagement activities and the reasons for decisions taken.

The Coalition government, and the following Conservative government, at least under the premiership of David Cameron, again leant strongly towards a choice- and market-oriented form of engagement, including in education, with the spread of academies and the creation of 'free schools', and the expansion of personal budgets in social care, but in addition sought to emphasise 'localism' and the 'Big Society'. Localism was sometimes characterised as being about giving responsibility for responding to problems to local authorities and communities, although without necessarily providing them with the resources to do so (Clarke and Cochrane, 2013; McLennan and Sullivan, 2013). Initiatives included a 'community right to bid' (but not a right to buy) for assets of community value that are put up to sale, and a 'community right to challenge' to run local services. The Big Society was a rather amorphous idea, closely linked to David Cameron (Kisby, 2010), which implied that non-state organisations, including local and community groups, should be much more involved in the provision of services. However, as an initiative it struggled to gain traction and gradually slipped down the policy agenda, even before Cameron's resignation as Prime Minister.

Challenges for participation and engagement

While it may be hard to argue against the idea of greater public engagement and participation, such initiatives are not unproblematic (Bochel *et al.*, 2008). For example, both elected representatives and public officials may see potential threats, as it is not always clear how public participation in decision making relates to the existing institutions of representative democracy (Newman, 2001; Bochel, 2006), and it raises questions about the weighting of professional expertise and judgement against citizens' views. It may also bring the risks of unrepresentative views dominating the process, and it may be difficult for participatory schemes to challenge the power imbalances of society, so that the average, and perhaps most influential, participant may be a middle-class, middle-aged, able-bodied white man. Consideration therefore needs to be given to how to address existing biases.

In addition, efforts designed to increase participation may create their own problems. For example, participation may involve a delay in taking action, as decision-making has to wait for people's involvement, and this may be further extended if there is a need to establish new groups or organisational structures prior to feeding into decision-making mechanisms. Similarly, there are the risks of raising expectations that it may not be possible to meet, so that the management of expectations may be an important element of such initiatives. For those who do participate, there are also dangers of incorporation and co-option, with individuals being drawn into participatory arrangements which could limit and divert their options for action and opposition to decisions. Similarly, participatory mechanisms may channel interaction and discussion towards a limited agenda, diverting attention from areas of potential conflict that those in power might wish to avoid (Lupton *et al.*, 1998; see also Chapter 2 on agenda setting).

Despite such challenges, however, there is a variety of different, but often overlapping, imperatives associated with attempts to encourage citizen engagement and participation, including both ideological and more pragmatically derived drivers. Appropriate forms of participation can also bring a variety of benefits, and it is therefore important that the purpose and parameters of engagement are clear to all of those involved (Bochel, 2006).

Behaviour change ('nudge' or 'think'?)

While the other topics in this chapter have fairly longstanding antecedents, the notion of governments actively seeking to enable behaviour change through 'nudges', even if not new, has come to prominence relatively recently. Indeed, the idea of encouraging individuals to change their behaviour, including through the application of 'behavioural economics', has been taken up by with enthusiasm by some politicians, perhaps not least as some have argued that it can achieve change at relatively low costs (Shafir, 2012). Under the Labour governments of 1997–2010 there was some attention to the idea of behaviour change (for example, Halpern *et al.*, 2004), but it was following the publication of Thaler and Sunstein's (2008) *Nudge: Improving Decisions about Health, Wealth and Happiness*, which suggested that it is often possible to influence what people do through reminders and cues, altering the 'choice architecture' within which people make decisions, rather than compulsion or control, that the idea was endorsed by David Cameron and the Conservatives and moved more towards the mainstream of policy activity. Cameron's fellow Conservatives, George Osborne (2008) and Andrew Lansley, were among the enthusiasts for such an approach, with Lansley suggesting that people could be nudged into making healthier choices around food, exercise, smoking and alcohol (for example, *The Daily Telegraph*, 2010), although he was criticised for attempting to nudge consumers into making healthier choices, and encouraging voluntary rather than regulatory agreements with big business to tackle obesity and alcohol abuse (Health Committee, 2011).

The Coalition government established a Behavioural Insight Team in the Cabinet Office only two months after the 2010 general election, which was intended to act as a champion for such ideas and to work across many areas of government (Hickman, 2011), and, indeed, a number of changes followed (for example, Cabinet Office, 2011), which were claimed to have saved £300 million by 2012 (Cabinet Office, 2012a). However, there appears to have been no further move to mainstream such ideas and activities within government, and from 2014 the Behavioural Insight Team became a free-standing company, part-owned by the government, its employees and Nesta.

Despite the enthusiasm of some, critics have argued that nudging may be insufficient to change behaviour (for example, House of Lords

Science and Technology Select Committee, 2011; British Medical Association, 2012), or that a combination of interventions may be necessary. Crawshaw (2013) contrasted the Coalition government's belief in the ability of individuals to change their own behaviours in relation to health with evidence from the Black Report (1980) to the Marmot Review (2010), which has emphasised the social determinants of health and the influence of social inequalities on health inequalities. He suggests that the behavioural turn in public health both seeks to place responsibility on individuals and reflects neo-liberal models of social and political life that seek to introduce market models into all aspects of social life. Vlaev *et al.* (2016), again examining attempts to change health behaviours, take a potentially more positive view. They suggest that behaviour change interventions appear to offer potentially powerful tools with which to influence individuals' decision making, but that there remain considerable uncertainties, such as how long nudge effects last, the impacts on different sections of the population, and whether there are compensatory or spillover effects (for example, if people who manage to stop smoking then overeat), and that there is the need for further rigorous evaluation of interventions.

There are, of course, a number of types of critique of nudging, with Leggett (2014) identifying three main forms: libertarian, focusing on nudge as a technocratic and top-down technology that may enhance rather than weaken state power; statist, seeing nudge as pro-market and an anti-state vehicle for extending neo-liberalism, spreading market relations and contributing to the retrenchment of the state; and critical democrat, drawing on Foucauldian perspectives and approaches based on deliberative democracy, the former seeing nudge as an invasive form of governing technology, and the latter being concerned with nudge threatening participative forms of democracy, although seeing the potential for the practical use of nudge, and emphasising preferences as revisable through reflection and public debate ('think').

Leggett argues for the potential for a social democratic approach that would: recognise the legitimacy of the state to shape behaviours in the public interest, including through longstanding tools such as bans, regulation and legislation; recognise the need to set behaviour change against the wider social and economic context and to tailor interventions to social circumstances; and see the state acting to protect citizens against proliferating attempts to shape their behaviours and subjectivity, which predominantly emerge from the commercial sector. He suggests that such a position could see the state deploying elements of both nudging and thinking, but also using the state to defend citizens against certain behaviour change interventions. Wilkinson (2013) suggests that nudging may be an imaginative and potentially valuable approach to policy making, but raises questions around whether nudging could be manipulative, and the consequent need for consent of the targets of nudge initiatives, and in the process also highlights Thaler and Sunstein's imprecision about what may or may not constitute nudges.

A somewhat different perspective, and one that is potentially valuable for those who are concerned about some of the difficult implications of nudging for more participative forms of democracy and for individual choice, has been presented by John *et al.* (2013). Drawing on a series of experiments on topics including recycling, volunteering, organ donation, voting and debating and deliberation, they have been prominent in supporting the idea of 'think', suggesting that while nudge may have a value in some instances, its limitations 'also argue for a potentially more profound tool to be considered, one that might lead to more long-term, systematic changes in citizen behaviour. This tool is discussion and deliberation – what we call think' (p. 149).

Globalisation

Taking a further, different approach to the idea of power, from the 1990s there has been considerable attention paid to what some have seen as the phenomenon of 'globalisation'. This is an argument that a complex set of processes – cultural, economic, financial, political and technological – means that the boundaries of the 'domestic' political and policy-making system are increasingly influenced by external pressures and events.

One of the key changes is generally seen as being the transformation of the global economy, with new modes of production and trade, the spread of deregulation, increased flows of capital and trade, and the growing power of transnational corporations and institutions (see also Chapter 6), reducing the ability of domestic policy makers to control their agendas and policies. From this perspective, 'global issues and problems interact with national issues and problems and national issues and problems interact with the local level' (Parsons, 1995, p. 236), while the boundaries between these different layers are becoming more interactive and permeable, and new tiers of policy making are also developing, such as the 'Europeanisation' of policy making for EU states. In addition, the growth of transnational or 'global' corporations, which organise production on a global basis, and which have the ability to rapidly move capital around the world, is seen by some as fundamentally weakening the capacity of national governments to determine their policies independently. The emphasis is increasingly on the world economy, as much as on national or regional economies. And the globalisation of communications and the media means that news, ideas and values are increasingly also being spread and are taking on a global nature.

While this is not entirely a new state of affairs, since agenda setting and policy making have long been affected and shaped by international or global influences, seen from this perspective the pace and nature of recent and continuing changes are such that our lives are increasingly affected by activities and events that take place in very different countries from those in which we operate as individuals. Some proponents of the globalisation thesis suggest that the importance of the nation state as the context in which agendas and policy are formulated is in terminal decline. Not only are the processes of globalisation proceeding rapidly, but also, in part due to cultural, social and economic convergence, the issues facing liberal democracies are essentially similar, such as ageing populations, crime, drug use, urban decay, environmental change and the threat of terrorism. In addition, the impact of global communications means that the ways in which these problems are defined are increasingly the same.

There have been a number of attempts to categorise the protagonists in the debate over globalisation. For example, Held (1999) identified three main strands of thought in relation to globalisation: hyperglobalists, transformationalists and sceptics. Hyperglobalists are those who argue that the world has been transformed into a single global economy, often linked with the view that the liberal market economy has, over time, helped uphold democracy and freedom, and has enabled prosperity (Wolf, 2004), with the nation states having lost their place as the key building block and now having to compete within new markets. Some supporters of this thesis argue that the focus of economic and political activity is shifting to regions, and in particular to a group of powerful cities, such as London, New York and Hong Kong (Ohmae, 1990). Transformationalists accept that globalisation is a significant social force, but that rather than nation states losing their role entirely, they are having to reinvent themselves in economic, political and social terms. Unlike hyperglobalists, who largely accept the dominance of economics, and in particular neoclassical views of economic behaviour, transformationalists see institutions as playing a stabilising role, creating some resistance to change and mediating external forces. Finally, as outlined further below, sceptics argue that the world has not become any more integrated or globalised than it has been in the past (Hirst and Thompson, 1999), that there is little evidence that nation states are converging on a particular model as a result of globalisation, and that they continue to develop in very distinct ways.

In the United Kingdom, successive governments have taken the view that the apparent ability of international financial organisations, multinational and transnational corporations to shift billions of pounds rapidly around the world, and potentially to relocate large parts of their operations, has required policies that are intended to attract and retain such companies, and this has impacted on tax rates, employment policies, education, and other policy areas, with an emphasis on labour market flexibility, and, for some, pressure for lower taxes and wages.

In addition to direct policy implications, such as the new global economy forcing states to cut social expenditure to maintain competitiveness (Esping-Andersen, 1996; Ellison, 2006), there are implications for the policy process, such as that issues and agendas will increasingly be determined by forces and changes outside the nation state, and which fall beyond the immediate influence of national policy making and governments. In addition, the emergence of health threats, such as AIDS, SARS and Ebola, has added new emphases to the global importance of health, as not only are such threats seen as potentially global problems, but there are strong arguments that they must be combatted at a global level. Similarly, from the 1980s and 1990s, 'problems' such as the supply and transportation of drugs, and refugees and economic migrants have come to be seen by many not simply as international problems, but as ones that require an international or global response, even if developing those responses has proved difficult.

However, as noted above, globalisation is not a phenomenon that is accepted without question, and some writers have challenged the view that nation states will continue to see their autonomy reduced. For example, some sceptics, perhaps best represented by Hirst and Thompson (1995 and 1999) and Hirst, Thompson and Bromley (2009), have questioned the evidence for a globalised, supra-national economic system. They argue that the increase in economic activity has been largely confined to the advanced capitalist states that are members of the OECD. They note that transnational corporations and right-wing political interests both benefit from arguments that states need to reduce their tax levels and consequently their spending, including on welfare provision. They also suggest that, even within an internationalised world market, nation states may be able to affect the agenda and make decisions, even if that is as part of an international polity rather than as a national entity, and point out that nation states retain a large degree of control over their own populations. In addition, they note that governing is not the sole preserve of nation states; it can be performed by a variety of public and private, state and non-state, national and international institutions, as with the EU, where not only do sub-national and national governments have very significant roles in determining policy and providing services, but even within the EU itself responsibility is split between the Commission, the Council of Ministers and other EU agencies. In addition, Deacon (2007) has argued that some international bodies, including some United Nations agencies, such as the International Labour Organization, pursue less of a neo-liberal agenda than others, and show more concern for social policy issues and social development.

Pierre (2013) makes four key arguments about the impact of 'globalisation' and the state: first, he suggests that the globalisation argument 'is static and underestimates the learning capacity of the state' (p. 143), so that governments are able to better understand the consequences of a more globalised and deregulated economy and its consequences for the domestic economy; second, he argues that similarities among different countries may be the result of similar problems rather than global pressures (economic growth, ageing populations, migration, etc.), and that some similarities in terms of policy and governance should therefore be expected, although he also notes international pressures, such as the diffusion of new public management ideas by organisations such as the IMF, the OECD and the World Bank; third, he suggests that the globalisation argument underestimates the diversity of national contexts, with the impact of globalisation depending as much on domestic factors as on global pressures; and finally, he claims that global ideas cannot penetrate nation state borders unless they are promoted by powerful carriers, and that they are not often the main driver of domestic reform, although he suggests that during states' financial crises, ideas are brought into domestic situations as part of the rescue packages provided by international financial institutions.

Among the key questions about globalisation, therefore, are the extent to which some issues will continue to be primarily local or national problems, while others, such as the world economy or the environment, will be seen as global problems, and what choices political actors will make (Hay, 2008) in the different national contexts within which they operate.

Conclusion

As considerable portions of this book have suggested, there are many perspectives that suggest that the distribution and exercise of power in contemporary society are not equal. While the participation of users and citizens may be seen as one way of addressing such inequalities, it is also arguable that it may simply reflect or even reinforce existing inequalities. In a review of literature on activism by middle-class service users in the UK, the USA and the Scandinavian countries, Matthews and Hastings (2013) point out that there is not a great deal of literature on the topic, but highlight four main causal theories: that middle-class interest group formation allows for the articulation of their demands and that service providers respond to that; that the nature and level of middle-class engagement with public services as individual consumers mean that services are more likely to be provided according to their needs and demands; that as the middle class is widely engaged in providing services, the shared cultural capital between middle-class service users and middle-class service providers confers an advantage; and that the needs of middle-class users, or their expectations of service quality, are 'normalised' in policy and practice, and that policy priorities can even favour middle-class interests. However, they conclude from their review that rather than any one of the theories, middle-class advantage 'would appear to accrue not simply via activism, but as a result of a complex interplay between the activities and attributes of service-users and providers as well as the broader policy and social context' (p. 85) so that there is a 'generally favourable pre-disposition towards middle-class needs within public services' (p. 85).

Further reading

On evidence in policy making, comprehensive overviews are given by:

Nutley, S. M., Walter, I. and Davies, H. T. O. (2007) *Using Evidence: How Research Can Inform Public Services*, Bristol: Policy Press.

Palfrey, C., Thomas, P. and Phillips, C. (2012) *Evaluation for the Real World: The Impact of Evidence in Policy-Making*, Bristol: Policy Press.

For policy transfer, ageing but important works are:

Dolowitz, D. (2000) *Policy Transfer and British Social Policy*, Buckingham: Open University Press.

Rose, R. (2005) *Learning for Comparative Public Policy*, London: Routledge.

For a good introduction to many of the issues covered here, including e-government, citizen engagement, co-production, partnership and elements of marketisation, see the chapters in:

Bovaird, T. and Loeffler, E. (eds) (2016) *Public Management and Governance*, London: Routledge.

On 'nudge' and the alternative 'think' strategy, try:

John, P., Cotterill, S., Richardson, L., Moseley, A., Stoker, G., Wales, C. and Smith, G. (2013) *Nudge, Nudge, Think, Think: Experimenting with Ways to Change Civic Behaviour*, London: Bloomsbury.

5
Central Government

While different tiers of government are examined in the following chapter, this chapter reflects the continued importance of central government in the determination of public policy, although also reflecting the variety of factors that limits its freedom to act. The chapter considers both legislative and policy-making functions, as well as the ability to influence policy in other ways, such as through fiscal controls, and even through emphasising particular goals or discourse. It outlines the variety of influences on the policy process at the level of central government, including ministers and the executive, the civil service, and Parliament, and their ability to make or control policy. The increasing role of legal and judicial mechanisms and the judiciary more broadly are examined. External influences such as supranational organisations, think tanks, pressure groups and the media are also considered.

What is central government?

One of the traditional ways of defining central government in the UK has been in terms of the Whitehall ministries and their outstations, staffed by civil servants, such as the Treasury, the Department for Work and Pensions, the Department for Transport and the Department for Environment, Food and Rural Affairs. However, it is also possible to consider a broader 'central state', which would also include other large agencies that report directly to ministers and to other central policy influences, such as the armed forces. Both of these approaches fit closely with the institutionalist approach discussed in the preceding chapter.

Central government can also be seen as consisting of a number of elements that might be characterised in different ways. While there is no one ideal, a fairly straightforward and common analysis can be based loosely around the following: the Prime Minister and Cabinet (which, together with some senior civil servants, are sometimes called the 'core executive'), ministers, departments and the civil service, and Parliament, effectively a combination of actors and institutions.

The core executive

In recent years the 'core executive' has been quite widely used as a model for the conceptualisation of the overlapping and interconnecting networks at the core of central government (for example, Rhodes and Dunleavy, 1995; Smith, 1999; Dorey, 2014). This section considers the 'core executive', taken here as the Prime Minister, the Cabinet, and the departments and committees that link them, including senior civil servants. It considers the principal ways in which control of the core executive is often portrayed: by the Prime Minister; by ministers as a group; or by central bureaucrats. However, it is worth noting briefly that some would point to the frequent common social and educational background of the core executive, and indeed senior members of the judiciary, and argue that this provides some grounds for considering the extent to which there is, if not a ruling elite as outlined in Chapter 3 (see also Jack, 2016), at least some case for questioning the commonality of interest among these groups.

The Prime Minister

While there is no constitutional definition of the role of the Prime Minister, they can be identified as fulfilling a number of significant functions including: head of the executive – overseeing the work of the civil service and government agencies; head of government policy – having a key influence over their party's election manifesto and the annual Queen's Speech outlining the government's legislative proposals for the coming year and being able to choose which policies they wish to promote or to play down, as well as determining the outcome of disagreements between Cabinet ministers; party leader – the Prime Minister is seen by the public as the person who leads and personifies their party, a role also highlighted by the Prime Minister's role in Parliament, and particularly in the weekly Question Time; responsibility for many appointments, including choosing the Cabinet and other ministers; and, with the growth of meetings and summits among governments, prime ministers are increasingly required to spend time participating in these activities as the UK's senior representative (see, for example, Jones *et al.*, 2001).

From the 1960s and 1970s it has frequently been argued that there has been a broad trend in many democracies towards party leaders becoming more autonomous from their parties (Webb *et al.*, 2012), and that in the United Kingdom, under prime ministers of different parties and with different leadership styles, there has been a move towards 'prime ministerial government'. This has largely been based upon the powerful position that prime ministers occupy in the core executive, together with the emphasis on prime ministers and party leaders in the media, and thus for the public. Supporters of this view argue that prime ministers have the power to choose their Cabinet, to structure agendas and to remodel procedures, and that Cabinet conventions have strengthened the pressures for group solidarity, while the growth of the Cabinet Office and the Prime Minister's personal staff have also provided additional support. In addition, except in times of personal or political weakness, prime ministers can be sure of a majority in both the Cabinet and Parliament for their policies. The apparent dominance of certain individuals as Prime Minister, such as Harold Wilson, Margaret Thatcher and Tony Blair, helped reinforce, for some, the impression of prime ministerial government, reflecting arguments that the powers of the Prime Minister have increasingly made the position more like that of a president, and that the Prime Minister and a few close allies are able to dominate decision making, with the Cabinet acting largely as a rubber stamp.

Prime ministers have used different mechanisms to support them. Margaret Thatcher, for example, drew significantly on sources independent of both the Cabinet and the civil service, with think tanks, promoting the virtues of the market, entrepreneurship and self-reliance, and operating outside the formal political institutions, being important influences on policy development during her period of office. This was reinforced by the close personal links and the interchange of personnel between the Prime Minister's Policy Unit and these think tanks. Under Tony Blair, in contrast, many commentators paid greater attention to the strengthening of the machinery at the centre of government, as discussed below.

The Prime Minister's Office, based in 10 Downing Street, deals with a variety of governmental responsibilities including: contacts with the government, documents and official engagements; liaison with the media; relations with the Prime Minister's party; advising the Prime Minister on a range of appointments and honours; and daily support, from security to computing, cleaning and catering. Under consecutive governments concerns have been expressed from some quarters about the growth and powers of the Prime Minister's Office, sometimes centred on key individuals, including the chiefs of staff, such as Jonathan Powell for Tony Blair, and press secretaries, or directors of communications, such as Bernard Ingham, under Margaret Thatcher, Alistair Campbell for Tony Blair, and Andy Coulson, who was forced to resign as director of communications for David Cameron in 2011 following allegations about phone hacking while he was editor of the *News of the World* newspaper. Amongst the reasons for this focus upon individuals are issues around access to the Prime Minister, in terms of both these people having constant and direct access, and also their control over access for others. In addition, some have expressed concerns over the growth in the size of the Policy Unit, which contains both civil servants and special advisers, and which not only provides advice to the Prime Minister but also works with other departments in the implementation of policy and contributing to speeches and publications.

Following the election of the Labour government in 1997, the new government's concern with improving the mechanisms of government was reflected in the creation of a number of new units within the Cabinet Office, including the Performance and Innovation Unit, which focused on a number of specific topics, including adoption, 'active ageing' and child care, and the Social Exclusion Unit, which was intended to encourage a 'joined-up' approach to social exclusion across government. Later in the Labour governments other new elements, including a Delivery Unit, an Office of Public Sector Reform and a Forward Strategy Unit, were also established. These were widely seen as enhancing the power of the Prime Minister at the centre of government. The Prime Minister's Delivery Unit was established in 2001, reflecting both Labour's broad concern with 'better' policy making and the challenges of implementation, as discussed in Chapter 2, and was intended to help deliver the government's domestic priorities (Barber, 2015). Richards and Smith (2006) suggested that this was effectively an attempt to re-impose a form of the top-down Westminster model to try to regain central control over policy outcomes, although they noted that the widespread use of targets for upward accountability was a crude tool, that improving local accountability might be a better tool for enhancing policy delivery, and that the demands on a Prime Minister are such that their attention to implementation is only ever likely to be partial.

During David Cameron's first term, leading the Coalition government with the Liberal Democrats, there was a significant reduction in the size of the Policy Unit, including the breaking up of the Delivery Unit and the Strategy Unit, and the replacement of many special advisers with civil servants, in part as a reaction to what the Conservatives saw as its inappropriate growth under Blair and Brown. However, by 2012 policy support for the Prime Minister was again growing, and by 2013 there were 22 special advisers supporting the Prime Minister, including a Policy Unit, headed for the first time by an MP, Jo Johnson. In addition, an Efficiency and Reform Group was created in the Cabinet Office, including units transferred from the Treasury, the Ministry of Justice and the Department of Work and Pensions, with the aim of ensuring that improvements in efficiency and reductions in costs would be central to government activities (Burnham and Horton, 2013). In July 2016 Theresa May appointed as Joint Chiefs of Staff Nick Timothy and Fiona Hill, and John Godfrey as Director of Policy, although they were forced to resign following the Conservatives' poor 2017 general election campaign.

There are, however, a number of significant criticisms that can be made of claims about the dominance of prime ministers. One of the most obvious is that no one individual can have a full understanding of the whole range of policy areas that governments are concerned with, and that prime ministers are unable to focus on more than a very limited number of policies, and even that may mean neglecting others to a greater or lesser extent. Arguably, therefore, prime ministers need to limit themselves and their intervention to a small number of issues, but even then they need to be aware of the risks of being seen as interfering by other ministers, who also have their own resources upon which to call. These include their own knowledge and that of their departments, as well as potentially support from within and outside the party. Indeed, many commentators argue that the power of prime ministers is contingent and relational (Smith, 1999), including varying with the state of the economy, the degree of party unity or discontent, the power of their colleagues, opinion poll ratings and the particular issue, while others have suggested that prime ministers are often constrained by external or global factors (Rose, 2001). Until the 2010 general election and the subsequent Coalition government, the ability of the Prime Minister to determine the date of a general election was also seen as an important power, over both their own and the opposition parties. The Fixed-term Parliaments Act 2011 appeared to make that power harder to exercise, as an early general election now requires either the passage of a vote of no confidence in the government or a two-thirds majority of the House of Commons supporting a motion for a general election, although the ease with which Theresa May triggered the 2017 general election suggests that there has been little real change (yet, at the same time, her loss of authority after the Conservatives lost seats and their overall majority in Parliament also reflects the contingent nature of prime ministerial power, as noted above). A further example that perhaps helps demonstrate that prime ministerial powers are limited was David Cameron's persistent attempts to promote the idea of the 'Big Society' (see, for example, Kisby, 2010). Having first set out the idea in opposition, in 2009, in government he sought to launch and re-launch it several times, but it failed to gain significant traction even within the Conservative Party and by the time he left office in 2016 it was barely registering on the political agenda.

For a variety of reasons, therefore, it can be argued that consideration of the wider core executive, with the awareness of interdependence and a need to cooperate in order to achieve policy goals, is more useful as an analytical tool than is a narrower focus on the role and power of the Prime Minister or the Cabinet, although it is also important to recognise the resources that the various actors possess.

Political leadership

Before moving on to consider the Cabinet and its role, a brief considera-tion of political leadership may be appropriate. As noted above, in recent decades much of the focus of the media and others has been on the Prime Minister and the leaders of the main political parties, but politi-cal leadership can also be given by many others. Elected politicians may be the most obvious example, including, for example, those who are or may become leaders of the devolved administrations, such as the Scottish government, or of local authorities. However, the analysis of leadership can also be extended to others who play important roles in influencing policy, including senior civil servants, and, at the local level, senior local government officers, as well as leaders of other influential organisations.

It is also possible to argue that one reason for the focus on political leadership in the UK and elsewhere has been that modern means of mass communication, and perhaps television in particular, have tended to emphasise personalities as much as policies, meaning that the manipu-lation of public images, both positive and negative, has become more important (Helms, 2012). Indeed, changes in decision-making structures have also tended to create new leadership roles, including within the devolved administrations as noted above, but also with Labour, Coalition and Conservative governments encouraging the shift to elected mayors within local government, with London being an early example of that, and other cities and regions being urged, or even required, to follow (for example, Stoker, 2004; Gains et al., 2007; Bochel and Bochel, 2010; Gains, 2015). While supporters of such moves claim that they will enhance accountability and potentially improve decision making, they inevi-tably also have the effect of pushing local leaders to the fore, in a way that more collective decision-making structures were less likely to do. However, while in common with much of the literature, the discussion here tends to focus on leadership in democratic regimes and as broadly associated with some form of electoral legitimacy (Hartley and Benington, 2011), it is also important to recognise that many others may be able to exercise some forms of leadership in relation to public policy, for exam-ple, senior bureaucrats, or social movement and trade union leaders.

In *Leadership: Theory and Practice*, Northhouse defines leadership as 'a process whereby an individual influences a group of individuals to achieve a common goal' (2016, p. 31), while Helms notes that although it is a contested concept, there is some agreement that it is about guiding others and about providing solutions to common problems. Some people view leadership as a trait, suggesting that certain people have innate characteristics or qualities that make them leaders, while others see leadership as a process that occurs in the interactions between leaders and followers, so that leadership can be learned. Clearly, to a considerable extent, political leaders are leaders because of their formal position in an organisation (assigned leadership) (Blondel, 1987), although others may also exercise leadership despite not necessarily having such a defined role (emergent leadership).

Some have also sought to identify a variety of styles of leadership, including: laissez-faire, with a 'hands-off' approach to political management, allowing leaders to concentrate upon key political matters while devolving responsibility to subordinates; transactional, with a focus on the unity and cohesion of government and party, with the leader negotiating compromises and attempting to balance different interests and factions; and transformational, where the leader is motivated by strong convictions, and has accompanying strength of character to put their beliefs into practice (see Burns, 1978). Recent work on leadership has also sought, for example, to examine 'authentic leadership', whether leadership is genuine; 'servant leadership', which suggests that leaders need to be attentive to the concerns of their followers and seek to empower them; and 'adaptive leadership', concerned with helping others to do what they need to do and to adapt to the challenges that they face (see Northhouse, 2016). It is, however, important to recognise that most political leaders are likely to demonstrate a variety of these characteristics, not least in response to different pressures and contexts, and that they inevitably have to respond to particular challenges and opportunities, while at the same time having to operate within particular institutional and political arrangements that may either empower or constrain them.

The Cabinet

The Prime Minister heads the Cabinet, a group of the most senior ministers and the main collective body of the political executive. The size of the Cabinet varies, but is usually around 20 ministers, with current legislation limiting the number of Cabinet ministers that can be paid a ministerial salary to 22, although others may attend Cabinet (in October 2016 Theresa May's Cabinet had 23 members, one of whom, Patrick McLoughlin, the Chancellor of the Duchy of Lancaster, was not paid for that position, with four other ministers also attending). Most members of the Cabinet are drawn from the House of Commons, and are accountable to it, including through Question Time, but some, most obviously the Leader of the House of Lords, are drawn from the upper House and are therefore unelected.

Cabinet ministers are normally the political heads of the main government departments, and are responsible for both the final determination of major policies and the coordination of the work of the various departments. The principle of 'collective responsibility' is widely applied to the Cabinet, so that whatever their differences, once a decision is made they will present a united front and defend it publicly. That principle does come under strain at times, and ministers have resigned over points of principle, as Robin Cook did in 2003 over the invasion of Iraq, while Iain Duncan Smith resigned from the Conservative Cabinet in 2016 over cuts to disability benefits, although at other times disagreements within the Cabinet have become clear, including during the Coalition government of 2010 to 2015, when, from time to time, some Cabinet ministers made known their unease about particular developments. The referendums on EU membership, in 1975 and in 2016, effectively saw collective responsibility suspended on the issue of Europe, enabling Cabinet ministers to campaign for different sides. At times, some Cabinet ministers may also voice thinly veiled criticisms of particular policies, and the leaking of documents may also be a means of attempting to circumvent collective responsibility.

Cabinet committees became an important part of the system of government during the Second World War, and were maintained and increased as government grew during the post-war years. They now make the bulk of decisions, and these have the same status as Cabinet decisions. At one time their existence was notionally secret, but as Prime Minister, John Major decided to take a more open approach, and the Cabinet Office now makes their existence and membership public. The creation of Cabinet committees, together with their membership and terms of reference, is the responsibility of the Prime Minister. There are two main types of Cabinet committee: those that deal with more or less permanent areas, such as economic affairs, home affairs and national security; and more *ad hoc* committees, which deal with more specific matters, such as the EU Referendum Committee, in 2016, and then the European Union Exit and Trade Committee. In March 2017, there were five Cabinet committees (a reduction from 10 when David Cameron left office the previous year), typically with 11–13 members, and a further nine sub-committees, four of which were sub-committees of the National Security Committee. In addition, reflecting ongoing concerns about implementation, David Cameron's Conservative government elected in 2015 introduced a number of 'implementation taskforces', 'to monitor and drive delivery on the

Government's most important crosscutting priorities' (Cabinet Office, 2016). These included Childcare, Digital Infrastructure and Inclusion, Exports, Tackling Extremism in Communities and Troubled Families. The idea of these taskforces was retained by Theresa May. While it has been suggested that, by making decisions on behalf of the Cabinet, committees erode the authority of the full Cabinet (and can empower the Prime Minister through the selection of their members (Peters and Helms, 2012)), others argue that it is only their existence that makes Cabinet government possible, given the volume and complexity of government business.

As noted above, outside the Cabinet, ministers have significant powers and responsibilities, and the ways that they pursue those, and indeed the challenges that may face them, have been subject to considerable attention, not least as a result of a number of former Cabinet ministers publishing diaries and memoirs that shed different lights on these (those by Crossman (1975, 1976 and 1977), Benn (for example, 1988) and Clark (1993) are arguably among the best known, although there are many more). Norton (2000) has suggested that there are five main types of minister: commanders – those who pursue policy goals based on personal experience or what they wish to achieve; ideologues, who pursue policies based on a clear political philosophy or doctrine; managers, who are generally more pragmatic and concerned with the efficient administration of their department; agents, primarily acting on behalf of others, such as the Prime Minister or the senior civil servants in their department; and team players, who prioritise collective decision making and seek to secure the support of as many of their Cabinet colleagues as possible. While Norton sees the commander and manager roles as the most common, Dorey (2014) highlights a trend towards more ministers playing proactive commander-type roles from the 1980s, associated with the increased use of special advisers, the focus on 'delivery' for senior civil servants, changes in particular policy communities, and the greater use of policy transfer and 'evidence-based' policy.

The Treasury

While the Treasury has always had an impact upon most areas of public policy, if only for its role in controlling public expenditure, in recent years its influence has perhaps come under greater scrutiny. One of the features of the Labour governments under Blair was the power wielded by the Chancellor, Gordon Brown, and the Treasury, which many commentators perceived to be unusually strong, as it arguably became more proactive in its relationship with other government departments, and rather than waiting for ideas to be brought forward by others, it was willing to generate ideas itself. This, taken together with the introduction of three-year spending rounds under the Comprehensive Spending Review, and the use of Public Service Agreements (scrapped by the Coalition government), which set out what departments aimed to achieve given the level of resources available to them, strengthened the power of the Treasury in relation to spending departments, such as Health and Work and Pensions. The Treasury also initiated both interdepartmental reviews, including on children at risk and the role of the voluntary sector in delivering services, and independent reviews, such as the Wanless review on the long-term resource requirements of the NHS (Wanless, 2002), which was followed by a significant injection of funds, the Barker review of housing supply (Barker, 2004) and the Stern review on the economics of climate change (Stern, 2006).

Under the Coalition and Conservative governments of 2010 and 2015, the Treasury remained influential, although in large part this was more similar to its previous role, in that it was responsible for managing public expenditure in a time of austerity, with major reductions in the budgets of some spending departments (see Table 5.1). Indeed, when Iain Duncan Smith resigned as Secretary of State for Work and Pensions in 2016, he highlighted the negative influence on attempts to create greater work incentives in the security system, arguing that '[t]here has been too much emphasis on money saving exercises and not enough awareness from the Treasury, in particular, that the government's vision of a new welfare-to-work system could not be repeatedly salami-sliced' (BBC News, 2016). Under the Coalition and Conservative governments, the spending reviews were retained (taking place in 2010 and 2013, and again in 2015). These reviews have arguably given departments greater certainty about their budgets and the ability to plan for a number of years, but are less well suited to dealing with issues that cross departments or to ensuring that departments seek to achieve value for money (National Audit Office, 2016c). The early months of Theresa May's governments appeared to suggest a somewhat more traditional role for the Treasury and the Chancellor, although later, particularly with the uncertainties created by the 2017 general election result, the dominance of discussions over exit from the European Union, and a potentially challenging economic climate, the picture was far from clear.

Ministers

While it is the relationship between the Prime Minister and the Cabinet that often receives the bulk of attention, there are other ministers in the government, as illustrated in Box 5.1 for the Department for Work and

Table 5.1 Total managed expenditure by department, 2010–11 to 2014–15

					£ million
	2010–11 outturn	2011–12 outturn	2012–13 outturn	2013–14 outturn	2014–15 outturn
Total Managed Expenditure by departmental group					
Education[1]	47,042	66,998	64,999	65,581	70,912
NHS (Health)[1]	89,450	122,426	124,101	127,901	135,292
Personal Social Services (Health)[2]	1,471	–	–	–	–
Transport	12,975	13,208	12,672	13,133	19,086
CLG Communities	10,353	4,970	3,781	5,638	6,555
Local Government	25,442	26,113	23,329	27,605	25,319
Business, Innovation and Skills	22,446	21,658	22,704	21,775	24,631
Home Office	14,589	14,030	13,405	13,183	14,137
Justice	9,491	8,882	9,410	7,550	7,302
Law Officers' Departments	656	618	598	584	564
Defence[1]	36,477	45,185	41,584	40,789	42,729
Foreign and Commonwealth Office	2,287	2,228	2,114	2,183	1,803
International Development	7,770	7,917	7,943	10,129	9,801
Energy and Climate Change	8,327	6,286	8,526	7,849	11,508
Environment, Food and Rural Affairs	2,301	2,314	2,360	2,143	2,437
Culture, Media and Sport	7,152	7,067	7,505	6,247	7,102
Work and Pensions	160,522	166,904	173,156	170,603	174,740
Scotland	31,704	30,789	30,858	31,354	33,206
Wales	15,395	14,934	15,003	15,339	15,643
Northern Ireland	14,369	18,541	18,541	18,543	19,592
Chancellor's Departments[3]	29,885	23,451	23,846	40,435	−16,109
Cabinet Office[1]	-5,009	11,187	11,941	11,168	13,442
Small and Independent Bodies	1,288	1,500	1,314	1,480	1,541
Total departmental expenditure[4]	**546,383**	**617,206**	**619,691**	**641,210**	**621,229**

Source: HM Treasury/Office for National Statistics (2016) *Statistical Bulletin: Public Spending Statistics April 2016*, London, HM Treasury/Office for National Statistics, p. 15.

Pensions and the Department for Environment, Food and Rural Affairs. Below the Cabinet comes the second tier, ministers of state. They work within particular departments and often have responsibility for particular functions, answering for those areas in the House of Commons or

---

Box 5.1   Department for Work and Pensions and Department for Environment, Food and Rural Affairs, 2017

In January 2017, the Department for Work and Pensions had the following ministers:

Secretary of State, Damian Green MP

Minister of State for Employment, Damian Hinds MP

Minister of State for Disabled People, Health and Work, Penny Mordaunt MP

Parliamentary Under Secretary of State for Pensions, Richard Harrington MP

Parliamentary Under Secretary of State for Welfare Delivery, Caroline Nokes MP

Parliamentary Under Secretary of State, Lord Henley (unpaid).

In January 2017 the Department for Environment, Food and Rural Affairs had the following ministers:

Secretary of State, Andrea Leadsom MP

Minister of State for Agriculture, Fisheries and Food, George Eustice MP

Parliamentary Under Secretary of State for the Environment and Rural Life Opportunities, Thérèse Coffey MP

Parliamentary Under Secretary of State for Rural Affairs and Biosecurity, Lord Gardiner of Kimble (unpaid).

---

the House of Lords, and may serve on Cabinet committees. It has been suggested that their departmental and policy-making roles have become more important in recent years (Public Administration Committee, 2011a). The most junior ministers are usually called parliamentary secretaries or parliamentary under-secretaries. They assist with particular areas of business and are often responsible for helping with the passage of legislation, for example in arguing the government's case on a clause-by-clause basis. The role and functions of junior ministers vary according to a number of factors, including their relationship with the Secretary of State and the size of the department (Theakston, 1987), although in their review of the junior ministerial role under the Labour governments of 1997–2010, Theakston (2014) notes that while there were a number of issues associated with such positions, they generally saw the development of ministers of state as policy makers with significant influence. There are also parliamentary private secretaries, who assist ministers with parliamentary duties, and who can also help them to keep in touch with the views on the backbenches. Although unpaid, this is often seen as being the first step on the ladder for those seeking ministerial office. The number of ministers in a department varies considerably, but does not necessarily reflect the size of a department in terms of either its staffing or budget. Finally, there are the 'whips', who are responsible for the timetabling of government business and ensuring that the government maintains a majority in votes. There are normally well over 100 members of the government, 140 as at April 2016.

Ministerial responsibility

Ministers are accountable to Parliament, and, according to convention, can be expected to take responsibility for failures by their departments, whether or not they were personally responsible. One of the most famous examples of that was the Crichel Down affair of 1954, when Sir Thomas Dugdale, the Minister of Agriculture, resigned over maladministration by his department, even though he had not been aware of it, while in 1982 Lord Carrington resigned as Foreign Secretary for the failure to forestall Argentina's invasion of the Falkland Islands. However, despite this example, and the existence of the 'convention', over the past three decades there is much greater evidence of ministers remaining in post despite failures by their departments (King and Crewe, 2013). In practice, it is impossible for ministers to be aware of the bulk of the work of their departments, and arguably, therefore, it may be difficult for them to be held responsible for their actions; and with the greater use of arm's-length bodies, operating with greater independence from ministers, there has been a further blurring of the line between the administrative failures of agencies and the policy failures of ministers. As a result, while there have been a number of ministerial resignations arising from personal failures or failures in policy areas, in recent governments few ministers have resigned over problems attributed to their department, with the failure of any minister to resign over the failures of the Child Support Agency in the 1990s being an obvious example. Even when Estelle Morris resigned as Secretary of State for Education and Skills in 2002, her resignation pointed more at the difficulties of managing a large department than at particular policy failures. Arguably, the most important factor is whether ministers retain the confidence of the Prime Minister and of their backbench MPs. It is perhaps unsurprising, therefore, that the House of Commons Liaison Committee has noted that while officials should appear before Parliament to report on matters of fact and the implementation of policy, '[i]t is important that Parliament should be able to hold to account those who are in reality responsible' and that on policy that is the minister (2012, p. 41).

Special advisers

A development that was much remarked upon during the Labour government of 1997–2001 was the increase in the number of special advisers to ministers, not just among the Prime Minister's staff, as noted earlier in this chapter, but across Whitehall, in part due to the appointment of more media advisers (Yong and Hazell, 2014). While there had been 38 special advisers under John Major in 1997 (the lowest number since 1988), there were 74 by 2001. Their numbers fell in the final years of the Labour governments and fell again when the Coalition government took office, with 63 appointed following the 2010 election. However, the numbers soon rose again, reaching over 100 in 2012. Under the Conservative majority government there were 95 special advisers in December 2015 (see Yong and Hazell, 2014; Everett and Falkner, 2015), although the number fell to 83 by December 2016. Among the arguments for these advisers is that they can reduce ministers' dependence upon civil servants, including in relation to political objectives, and can provide a broader range of advice, helping negate some of the concerns over the power of civil servants, while they can also perform the more political tasks that might be seen as inappropriate for civil servants (see, for example, Gains and Stoker, 2011). However, such a view can also be interpreted as undermining the advisory role of civil servants. In 2001, the government introduced a code of conduct for special advisers, including that they should respect the political impartiality of civil servants, although there have continued to be a number of sporadic instances of disagreement over the role of individual advisers.

The civil service

Senior civil servants

British ministers are dependent upon career civil servants to an extent that is unusual in most other Western democracies. The traditional constitutional position has been that officials advise and that ministers make decisions. This has been underpinned by features such as the permanence of civil servants, who do not change when the political composition of the government changes; anonymity, with ministers being answerable to Parliament and the public, while civil servants remain in the background; and neutrality and impartiality, with civil servants seen as being uninfluenced by their own opinions and carrying out ministers' decisions whether or not they agree with them. While, as discussed in a number of places in this book, few now accept such a view unquestioningly, not least because senior civil servants have long played a role in the detailed formulation of policy within their departments, it nevertheless helps to highlight important distinctions in their roles and underpins their behaviour, and it allows ministers to be seen as decisive and accountable, reflecting their democratic legitimacy, and civil servants to be regarded as neutral advisers on policy.

However, there are critics, including from the political left and right, who argue that in reality the Cabinet and individual ministers have relatively little control, with the majority of policy decisions effectively being shaped by the ways in which issues are processed within the civil service. For the left, this was underpinned by the reported experiences of Tony Benn, Barbara Castle and Tony Crossman during the 1960s and 1970s, with some seeing a civil service elite blocking radical reforms by Labour governments through the work of inter-departmental commit-tees, civil service control over the flow of information to ministers, and the ability to route potentially difficult issues past 'awkward' ministers, including straight to the Prime Minister. Similarly, on the right some have argued, often building on rational choice critiques of bureaucracies (see Chapters 2 and 3), that civil servants blocked radical initiatives under the Thatcher governments, including attempts to achieve major reductions in public expenditure. However, there were significantly fewer such claims from former ministers in the Labour governments of 1997 to 2010 and the Coalition government of 2010 to 2015 (although Francis Maude, the Cabinet Office minister, did argue in 2012 that some senior civil servants intentionally frustrated Coalition policies (http://www.bbc.co.uk/news/uk-politics-19797736, accessed 8 November 2016)).

It is certainly the case that senior civil servants, in providing policy advice to ministers, are potentially able to select what information they provide and to steer ministers towards particular decisions. However, as Smith (1999) has pointed out, while officials do have significant resources, so too do ministers, in particular political authority and legiti-macy, and special advisers (see earlier in this chapter), and the relation-ship between the two is more typically symbiotic than conflictual. While ministers need the advice and expertise of civil servants, so officials need strong ministers who can gain resources, space in the government's leg-islative programme, and inter-departmental support. Indeed, policy mak-ing can be messy, as portrayed in Rhodes' (2011) qualitative study, which included the relationships between civil servants and politicians, and presents a picture of day-to-day events and pressures, including from the media, confusing and complicating policy making.

Policy network approaches would also highlight that not only is the policy process not as top-down as some analyses might suggest, but also that the variety of actors involved, and the complexity of policy making and implementation, means that power may be more dispersed across a range of organisations than is implied in simple hierarchical models.

By convention, a department's permanent secretary can refuse to implement a minister's decision if they feel that it is unjustified, either because they view it as a waste of time, or because it is improper. The minister can then overrule that by issuing a 'ministerial direction' instructing officials to carry out the decision. That happened 13 times under the Conservative governments from 1990 to 1997, 37 times under the Labour governments of 1997–2010 (one of which followed the discovery that errors in the benefits system had led to hundreds of disabled people being paid benefits to which they were not entitled – Alistair Darling, then Secretary of State for Social Security, decided that it was unacceptable that they should be required to repay this money and ordered officials not to recover the overpayments), only three times under the Coalition government of 2010–2015, and at least three times in the first three months of the Conservative government elected in 2015 (one of which related to the funding of the Kids Company charity, which collapsed shortly after, despite the additional £3 million given by the government), the great majority of which related to value for money (see Freeguard, 2015).

The wider civil service

Outside the core executive, and beyond the most senior civil servants who have regular contact with ministers, is the remainder of the civil service. A working definition of civil servants is that they are staff of all of the government departments that work for ministers. However, in contrast to the senior civil servants discussed above, the majority of civil servants do not work in departmental headquarters, are located outside London, and in recent years many have become part of 'agencies', as discussed below and in Chapter 7.

The numbers of civil servants have fluctuated considerably over time. In 1977, there were 746,000 civil servants, the highest level in the past 50 years, but that had fallen to 478,000 by early 1999, in large part as a result of reductions under the Conservative governments of 1979–1997. The numbers then rose to 536,000 in 2005, before falling again to 444,000 in 2011, the lowest level since the Second World War; figures for 2015 showed 440,000 civil servants (Office for National Statistics, 2015a). The largest numbers of civil servants work in the Department for Work and Pensions, the Ministry of Justice, HMRC and the Ministry of Defence. Despite the common perception, and the use of terms such as 'central government' and 'Whitehall', only a relatively small proportion of civil servants work in the London headquarters of their departments (as at 31 March 2016 fewer than one in five civil servants worked in London (Office for National Statistics, 2016a)) with the great majority involved in delivering government services and collecting revenue to pay for them, including paying pensions and benefits, running immigration and asylum services, and collecting taxes such as income tax, national insurance and VAT. Traditionally, departments had formal, hierarchical structures, with the most senior civil servant, the permanent secretary, reporting to the minister, and below them, deputy under-secretaries, assistant under-secretaries, and so on down the ranks. More recently, however, boards have been established to be responsible for the management of departments, including some with non-executive members, as illustrated in Box 5.2.

From the 1980s, there have been a series of significant changes affecting the civil service, arguably based at least in part upon the rational choice theories discussed in Chapter 3 (note also the discussion of bureaucracies in Chapter 2). In the early 1980s, there was an emphasis on cost-cutting and value for money, with attempts to streamline the bureaucracy and bring business efficiency methods to the civil service (Pilkington, 1999). That was followed by the 'Next Steps' initiative, which originated in a report by Sir Robin Ibbs, head of the Downing Street Efficiency Unit, called *Improving Management in Government: The Next Steps*, that argued that 'agencies should be established to carry out the executive functions of government within a policy and resources framework set by a department' (Ibbs, 1988, p. 9), with the agencies to operate at arm's-length from their parent department, and chief executives of the agencies having considerable managerial freedom, although remaining ultimately accountable to the department (see Chapter 7). While the idea of functions being delegated to agencies was not new, with, for example, the NHS Management Board having had responsibility for oversight of regional and district health authorities, and the Manpower Services Commission and the Training Agency having played significant roles for the Department of Employment, the scale of change proposed was unprecedented, with the argument being that the bulk of the policy implementation and service delivery work of the civil service could be done by agencies. Indeed, by 1997, three-quarters of civil servants were operating within agencies, with framework agreements setting out the aims and objectives of each agency, the relationship with the parent department and the financial accountabilities.

As discussed in greater depth in Chapter 7, one of the issues associated with the creation of agencies was the nature of accountability, with an early example being that of the Child Support Agency. While

Box 5.2 Department of Health and Ministry of Defence Boards, November 2016

Department of Health Board:

Jeremy Hunt MP, Secretary of State for Health

Philip Dunne MP, Minister of State for Health

Nicola Blackwood MP, Parliamentary Under Secretary of State for Public Health and Innovation

David Mowat MP, Parliamentary Under Secretary of State for Community Health and Care

Lord Prior, Parliamentary Under Secretary of State for Health (Lords)

Chris Wormald, Permanent Secretary

Professor Sally Davies, Chief Medical Officer

David Williams, Director General, Finance and Group Operations

Charlie Massey, Director General, Acute Care and Workforce

Tamara Finkelstein, Director General, Community Care Group

Professor Chris Whitty, Chief Scientific Adviser

Peter Sands (lead non-executive)

Chris Pilling (non-executive)

Gerry Murphy (non-executive).

Ministry of Defence Board:

Rt Hon Sir Michael Fallon MP, Secretary of State for Defence

Rt Hon Earl Howe MP, Deputy Leader of the House of Lords and Minister of State for Defence

Stephen Lovegrove, Permanent Secretary

Sir Stuart Peach, Chief of the Defence Staff

General Gordon Messenger, Vice Chief of the Defence Staff

Louise Tulett, Director General, Finance

Gerry Grimstone (lead non-executive)

Graham Williams (non-executive)

Paul Skinner (non-executive)

Danuta Gray (non-executive).

agencies had been developed based upon the view that there was a reasonably clear divide between the policy-making role of ministers and the implementation and managerial role of civil servants, in the case of the Child Support Agency, the policies that underlay its creation were flawed, and the policy failings of ministers were thus reflected in the managerial failings of the agency as it failed to meet targets and created large numbers of complaints from the people it was contacting. Under John Major the process was extended further, with regular agency reviews, which included consideration of whether an activity should be contracted out, privatised or abolished.

On Labour's return to government in 1997, the commitment to the modernisation of government included the role of the civil service, and in particular, as illustrated in the 1999 White Paper *Modernising Government* (Cabinet Office, 1999), a desire to improve working across boundaries to achieve 'joined-up' government. This was reflected in initiatives such as the creation of Cabinet sub-committees and ministerial working parties to encourage policy coordination across departments, and the growth of the Cabinet Office and its coordinating role, including units such as the Social Exclusion Unit and the Women's Unit (Flinders, 2002), while the introduction of units such as the Performance and Innovation Unit was in part intended to give a greater sense of direction and focus on results to the civil service (Gray and Jenkins, 2002). In 2012, the Coalition government published *The Civil Service Reform Plan* (Cabinet Office, 2012b). In some respects it reflected elements of the previous Labour governments' approach, with an emphasis on improving policy-making capability, better implementation, and using evidence on 'what works'. However, it also differed from previous governments in that it argued for opening up the development of policy to external sources, in place of what it described as Whitehall's 'virtual monopoly' (p. 14), and made clear that the civil service would become smaller, and that the delivery of services should move to a 'Digital by Default approach' (p. 11).

As with many countries, such as Canada and the United States, in the United Kingdom there have been a number of attempts under consecutive administrations to improve the performance of government departments through the use of policy goals. Alongside Labour's Comprehensive Spending Reviews, Public Service Agreements (PSAs) were introduced, setting out what departments would achieve with a given level of resources. Service Delivery Agreements (SDAs) were added, with a greater emphasis on outputs and processes (Flynn, 2012). In 2006, a Capability Reviews programme was initiated, as part of the wider reform of the civil service, intended to help departments meet future challenges. However, while initially seen by senior civil servants and ministers as useful, these were soon seen as becoming bureaucratic, while peer review was largely replaced by self-assessment (Panchamia and Thomas, 2014). Under the Coalition government, PSAs and SDAs were replaced by business plans for each department, and the Capability Reviews with Departmental Improvement Models and Departmental Improvement Plans. Then under the Conservatives, in 2016, Single Departmental Plans were introduced, intended to help align spending agreements with key manifesto commitments and plans for departmental reform. The National Audit Office (2016a) reported on progress with single departmental plans in July 2016, and concluded that the government had put considerable effort into developing SDPs, including learning from the past, and that they were helpful in planning and tracking progress at the centre of government and for departments, but for the public and Parliament they did not at that time provide the transparency and accountability that the government had promised.

Aside from the reform efforts of governments as outlined above, from 2010 the civil service was significantly affected by 'austerity' and cuts in public expenditure. Burnham and Horton (2013) suggest that the Coalition government's financial strategy had four main components: reducing the state's operations to core services and doing 'better for less'; saving central costs, including by pushing responsibility for cuts down to local bodies; reducing benefits for people of working age, with savings directed to young people and pensioners; and cutting back contracted goods and services, unless they helped economic growth, with the first two of these, in particular, impacting directly on the civil service. Following the 2010 Spending Review, most departments were required to make savings of 25 per cent over four years, with 33 per cent savings from administrative costs, although health and overseas aid budgets were 'protected', while education and defence were asked to find smaller reductions. Further cuts were set out in the 2015 Spending Review, although with the impact of Brexit and the installation of a new Prime Minister and Chancellor, some of the main austerity targets of the government appeared likely to be downgraded, while the 2017 general election result added a further element of uncertainty. However, it is clear that from 2010 the costs of administering government departments have fallen, with the Cabinet Office's Efficiency and Reform Group claiming to have saved £18.6 billion against a 2009/10 baseline 'through efficiency and reform, and tackling fraud, error and uncollected debt' (Cabinet Office, 2015), although the £18.6 billion was actually a cumulative figure, with most of the savings made between 2012 and 2014 (Freeguard et al., 2015).

Departments' budgets are divided between Departmental Expenditure Limits (DELs), which are usually relatively known quantities for plans that the department is committed to, as through Spending Reviews they cannot overspend (although they may underspend), and Annually Managed Expenditure (AME), which is harder to predict, often because it is demand-driven, such as social security benefits or pensions. Freeguard *et al.* (2015) suggest that departments can be grouped into different categories in terms of how they manage their resources: direct-management, where the majority of spending is managed directly, as with the Ministry of Defence, the Department for Work and Pensions, and HM Treasury; those that manage the majority of their spending through arm's-length bodies, such as Defra, the Department for Culture, Media and Sport and the Department of Health; and those that allocate their resources largely through system and grant funding, including the Department for International Development, the Home Office and the Department for Communities and Local Government. There is also the use of markets and contracting, the model used by the Department for Education for the academy schools programme, although no department uses those mechanisms for the majority of its resources.

Devolution has also clearly impacted on the civil service, not only because of different policy priorities, but also because of different strategic steers for the civil service. For example, in Scotland, under both Labour and SNP governments, sustainable economic growth has been a key strategy for all of the public sector. Initially, a Best Value approach, broadly similar to that adopted by the UK Labour government for local government in England and Wales, was adopted (Burnham and Horton, 2013), seeking to balance quality and cost, while also ensuring equal opportunities and emphasising the customer. There were also debates on reform of the civil service, culminating in a report in 2010, *Shaping Up*, which highlighted the need for more strategic direction from senior staff, together with improvements in leadership and better coordination and more effective communication (Scottish Government, 2010). In Wales, too, the strategic emphasis has been on sustainable development and improving the quality of life, with Spatial Plan Area Groups being used to draw together the variety of actors involved in each area (Burnham and Horton, 2013). In Northern Ireland, the power-sharing Executive appointed in 2007 set out a series of principles and strategic priorities intended to raise standards across government and deliver improved and fair outcomes for the population.

Parliament

From a pluralistic perspective, it might be expected that an elected body such as the House of Commons would be a significant power centre. However, for well over a century, as discussed above, the executive has been viewed as the dominant body in British government, while Parliament (with the emphasis generally having been on the House of Commons) has not been seen as playing a significant role in policy making. Of course, the powers of government are such that not all policies require legislation, and even where legislation is concerned, the bulk of it emerges from the executive and emerges more or less intact following its passage through Parliament, although Parliament arguably does provide a forum for debate between the government and its critics, and publicises the executive's legislative proposals and actions. However, strong partisanship, party discipline and the manner of operation of the House of Commons all work to enable governments to control debate and maintain a strict legislative timetable. In addition, any measures proposed by backbenchers through the private members' bills procedures that might have financial implications are excluded from consideration, at least without government support. Debates and questions to ministers are major activities, but scrutiny of new legislation (largely by public bill committees, with the specialist select committees playing no formal role in the legislative process (Russell and Benton, 2013)) has generally been seen as relatively ineffective, although, as discussed below, this may be changing somewhat, at least in some cases. Strong party loyalties also mean that there is little sense of a corporate identity in Parliament, and that scrutiny of government actions and finances can regularly turn into inter-party arguments. The House of Lords' powers are limited by the Parliament Acts of 1911 and 1949, so that it cannot delay or amend a 'money bill' (financial measure), although it can delay other bills for up to a year.

Nevertheless, Parliament can be seen as playing a variety of roles in relation to public policy (with scrutiny being discussed further in the next section). For example, some politicians have argued that there are limits to what the democratic polity will tolerate, whether it be levels of unemployment, taxation or public expenditure, and that concerns can be expressed and regulated through Parliament, and the House of Commons, as the elected chamber, in particular, especially when there is significant discontent (Judge, 2005). In addition, Parliament serves to legitimise the policies and actions of governments, and issues of legitimacy may act as important constraints on what a government can do, so that political and electoral pragmatism can limit the extent to which reforming governments are able to pursue their most radical policies. Finally, parliamentary institutions act as channels of influence. The impact of this may run in different ways: the use of lobbying tactics by influential groups and interests may be seen as advancing special against mass interests, and therefore either unfair or potentially delegitimising; or the capacity of political institutions to enable such lobbying to take place can be seen as a significant factor in preserving sufficient consensus to allow government to continue in a divided society.

Of course, the House of Commons may be a representative institution, in that it is elected, but it is far from representative in socio-economic terms, being largely white, middle-class and male. The post-war years saw something of a convergence in the socio-economic backgrounds of MPs, with the proportion of Conservatives who had been to state schools, and to universities other than Oxbridge, increasing (although of Conservative MPs in 2015, half had still attended fee-paying schools), while on the Labour side the proportion coming from manual occupations fell (only 7 per cent of Labour MPs in 2015) and the numbers who are university-educated and from middle-class professions grew. At recent elections, a notable development has been an increase in the proportion of MPs who have formerly been involved as politicians or political organisers, from 7 per cent in 1992 to 17 per cent in 2015. The 1997 general election was significant for a surge in the number of women elected to Parliament, to 120, 101 of whom were Labour, and since then the proportion of MPs who are female has risen further, reaching 29 per cent in 2015, following significant increases in the number of Conservative and SNP women MPs, and 32 per cent in 2017. The number of MPs from non-white backgrounds has also increased, from 15 in 2005 to 27 in 2010, 41 in 2015 (House of Commons Library, 2016b) and 52 in 2017.

Until the 1999 House of Lords Act, the majority of members of the House of Lords were hereditary peers. One of the major criticisms was that this hereditary component heavily biased control of the House against Labour and towards the Conservatives. The removal of all but 92 of the hereditary peers, and the increased number of life peers, has somewhat redressed the balance, although the desire of the Coalition and Conservative governments elected in 2010 and 2015 to increase the number of their supporters in the House resulted in a significant rise in the number of peers, from just over 700 in 2010 to more than 800 in 2016. Conservatives constituted about 31 per cent of the House, Labour about 25 per cent, Liberal Democrats about 13 per cent and crossbenchers 22 per cent, with the remainder being non-affiliated and the 26 Church of England bishops. From 2014, peers were able to retire more easily, after which they can play no role in the House. Despite the introduction of life peerages, the House of Lords remains atypical of the population in terms of class, gender and ethnicity. Since the 1999 reforms, consecutive governments have been elected promising to further reform the House of Lords, although all have failed to make significant progress with their proposals.

Scrutiny

Parliament has a variety of opportunities to scrutinise both legislation and the actions of the executive. These include examining and debating bills. Every bill has to go through three readings, a committee stage and, normally, a report stage. The general pattern is outlined in Figure 5.1.

For most bills, the main scrutiny in the House of Commons takes place in the public bill committee. These are established for each bill, and their membership reflects the strength of parties in the Commons. Public bill committees are not able to reject bills, or to make changes that are not in line with the principle that has been approved on second reading, but they are able to make amendments. Since 2006–07, public bill committees have gained the ability to receive written and oral evidence (although not for bills that are introduced in the House of Lords), and this has arguably increased their knowledge of the implications of legislation (Thompson, 2013 and 2016), and to divide their time between taking oral evidence and line-by-line scrutiny of the bill. Each bill is discussed clause by clause, and any proposed amendments are discussed before a motion is taken that the clause remain part of the bill, although there are often significant time constraints (Norton, 2013). However, given that the government normally has a majority on the committee, and that the progress of legislation is monitored by the party whips, even though a government may lose the argument, most bills are enacted with few changes other than those desired by the government.

In the House of Lords there is often more time to debate bills in greater detail, and the number of amendments made in the Lords is much greater than in the Commons (perhaps in part because party ties may be less strong, while governments may also be more willing

Figure 5.1 The passage of a bill

Source: http://www.parliament.uk/about/how/laws/passage-bill/, accessed 6 June 2016.

to accept amendments made in the upper House), making it an important forum for revision of legislation. Accountability (or rather the lack of democratic accountability and therefore legitimacy) remains a significant issue, as is frequently highlighted when the unelected Lords, on occasion, attempts to delay or reject legislation passed by the Commons, as for example, in 2014, when the Lords voted against the Coalition government's plans to restrict access to judicial review. Supporters of the House of Lords often highlight the expertise that exists within it (Joint Committee on House of Lords Reform, 2002; Bochel and Defty, 2010), although critics have noted that the depth of expertise varies considerably across policy areas, and that the House of Commons, too, possesses considerable expertise, including knowledge that MPs gain from the first-hand experiences of their constituents (Bochel and Defty, 2010).

While bills are primary legislation, they often contain powers that allow regulations to be made under their authority once they are enacted. This is called delegated legislation (statutory instruments), and can be made subject to parliamentary approval. However, the procedures for introducing such regulations can vary, and while the House of Commons undertakes some scrutiny through a Select Committee on Statutory Instruments, there are concerns that there can be little time for proper consideration and debate. In addition, the House of Lords has played an important role in the scrutiny of secondary legislation, which gives ministers the power to make orders (usually in the form of statutory instruments) some of which require parliamentary approval (Norton, 2013), but this, too, has been contentious at times, as when the Lords blocked the government's proposed changes to reduce the value of certain tax credits in 2015.

Parliament also has a number of means of scrutinising the actions of government, of which the most obvious to the public are perhaps those that occur on the floor of the House of Commons – debates and Question Time, particularly Prime Minister's Question Time. However, these are frequently highly adversarial, and are often seen as an opportunity for political point scoring, rather than for real debate and deliberation. In the House of Commons, select committees provide another means of scrutiny. There are a number of types of select committee, including 'domestic committees', which advise on the running of the House; 'scrutiny committees' that examine topics such as delegated legislation and European legislation; departmental select committees that monitor the work of the major government departments; and other committees that consider external matters, such as the European Union Committee, which assesses the legal and political importance of draft EU legislation, the Public Accounts Committee, which focuses on the value for money and effectiveness of public spending, and the Public Administration and Constitutional Affairs Committee, which examines constitutional issues and the standards of administration of the civil service, along with the recently created Petitions Committee, which considers public petitions and e-petitions to the House.

The current system of departmental select committees was established in 1979, and reflects the changing shape of government departments, with committees changing their name and scope in line with the departments. In 2016, these included the Culture, Media and Sport Committee, the Education Committee and the Treasury Committee. The membership of committees approximately reflects party proportions in the House, while the positions of chair are divided between the parties, although they do provide opportunities for MPs to develop a degree of collegiality, away from the prevalence of party in many parliamentary activities (Tyrie, 2011). The committees can undertake in-depth analysis of government policy and actions, and can examine subjects in detail and produce evidence that might not otherwise be available. Normally the committees select topics for inquiry, and then collect information, including both oral and written evidence. They are able to question ministers, civil servants and others, and can tackle a wide range of topics. The number of reports produced in a parliamentary session varies considerably (see Box 5.3 for examples of committee reports). Despite generally having a government majority, committees can produce critical (sometimes damning) reports, with examples including a highly critical report on the collapse of Kids Company in 2015 (Public Accounts Committee, 2015) and the government being accused by the Health Committee in 2016 of having broken its pledge on NHS funding (Health Committee, 2016). However, the scope of their investigations is restricted by time, resources and the general aim of achieving consensus on reports. In addition, while their recommendations are often accepted by government (Russell and Benton, 2013), that is most likely when they are in line with existing policy, and they are largely dependent upon the media and pressure groups taking up issues if they are to have any real impact on policy. Arguably, where the committees can have real value is in their ability to question ministers and civil servants on potentially key areas of policy, in making significant amounts of information available, and from time to time in producing authoritative and persuasive reports. Committees have also made some impact in calling witnesses from beyond those normally associated with the making and implementation of public policy, as with senior bankers over the banking crisis of 2008–09 (Treasury Committee, 2009), Rupert Murdoch over phone hacking (Culture, Media and Sport Committee, 2012) and Mike Ashley over working practices at Sports Direct (Business, Innovation and Skills Committee, 2016).

Box 5.3   Examples of House of Commons Select Committee reports, 2015–16 session

Communities and Local Government Committee – three reports:

1st report – *Devolution: the next five years and beyond*

2nd report – *Housing associations and the Right to Buy*

3rd report – *Department for Communities and Local Government's consultation on national planning policy.*

Home Affairs Committee – seven reports:

1st report – *Psychoactive substances*

2nd report – *The Work of the Immigration Directorates (Q2 2015)*

3rd report – *Police investigations and the role of the Crown Prosecution Service*

4th report – *Reform of the Police Funding Formula*

5th report – *Immigration: skill shortages*

6th report – *The work of the Immigration Directorates (Q3 2015)*

7th report – *Police and Crime Commissioners: here to stay.*

Work and Pensions Committee – 11 reports:

1st report – *Pension freedom guidance and advice*

2nd report – *Welfare-to-work*

3rd report – *A reconsideration of tax credit cuts*

4th report – *Benefit delivery*

5th report – *The local welfare safety net*

6th report – *Understanding the new state pension – interim report on pension statements*

7th report – *Communication of state pension age changes*

8th report – *Communication of the new state pension*

9th report – *Support for the bereaved*

10th report – *In-work progression in Universal Credit*

11th report – *Automatic enrolment.*

The House of Lords also has a number of select committees, although, in general, attempts have been made to ensure that these do not merely duplicate the coverage of the Commons' committees, so that they often cover broad areas that might cut across the work of government departments, such as the Constitution Committee, while others have more focused topics and fixed life spans such as the Long Term Sustainability of the NHS Committee. The House of Lords' EU Select Committee, and its sub-committees, including the EU Financial Affairs Sub-Committee and the EU Justice Sub-Committee, has played an important role as the primary mechanism for scrutinising EU legislation in the UK Parliament. Similarly, the Secondary Legislation Scrutiny Committee examines secondary legislation and draws the attention of the House to any 'which it considers may be interesting, flawed or inadequately explained by the Government' (http://www.parliament.uk/business/committees/committees-a-z/lords-select/secondary-legislation-scrutiny-committee/role/, accessed 6 June 2016).

Finally, there are a number of joint select committees with members from both Houses, some of which are permanent, such as the Joint Committee on Human Rights and the Joint Committee on the National Security Strategy, while others may relate to a particular matter, such as a draft bill or House of Lords reform.

As with other means of parliamentary scrutiny, it is difficult to measure the effectiveness and influence of select committees, although many suggest that they can and do influence government (for example, Hindmoor et al., 2009; Liaison Committee, 2012). Indeed, Benton and Russell (2013) have argued that there is a variety of forms of influence: direct government acceptance of committee recommendations, which they suggest happens in more than two-fifths of cases, while it is relatively rare for recommendations to be ignored completely; influencing policy debate; spotlighting issues and altering policy priorities; brokering in policy disputes; providing expert evidence; holding government and outside bodies accountable; exposure of wrongdoing or poor policy making in a public arena; and generating fear (anticipated reactions).

A further resource for Parliament is the National Audit Office (NAO), which scrutinises public spending, including through undertaking audits and producing value-for-money reports that are considered by the Public Accounts Committee and other select committees. For example, in 2016 it produced a report on *Transforming Rehabilitation* (National Audit Office, 2016d; see Box 5.4 for further examples of NAO reports). This focused on changes to probation introduced from 2013, intended to reduce reoffending rates. In terms of value for money, it concluded that the Ministry of Justice 'has successfully restructured the probation landscape, avoiding major disruptions in service ... [b]ut ... it needs to

---

Box 5.4   Examples of National Audit Office reports, 2016

Delivering value through the apprenticeships programme

Discharging older patients from hospital

Financial sustainability of local authorities: capital expenditure and resourcing

Introduction of the new state pension

HMRC's approach to collecting tax from high net worth individuals

Investigation into the UKTI specialist services contract with PA Consulting

Investigation: The Department for Transport's funding of the Garden Bridge

Modernising the Great Western railway

Shared service centres

---

address operational problems, such as the underlying capacity issues, weaknesses in ICT systems and performance data, and improve working relationships between NPS [National Probation Service] and CRC [community rehabilitation companies, which supervise low- and medium-risk offenders] staff' (p. 10). The report contained 12 'key findings', including that there were limitations around data quality and availability and that both NPS and CRC staff considered that high workloads have reduced the supervision and training that they receive and the service that they provide, and seven recommendations, including that the National Offender Management Service (an executive agency of the Ministry of Justice – see Chapter 7) needed a deeper understanding of the financial and service viability of CRCs, and that the Ministry should, as a matter of urgency, ensure that data were available to support the contract and performance measurement of CRCs and the NPS.

Influence

As noted earlier in this chapter, the policy influence of Parliament has often been seen as very limited, although in recent years a number of arguments have been made that suggest that it may be greater than often suggested. However, in addition to the scrutiny processes outlined above, there are a number of other methods that backbench MPs and peers can use to gather information and attempt to influence government. Indeed, recently, the view of Parliament's subservience has been challenged (for example, Cowley, 2002 and 2005; Flinders and Kelso, 2011), with Russell and Cowley (2016) arguing that some critics of Parliament have tended to focus on the policy decision-making stage, rather than the earlier and later stages of the policy process, and on visible and measurable influence, rather than, for example, considering the extent and impact of governments anticipating the reactions of Parliament and taking that into account in the formulation, implementation and evaluation of policy (see also Russell *et al.*, 2016). While voting against one's party, or even threatening to do so, tends to be a mechanism of last resort for many parliamentarians, it is certainly the case that, at times, backbench parliamentarians, either working behind the scenes, or occasionally by threatening to vote against their party, can force the government to rethink its policies, as with proposals to amend the 'purdah' rules on government activity for the EU referendum campaign in September 2015, and the rejection of military action against Syria in August 2013. Government defeats in the House of Lords are much more frequent than in the House of Commons, not least because of the lack of a majority for any one party. In attempts to influence government measures, or in initiating private members' legislation, backbenchers are helped considerably if there is support that runs across parties, and/or from pressure and interest groups, the media and public opinion.

MPs and peers are also able to introduce proposals for legislation (see Norton, 2013), with the annual ballot in the House of Commons being the best-known example, although these often originate from lobbying organisations or even government departments. Legislation concerned with ethical and moral issues is often left to private members' bills, as with major reforms such as the abolition of the death penalty, and the legalisation of homosexuality in the 1960s, while more recently attempts to legislate on abortion have also come from the backbenches. However, only a small proportion of private members' bills ever become law.

Parliamentary questions, certainly in written form, are used largely to request information on issues topical at the time, and in this they appear to be a useful tool (Franklin and Norton, 1993; Martin, 2011). Pressure groups and other lobbying groups can also help by providing information, and can encourage MPs and peers to make representations to the government on some issues.

One means by which pressure group activity and views can be fed into the parliamentary arena is through all-party groups within Parliament. These are unofficial groups, consisting of backbench members of both Houses, and tend to cover subjects that are not generally contentious in party political terms, some of which receive administrative and/or financial support from pressure groups. There are a large number of these groups (around 500 subject groups, and well over 100 country groups in 2016) and they vary widely in the subjects that they cover, including, for example, antisemitism, carers, energy storage, human trafficking and modern slavery, and social enterprise. Groups' activities typically include meetings and sometimes visits, the issue of occasional publications or newsletters, and the production of briefing papers and suggestions for action in Parliament. The groups represent a channel to MPs and peers, and through them to ministers, of a more organised nature than might be envisaged from a simple pluralistic perspective in which individual organisations would make their own advances to individual MPs. In turn, this could mean that interests around which it is possible to gather all-party support, and to establish a group, might have an advantage over other interests.

Overall, views vary on the ability of Parliament to influence the executive and public policy. In some respects, Parliament appears weak compared with the executive, and developments such as the use by governments of quasi-governmental mechanisms, the growth in influence of the European Union, and devolution within the United Kingdom have further dispersed power from Parliament. In addition, as outlined in Chapter 3, elite, Marxist and rational choice perspectives can all lead to questions over Parliament's role in the policy process, including fundamental features such as accountability and representation, aspects of which are discussed in Chapters 6 and 7, and even the nature of parliamentary democracy. At the same time, as is noted above, there have been arguments in recent years that moving away from less visible signs of conflict and towards a broader view of the policy process suggests that the impact of Parliament has been underestimated.

Parties, think tanks and organised interests

Political parties

For present purposes, political parties can be seen as having four main functions:

1. *integration and mobilisation* – parties are concerned to organise and express the views of citizens who share common ideals and interests, and to establish grass-roots organisations that will help to mobilise electoral support;

2. *influencing of voting* – to a considerable extent voting behaviour is influenced by voters' support for particular parties, rather than the personalities of individual candidates. In order to win political power, therefore, it is necessary for individuals to have the backing of a political party;

3. *elaboration of policies* – parties generally present themselves as potential governments, and put forward sets of policies, normally in a manifesto. They therefore develop a range of policy proposals that they set before the electorate, although, as noted throughout this book, these are conditioned by the wider environment, including economic circumstances, international affairs, and their awareness of and relations with other powerful interests, including business, the media and trade unions;

4. *recruitment of political personnel* – virtually all MPs and members of the devolved legislatures come from political parties, and even at the level of local government the proportion of independent councillors has been steadily diminishing, although there remain significant numbers, particularly in rural areas.

While there have been significant changes in the environment within which parties operate, including a broad long-term decline in turnout at elections, and consequent concerns over democracy, accountability and even legitimacy, and the growth of the Internet and social media as forms of communication, they continue to play a central role in the development of policies, and they act not only as catalysts for the view of their members but also as channels of communication more generally. It has been argued that much of the agenda of governments is dominated by routine or institutionalised agenda setting (for example, Kingdon, 1984), and that its influence on policy is often indirect rather than direct. However, parties are clearly able to make some choices, despite economic and political constraints. For example, faced with a large fiscal deficit following the financial crisis of 2008–09, the parties differed in the speed with which they proposed to reduce it, and the extent to which they sought to do so in terms of the balance of public expenditure cuts and increases in taxation. Similarly, parties can choose the extent to which they use the market or the public sector to deliver public services, as is evidenced by the growing use of private and not-for-profit sectors in the NHS in England under Labour, Coalition and Conservative governments, with much less change in Scotland and Wales, where most of the parties oppose such moves.

Interest groups and think tanks

The existence and operation of organisations representing interests and groups in society, and competing for access to power, underpin much of the notion of a pluralist society, as outlined in Chapter 3. A wide variety of terms is used when discussing organised interests in the policy process, including pressure groups, organised interests and civil society organisations. While these sometimes can be used to identify real differences, here they are broadly treated under the overall heading of 'interest groups'. Interest groups can be described as organisations that are concerned with influencing government, either to produce changes desired by the group or to prevent changes which may be undesirable for them. Unlike political parties, they do not seek to govern themselves. They may range in size from national or even international bodies that represent large numbers of members, to local organisations representing only a few people. As discussed in Chapter 3, pluralists see the lobbying activities of interest groups as crucial factors in strengthening civil society and maintaining an effective democracy, while others may see them as increasing the influence of particular interests at the expense of others. In recent years, the numbers of people who have been members of pressure groups have far outstripped those who join political parties, although the numbers that participate in elections through voting are clearly much greater still. Interest groups are therefore a significant mechanism for participation and representation, including, importantly, in the period between elections. However, critics have argued that they can undermine democracy as they campaign for specific sectional interests, whose aims may not coincide with those of society as a whole.

Interest groups have been categorised in many different ways, but for the purposes of this book it is perhaps worth noting the differences between 'sectional' and 'cause' groups. Sectional groups seek to represent the interests of particular groups in society, including, for example, trade unions and professional organisations such as the British Medical Association, the Police Federation and the British Association of Social Workers. Cause groups promote causes based on shared values and beliefs, which may not be directly related to the interests of their members. They include bodies such as Child Poverty Action Group, Shelter, Greenpeace, the Society for the Protection of the Unborn Child, and Amnesty International. This category would also include *ad hoc* groups, such as those that might be formed to oppose the closure of a local hospital or school, or the building of a new road.

Groups can also be classed as 'insider', those that are 'regarded as legitimate by government and are consulted on a regular basis', or 'outsider', which 'either do not wish to become enmeshed in a consultative relationship with officials, or are unable to gain recognition' (Grant, 1995, p. 15). While the status of an insider group might appear more favourable, it is also likely to require some acceptance of constraints, such as a willingness to compromise, and a preference for discussion rather than direct action.

Interest groups have the opportunity to play a significant role at different stages in the policy process. For example, they may be involved in attempting to get issues onto the agenda, including through the use of the media and influencing the opinions of policy makers and the public. Network approaches (see Chapters 2 and 3) suggest opportunities for interest groups including as part of policy communities or policy networks, or advocacy coalitions. And for views grounded in the process through which legislation passes, as outlined earlier in this chapter, they may seek to access people in the core executive, such as ministers or senior civil servants directly, or through Parliament, which remains an important access point for many groups, and they are also likely to be involved in Parliament during the passage of legislation. These analyses are also generally applicable to interest group activity at different tiers of government (see, for example, Chapter 6).

While organisations have long contributed ideas, including directly to the political parties, as with the Fabian Society and the Labour Party, from the 1970s this has been more apparent, with many of the radical policy ideas of the Conservative governments from 1979 to 1997 originating from 'think tanks' (see Pautz, 2011, for a discussion of what might constitute a think tank) such as the Adam Smith Institute, the Centre for Policy Studies, the Institute of Economic Affairs and the Social Affairs Unit. During the 1990s, two newly created think tanks, Demos and the Institute for Public Policy Research, in addition to the Fabian Society, had close links with the Labour Party, including when the party was in power from 1997 (Pautz, 2010). Similarly, think tanks on the right, both older and newer, such as Policy Exchange and the Centre for Social Justice (CSJ), were active in seeking to influence the Conservative Party before and after the 2010 general election (Pautz, 2013), with the CSJ frequently being credited with considerable influence on welfare policy during that period.

There has also been a general growth in the number of think tanks, some of which are politically neutral, such as the Institute for Fiscal Studies and the Institute for Government, while, as noted above, others may have loose or close links with the political parties. Alongside this, there has been a growth in the lobbying industry, which, while not yet operating on the scale of that in the United States, has raised questions about the appropriateness of this activity, including when it employs former 'insiders' from the political parties and the civil service, and about its ability to exploit relationships with government on behalf of particular clients or interests.

Perhaps unsurprisingly, lobbying in general and professional lobbying in particular have become a sensitive topic for lobbyists and government alike, not least because of a series of scandals from the 1990s on, exposed by the media, that have highlighted the ability of special interests to seek privileged access to those perceived to be able to exercise influence. Indeed, arguably the key benefit of using a professional lobbyist is that they are able to offer access to government, including those who may be able to make or influence decisions. However, the use of paid lobbyists is, by its nature, likely to be limited to interests that have significant resources, and this, in turn, is likely to reflect, and perhaps reinforce, existing imbalances of power. One response has been to try to increase transparency, with the government having established a Register of Consultant Lobbyists in 2015, overseen by the Office of the Registrar of Consultant Lobbyists (registrarofconsultantlobbyists.co.uk), for lobbying as defined by the Transparency of Lobbying, Non-Party Campaigning and Trade Union Administration Act 2014, although this did not include those lobbying others in potentially powerful positions, while 'in-house' lobbyists were also excluded, such as those employed by an alcohol (see Box 5.5) or tobacco company and lobbying on their behalf. As of September 2016, 137 firms were on the Register, with, for example, between April and June 1915, Daniel J Edelman Ltd having represented the taskforce on Shale Gas, UKTV and Fujitsu, and from April to June 1916, PB Political Consulting having represented the College of Occupational Therapists, the Religious Education Council, Brain Tumour Research, the Medical Technology Group, UK Sepsis Trust and the All Party Parliamentary Group on Sepsis. In addition, in 2015 the Chartered Institute of Public Relations launched the UK Lobbying Register, a voluntary register intended to allow all professionals involved in lobbying to register, beyond the limits of the Registrar of Consultant Lobbyists, while the Association of Professional Political Consultants also maintains a register. However, while these statutory and voluntary registers may increase transparency in terms of showing who represents particular interests, they do not of themselves address the issues of how lobbying takes place or of the unequal access to decision makers.

Box 5.5   The influence of the alcohol industry

Hawkins and Holden (2014) argue that 'alcohol industry actors enjoy significant access to key policy actors through a range of different channels and forums' (p. 67), including contacts with politicians and officials, official consultations, all-party groups and party conferences, which provide both networking and lobbying opportunities, and that they have been able to 'cement their position as partners in the policy process through the provision of specific, practical expertise and through their apparent ability to implement policy initiatives on behalf of the government, often in place of mandatory regulation' (p. 67). They highlight the ongoing role of the Portman Group as a conduit between government and the industry. Hawkins and Holden argue that while some level of consultation between government and industry is desirable, for example in leading to more effective policy, it is also possible for such involvement to impinge upon the public interest, and that it may not be appropriate for corporate actors to have the same or greater influence as practitioners and experts within a given field.

Most writers on pressure groups (for example, Grant, 1995; Coxall, 2001; Klüver, 2013) and think tanks (for example, Pautz, 2013) point out that there are significant difficulties in assessing their effectiveness in influencing policy, and that a variety of factors are likely to affect that, including their objectives, the resources available to them, the level of public support, and the wider economic and political environment. In addition, simply because a government adopts a policy advocated by a particular group, it does not necessarily follow that it chose it for that reason.

Social movements

Social movements are difficult to define, but reflect the mobilisation of large numbers of people away from traditional organisations such as political parties and trade unions, and beyond conventional approaches to lobbying government, but which also provide some continuity to collective action with regard to an issue over which there is conflict (see, for example, della Porta and Dani, 2006; Kriesi, 2011; Goodwin and Jasper, 2015), sometimes around issues which are new to the political agenda, and frequently through the use of direct action. These might range from the women's movement and the disability movement to environmental and animal rights concerns, and other issues such as the anti-capitalist demonstrations of the 1990s and 2000s, including the Occupy movement. The most common forms of participation are peaceful protests, such as demonstrations and marches, but others involve civil disobedience, such as occupying land and sometimes attacks on property. In the United Kingdom, such forms of direct action are not new, with reforms such as the abolition of slavery and the extension of the franchise (including to women) having been linked to such activities, while in the 1960s the Campaign for Nuclear Disarmament held many large public demonstrations. However, from the 1990s there has been something of a revival of a range of less orthodox forms of action (della Porta and Dani, 2006), which some have linked to globalisation processes and the large-scale flows of information and means of communication made possible through technological developments. While they are sometimes seen as seeking to represent the concerns of civil society, in what is essentially a pluralist manner, their tactics and frequently their answers to problems, such as the need for more inclusive and participative forms of politics, do not always fit easily with such a view.

As with other groups, it is difficult to assess the degree of change brought about by social movements (Gamson, 2015), not least as they are rarely the only or even the most significant of actors or influences, and because they frequently have a variety of goals (Goodwin, 2015). It is certainly possible to highlight many examples of issues reaching or moving up the political agenda as the result of their actions, and it may be that also they play a role in helping encourage norms at the national or transnational level, or in encouraging procedural changes, such as the acceptance of new ways of accessing the political system, such as greater use of forms of direct or participatory democracy.

The judiciary

While not strictly part of central government, and indeed real attempts are frequently made to maintain a distinction between the executive and the judiciary, it is worth noting that over the past four decades there has been an increased role for the judiciary in relation to public policy. There have been a number of aspects to this. First, there has been the greater use of the courts to seek to challenge the actions and decisions of government, including at a European level, while the incorporation of the European Convention on Human Rights into UK law through the 1998 Human Rights Act made it possible for the domestic courts to be used by individuals who believe their human rights have been infringed. Second, there has been a significant increase in the use of judicial review to attempt to challenge decisions. Judicial review is a mechanism through which the courts can be asked to review the legality of actions or decisions either on the grounds that they are outside the powers granted to ministers by the relevant legislation, or on the grounds that they are not in accordance with natural justice. And third, there has been a tendency for governments to use judges to head enquiries into a variety of incidents and issues, such as the 1981 Scarman report on the causes of riots in Brixton, the 1999 Macpherson report on the death of Stephen Lawrence, the 2012 Leveson report on the culture, practices and ethics of the press, and the 2016 Chilcot report into the Iraq War.

In 2009, judicial authority was transferred from the House of Lords with the creation of a Supreme Court for the United Kingdom, which became the final court of appeal for all civil cases in the UK, and for criminal cases from England, Northern Ireland and Wales (the Court of Session plays that role for Scotland). As with other UK courts, the Supreme Court has a duty to interpret legislation so that it is compatible with the European Convention on Human Rights, in as far as it is possible to do so. If the court decides it is not possible to interpret legislation in such a way, it issues a 'declaration of incompatibility', which does not require the government to change the law, but provides a strong message to government that it should bring the legislation into line with the ECHR. The Supreme Court is also able to effectively send issues back to the European Court of Human Rights, although it does so very rarely.

From the perspective of national and local administration, the High Court can be seen as playing the role of a supervisory court, with the purpose of its activities being to ensure that governmental and public authorities follow the proper procedures and fulfil their legal duties and responsibilities. This is effectively carried out by the judicial review process, which can be initiated by an individual or organisation that is unhappy about the decision of an inferior court, tribunal or administering body. For most of the past decade the great majority of applications for judicial review have been in relation to asylum and immigration (more than 13,000 in 2013), while there have typically been around 2,000 other civil applications and 300 criminal applications lodged.

At the supra-national level, the European Court of Justice is the final arbiter on questions relating to the interpretation of European Union law (see Chapter 6). It makes decisions where there is conflict on the interpretation and application of EU law between member states, between institutions, or between institutions or member states and individuals. Where there is conflict, EU law takes precedence over national law.

The European Convention on Human Rights was ratified by the United Kingdom in 1951, although successive governments refused to take the step of incorporating it into law, arguing that human rights were already protected under domestic law, and reflecting the concept of the sovereignty of Parliament. As a result, UK citizens who felt that their human rights had been infringed could not appeal to the British courts on the basis of the convention, although they could appeal to the European Court of Human Rights in Strasbourg, albeit that this was frequently a lengthy and expensive process. The Court found against the British government on many occasions, including over the treatment of suspected terrorists in Northern Ireland and the use of different ages of consent for heterosexual and homosexual acts, and while the UK was not bound to comply with the decisions, it consistently did so by introducing changes in domestic law to bring it into line with the judgments of the Court. The passage of the Human Rights Act 1998 meant that those who feel that their human rights have been infringed now have recourse to the domestic courts.

Conclusion

The use of an analytical approach to central government grounded in the notion of the core executive is appealing, directing attention at some of the key actors in the policy-making process, and reflecting the complexity of the relationships between ministers and senior civil servants. However, it is also clear that prime ministers are able to exercise considerable power, although this may be constrained by their relations with their Cabinet colleagues and to some extent with their party in Parliament. Whether there is a trend towards a more prime ministerial style of government remains hard to discern amongst the constantly changing conditions, including the strengths of other members of the Cabinet, the degree of internal party unity or division, the size of a government's majority in the House of Commons, and the salience of particular issues. The idea of the core executive is therefore not only attractive, but it can also help in extending consideration of the exercise of power towards the larger networks of power relationships that exist not only within Westminster and Whitehall, but also beyond them. However, the ability of Parliament to exercise sufficient scrutiny over the actions of the executive remains a significant question for many.

The Labour governments of 1997–2010 placed considerable emphasis on attempts to 'modernise' government, in addition to building upon their Conservative predecessors' commitment to improving the performance of the civil service, including through the continued use of agencies. They also made significant use of special advisers to support ministers. The Coalition and Conservative governments maintained the same overall approach, although they paid less attention to attempts to improve policy making, while at the same time enforcing considerable change, not least through cuts in public expenditure and reductions in the size of the civil service.

Under governments of all parties the role of judges and the courts has continued to develop, in particular through the application of judicial review, while attempts to expand and limit freedoms, whether through anti-discrimination legislation or legislation designed to tackle terrorism, have also brought additional focus to the role of the courts. However, it is important to be aware of the distinction between political decisions and judicial decisions. Political decisions are those that involve choices between alternative courses of action. These should be made by elected politicians and may properly reflect the political outlook of the government of the day. Judicial decisions are procedural or mechanistic decisions based on the laws already laid down by Parliament. They should be concerned with applying the law, not making the law. These should therefore be limited in scope and politically unbiased.

Finally, returning to some of the ideas put forward in the early chapters of this book, it is important to note that the policy process is much more complex and fragmented than might be seen from a simple reading of this chapter. Approaches such as those highlighting the role of networks have suggested that much policy making and implementation is developed through the existence of informal networks, with relationships built upon varying degrees of interdependence. In addition, arguments around globalisation and multi-level governance, with power variously being seen as shifting upwards towards multinational corporations or transnational organisations, or downwards towards regional levels of government, also suggest a need to take account of diverse and fragmented sources of power and to emphasise patterns and modes of coordination. There are also those who, reflecting elite theory, would suggest that many of the groups covered in this chapter, such as Cabinet ministers, senior civil servants and senior members of the judiciary, often share a common background, including social status, school and university education, with many having attended the major private schools and Oxford or Cambridge, whilst also being overwhelmingly white and male, and that they may therefore possess common values and interests. In some senses, therefore, attempts to develop a comprehension of central government mirror the debates in the early chapters of this book. Much of this chapter essentially takes an institutionalist approach to its topic, seeking to provide a basic understanding through outlining some of the main institutions; but our appreciation can only be further developed through a wider and more diverse approach which takes account of the true nature of the policy process in contemporary society.

Further reading

The following work goes into considerable depth on some of the topics covered here, such as political parties, the core executive and parliament:

Dorey, P. (2014) *Policy Making in Britain*, London: Sage.

Although taking a different approach, this reference provides many examples relevant to this chapter:

Cairney, P. (2012) *Understanding Public Policy: Theories and Issues*, Basingstoke: Palgrave Macmillan.

Finally, a comparative perspective on some of the topics covered can be found here:

Knill, C. and Tosun, J. (2012) *Public Policy: A New Introduction*, Basingstoke: Palgrave Macmillan.

6

Multi-level Governance

This chapter reflects the growth in awareness of multi-level governance and the arguably significant spread of powers to different levels of decision making over the past three decades. While there is an emphasis throughout this book on policy change, the key areas of this chapter perhaps encapsulate that particularly well, as during a six-month period during 2016 the United Kingdom voted to leave the European Union in a referendum, albeit with great uncertainty over what 'Brexit' might entail and what the future might look like; the further progression of 'devolution' within England was called into question as its main proponent, George Osborne, the Chancellor of the Exchequer, left the Cabinet when Theresa May replaced David Cameron as Prime Minister; and Scotland's First Minister, Nicola Sturgeon, announced plans to consult on legislation for a second referendum on independence for Scotland. The chapter considers the development of supra-national organisations, including the European Union, devolution to Northern Ireland, Scotland and Wales, and the position of local government, its powers and provisions.

Sovereignty has long been based upon the nation state, with even international law being widely viewed as the outcome of intergovernmental bargaining and resting on the voluntary compliance of states (Palumbo, 2015). More recently, the term 'multi-level governance' has been used to describe a situation where state sovereignty has been dispersed, downwards and upwards, to different tiers of government, such as new forms of regional government and the European Union. While the previous chapter focused upon central government, and illustrated the continuing centrality of Whitehall and Westminster as the main executive and legislative bodies within the United Kingdom, particularly with respect to areas such as economic policy and foreign policy, this chapter is concerned with other tiers of government, some of which have received considerable attention in recent years, particularly with the referendum vote in 2016 in favour of leaving the European Union, and the referendum on independence for Scotland in 2014, and indeed the continued debate over whether Scotland will remain in the United Kingdom.

In terms of theoretical analysis, while much work remains concentrated on central government, many of the ideas discussed in Chapters 1 to 3, and to a considerable extent those in Chapter 4, are easily transferable to and can assist in our understanding of the policy process at other levels.

It is clear that among the major developments affecting the United Kingdom state over recent years have been those in relation to newer levels of governmental power, in particular the European Union and the devolved administrations of Northern Ireland, Scotland and Wales. In addition, local government has been subject to significant structural reform and other initiatives from central government. These changes have encouraged analysts to move away from a focus upon the United Kingdom as a unitary state, where, it was often possible to argue, power was relatively centralised. This chapter considers these developments and their implications for public policy.

It is perhaps worth returning briefly here to the use of the term 'governance' rather than 'government'. As discussed in Chapter 1, while the former has a variety of meanings, it is increasingly used to imply, for example, a lesser role for government and the state, the use of a wide variety of mechanisms for the management and delivery of public services, institutional and constitutional reform, and a recognition of the need for policy to be made and implemented through complex networks of groups drawn from public, private and not-for-profit sectors. Multi-level governance is often associated, therefore, not only with shifts of power between different levels of government, but also with the blurring of boundaries between formal and informal sources of authority, including between public and private actors.

The European Union

Despite the decision made in the 2016 referendum that the United Kingdom should leave the European Union, at the time of writing this book it remained an important element in the policy process, and was likely to do so for some time. This was the case not simply because the United Kingdom was unlikely to leave the EU before 2019, nor because it was unclear what the relationship would be after that point, but also because it was possible, if not likely, that the EU would remain an influence, including because of its position as a major trading partner, as well as its role in some areas of international affairs.

In addition, the European Union is an important example of states formally transferring powers to a supra-national authority (Howlett, 2011), which is then able to limit both what national governments can do and the tools or instruments that they use to do it (Kassim and Le

Galés, 2010). It is therefore retained as a major component of this chapter. Yet the European Union's immediate impact on public policy has varied considerably from area to area, and nation states have often been able to develop their own responses to policy problems. While it can perhaps be seen as having been quite influential in some areas, such as employees' rights and aspects of gender equality, in major fields such as education, health and social care, its role has been relatively minor (see, for example, Dodds, 2013; Dorey, 2014). However, the scale of the EU and its actual and perceived impact upon society and the state mean that it has been widely seen as being of importance. The main EU institutions are:

➢ *the European Council* – The heads of state or heads of government of the member states, together with the European Council President and the President of the European Commission, with the Prime Minister being the UK's representative, set the EU's strategic direction. The European Council meets at least every six months. It is chaired by the President of the European Council, who is elected for two and a half years, which can be renewed once. The aim is generally to make decisions by consensus, although where the EU treaties allow, qualified majority voting can be used;

➢ *the Council of the European Union* – Together with the European Parliament, the Council is the chief legislating body, consisting of a minister from each of the member states, with the membership changing according to the subject. Decisions are usually made by qualified majority voting, although sometimes require unanimity. Where there is unanimity the Council sometimes needs only consult the Parliament, although in most areas legislative and budgetary powers are shared;

➢ *the European Commission* – Based in Brussels, the Commission's role is to initiate EU policy, including proposing legislation, to implement decisions of the Council of the European Union and the European Parliament, to act as guardian of the European treaties, and to ensure that European legislation is implemented in the member states. It also represents the EU outside Europe, for example in negotiating trade agreements with other states. Having been proposed by the European Council, the President of the Commission is elected for a five-year term by the Parliament. There is a commissioner from each member state, selected by the President-elect on the basis of suggestions by the member states, with the Commission as a whole being approved by the Parliament. The Commissioners undertake to act for the Union rather than as representatives of the state from which they come. These include commissioners for Economic and Financial Affairs, Employment, Social Affairs and Inclusion, Justice and Consumers,

Maritime Affairs and Fisheries, and Mobility and Transport, each with a Directorate-General, staffed by the Commission's 'civil servants';

➤ *the European Parliament* – There are 751 Members of the European Parliament (MEPs), of whom 73 have been elected from the UK. Despite its name, until relatively recently the European Parliament has had relatively little influence on legislation, and its principal roles have arguably been to scrutinise, largely through its committees, proposals from the Commission and the work of its Directorates-General, and to approve the appointment of the Commission and the EU budget. More recently, it has become involved in joint decision making with the Council of the European Union in some areas, so that it has the power to reject some proposals, as when it rejected the Council's long-term budget proposals in 2013, or rejected the plans to enable each member state to restrict or prohibit the sale of certain genetically modified foodstuffs in 2015;

➤ *the European Court of Justice* – The Court (ECJ) consists of 28 judges and 11 advocates-general who are appointed for six-year terms by the governments of the member states acting together. Membership of the EU carries with it an obligation to accept the ECJ as the ultimate court of appeal on EU law, and EU legislation takes precedence over national legislation, so that one of its functions is, therefore, to make decisions in disputes between the Commission and national governments. It has made judgments on a wide variety of cases, such as the freedom of movement of workers and their families, including migrant workers, and equal pay for women, as well as on rights of European citizenship;

➤ *the European Economic and Social Committee* – This advisory committee comprises representatives of civil society (employers' organisations, trade unions and other groups), and gives opinions on proposals for EU legislation. It also seeks to use its role to develop a more participatory European Union;

➤ *the European Ombudsman* – Appointed by the European Parliament, its brief is to investigate complaints of maladministration against EU institutions;

➤ *the European Central Bank* – The central bank for the Eurozone is responsible for price stability, including interest rates, and the European Investment Bank, which facilitates the financing of long-term capital projects.

The 1957 Treaty of Rome, which established the then European Economic Community, emphasised primarily the economic dimension, with relatively little allowance for a social dimension, and in the early years the emphasis was largely on the free movement of workers and the establishment of a common market. In 1986, the Single European Act extended qualified majority voting in the Council, and also gave some greater space for the development of the social policy dimension within the EU, particularly as it related to employment, such as in the areas of health and safety at work, and economic and social cohesion. The Maastricht Treaty of 1991 established the European Union, gave the Parliament more say in decision making, and again took the social dimension a step further, although the UK initially opted out of the social chapter. The 1997 Treaty of Amsterdam consolidated the mechanisms established under the Maastricht Treaty and gave further support for some aspects of social policy, particularly as it related to employment, with the Labour government signing up to the social dimension, unlike its Conservative predecessors. The 2007 Treaty of Lisbon gave the European Parliament further powers, changed the foreign affairs and diplomatic structures of the EU, and introduced the possibility for citizens' initiatives.

In general, despite the number of treaties, it is important to recognise that the power of the EU and member states varies considerably from area to area, generally being greatest with regard to the single market and smallest with regard to issues such as national security, law and order, health care, national transport, and treaty changes outwith the competencies of the EU, and that member governments remain very significant factors in the development (or otherwise) of policies at the European level, although there has undoubtedly been some diffusion of power upwards. Perhaps the most notable areas where the European Union has had an impact have been the greater linkage of the economy of the United Kingdom with those of other member states, including in relation to the standardisation of many aspects of economic life; in relation to the social dimension, arguably development of policy over equality between men and women, which has impacted in particular on working women; and in politics the UK's relationship with the European Union, as highlighted most markedly in the referendum decision in 2016 to leave the EU.

In terms of the policy process, in the same way as there are concerns about a democratic deficit in relation to the use of quasi-governmental organisations in the United Kingdom (see Chapter 7), so, too, have some raised concerns about this at the European level. These tend to be fairly obvious, with the European Parliament, although directly elected, having had relatively limited ability to influence European legislation, while the lack of Europe-wide political parties, and clear leaders, as well as a means of communication, have also been seen by some as hindering the processes of democratic accountability. Similarly, the European referendum of June 2016 highlighted the concerns of many about the role and powers of the EU, including the perceived bureaucracy and red tape, and that these can increase prices to consumers (tampon tax) and business (energy), the difficulty of controlling immigration as part of the EU, and the supremacy of European laws and the European Court of Justice. Given such concerns, and the complexity and the degree of networking that take place at the European level, as well as the existence of a European Union bureaucracy (albeit small compared with those of national governments), ideas such as agenda setting, policy networks and the advocacy coalition framework, and perspectives on bureaucracies, discussed in Chapters 2 and 3, are clearly useful tools for analysing decision making and implementation, while, as with nation states, the EU has made use of agencies (see Chapter 7; see also Ongaro *et al.*, 2012).

It is possible to argue that the European Union, in part because of its broadly consensual approach to policy making, and the dependence of its policy makers on the information that groups supply, has been relatively open to groups that may be seeking to influence policies, particularly those that are willing to try to exploit the variety of different opportunity structures within the EU (Coen and Richardson, 2009), as arguably happened with elements of gender equality (Mazey, 1998; Duncan, 2002). In addition, as Klüver (2013) notes, the considerable fragmentation of EU institutions has provided many access points to the decision-making process, while the institutions have also made efforts to include interest groups, in part as a response to criticisms of the democratic deficit (Kohler-Koch and Finke, 2007). Klüver suggests that at the EU level, lobbying can be conceived of as involving an exchange of goods, with interest groups demanding influence while the EU institutions seek policy-relevant information, citizen support and economic power from the groups, and that it is helpful to consider lobbying in terms of the issue-specific alignment of coalitions of interest groups that pursue the same objectives. However, it has been noted that business interests tend to be better represented than cause groups (for example, Persson, 2007; Klüver, 2013), although Klüver also suggests that if other organised interests represent large numbers of citizens and are able to supply considerable amounts of information to the Commission, the Council and the Parliament, they, too, have the possibility of influencing policy outcomes.

Palumbo (2015) notes that lacking the ability to impose new taxes from which to derive revenue, and in its attempts to take integration forward without antagonising national governments, the EU has experimented with new forms of regulation including common guidelines that are translated into national policy, and the open method of coordination, using committees composed of experts, national representatives, eurocrats and NGOs, benchmarking and comparative analysis of policy performance, with states submitting data for peer review with the aim of improving policy effectiveness, having been widely used as a policy

instrument (see Chapter 3) (Weale, 2011). However, the use of negotiated rule-making and the complexity of multilevel governance raise
questions of political accountability, not only but particularly for the EU
(Weale, 2011).

In terms of impact on public policy in the UK, Dorey (2014) highlights
the uneven impact of the EU, noting Bulmer and Burch's (2009) suggestion that an 'inner core' of Whitehall departments, including the Treasury,
the Department for Environment, Food and Rural Affairs and what is now
the Department of Business, Innovation and Skills, has been most affected
by the EU as its concerns with competition and trade, the environment
and agriculture have had significant implications for them, and an 'outer
core', which is affected only sporadically or on a narrower range of issues,
such as the Department for Education and the Department of Health,
although he suggests that it is possible to identify an 'intermediate layer'
of departments that have found some elements of their role increasingly
affected by European activities, such as the Home Office, the Ministry of
Defence and the Department for Work and Pensions.

Other supra-national organisations

Increasing attention has been paid to the influence of the international
system and its role in shaping public policy at the domestic level. One
way of considering this is to look at international regimes, sets of governing arrangements, rules or norms that impact on behaviour (Keohane
and Nye, 1987 and 1997). These may be based on explicit treaties or on
conventions that develop over time, and some may be administered by
formal organisations while others are effectively more or less accepted
behaviours. They may affect policy, including by promoting certain preferences and limiting others. Obviously, at the international level power
is not equal, with the United States, for example, being able to exercise
considerable influence in some areas, perhaps in particular by blocking
initiatives which might be seen as unfavourable to it, while the growth in
the economic power of China, especially, has been evident in recent years.

Of course, the United Kingdom is also a party to many other organisations that can impact upon public policy. One of the most obvious of
these is the European Convention on Human Rights, which was ratified
by Britain in 1951, although it was not incorporated into UK law until
the Human Rights Act 1998, with successive governments arguing that
human rights were already protected by domestic law and that Parliament
was sovereign. Despite that, British citizens were able to appeal to the
European Court of Human Rights, and over time the Court found against
the British government on many occasions, including the treatment of

suspected terrorists in Northern Ireland and the use of different ages of consent for heterosexual and homosexual acts. The Human Rights Act 1998 made it possible for individuals who believe that their human rights have been infringed to take cases to the domestic courts. Despite opposition from some quarters, particularly within the Conservative Party, which has proposed scrapping the Act and introducing in its place a British bill of rights, the Act has had a considerable impact on public policy, particularly around personal privacy and equality.

Other organisations may affect public policy in the United Kingdom in a variety of ways. For example, the UK is a member of the United Nations (with treaties such as the Kyoto Protocol committing states to setting binding emissions reduction targets) and its agencies, such as the World Trade Organization, the World Health Organization and the International Labour Organization. While these organisations frequently tend to rely on harmonisation and diffusion (see Chapter 4 on policy transfer and Chapter 3 on globalisation), or on encouraging states to opt into agreements, rather than having strong enforcement powers, they can nevertheless be seen to have an influence on policy, particularly over time. For example, the World Health Organization plays an important role in collecting and transferring information between countries, and in advising on potential global diseases, such as SARS, while the International Labour Organization sets core labour standards, and in the debate about the nature of Britain's exit from the European Union, it was sometimes argued that the default position might be that World Trade Organization rules would apply to tariffs on imports. While some inter-governmental organisations are well known and recognised as making and influencing public policy, many may be obscure, although, as Davies and Woodward (2014) note, they can nevertheless have influence over daily life, as with the International Telecommunications Union (another United Nations agency) and its allocation of radio frequencies for use by radio and mobile phones.

Another example of an organisation having an impact on UK policy (and indeed that of other states) is the Organisation for Economic Co-operation and Development's Programme for International Student Assessment (PISA) tests (Baird et al., 2011), which have become widely quoted by politicians and others as comparative measures of schoolchildren's performance, including in mathematics, reading and science, and consequently of education policy as a whole.

In addition, the UK is part of many other international bodies, including: some that focus to a considerable extent on Europe, such as NATO, the Council of Europe and the Organization for Security and Co-operation in Europe (OSCE); the Commonwealth; Interpol (the International Criminal Police Organization); international scientific organisations, such as the Centre for European Nuclear Research (CERN) and the European Space Agency; and transport and communication organisations, including the International Telecommunications Union (as noted above), the International Civil Aviation Organization and the International Maritime Organization.

There are different approaches to classifying intergovernmental organisations, including by their membership (restricted or open), competencies (from many policy areas, such as the EU or the UN, to very specific issues, as with the European Space Agency), functions (with operational organisations seeking to use bilateral and multilateral resources to achieve the outcomes of their mandates, as with peacekeeping, humanitarian relief or undertaking scientific projects, while programme organisations tend to support international cooperation through collating, analysing and disseminating information, including for the development of rules and norms for expected standards of behaviour), or authority (with some having greater autonomy and authority, while others are almost entirely dependent upon their members' approval in order to undertake activities) (Davies and Woodward, 2014).

It is not the purpose or intention of this chapter to draw in depth on the substantial literature, particularly in the field of international relations, that seeks to analyse and theorise the existence of international organisations. Nevertheless, it may be worth highlighting four schools of thought that may assist in our understanding of them and how they operate:

1. *Realism* – sees the international political system as anarchical, and states as motivated by self-interest, meaning that states seek to bolster their own security, largely by building up military power, so that the best way of maintaining peace in the international system is through working towards a balance of power. While generally pessimistic about the possibilities for international cooperation, realists do recognise that international organisations can be created and sustained only when they are in the interests of the most powerful states, and they reflect the current distribution of power in the international system. As a result, international organisations are not independent actors, but, at best, are entities through which states pursue their national interests.

2. *Liberalism* – while many liberal perspectives exist, the most influential have arguably been functionalism and liberal institutionalism. *Functionalist* approaches see international organisations emerging spontaneously as a response to the challenges arising from economic and technological change, with pressure for government functions to be organised regionally or globally through expert international organisations, and from which cooperation and common values can

develop. Neo-functionalists suggest that rather than international organisations arising spontaneously, they are underpinned by political calculations, but nevertheless they can encourage further political integration. *Liberal institutionalists* argue that international organisations are mechanisms that support the efforts of states to respond to collective problems, rather than being stepping stones to global government, and they exist simply to regulate relations between states. At the same time, they accept that cooperation through such bodies can affect state behaviour through making them more predisposed to cooperate.

3. *Constructivism* – this perspective highlights that the interests of actors are socially constructed, with the interests and actions of states being constrained by social structures (such as ideas, values and norms) amongst actors in the international system, creating a view of what might be seen as legitimate courses of action: the logic of appropriateness. This might include the ways in which human rights have often been seen as associated with the identity of legitimate states at the international level. For constructivists, therefore, international organisations are more than the sum of their member states, and can be at least semi-autonomous actors.

4. *Critical theories* – there is a variety of approaches that do not fit in with the mainstream visions of international organisations and their place in international relations. In particular, they do not regard states as the starting point for analysis, recognising that social power exists in other political places. And, frequently, they possess strong normative elements, suggesting that alternatives to the status quo are possible.

Perhaps even more than with the European Union, it can be argued that accountability is a challenge for supra-national organisations, so that Barnett (2016), for example, suggests that 'global governance institutions are much better at preaching accountability than living it' (p. 134). He suggests that the discourse of modern governance includes two key characteristics that do not always coincide: one is effectiveness, including an emphasis on experts who are both capable because of their training and knowledge and motivated to act in the public interest; and accountability, which is necessary for other desired outcomes as well as being a defining feature of democratic regimes. He goes on to argue that expertise is more likely to be favoured than democratic accountability in global governance for three reasons. First, while it is relatively easy to identify the 'public' in the domestic sphere, and also expectations of democratic accountability, there is no readily identifiable 'public' or expectations for accountability mechanisms in global governance, and the demands for expert knowledge are therefore likely to outweigh those for accountability.

Second, global governance remains defined by states, with account-ability mechanisms largely established by and run through states, and while the state might be expected to represent the interests of its people in holding global actors to account, that 'remains more of an assumption than an empirical tendency' (p. 144). And third, the discourse of expert knowledge contains strong elements of paternalism that justify and legitimise an anti-democratic stance, a feature that he argues is particularly pronounced in the context of relations between the developed and the developing world, including humanitarian governance, where discourses of inequality remain strong.

Finally, critics have argued that some international organisations that have had significant influence, not least because of their claims for expertise, as well as the financial and other resources that they have available, such as the International Monetary Fund and the World Bank, have tended to favour neo-liberal arguments and approaches, and to have embraced marketisation and privatisation with harmful effects, particularly on poorer nations (for example, Stiglitz, 2001), although some have suggested that other bodies, such as the International Labour Organization, have provided a more balanced approach to economic and social policies (for example, Deacon, 2007).

Sub-central government

While much of the discussion above has been concerned with argu-ments that the existence of the European Union and other transnational organisations has seen a shifting of power upwards, away from the United Kingdom government, it is equally important to recognise that the past two decades have seen significant developments in sub-central govern-ment in the United Kingdom, with the Labour governments of 1997–2010, in particular, but also their Coalition and Conservative successors, seeking to devolve power downwards, at least in some respects, although frequently simultaneously demonstrating considerable centralising ten-dencies (see Table 6.1).

The introduction of devolution to Scotland and Wales by the 1997–2001 Labour government resulted in significant change, in terms not only of the structure of government but also, arguably, in public percep-tions. In September 1997, Scots voted overwhelmingly in favour of a Scottish Parliament (74.3 per cent), and substantially for it to have tax varying powers (63.5 per cent), and a week later the Welsh people voted narrowly in favour (50.3 per cent to 49.7 per cent) of a Welsh Assembly. Both took power on 1 July 1999. Labour also followed through the

Table 6.1 Areas of devolved powers in the UK

	Scotland	Wales	London	Northern Ireland	Combined authorities (proposals, including Greater Manchester)
Taxation	Local seat of government and UK Parliament	Subject to referendum	UK Parliament	Local seat of government and UK Parliament	UK Parliament
NHS	Devolved	Devolved	UK Parliament	Devolved	Optional
Transport	Devolved	Local seat of government and UK Parliament	Devolved	Devolved	Devolved
Education	Devolved	Devolved	UK Parliament	Devolved	UK Parliament
Policing	Devolved	UK Parliament	Devolved	Local seat of government and UK Parliament	Transferred from Police and Crime Commissioner to mayor
Housing	Devolved	Devolved	Housing and planning strategy devolved	Devolved	Devolved

Source: Coleman, A., Segar, J. and Checkland, K. (2016) 'The devolution project in Greater Manchester: Introduction to the special issue', *Representation*, 51(4) 377–384, p. 380 (copyright © McDougall Trust, London, reprinted by permission of Taylor & Francis Ltd., http://wwwtandfonline,com, on behalf of the McDougall Trust, London).

Conservatives' approach to the peace process in Northern Ireland with the creation of the Northern Ireland Assembly, which sat for the first time on 1 July 1998. These new decision-making bodies provided a new dimension to the public policy process, and each is discussed below.

In terms of multi-level governance, there is also a significant link between devolution to Northern Ireland, Scotland and Wales, and the European Union, as the devolved administrations have also sought to influence EU policy making and resource allocation, and each has maintained an office in Brussels. Europe's Committee of the Regions has also provided one institutional channel for such approaches for sub-national tiers of government, although it has frequently been criticised as weak, and Scotland, together with some other regions within Europe, has sought a greater role for regions within the EU.

England

Before moving on to a consideration of the devolved administrations, it is worth noting that there have also been developments in England. Elements of regional government (or at least regional administration) existed to a greater or lesser degree for much of the twentieth century, depending on the fashions and needs of governments. For example, during the 1960s, 11 regional boards were created for economic planning, consisting of employers, trade unionists and local councillors, but they were abolished in 1979, while the privatisation of the water industry led to the end of water boards, although the NHS continued to operate Regional Health Authorities until 1996. In 1994, the Conservatives brought together elements of a number of central government departments into Government Offices of the Regions, which had particular responsibilities for promoting the competitiveness of their regions, as well as supporting regeneration and social exclusion, although these were abolished by the Coalition government in 2011.

The idea of elected regional government began to re-emerge on the agenda during the Conservative governments of 1979–97, fuelled in part by discontent in some areas about the centralisation of government, the reduction in the autonomy of local government, and an awareness of the regional dimension within the EU, to which England's existing structures could not easily respond. In a White Paper in 2002 the Labour government outlined the potential for regional assemblies for England, but in a referendum in 2004 voters in the North East rejected such a proposal and the idea was subsequently dropped. Then in 2014, immediately following the defeat of the referendum on independence for Scotland, David Cameron announced that the government would seek to implement the idea of 'English votes for English laws', reducing the ability of MPs from Northern Ireland, Scotland and Wales to vote on legislation that only affected England. Following the Conservatives' victory in the 2015 general election, and the surge in support for the SNP, the plans were passed in the House of Commons, although the difficulty of distinguishing what might constitute an 'English law' remained significant.

In addition, in November 2014 the Coalition government announced that, with the agreement of the region's councils, Greater Manchester was to have a directly elected mayor, with powers over transport, social care and housing, as well as police budgets, while responsibility for the health and social budget was added later, with the first mayor to be elected in 2017. Following that, the idea of regional devolution, in each case including a directly elected mayor, was extended to a number of other areas, including Sheffield, West Yorkshire, Liverpool and Greater Lincolnshire, albeit with different powers over different matters (House of Commons

Library, 2016a), although not all of these transfers took place, with, for example, a number of local authorities in Lincolnshire opposing the proposals. While there appeared to be considerable support within these areas for such developments, fears were raised about the implications of funding pressures, including further cuts in public expenditure and the localisation of blame as a result, and about how clear accountability would be. There have also been concerns that devolution for England, even more so than in Northern Ireland, Scotland and Wales, has been largely designed and imposed by central government (Richards and Smith, 2015) (albeit recognising the significant demand for devolution in many areas), and that there has been a lack of consideration of public engagement, consultation and the design of democratic arrangement (Richards and Smith, 2015; Gains, 2015).

The departure of David Cameron as Prime Minister, and perhaps even more so George Osborne as Chancellor of the Exchequer, following the 2016 referendum result in favour of leaving the European Union, meant that the English devolution initiative had arguably lost its strongest supporters in government, and the new Prime Minister Theresa May and her Cabinet generally appeared less enthusiastic about the idea.

Scotland

It is important to be aware that while the Scottish Parliament and Scottish government may be relatively new institutions, Scotland has long had its own legal system, education system, established church and arrangements for government (particularly through the Scottish Office, created in 1885), and similarly that policy had been distinctive in many areas prior to 1997. Devolution did, however, introduce a new tier of democratic accountability through the Scottish Parliament, elected using the additional member system, a more proportionate electoral system than at Westminster, that was expected to make coalition or minority governments more likely to occur.

The Scottish Parliament can make laws in relation to devolved matters in Scotland, and can amend or repeal existing Acts of the UK Parliament in relation to devolved matters. From its creation, it had substantial powers, including on health, including the NHS in Scotland, education, local government, social care, housing, economic development, transport and the criminal law. The powers reserved to the UK Parliament included the fiscal, economic and monetary system (with the exception of the tax-varying powers in Scotland), employment legislation, social security, health matters such as abortion and human fertilisation and embryology, equalities legislation, and defence and foreign affairs.

Even early in the life of the devolved administrations, when both the UK and Scottish governments were controlled by Labour, there were areas where Scotland took a different approach to that at Westminster, with notable examples being the abolition of student tuition fees for higher education and the provision of free social care for older people. Since then, under both Labour and then SNP administrations, the divergence with the UK Coalition and Conservative governments has grown, with apparently stronger support for the welfare state and universalism in Scotland (Mooney and Scott, 2012), even if more at the level of rhetoric than through radical policy development (Birrell and Gray, 2016). Of course, it is not only policies that have been to some extent distinctive, but also the ways in which they are made and implemented, with considerably less emphasis in Scotland on marketisation and new public management than in England (for example, Birrell and Gray, 2016), and perhaps more attempts to involve professionals (for example, Greer, 2007). However, Cairney (2016) considers the extent to which there is a 'Scottish approach' or policy style, examining the cases of prevention of inequalities and transition from child to adult services, and concludes that while the Scottish government may have a reputation for doing things 'better' than its UK counterpart, where issues are difficult to define and manage, at present problems of ambiguity and fragmentation remain.

Deaner and Phillips (2013) have reflected the arguments by others that Scotland has a somewhat higher level of spending than England, around 9.3 per cent of government spending in the UK, compared with an 8.4 per cent share of the UK population (although they note that fluctuations in the economic output associated with the North Sea, which varies significantly over time, can make such calculations problematic), and that it is spending on public services that accounts for most of the difference in spending per person between Scotland and the UK, with spending on education, economic development, housing and social services being substantially higher than in the rest of the UK.

As devolution has become more embedded there have been additional transfers of powers, including through the Scotland Act 2012, which allowed for the introduction of a Scottish income tax, and most recently, following the referendum on independence for Scotland in 2014 and the subsequent Smith Commission (2014), the Scotland Act 2016 devolved further powers, including over abortion law, income tax and VAT, significant elements of the social security system, and powers in other areas such as oil, gas and transport. The decision that the United Kingdom would leave the European Union also raised questions about how the powers returned to the UK, such as in relation to agriculture and fisheries, would be distributed between Westminster and the devolved legislatures.

Wales

Like Scotland, Wales had retained some historical differences with England, particularly around the Welsh language and culture, although these had attracted much greater support in rural and northern Wales than in urban and south Wales. In addition, a Welsh Office was established in 1964, and a Welsh Grand Committee created to debate Welsh bills, but neither of these was as powerful as its Scottish counterparts. It was perhaps unsurprising therefore that support for devolution in Wales was more lukewarm, and that the National Assembly for Wales was created with considerably weaker powers than those of the Scottish Parliament.

Like the Scottish Parliament, the National Assembly for Wales is elected by the additional member system, giving a degree of proportionality and making one-party majority government harder to achieve. Initially the Assembly had no primary legislative and only limited secondary legislative powers, while it also had no ability to vary taxation. However, it did inherit most of the powers of the Secretary of State for Wales, giving it responsibility for many aspects of health, education, local government, the environment and economic regeneration. Indeed, in the years immediately following devolution the Welsh government abolished tests for primary school children and the publication of school league tables, abolished prescription charges for people under 25, and introduced free dental checks for those under 25 and over 65. Policy divergence continued under the Coalition and Conservative governments at Westminster, for example in health and social care, and in the greater emphasis on tackling poverty by the Welsh government.

The powers of the Assembly have also increased over time, including through the 2006 Government of Wales Act, while the Wales Act 2014 devolved some tax-raising powers to the National Assembly, including stamp duty and the landfill tax, and some powers over income tax, subject to approval in a referendum. It also removed the possibility for the same person to sit in the Assembly and the House of Commons at the same time.

Following the second Silk Commission report (2014), the Wales Act 2017 was introduced to establish a reserved powers model of devolution for Wales and to devolve further powers, including over road transport and harbours and ports, to Welsh ministers.

Northern Ireland

Unlike Scotland and Wales, Northern Ireland did possess its own parliament for much of the twentieth century (from 1921 to 1972), with the Unionists, representing the protestant community, having a permanent majority, and the minority Roman Catholic population being excluded from power and often experiencing discrimination by the government, for example in terms of housing and employment. Following the onset of the 'troubles', the UK government initially took on responsibility for law and order, and then for all aspects of government, through the Secretary of State. While that arrangement was never intended to be permanent, the obstacles to the re-establishment of devolved government could not be entirely addressed until the late 1990s, but in April 1998 the Good Friday Agreement was approved by 71.1 per cent of those voting, helping clear the way for the establishment of the Northern Ireland Assembly and an executive in November 1999. However, given the political situation in Northern Ireland, the early years of the Assembly have seen a rather on-off existence.

The Assembly has full legislative and executive authority for devolved matters, including for education, health, social care and social security. However, the nature of power-sharing in Northern Ireland has made it harder to achieve consensus, so that commitments to policies often reflect a lowest common denominator approach (Gray and Birrell, 2012). Indeed, while in some respects Scotland and Wales have been seen as more 'progressive' than the Westminster government, on issues such as abortion, sexual orientation and same-sex marriage, Northern Ireland has taken a more conservative approach (Gray and Birrell, 2012).

Devolution: summary

While devolution has been followed by policy divergence, Mooney and Scott (2012) have argued that it 'has not produced radically different forms of government across the UK, nor has policy making across the devolved countries and England been as significantly divergent as was anticipated' (p. 8). Wright (2014) notes two potential reasons for this: first, oppositional politics, perhaps linked to proportional representation, mean that compromises have been necessary in respect of policy change; and second, despite the rhetoric about change, there have been limitations on funding, including the Barnett Formula for block grants from Westminster, although she notes that the devolved governments have been very reluctant to use their powers to increase borrowing or taxation, the latter having been an option available to the Scottish government in particular (Gray and Birrell, 2012).

In general, ideological differences between the devolved governments and the Westminster government have widened since the election of the Coalition government in 2010 and the Conservative governments from 2015, and there has been no enthusiasm for the austerity agenda in the devolved administrations (Mackinnon, 2015; Gray and Birrell, 2012), although, equally, in Scotland the SNP administration has been unwilling to use its powers over taxation to increase public expenditure.

There have also been debates over the financial arrangements for devolution, which have been dominated by the Barnett Formula, which allocates more than half of public expenditure to the devolved nations. This has allocated the highest level of per capita spending to Northern Ireland, followed by Scotland and Wales and then England. At the same time, social security, which accounts for a large proportion of public expenditure, has not been devolved in Scotland and Wales, although the Scotland Act 2016 and the Wales Act 2017 mean that further powers over are being passed to the two legislatures.

Local government

During the late nineteenth and early twentieth centuries, local government pioneered the provision of public services, including public libraries, schools, public health, hospitals, public housing, public transport, electricity, gas and water supplies and sewage. However, from the 1940s onwards, local government has lost many of its powers and responsibilities, initially for electricity and gas, then for hospitals, with others following. Part of the reason for this is that in the United Kingdom local authorities have no independent right to exist, and derive their powers from Westminster in England and from the devolved administrations in Northern Ireland, Scotland and Wales, including their responsibilities for governing a range of services and responsibilities at the local level. This is different from the position in some other countries, and is reflected in the relatively frequent reorganisations and the lack of independent fundraising powers. Given this, it is unsurprising at the local level, as Stoker (2000) has pointed out, reflecting some of the debates outlined in Chapter 1, that:

> ...a key concern in the study of local politics has become 'governance', which can be broadly defined as a concern with governing, achieving collective action in the realm of public affairs, in conditions where it is not possible to rest on recourse to the authority of the state...Governance recognises the capacity to get things done which does not rest on the power of government to command or use its authority. Governing becomes an interactive process because no single actor has the knowledge and resource capacity to tackle problems unilaterally. (p. 3)

Stewart (2000) has noted that one of the key characteristics of local government is that it is part of a substantial network of institutions, including other local authorities and other public sector bodies, as well as the variety of private and not-for-profit organisations that undertake functions on behalf of government. If one of the key roles of local government is to play a leading role in the economic, social and environmental well-being of its area, then its relationship with these other organisations will be crucial. For many years, local government was an important provider of services such as education, housing and social care, meaning that it was both useful to central government and frequently in direct contact with large sections of the public. However, under the Conservative governments of 1979–97 many of the powers of local government were eroded, including through its ability to raise income through local taxation (initially property rates, then the poll tax and most recently council tax), pressure to contract out some services, the application of stricter central government guidance and other requirements. Indeed, Copus (2013) argues that central control has developed to such an extent that 'the viability of democratic, representative local government is challenged' (p. 390). While these changes may perhaps have been most noticeable in England, the same broad pattern can be observed and has continued across the UK under governments of all parties.

There are, however, significant, and arguably growing differences in both the structures and processes of local authorities across the UK, as outlined below.

England

The Local Government Act 1972 introduced a new pattern of local authorities for England, but barely a decade later the Conservatives' Local Government Act 1985 made further changes, abolishing the Greater London Council and six metropolitan counties in England and leaving a mix of two tier (39 county and 296 district (these were three tier if parish councils were included)) and unitary (36 metropolitan districts and 32 London boroughs, along with the City of London) councils that remained in place until 1995. The county councils were broadly responsible for education, structure planning and social services and the districts for housing, environmental health and refuse collection. However, in the early 1990s the Conservatives established a Local Government Commission to review the structure of local government, with the changes resulting from its recommendations leaving 115 unitary authorities and in other areas 34 counties with 238 district councils below them.

When Labour returned to office in 1997, an elected Mayor for London and a Greater London Authority were created following a London-wide referendum in May 1998. Other than the unsuccessful attempt to introduce devolved regional government, noted earlier in this chapter, the

Labour governments did not introduce any further structural changes, but did seek to change the decision-making processes of local government, arguing that they could lead 'to inefficient and opaque decision making' (DETR, 1998, p. 25). Labour sought to encourage councils in England to adopt either a cabinet and leader model, or a directly elected mayor, to drive decision making and the implementation of policies, with the remaining councillors playing more of a scrutiny role, although relatively few authorities were keen to adopt the latter model, despite the high profile of the London Mayor.

Although they placed less emphasis on decision-making structures, from 2010 the Coalition and Conservative governments appeared to share the desire to encourage the use of mayors, as noted in the discussion about devolution within England earlier in this chapter, although local communities did not necessarily appear to share such enthusiasm (for example, Fenwick and Elcock, 2014). Nevertheless, decision making has generally moved away from committees, and most councils in England now have cabinet-leader structures. The Coalition government also placed considerable emphasis on 'localism', most notably in the Localism Act 2011, which set out a range of measures intended to shift powers away from central government, although while these included the granting of supposed freedoms and flexibilities for local government, many were intended to empower 'communities' including in challenging and bidding to run local authority services (see, for example, Bochel, 2016). However, by 2015 little use had been made of powers such as the 'community right to challenge' and the 'community right to bid', and with the apparent demise of David Cameron's Big Society ideas, it was unclear what future there was for such initiatives.

In terms of spending, Table 6.2 sets out budgeted expenditure by service for local authorities in England, which highlights both the large areas of education, social care and mandatory housing benefits, and provides some indication of the reductions in spending that local governments have been affected by since 2010.

Interestingly, despite all of the developments outlined above, John (2014) is able to argue that from an institutional perspective local government in England displays a high degree of path dependence, in part because it has been efficient, other proposals for reform have frequently not been fully considered, and participatory initiatives in the 1970s, 2000s and 2010s failed to take root. Indeed, the continuing focus on networks and community governance has suggested that local authorities have had the knowledge to manage the relationship between hard and soft power (Stoker, 2011), and to balance out local interests (Cole and John, 2001), and as a result they may continue to play a significant role in the policy process.

Table 6.2   Budgeted net current expenditure by service, 2014–15 and 2015–16, England

	Net current expenditure 2014-15	Net current expenditure 2015-16	£ million £ Change	% Change
Education	35,835	34,976	-860	-2.4
Highways & transport	4,814	4,922	108	2.2
Social care	22,090	21,779	-310	-1.4
of which:				
Children and Families Social Care	*7,726*	*7,698*	*-28*	*-0.4*
Adult Social Care	*14,364*	*14,081*	*-283*	*-2.0*
Public Health	2,849	3,321	473	16.6
Housing (excluding Housing Revenue Account)	1,945	1,742	-203	-10.4
Cultural, environment & planning	9,029	8,695	-334	-3.7
of which:				
Cultural	*2,614*	*2,496*	*-117*	*-4.5*
Environmental	*5,139*	*5,048*	*-91*	*-1.8*
Planning and development	*1,276*	*1,151*	*-125*	*-9.8*
Police	11,121	10,951	-170	-1.5
Fire & rescue	2,123	2,080	-43	-2.0
Central services	3,686	3,112	-573	-15.6
Mandatory Housing Benefits	21,001	21,094	93	0.4
of which:				
Rent Allowances	*16,069*	*16,156*	*87*	*0.5*
Rent Rebates to Non-HRA Tenants	*531*	*542*	*11*	*2.1*
Rent rebates to HRA tenants	*4,401*	*4,396*	*-6*	*-0.1*
Other services	224	281	57	25.7
Appropriations to(+) / from(-) accumulated absences account	-4	-6	-3	78.1
Total net current expenditure	**114,711**	**113,089**	**-1,623**	**-1.4**

Source: Department for Communities and Local Government, 2015.

Scotland

In Scotland, the Local Government (Scotland) Act 1973 created two tiers of nine regional councils and 53 district councils, together with three all-purpose authorities for the island areas (the Orkney and Shetland Islands and the Western Isles). However, in the 1990s the Conservatives introduced further changes through the Local Government (Scotland) Act 1994, leaving 29 new unitary councils together with the three island councils.

Under devolution, the McIntosh Commission was established in 1999, to consider the implications of the creation of the Scottish Parliament for local government, with its best-known proposal being for the use of proportional representation for local elections, which was eventually introduced in 2007 with the use of the single transferable vote. The Commission, however, also recommended that Scotland retain a diversity of approaches to decision-making structures in local government, in contrast to the drive for leader-cabinet or elected mayor models in England.

Labour's Best Value approach was taken up voluntarily by a number of councils in Scotland, and was made statutory from 2003, but was implemented very differently from in England with less central direction and inspection and less use of league tables (Wilson and Game, 2011).

As in England, the funding of local authorities has remained problematic under consecutive administrations. At the 2007 Scottish Parliament elections the SNP pledged to replace council tax with a local income tax, but having won the election they did not do so. Instead, the SNP government did introduce a freeze on council tax in 2008–09, with authorities receiving a compensatory share of a sum set aside by the government, although a number of local authorities have continued to make a case for the freeze to end and for them to be able to raise more income locally, including through the levying of other taxes.

Wales

As with England, the Local Government Act 1972 introduced a two-tier system of eight counties and 37 districts, with responsibilities similar to their equivalents in England, with the option of community councils (the equivalent of parish councils in England) being taken up in some areas. The situation then remained unchanged until the early 1990s, when the Local Government Act 1992 established unitary authorities. Responsibility for the structure of local government passed to the National Assembly for Wales as part of the devolution process.

As in other parts of the United Kingdom, the delivery and governance of local public services has remained a significant topic. A Wales Programme of Improvement was launched from 2002, taking a risk-based, self-assessment approach to performance management (Wilson and Game, 2011), an approach that underwent some revision in 2009 in an attempt to encourage greater linkages between annual planning and longer-term strategic planning. In 2014, a report recommended that the number of local authorities be reduced to between 10 and 12, through a process of mergers (Commission on Public Service Governance and Delivery, 2014), although, despite the publication of a draft bill, the Welsh government decided that there was no consensus on structural reform.

Northern Ireland

Despite a longer period of continuity, Northern Ireland has not been immune from the restructuring of local authorities. The Local Government (Northern Ireland) Act 1972 had created 26 unitary councils responsible for a limited range of services, including refuse collection, cemeteries and tourism. However, in 2015 these were replaced by 11 new councils, which gained some responsibilities, such as for local planning and local economic development. In addition, where there had previously been systems of regional boards (such as four Health and Social Service Boards and five Education and Libraries Boards), consisting of appointed members, these were centralised into a single library authority and health and social care board in 2009 and a single education authority in 2015.

Decision making in local authorities

Running parallel to local authorities' political decision-making structures are those of their departments. These vary significantly across authorities, in part depending on the type of authority and its responsibilities, although for some types of council certain services are mandatory. Most councils have a chief executive or manager who is the most senior officer of the authority and who normally takes responsibility for corporate activities. The chief executive's department, itself comprising various elements, heads and generally coordinates this structure, below which there is a variety of departments which may or may not be hierarchically organised depending on the particular local authority structure. Each department is headed by a chief officer or director and staffed by specialist and generalist officers. Many have a long history, with, for example, the term 'local education authority' dating back to before 1902 (Stewart, 2000), although in England the academisation of schools under the Coalition and Conservative governments appeared to threaten the existence of education departments. Some departments, such as education, housing, children's services and adult social care, have traditionally provided services directly to the public, although the pressures from consecutive governments for councils to shift towards more of an enabling role mean that has reduced considerably since the heights of the 1960s and 1970s, while others provide services and support to other departments within the authority. The role of departments and the officers within them is to implement the decisions and policies determined by the elected members of the council, although, as with civil servants, they also have the potential to influence policy choices.

Within departments, the role of the chief officer is a key one and has traditionally been defined by the services for which their department is responsible. This set parameters for the relationship with the elected councillor responsible for chairing the corresponding council committee, or, more recently, particularly in England, the cabinet member responsible for the area. While the professional role and judgement of the chief officer can affect the relationship, the electoral legitimacy of the cabinet member or committee chair can also be a powerful tool, so that while chief officers do possess some delegated powers, few chief officers would be willing to exercise them in any new and significant way without consulting the relevant member.

The relationship between chief officers and the council lead on their area has undergone significant change over recent decades. The rise of political partisanship in council elections, increasing financial constraints on local authorities, and the growing assertiveness of elected members have all resulted in elected councillors being more willing to challenge officers. The traditional view, that members are responsible for the formulation of policy and officers for its implementation, has generally been replaced by an awareness that, as in central government, formulation and implementation are inextricably linked, and that there is a significant role for officers in the making of policy and for members in carrying it out, although the reality varies widely from authority to authority. In addition, further down the hierarchy, many of the employees of local authorities do have a significant degree of discretion, as is clearly the case with social workers and teachers, who can therefore have a considerable impact upon the way in which policies are actually implemented and delivered to users (see also the discussion of street-level bureaucrats in Chapter 2).

While departments are the key building blocks in the council structure, there has always been significant variation in departmental structures, and recent years have seen this amply illustrated, with many authorities seeking to reduce the number of departments as part of efficiency drives, while there have been other influences, including the requirement of the Children Act 2004 that children's social services be integrated with education and separated from adult social services, the move towards commissioning rather than providing services, the emphasis on multidisciplinarity in service provision, and an awareness of the need to work across existing professional and departmental boundaries.

Like the civil service and parts of the NHS, local authorities are in many cases large-scale bureaucracies, and many of the perspectives from Chapter 2 can usefully be applied to them. The fact that parts of local authority provision have been largely professionalised, including social work and to some extent housing management, brings strengths in terms of training and knowledge, together with a recognition of expertise and professional qualifications, but can also sometimes be accused of encouraging uniformity and rigidity of provision and resistance to change (Stewart, 2000).

Wilson and Game (2011) present four models that can be used to analyse the distribution of power and influence within local authorities. The 'formal model', perhaps unsurprisingly, suggests that councillors make policy, while officers advise them and implement policy. While critics point out that the reality is significantly more complex, and that the model might perhaps say more about what should happen than what does, it does help highlight the different roles of councillors and officials. The 'technocratic model' sees officers as the dominant force, with their power lying in their technical and professional knowledge. However, councillors do have the democratic legitimacy associated with having been elected, while many councillors, and perhaps particularly those in executive (and potentially full-time) positions, have experience, knowledge and political skills, which they are able to use in their relationships with officers. In addition, Wilson and Game note that the intensification of the role of parties in local government from the 1970s has helped shift power towards councillors, although where strong elected leadership is lacking, they suggest that officers are well placed to fill any policy vacuum. The 'joint elite' model argues that policy making is often dominated by a small group of leading councillors (from the majority party or parties) and senior officers, although it can be questioned to what extent such united and cohesive groups typically exist, and whether the model underplays the tensions and conflicts that occur in the real world. Finally, they note Gains' (2004) 'dynamic dependency' model, which suggests that all behaviour, including that of councillors and officers, is the outcome of the interplay of institutional understandings (relating to things like both formal and informal 'rules', 'world views') and the skill of different actors in exercising their respective resources. Gains argues that a dynamic model provides a better understanding of how member-officer relations vary across authorities and over time, while Wilson and Game conclude that 'it does not see the balance of power between ... officers and members, in zero-sum terms, but rather as a dynamic and dependency-based relationship, varying from one institutional setting to another. It thereby adds a helpful nuance to our understanding of local policy making' (p. 337). They also highlight that there are many other factors that can influence policy making, including the ruling party (or parties), non-executive (sometimes called 'backbench') councillors, and tensions both between and within departments within an authority, presenting this diagrammatically (see Figure 6.1).

Finance

As noted earlier in this chapter, from the 1980s, central government has maintained tight control over local government's ability to spend money on capital, limiting its borrowing powers (although in the second half of the Labour government these were slackened somewhat), its

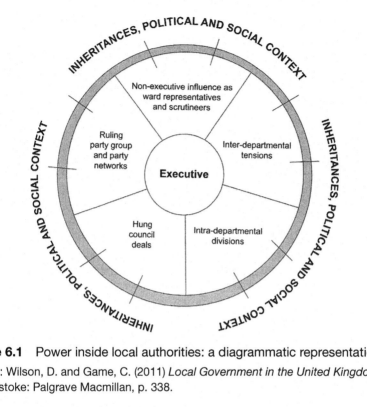

Figure 6.1   Power inside local authorities: a diagrammatic representation
Source: Wilson, D. and Game, C. (2011) *Local Government in the United Kingdom*, Basingstoke: Palgrave Macmillan, p. 338.

ability to spend the money raised through selling assets, such as land or buildings, and ring-fencing many aspects of capital grants from the centre. Councils are able to finance current spending through government grants (which vary considerably, but might typically be seen as accounting for well over half of local authority spending in England), the Business Rate Retention Scheme, the council tax (accounting for around one-quarter of local authority spending in England), and fees and charges (such as for car parks and leisure facilities). The Conservative governments of the 1980s and 1990s introduced the 'capping' of the budgets and taxes of local authorities, so that central government was effectively setting the spending limits for councils, leaving councillors only with the ability to frame budgets within those constraints. The subsequent Labour governments also used capping, although more selectively, while the Coalition government effectively replaced it with a 'tax lock' that required agreement through a local referendum for higher council tax increases. In Scotland, the SNP government also froze council tax, although in Wales councils have been able to increase council tax.

Central–local relations

Wilson and Game (2011) highlight three models of the relationship between central and local government (primarily in England, although all three can be useful in exploring the extent and nature of the relationship in other parts of the UK):

- [T]he agency model sees local authorities essentially as subordinate to central government, with little or no discretion in the implementation of national policies. However, they suggest that such a view is too simplistic, and they point out that there is still considerable diversity in levels of expenditure and the policy priorities and delivery of services[.]
- [T]he power-dependence model sees central government and local authorities as each having resources (legal, financial, knowledge, political, etc.) and that power is exercised via a process of bargaining and exchange. This view can be criticised for understating the power of central government, as well as for paying insufficient attention to the internal politics of organisations and to the broader (capitalist) economic and political system within which inter-governmental relations take place (see, for example, the discussion of Marxist interpretations of power in Chapter 3)[.]
- [T]he idea of policy communities and policy networks (see also Chapter 3) recognises that most local authority policy making takes place within particular policy communities, such as social care or planning, and Wilson and Game suggest that this, with its emphasis on professional interests, can be seen as being applicable to 'the profession-based world of British local government'.

(p. 205)

Conclusion

As is clear throughout this chapter, the scale of change in relation to multi-level governance has been, and continues to be, substantial, although the implications for public policy vary from area to area. The shape and impact of the United Kingdom's exit from the European Union themselves are likely to be a major factor in government and public policy for a number of years, while there will be knock-on effects to many other areas of policy, including the economy, the powers of the devolved legislatures, and also potentially the future of Scotland within the UK. Other developments, such as the Trump presidency in the United States, also raised questions about key elements of the wider international system, including whether the USA might take a more 'isolationist' approach than it has in recent times.

Within the United Kingdom, devolution continues to perhaps best be seen as a process, rather than an end, with further powers having been granted to the devolved administrations, the experiments with devolution in England, and major questions over how sub-national governments should be funded. These, in turn, have created new dynamics in the policy process, and have highlighted the greater possibilities for policy divergence (and for that matter policy transfer).

Given such developments, and returning to the themes discussed in the first four chapters of this book, while centralised top-down models of policy making may still have a relevance for some policy areas, for others it is much more appropriate to consider approaches that emphasise complexity and fragmentation, along with questions over how best to manage policy making and implementation in these changing times.

Further reading

The following contains a useful chapter on the internationalisation of policy making:

Dorey, P. (2014) *Policy Making in Britain*, London: Sage.

For a more comparative perspective, try:

Dodds, A. (2013) *Comparative Public Policy*, Basingstoke: Palgrave Macmillan.

Knill, C. and Tosun, J. (2012) *Public Policy: A New Introduction*, Basingstoke: Palgrave Macmillan.,

Also of value is:

Wilson, D. and Game, C. (2011) *Local Government in the United Kingdom*, Basingstoke: Palgrave Macmillan.

And a detailed examination of devolution is provided by:

Birrell, D. (2012) *Comparing Devolved Governance*, Basingstoke: Palgrave Macmillan.

7

Government at Arm's Length

From the 1980s, the idea of 'arm's-length' decision making and implementation has become an important feature of the policy process under successive governments, whether through more 'formal' approaches such as agencies and quangos, or through less formal mechanisms such as the removal of schools from local authority control or increasing the role of private and voluntary providers in state provision. In addition, the contracting out and privatisation of a whole range of government activities and services has arguably significantly changed their relationship with both governments and recipients.

This chapter considers the arguments around government at arm's length, together with a variety of associated issues such as accountability, regulation, scrutiny and the politicisation or de-politicisation of policy making and provision.

An understanding of arm's-length government and the issues surrounding it is important for those interested in public policy because many of the bodies that now deliver and regulate services either are arm's-length bodies, or can to some extent be understood through an appreciation of the concept.

From the 1970s and 1980s, in particular, arm's-length bodies have been seen as important for a number of reasons, not least because the proportion of public expenditure and the range of governmental activities that they are responsible for have increased markedly, combined with the unelected status of those responsible for making what are often important decisions, and the extent to which this can be seen as effectively bypassing representative government, and consequent questions such as those associated with democracy and accountability, as explored further in this chapter. While the focus here is on the United Kingdom, it is important to note that there has been a broad movement towards the use of such organisations across many developed countries, and that it is possible to consider their use from a comparative perspective (see Durose *et al.*, 2015; Verhoest *et al.*, 2011).

What is arm's-length government?

Even a fairly cursory examination of the public sector in the United Kingdom shows that much of it does not fall easily into the categories of local or central government as outlined in the preceding chapters of this book, and that there is a wide variety of organisations that undertake elements of the work of government. These can be important in the policy-making and implementation process and include major bodies such as NHS England, the BBC, the Equality and Human Rights Commission and the Driver and Vehicle Licensing Agency, as well as smaller bodies with specific responsibilities, such as the Copyright Tribunal and the Victims' Commissioner.

The very utility of these organisations, and their consequent diversity, does, however, complicate our attempts to understand them, a theme that runs throughout this chapter, and a situation that is not helped by the variety of terminology and definitions that have been and are applied to some or all of them. These include 'quasi-autonomous non-governmental organisations' (quangos), 'non-departmental public bodies', 'fringe bodies', 'semi-autonomous authorities', 'hybrids' and even 'extra-governmental organisations'. Nevertheless, while the observation of Doig (1979) that 'there is no one characteristic, or lack of characteristic, that distinguishes quangos or non-departmental public bodies from other organisations in the structure of government' (p. 311) remains apposite, it is clearly important to be able to identify them and their roles. Here, the emphasis is therefore on the 'arm's-length' nature of their relationship with government, and with organisations having some or all of the following characteristics (see also, for example, Pollitt, 2016a):

➤ undertaking some of the functions of government;

➤ having a status defined largely or entirely in public law;

➤ being funded entirely or to a large extent by government;

➤ keeping the appointment of leading officers under the control of a minister or department;

➤ having a degree of independence from ministers and departments, particularly in their day-to-day operations;

➤ being potentially less subject to scrutiny by Parliament than are government departments (for example, Public Administration Committee, 2014).

In 1979, when Margaret Thatcher first came to power, she asked Leo Pliatzky (1980) to undertake a review of government agencies, with the aim of reducing the costs and numbers of such organisations, and for that he adopted the Whitehall term 'non-departmental public bodies' (NDPBs), within which he identified three categories – executive, advisory and tribunals – and more recent official government definitions and statistics have built upon that approach. Others have argued for different terms, and have suggested that many other bodies could and should be included in such statistics (Weir and Hall, 1994; Taxpayers' Alliance, 2008), including at the local level. Different definitions clearly lead to different figures, so that, for example, in 2009 the White Paper, *Smarter Government,* found 752 arm's-length bodies, and a Cabinet Office report identified 766 non-departmental public bodies sponsored by the UK government, while the Taxpayers Alliance (2008) listed 957 'semi-autonomous bodies'; in addition, an earlier report by the Public Administration Committee (2001), *Mapping the Quango State,* had identified more than 5,000 'quangos' (of which around half were registered social landlords and housing associations); and the numbers of staff employed by these organisations and the levels of spending by them similarly vary according to the definition adopted.

Classifying arm's-length bodies

Pliatzky's categorisation remains useful, and provides some indication of the variety of arm's-length bodies:

➤ *executive* – those that are direct instruments of government policy, for example in terms of education, housing, health and environmental protection (such as the Committee on Climate Change, the Environment Agency, the Homes and Communities Agency and Public Health England);

➤ *advisory* – those, once described by Hall and Weir (1996) as '… a near invisible layer of government, even though they shape government decisions of vital importance which touch people's lives where they are most vulnerable' (p. 4), that include the Advisory Council on the Misuse of Drugs, the Commission on Human Medicines, the Law Commission, the Senior Salaries Review Body and the Social Mobility Commission;

➤ *tribunals* – those that have a licensing or appeals function based in a specific area of law, such as the Investigatory Powers Tribunal, the Pensions Ombudsman and the Valuation Tribunal for England.

To these, it is worth adding public corporations, such as the BBC, Channel 4 and the Civil Aviation Authority, and non-ministerial departments, such as the Land Registry, Ofsted and the National Archives. Non-ministerial departments (NMDs) are government departments that do not have their own minister, and are normally headed by a statutory board. However, as Rutter (2013) has pointed out, their strange status does raise questions of accountability, and the non-ministerial departments themselves appear inconsistent in their views of accountability relationships. One example of this lack of clarity is Ofsted, which is categorised as a non-ministerial public body, but which might be viewed either as enforcing the views of the Department for Education, or as an independent body overseeing professional standards. In addition, in its listing of 'Departments, agents and public bodies', the government now also notes 'other' organisations such as the Commissioner for Public Appointments, HM Inspectorate of Prisons, the Local Government Ombudsman and Ofcom. Arguments about the classification of arm's-length bodies continue to figure significantly, not least as the lack of clarity about classification is seen by many as contributing to concerns about the lack of transparency and accountability of such organisations (for example, Gash et al., 2010; Rutter, 2013; Public Administration Committee, 2014), with Gash et al.'s categorisation being shown in Figure 7.1.

Given the definitional problems discussed above, the constantly changing picture arising from mergers, abolition of some bodies and creation of others, and, in turn, the variety of tiers of government involved (and the different categorisations used by them), it is almost impossible to give an agreed figure on the number of arm's-length bodies. However, during 2016, the UK government's official definitions of 'Departments, agencies and public bodies' showed, in addition to the 25 ministerial departments, 21 non-ministerial departments, 373 agencies and other public bodies and 10 public corporations; the Scottish government identified a further seven non-ministerial departments, 36 non-departmental public bodies, seven executive agencies, four public corporations, 23 'health bodies', and six commissioners and ombudsmen; the Welsh government identified one non-ministerial department, nine executive bodies, nine tribunals, 11 executive bodies and 12 public companies or subsidiary companies.

As a final point for this section, while many accounts tend to emphasise the degree of continuity in the use of arm's-length bodies (for example, James et al., 2011; Flinders and Skelcher, 2012), and particularly agencies, over time, Elston suggests that this may be overstated, and that it is not at all clear that the agency idea means the same now as it did 25 years ago. However, for the purposes of this chapter and book, it is possible to argue that the challenges associated with arm's-length bodies remain broadly similar, even if there is less continuity in their nature and use than may sometimes be implied.

1 **Advisory NDPBs:** Committees or boards which provide expert advice to ministers on specific policy issues. Usually set up without legislation and supported by staff from the parent department, with no significant budget.

2 **Executive NDPBs:** Bodies which play a role in national government but are not part of any department, deliberately established to operate at arm's length from ministers. Usually set up by statute, they can hire their own staff and the chief executive is accounting officer for the budget allocated to them. They are, however, sponsored by a parent department which holds the body to account and whose ministers are responsible for appointments of board members. Most executive NDPBs receive a significant grant-in-aid from their parent department to fund all or some of their work. Some also raise funds from other sources (e.g. regulatory levies).

3 **Independent monitoring boards ('other' NDPBs):** Every prison and immigration removal centre (and some short-term holding facilities) has an independent monitoring board which monitors day-to-day life to ensure proper standards of care and decency.

4 **Tribunal NDPBs:** These bodies have jurisdiction in a particular area of law. They are coordinated by the tribunals service, an executive agency, and supervised by the Administrative Justice and Tribunals Council.

5 **Executive agencies:** Agencies carry out services or functions with a focus on delivering specific outputs. They usually have no statutory basis and, in law, are indistinguishable from their parent department. However, their chief executives are accounting officers and responsible for their expenditure; they will also have a separate organisational identity from the parent department and often have more human resources and financial flexibilities available to them than the parent department.

6 **NMDs:** A department not headed by a government minister but represented by the minister of another department in Parliament. NMDs are normally set up under legislation and funded through the Treasury.

7 **Public corporations:** Market bodies that derive more than 50% of their income from the sale of goods and services. Some charge for regulatory activities where these provide a significant benefit to the person paying the fee. They are owned or controlled by central government but they have substantial day-to-day operating independence so that they should be seen as institutional units separate from their sponsor departments. Otherwise may have similar features to executive NDPBs as detailed above.

8 **Independent statutory bodies:** These bodies (which include the five HM inspectorates) enjoy statutory powers and are not part of government departments but receive their budget through a departmental vote.

9 **Special health authorities:** Special health authorities are health authorities set up to assume a delegated responsibility for providing a national service to the NHS or directly to the public. They are established under statute. Ministers retain a formal power of direction to ensure ultimate control over their activities. In terms of governance, they are in most respects akin to an executive NDPB.

10 **Parliamentary bodies:** There are currently five independent parliamentary bodies or 'constitutional watchdogs': Comptroller and Auditor General, Parliamentary Ombudsman, Parliamentary Commissioner for Standards, Electoral Commission and Office of the Information Commissioner. These are formally independent institutional units that review the actions of government on behalf of (and report to) Parliament rather than the executive.

11 **Central bank:** The Bank of England appears to have a unique constitutional position.

Figure 7.1   Types of arm's-length body

Source: Gash *et al.* (2010) *Read Before Burning: Arm's Length Government for a New Administration*, London, Institute for Government (reproduced with permission from the Institute for Government, copyright © Institute for Government).

The origins and growth of arm's-length government up to 2010

Despite the attention devoted to arm's-length bodies by politicians, academics and the media from the 1970s, such forms of government are not new. Flinders *et al.* (2014) note that there has been a long history of appointed boards in the United Kingdom, and that 'the British political tradition emphasised flexibility and ministerial capacity over constitutional rigidity and rules' (p. 60), so that, for example, in the nineteenth century, for ministers and their officials, they were not so much a problem as a solution to an increasing range of social challenges. The Crown Agents, while privatised in 1997, dated from the mid-nineteenth century, and the Horserace Totaliser Board (the Tote) was established in 1928, although it was privatised in 2011. Similarly, the potential value of such bodies to governments is such that even during one of the main periods of government growth, the Fulton Committee (1968), reporting on the civil service, suggested that further consideration should be given to the hiving-off of functions to non-departmental organisations, a practice that has ebbed and flowed somewhat in the period since then.

Skelcher (1998) identified three phases of growth of arm's-length bodies in the twentieth century. Up to the 1950s, appointed bodies were generally used to manage public enterprise in the form of public corporations, such as the BBC and the Forestry Commission. In the 1960s and 1970s the approach was extended to incorporate 'key interests' into tripartite boards involving government, employers and unions, reflecting the shift towards a more corporatist model of decision making (see Chapter 3). During the Conservative governments of the 1980s, despite an initial concern to reduce the number of 'quangos', as noted above with regard to the Pliatzky report, a more 'business-like' model developed, reflecting not only the idea of public managerialism at arm's length, but also an influx of business representatives onto the boards of many organisations. This was stimulated in large part by a report by Robin Ibbs (1988), then Head of the Efficiency Unit in the Cabinet Office, *Improving Management in Government: The Next Steps*, which suggested a clearer differentiation between policy making and policy implementation and recommended that the parts of departments responsible for implementation should be given greater autonomy in the form of 'executive agencies' (sometimes referred to as 'Next Steps agencies'). This saw the creation of agencies for which governments established the broad parameters of policy, while the agencies took responsibility for delivery (Jordan, 1995; Judge, 2005). The types of activity undertaken by arm's-length bodies can therefore be seen to vary considerably with changing government priorities and approaches, so that while the demise of nationalised industries and the reduction in direct government intervention in the economy saw activity in those fields significantly reduce, there was an expansion of the numbers and activities of bodies involved in regulatory activities and in areas of social provision, including education and health.

By the 1970s, the perceived growth in the number and scope of such organisations was giving cause for concern, and was highlighted in academic work, by politicians and in the media. As noted earlier, soon after her election in 1979, Margaret Thatcher made clear her intention to reduce the numbers, power and costs of arm's-length bodies. However, changes in the use of arm's-length government, along with the definitional and classificatory difficulties discussed above, meant that it was possible for the Conservative governments of the time to argue that they had reduced the number of non-departmental public bodies (see Figure 7.2), while simultaneously critics were claiming that the number of arm's-length bodies had increased and that expenditure by them had grown from £42 billion in 1978–79 to £60 billion in 1994–95 (Hall and Weir, 1996). There are a number of explanations for these developments, including changes in the nature of the work undertaken by these bodies, so that with the demise of the nationalised industries and the reduction in direct state intervention in the economy, activity in this field was significantly reduced, but at the same time there was an increase in the use of arm's-length government in the fields of education, health and housing, not least as part of the shift from 'government' to 'governance' and the Conservatives' desire to hive off what they saw as 'non-essential' tasks to private and not-for-profit organisations (Gash *et al.*, 2010), which

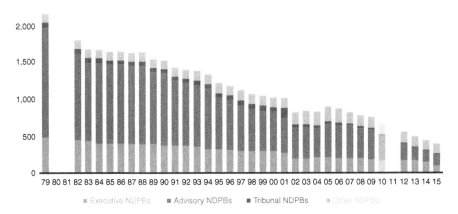

Figure 7.2 Number of non-departmental public bodies, 1979–2015

Source: Freeguard, G., Andrews, E., Devine, D., Munro, R. and Randall, J. (2015) *Whitehall Monitor 2015: The Coalition in 163 Charts*, London: Institute for Government, p. 11 (reproduced with permission from the Institute for Government, copyright © Institute for Government).

they also suggested might have the specialist expertise to undertake such functions. The greater use of policy instruments such as privatisation, internal markets, contracting out and deregulation saw new arm's-length-type bodies come into being in some areas, and also required that regulatory bodies be set up to monitor the operation and standards in services that had previously been state-run, including the creation of bodies such as Ofgas (later incorporated into Ofgem), Ofwat and Oftel (later becoming part of Ofcom), with Howlett (2011) noting that quangos and agencies as an organisational tool were useful in attempts to create some market mechanisms where there was not a competitive marketplace. In addition, as with governments before and since, the Conservatives used arm's-length bodies as a mechanism to bypass local government, enabling them to put their policies into practice without having to encounter direct opposition at the local level. The creation of bodies such as locally managed schools, Economic Development Agencies and housing associations therefore arguably enabled the government to keep a tighter rein on both policy direction and expenditure, because, rather than being funded by local authorities, they were directly funded by central government (Burnham and Horton, 2013). Finally, the creation of executive agencies is straightforward in the UK, in comparison with many European states, where legislation would be required for change on the scale of the UK (Pollitt, 2007).

Under the Labour governments from 1997 there was some reduction in the total number of NDPBs (a fall from 305 in 1997 to 192 in 2009 (although see Dorey, 2014), with a part of that fall being a result of devolution and some NDPBs moving from being the responsibility of Westminster to the devolved legislatures. However, there was a continued increase in the levels of expenditure going through them (from £22.4 billion in 1997 to £46.5 billion in 2009) (Flinders et al., 2014), together with the creation of many new arm's-length bodies, some of which reflected long-established functions, such as the Independent Police Complaints Commission, which replaced the Police Complaints Authority in 2002, but some of which were associated with Labour's flagship policies, such as the New Opportunities Fund, the Youth Justice Board and the Low Pay Commission. From 2003 to 2007 there was something of a period of rationalisation, although a number of proposals for reform of specific bodies were not taken forward, and the National Audit Office (2010) noted that much of the restructuring of that period had not been carefully planned.

Arm's-length government since 2010

The Coalition, and the following Conservative governments, argued that public functions should in general be undertaken by a body that is democratically accountable at either local or national level, and should only exist as an arm's-length body if it met one of three tests: it performs a technical function; its activities require political impartiality; or it needs to act independently to publish facts (for example, Cabinet Office, 2015). The Coalition government announced a review of a range of 901 arm's-length bodies, with the initial objectives being stated as to improve accountability of ministers to Parliament by bringing functions back into their departments, and to contribute to reductions in public expenditure, although it rapidly became clear that both the motives and the results were more mixed (for example, Public Administration Committee, 2011a). The review announced that 192 of these bodies would cease to exist, while a further 181 would be merged with other public bodies and 171 would be substantially reformed, although most of the functions would continue to be carried out, usually within departments. Following the Public Bodies Act 2011, by the end of December 2013 there were 283 fewer bodies as a result of the government's reforms (National Audit Office, 2014b) (see Table 7.1 for the Home Office's non-departmental public bodies following the review). The government also introduced triennial review for non-departmental public bodies, intended to gather evidence on them and to challenge whether functions continue to be needed or whether alternative models of delivery might be appropriate. Although recognising some benefits, the Public Administration Committee (2011b) was critical of the review on a number of fronts, including the criteria (or lack of them) used, and the lack of consultation, while Flinders and Skelcher (2012) have pointed out that simply abolishing bodies without abolishing their functions does not of itself save money, and that there may even be unexpected costs.

The lack of consistency highlighted by many critics clearly continued. For example, while *Public Bodies 2015* (Cabinet Office, 2015) showed that as at 31 March 2015 there were 146 advisory NDPBs, 111 executive NDPBs, 42 executive agencies, 23 non-ministerial departments, 13 tribunal NDPBs and 133 other NDPBs, the number of NDPBs varied widely by department, with, for example, the Department for International Development and the Treasury each having only two (one advisory and one executive each), while the Ministry of Justice had 199 (60 advisory, seven executive and 132 other).

Indeed, the Coalition government was also not immune from the creation of new organisations, with the Office of Budget Responsibility being an obvious and important example. Some commentators also raised questions about whether there was any significant improvement in accountability or significant savings in terms of expenditure. The National Audit Office (2014b) reported that many of the bodies that were proposed for abolition had incurred no spending in 2009–10 and that more than half were advisory, rather than having executive functions. The government's reforms also excluded the Department of Health, and because of that NHS England, described by Rutter (2014), following the Health and Social Care Act 2012, as 'the mother of all NDPBs' (p. 150), which is important as the NHS in England is effectively run by arm's-length bodies. Walker (2014) highlights three 'giant' quangos in the NHS, adding Monitor (which then became part of NHS Improvement in 2016) and the Care Quality Commission (responsible for regulating health and social care in England), and the many other bodies, such as clinical commissioning groups and foundation trusts, with the role of the Secretary of State limited to setting its objectives, determining the size of its budget and then holding others to account for performance. The growth of academies in education also resulted in a significant fall in the proportion of the Department for Education's spending through grants to local authorities, and a shift towards the direct funding of schools.

The 111 executive NDPBs employed almost 77,000 staff and were responsible for total government spending of more than £18 billion (in addition to NHS England with its budget of around £100 billion), and total spending of over £22 billion (Cabinet Office, 2015). The 42 executive agencies employed more than 110,000 staff and were responsible for more than £76 billion of government spending (of which £59 billion went on education and skills through the Education Funding Agency and the Skills Funding Agency) and total spending of nearly £79 billion. The non-ministerial departments accounted for much lower levels of spending (£2.3 billion of government funding and £3.1 billion overall), but still employed more than 26,000 staff.

However, Flinders and Tonkiss (2016) have argued that more significant than the structural reforms was the increase in the capacity of departments to control their non-departmental public bodies, driven by the Cabinet Office. This included a new controls framework, which Flinders and Tonkiss suggest includes much tighter operational control (see also Dommett and Flinders, 2014), and also the new triennial review procedure, which questions both the governance of each public body and also whether the functions still need to be provided at arm's length. However, they also note that this new approach has been restricted to the relatively narrow sphere of non-departmental public bodies, rather than being rolled out to the full range of arm's-length organisations. Dommett and Flinders argue that while the government emphasised control, it underplayed order in its reforms. Similarly, Dommett and MacCarthaigh (2016) suggest that despite the Coalition government's reforms there is a need for further progress, including in regulating the full range of arm's-length bodies, ensuring the efficient and effective management of agencies by their sponsor departments while balancing central control and agency autonomy, and ensuring coordination across the complex environment.

Table 7.1 Home Office non-departmental public bodies, December 2015

Name	Type	Description
Advisory Council on the Misuse of Drugs (ACMD)	Advisory	Advisory, statutory, NDPB as constituted under the Misuse of Drugs Act 1971.
Animals in Science Committee (ASC)	Advisory	To advise the Secretaries of State for the Home Office and the Northern Ireland Office on their duties under the terms of the Animals (Scientific Procedures) Act 1986 as amended. It is also responsible for exchanging information with similar EU National Committees in other member states and sharing best practice within the EU on the operation of animal welfare bodies.
Disclosure and Barring Service	Executive	Provides criminal records checks and barring decisions.
Gangmasters Licensing Authority	Executive	The GLA operates a licensing scheme that regulates businesses that provide workers to the fresh produce supply chain and horticulture industry, to make sure they meet the employment standards required by law. It also enforces the criminal offences in the Gangmasters Licensing Act 2004 on behalf of the Home Office.
Independent Police Complaints Commission (IPCC)	Executive	Has a dual purpose to act as an overall guardian ensuring the effectiveness and efficiency of the operation of the whole police complaints system and also to take a role in individual cases.
Investigatory Powers Tribunal	Tribunal	A statutory body established to consider proceedings brought under Section 7 of the Human Rights Act 1998 (HRA) against the intelligence services and certain public authorities in respect of their investigatory powers and conduct. To investigate complaints regarding actions by those intelligence services and public authorities who hold powers under the Regulation of Investigatory Powers Act 2000 to ascertain whether they have used those powers lawfully.
Migration Advisory Committee	Advisory	Provides independent, evidence-based advice to government on migration, particularly shortages in the labour market where migration can contribute.
National Crime Agency Remuneration Review Body (NCARRB)	Advisory	Makes independent recommendations to the government on the pay and allowances of National Crime Agency (NCA) officers designated with operational powers. These officers are subject to legislative restrictions on industrial action.
National DNA Database Ethics Group (NDNADEG)	Advisory	To provide independent advice on ethical issues around the operations of the National DNA Database.

Office of Surveillance Commissioners	Tribunal	To keep under review public authority use of covert techniques under the Regulation of Investigatory Powers Act, the Regulation of Investigatory Powers (Scotland) Act and the Police Act.
Office of the Immigration Services Commissioner	Executive	To regulate those who provide immigration advice and services by promoting good practice and investigating complaints.
Police Advisory Board of England and Wales	Advisory	Discusses matters other than those relating to police pay and conditions; provides advice to the Home Secretary on matters related to policing.
Police Discipline Appeals Tribunal	Tribunal	To consider appeals by police officers against decisions taken in relation to misconduct or unsatisfactory performance procedures.
Security Industry Authority (SIA)	Executive	Responsible for regulating the private security industry. It is an independent body reporting to the Home Secretary, under the terms of the Private Security Industry Act 2001.
Technical Advisory Board	Advisory	To advise the Home Secretary on whether obligations imposed on communications service providers under the terms of the Regulation of Investigatory Powers Act 2000 (RIPA) are reasonable.

Source: Cabinet Office (2015) 'Public bodies 2015 data directory update as at 31 December 2015', https://www.gov.uk/government/publications/public-bodies-2015, accessed 20 May 2016.

This gave the agencies a considerable amount of freedom, and also enabled governments to distance themselves from unpopular decisions while still being able to take the credit for success. It tended to fit well with specialist functions, such as the UK Atomic Energy Authority and the Forestry Commission, and with the NHS, where despite the emphasis on a national service, the scale meant that there was an argument for some degree of more devolved management. At the same time, these changes also meant that policy delivery was increasingly moved into the hands of unelected, professionally dominated and largely unaccountable elite groups, made it easier for the incorporation of private sector ideas and indeed provision into service delivery, and eased policy making and implementation more towards the domain of policy networks and inter-agency negotiation (Hudson and Lowe, 2009).

Dommett and Flinders (2015) suggest that the Coalition government's anti-quango stance was more measured and reflective than had been that of the Conservative government in 1979, but conclude that at the level of meta-governance ('the governance of governance' (p. 2)) the Coalition government largely failed to reform or address key concerns about the architecture of the state.

As noted above, there are also large numbers of bodies at the local level, including in education, health care, housing and social care, that display arm's-length characteristics, in that they operate with varying degrees of independence from the formal structures of local democratic control, a considerable number of which have been created by the hiving-off of functions from local authorities to single-purpose bodies with independent governing arrangements, particularly in education and housing (Wilks-Heeg *et al.*, 2012). And, at the regional level, while the Coalition government removed some arm's-length bodies in England, such as the Regional Development Agencies, it also created new unelected ones, such as the Local Enterprise Partnerships, which are partnerships between the private sector and local authorities that are intended to steer economic growth strategically in their areas and were responsible for spending up to £12 billion of the Local Growth Fund for 2015–16 to 2020–21 (see, for example, National Audit Office, 2016b).

Arm's-length bodies and devolved government

In the early days of devolution, Democratic Audit raised concerns about the role of unelected bodies in sub-national governance (Weir and Hall, 1999; Beetham *et al.*, 2002), and in 2012 they returned to that topic (Wilks-Heeg *et al.*, 2012). While each of the devolved governments has considerable powers over arm's-length bodies, other than those associated with reserved powers (see Chapter 6), Democratic Audit suggest that although there have been reforms in each area, they have not been as substantial as the rhetoric of the parties or governments, and that much of the change, and indeed the reduction of numbers, has been either associated with the amalgamation of some with other non-departmental public bodies, or a result of their reclassification. In Scotland, where a report in 2007 recommended widespread reforms (Crerar Report, 2007), the number of bodies has fallen, from around 180 in 2000 to fewer than 120 in 2016, although some new organisations have also been created. In Wales, where the Assembly was prohibited from abolishing bodies that had been established by royal charter, while the number of executive bodies and levels of expenditure by them have fallen, other bodies have been created, some of which are not included in official lists (Wilks-Heeg *et al.*, 2012). In Northern Ireland, until devolution, many public services had been delivered either through the Northern Ireland Office or by executive bodies. Following a review in 2003 (Review of Public Administration, 2003) there has been a significant reduction in the number of arm's-length bodies, although this has to a considerable extent been achieved through the creation of what Wilks-Heeg *et al.* (2012) describe as 'super-quangos'.

Of course, as in England, arm's-length bodies are also used at the local level in the devolved administrations. For example, the Scottish Parliament's Local Government and Regeneration Committee (2016) has examined 'arm's length external organisations' (ALEOs), which were defined as formally separate from a council but subject to its control and influence. The report noted the considerable increase in ALEOs from the 1980s, and highlighted the lack of a legal definition of ALEOs and consequent confusion as to the levels of reporting by the organisations and of scrutiny and monitoring by councils, while the fact that some ALEOs are also charities made those organisations subject to charities legislation and further disagreement over their status. The Committee recommended greater clarity over classification, explicitly linked to form and function, more emphasis by local authorities on monitoring service performance, and suggested that those who work for ALEOs should not be employed on pay and conditions inferior to those who work directly for councils. It also noted concerns that the use of ALEOs made the organisations less accountable to local communities.

The uses and abuses of arm's-length government

Given the developments outlined above, it is unsurprising that the approach to arm's-length bodies in the United Kingdom is often described as '*ad hoc*' (for example, Burnham and Horton, 2013), and this has arguably led to a more complex and less comprehensible system than might have been the case with greater planning and consistency.

Nevertheless, cogent arguments can be deployed not just against the use of arm's-length bodies in policy making and implementation, but also in support of them (see Table 7.2). Indeed, while all of the major parties have criticised them, they have also made use of them when it has suited them, and, as Hogwood (1995) pointed out, our perspective on such bodies tends to vary with the issue. Unsurprisingly, therefore, it remains the case that arm's-length government is an important feature of British government, and that it continues to play a significant role, including in relation to the delivery of services at local and national levels.

One of the issues arising from these shifts is that the actual process of governing becomes more complex and fragmented because of the number of organisations involved, lending further credence to network approaches which emphasise such characteristics, and those that move away from simplistic top-down models of the policy process (see Chapter 3), and can lead to challenges in relation to implementation, with attempts to put policy into practice being hindered even by relatively small differences in focus among a number of organisations responsible for it (see Chapter 2).

The dominant perspective sees arm's-length government resulting from a political principal passing some of their authority to an administrative agent that then has some discretion in how it is exercised (see Chapter 2). That can be seen as having a number of potential advantages: from the perspective of the principal it may improve their political security by producing ties of mutual obligation; it may also enhance the deliverability of the principal's goals by emphasising political responsiveness over neutral competence in bureaucrat recruitment. However, Howlett (2011) notes that there can also be significant principal-agent problems, with Koppell (2003), for example, suggesting that in the USA 'hybrids' may be less reliable as agents than traditional government agencies. In addition, maintaining the arm's-length relationship can be difficult, and agencies may not have sufficient autonomy for governments to avoid the consequences of scandals or other problems associated with them – so the relationships can become too close (so that there is day-to-day interference) or too distant (with agencies becoming powers unto themselves). Howlett also points out that many agencies do not have to face market discipline in terms of expectations of profitability, and may therefore not act in a cost-efficient manner.

However, for many the major issues with arm's-length government relate to the accountability of such organisations, and, to a lesser but still significant extent, to the system of appointments with the associated questions over patronage and a lack of diversity among appointees, as discussed further below.

Accountability and the democratic deficit

One of the key concerns about the use of arm's-length government mechanisms is the extent to which they are accountable and subject to democratic control. Even in 1979, Chester argued strongly that:

> the growth of fringe bodies is a retreat from the simple democratic principle evolved in the nineteenth century that those who perform a public duty should be fully responsible to the electorate – by way either of a minister responsible to Parliament or of a locally elected council. The essence of the fringe body is that it is not so responsible for some or all of its actions.
>
> (p. 54)

Since then, arm's-length government has become, in many respects, more open and less secretive than it was, with clearer requirements to publish information such as the agendas and minutes of meetings and registers of members' interests, while some have sought to go beyond the minimum

Table 7.2   Arguments for and against the use of arm's-length bodies

Arguments for arm's-length government:	Arguments against arm's-length government:
allows particular expertise to be brought into government;	allows representative government to be bypassed;
speeds decision making by reducing the overload of information that can occur at the upper reaches of a centralised hierarchy;	can reduce the opportunities for economies of scale and for uniform national levels of service;
decisions made closer to the users of a service are more likely to be responsive to their needs and can reflect local and regional differences;	can blur lines of accountability and place functions in the hands of unelected, sometimes unaccountable individuals;
encourages innovation as ideas do not have to be approved centrally;	the democratic deficit undermines the legitimacy of elected tiers of government;
can depoliticise decision making, with judgements about the application and interpretation of policy being made by individuals who are independent of government;	can make the coordination of policies and programmes more difficult;
single-purpose boards offer potential for focus on specific policies, and tasks which may be inappropriate for political control, such as the BBC;	the role of elected politicians is constrained by distancing themselves from some fields of governmental decision making;
can allow stakeholders to be brought onto the board in a way that may not be possible in representative government;	depoliticising decision making can allow politicians to distance themselves from potentially unpopular decisions;
policy implementation may be enhanced where those who are responsible are sympathetic to the policies;	there is a frequent lack of rationale for the allocation of executive functions between elected and appointed bodies;
delegation of authority reduced demands on centres of elected decision making;	the number of bodies can cause problems of coordination, strategic and joined-up government;
allows for greater recognition of local contexts and differences;	claims of independence can be undermined by the potential for political bias in appointments;
can allow large numbers of people to take part in public life, with the great majority being unpaid volunteers.	certain groups may dominate and others may lose out among patronage posts.

Source: Adapted from Skelcher, C. (1998) *The Appointed State*, Buckingham: Open University Press, p. 179, and Pollitt, C. (2016b) 'Decentralized management: agencies and "arm's-length bodies", in Bovaird, T. and Loëffler, E. (eds) *Public Management and Governance*, Abingdon: Routledge.

levels of transparency required of them. However, the use of arm's-length bodies has continued to grow, and there are frequent arguments made that the degrees of transparency and accountability vary considerably across arm's-length bodies, with the Public Administration Committee's

(2014) call for an online 'Directory of Governance' to include annual reports, minutes of meetings and other information being one example (see also Gash *et al.*, 2010). It is unsurprising that such criticisms have continued to be raised, including by Hall and Weir (1996), Gash *et al.* (2010) and the Public Administration Committee (2014). While it is certainly true that there are a variety of mechanisms for regulating and holding accountable arm's-length bodies, including their contractual agreements and obligations, investigations by parliamentary select committees, auditors and ombudsmen, as well as the courts, in addition to the role sometimes played by the media in taking up such issues, it equally remains the case that these are not applied rigorously or consistently. Even within Parliament, while departmental select committees, the Public Accounts Committee and the Public Administration and Constitutional Affairs Committee can all undertake some investigations, there is no mechanism to enable Parliament to take a strategic view of the development and actions of arm's-length bodies (Public Administration Committee, 2014; see also Gash *et al.*, 2010). Building on its 2011 report *Smaller Government: Shrinking the Quango State*, the Public Administration Select Committee (2014) has argued that:

> [o]rganisational forms and names are inconsistent. Most public bodies answer to Ministers but some are directly accountable to Parliament. There is no agreement on how many types of body exist. There are overlaps and blurring between categories. Accountability arrangements and reforms so far have been ad hoc.
>
> (p. 3)

The Committee went on to argue for a clear taxonomy of public bodies: constitutional bodies, independent public interest bodies, departmental sponsored bodies and executive agencies. It suggested that all public bodies should only sit in one category, so that it is clear how it is governed and sponsored, and that, in turn, would help clarify accountability. The Committee also considered the appointment of individuals to the boards of public bodies, and called on the government to clarify which appointments are regulated by the Commissioner for Public Appointments and which are not, and the reasons for those decisions. In terms of accountability (see Table 7.3), the Committee suggested that mechanisms might include:

➤ responding to parliamentary questions;

➤ giving evidence to select committees, pre-appointment and post-appointment hearings by select committees;

➤ publishing or laying before Parliament an annual report and accounts;

➤ publishing a register of members' interests;

➤ agreeing strategic objectives and performance targets and corporate plans with the sponsor department;

➤ holding board meetings in public and making minutes available;

➤ making media appearances and answering journalists' questions;

➤ listening to the views of the public and stakeholders and taking these views into account.

This would reflect different levels of accountability: to Parliament, to the sponsor department, to the media and to the public.

Following calls by some for the creation of bodies to be for a fixed term, with automatic abolition, or at least a major review (Gash *et al.*, 2010), the introduction of triennial reviews for non-departmental public bodies by the Coalition government was seen by many as a positive step, although it was not extended to non-ministerial departments, executive agencies, NHS bodies or other such organisations, while Rutter *et al.* have identified a number of other ways in which the relationships between departments and arm's-length bodies could be improved, including improving the quality of sponsorship by departments and using more contractual relationships for smaller bodies (Rutter *et al.*, 2012a).

Table 7.3 Accountability tensions between public bodies and government

Greater focus if a function is performed in a separate body	⇔	Greater potential for coordinated working if a function is performed in a central government department
Public bodies take responsibility for their own work in the event of failure	⇔	Greater ministerial control if a function is performed centrally
The desire for simplicity and greater public understanding	⇔	Adapting to the particular circumstances and complexities of a sector
Strong and close relationships between central government departments and public bodies	⇔	Seeking challenge and scrutiny
Having expertise and specialists in public bodies	⇔	Retaining expertise in departments, so that Ministers are well informed

Source: Public Administration Committee (2014) *Who's Accountable? Relationships between Government and Arm's-Length Bodies*, London: The Stationery Office, p. 6.

One response to issues of accountability, particularly from those who favour market-type approaches, has been to suggest that arm's-length bodies often offer accountability to customers, so that in the case of academy schools, or contracted-out local authorities, people may be able to make alternative choices. It is also possible to argue (from a broadly pluralist perspective) that the system of appointment to arm's-length bodies may enable the participation of actors who might otherwise be marginalised, for example, through the incorporation of representatives of particular interests, or due to a specific functional responsibility, such as the Equalities and Human Rights Commission in the UK. However, such choice, or other forms of redress, may not always be available, while these arguments also neglect accountability to citizens as a whole through representative institutions.

Taking a rather different approach, Durose *et al.* (2015) seek to challenge the idea that arm's-length government necessarily involves a democratic deficit. While they recognise some of the criticisms that arise from the delegation of functions by politicians to agencies, they suggest that rather than the traditional state-centric approach that is associated with such views, it is possible to develop a polycentric and pluralist model that emphasises local self-determination rather than the central state as its starting point (for example, Ostrom, 1990), with many centres of decision making capable of recognising the preferences of smaller communities. They argue that this 'offers the possibility of simultaneously accomplishing both democracy and efficiency in public administration' (p. 142) because 'it enables the specific needs of individuals and groups to be met while at the same time enabling that community to see itself in relation to others and to the wider polity' (p. 143). As illustrations of how this might work with arm's-length bodies, they suggest examples of 'private government', such as residential community associations (sometimes called homeowners' associations) from the United States, and free schools from England, which they suggest can enhance democracy by enabling the specific needs of individuals and groups within a self-identifying community to be met, and also enabling that community to see itself in relation to others and the broader polity (Durose *et al.*, 2015). However, they also recognise that if the public are to be encouraged to participate in arm's-length government then institutional design is crucial (see also, John, 2009), with citizens subscribing to the philosophy of civic republicanism and the creation of 'popular' spaces that can be organised and let by citizens. Importantly, of course, such an approach would require a significant shift away from traditional ideas of arm's-length government having powers delegated from while being accountable to representative institutions, but it does reflect other wider debates about changing forms of democracy and the development of forms of direct and deliberative democracy.

Finally, particularly for those arm's-length bodies that are responsible for delivering services, it is possible to identify other models, with the Public Chairs' Forum (2010) suggesting: employee mutualism, moving the activity outside the public sector; moving activities entirely to the private sector through selling or transferring staff and assets; establishing joint ventures between arm's-length bodies and the private sector; or simply outsourcing the activity to the private sector. However, there remain a number of barriers to such shifts, including the challenges in adopting alternative models and the relative lack of examples of best practice that might be shared, and the concerns of departments that might be risk averse (for example, Tonkiss and Noonan, 2013).

Appointments

Appointments (and indeed re-appointments) to arm's-length bodies have also been a significant point of criticism, with external scrutiny having in the past been very limited. Following concerns in the mid-1990s about the behaviour of politicians and some quango appointments, the Committee on Standards in Public Life (1995) set out seven principles of public life (selflessness, integrity, objectivity, accountability, openness, honesty and leadership) and made a number of recommendations about appointments, one of which was for a Commissioner to monitor, regulate and approve departmental procedures, while another was that appointment should be on merit. In 1995, the first Commissioner for Public Appointments was appointed, and since then they have had a responsibility for regulating some appointments, independent appointments commissions have been created (such as the Judicial Appointments Commission and the NHS Appointments Commission) and Parliament has held pre-appointment hearings for some posts since 2007, although a recommendation from the Liaison Committee in 2011 that Parliament's role be increased somewhat was rejected by the government. Over time, therefore, the discretion of ministers in relation to appointments has become more limited (Flinders and Geddes, 2014).

While there have been improvements in the system of appointments to the boards of many arm's-length bodies, including the advertising of vacancies, job descriptions, application forms and requirements to observe equal opportunities practices, the Public Administration Committee (2014) has nevertheless concluded that '[p]ublic appointments are not sufficiently transparent, representative or accountable' (p. 27), and recommended greater clarity over who is involved in an appointment, that it should be made clear to appointees whether their appointment is for one or more terms, and that organisations should seek out able people from under-represented backgrounds and groups. In relation to that final point, although there has been progress in increasing the diversity of the people who fill public appointments, they remain somewhat unrepresentative of the wider population. In 2015–16, the Commissioner for Public Appointments (2016) reported that 47 per cent of appointees were women (up from 46 per cent the previous year, although the percentage of chair appointments that were women fell from 36 per cent to 23 per cent). Following something of a trend in recent years, the proportion of appointees from black and minority ethnic communities reached over 10 per cent for the first time in 2015–16, although again the proportion of chair appointments fell, from 8 per cent to 5 per cent. The proportion of appointments of disabled people remained at around 4 per cent. Around 30 per cent of appointments were people aged 66 or over, while only just over 10 per cent were under 45.

Conclusion

Arm's-length bodies continue to play important roles in many areas of public policy, despite considerable concerns about accountability and transparency, and the promises of politicians of all parties to reduce the use of such organisations, particularly while in opposition. The widespread, *ad hoc* and inconsistent use of such organisations by governments also fits with ideas about the complexity of the policy process, and can perhaps best be understood using a variety of analytical approaches. For example, their existence can be seen as creating additional power centres which may be available to interest groups, although at the same time they can be shown to be diverting power away from representative institutions. It is also helpful to be able to draw upon institutional approaches to the policy process, as well as those that highlight the complexity of decision making and implementation, such as policy networks, while, for some larger bodies and those that deliver services, analysis might usefully draw on ideas about the power of bureaucratic institutions and street-level bureaucrats. The risks and benefits of arm's-length government can also be better understood through the application of ideas such as interest representation on the one hand and co-option and agenda setting on the other.

As noted above, it is possible to build arguments both for and against the continued use of arm's-length bodies. In many respects they are valuable, not least for bringing expertise to bear on particular policy areas, for being able to bring together a range of interests, and in some instances for enabling decisions to be made away from the mainstream political arena. Arm's-length objectivity is also particularly important in the quasi-judicial role played by tribunals. However, the weaker standards of accountability of many arm's-length bodies to elected representative institutions is inevitably a cause for concern, along with other aspects of the 'democratic deficit', including the lack of clarity and scrutiny of many appointments to boards, and the continuing unrepresentativeness of appointees. While the value of arm's-length bodies means that they are likely to continue to play a significant role in public policy, so too do their shortcomings mean that debates about openness, transparency and accountability will persist.

It is also worth noting that whatever the motivation for delegation to quasi-independent bodies, the result is to reframe certain classes of decision as technical in nature, and thus best determined by experts, rather than being matters of contestation in the political process, and that this can be seen as fitting with the broad acceptance of new public management ideas that promote the withdrawal of politicians from detailed involvement in policy domains.

Further reading

The work of parliamentary select committees provides some of the best information on arm's-length government, including:

Public Administration Committee (2011a) *Smaller Government: Shrinking the Quango State*, London: The Stationery Office.

Public Administration Committee (2014) *Who's Accountable? Relationships between Government and Arm's-Length Bodies*, London: The Stationery Office.

For consideration of the impact of the Coalition government's reform programme for public bodies, see:

National Audit Office (2014b) *Progress on Public Bodies Reform*, London: The Stationery Office.

For an assessment of the state of democracy in the United Kingdom, including some of the accountability challenges associated with arm's-length bodies, refer to:

Wilks-Heeg, S., Blick, A. and Crone, S. (2012) *How Democratic Is the UK? The 2012 Audit*, Liverpool: Democratic Audit.

For a comparative perspective, see:

Verhoest, K., Van Thiel, S., Bouckaert, G. and Laegreid, P. (eds) (2011) *Government Agencies: Practices and Lessons from 30 Countries*, Basingstoke: Palgrave Macmillan.

8
Evaluating Policy

While the importance of policy evaluation has in the past sometimes been underplayed, particularly by governments (and sometimes for understandable reasons), but also occasionally by academics and others, it is an important part of the policy process, and indeed the extent to which policies do or do not achieve their goals is clearly linked to many of the other topics in this book.

This chapter therefore discusses why there is a need for policy evaluation, approaches to and methods and techniques of policy evaluation, and some of the problems and challenges associated with policy evaluation. It also considers tools such as audit and inspection, which have been widely used by governments in recent years, although arguably as much as management mechanisms as to inform the assessment and future development of policy.

The monitoring and evaluation of policies have long been seen as a key element of the policy process (for example, Davies *et al.*, 2000a; Hogwood and Gunn, 1984; Pollitt *et al.*, 1979), particularly for judging the degree of success or failure of policies, and for feeding back into the formulation and implementation of new or revised policies, and in recent years the emphasis on this has grown further (for example, Howlett *et al.*, 2009; Knill and Tosun, 2012; Palfrey *et al.*, 2012; Parsons, 2017), linked not only to concern about the effectiveness (or otherwise) of policies and the much wider use of performance management tools, but also to the greater emphasis on the use of evidence in policy development (see Chapter 4).

If decisions are made and policies developed that are aimed at achieving particular goals, it would seem natural and appropriate that those who make those decisions, at whatever tier of government, would wish to determine the effects of their decisions or actions. However, as much of this book illustrates, the policy process is complex, there are many different competing and even contradictory pressures, and, as a result, the practice of evaluation is often not straightforward, if indeed it happens at all. Even as new policies are being devised, the social, political and economic environment within which they are intended to have an impact is likely to be changing, and that in turn will affect their implementation and any outcomes, as well as potentially the desire and priorities of policy makers in terms of evaluation. In addition, policies impact on other policies, and will sometimes create new and unanticipated problems, which then also need to be addressed. Given these challenges, it is perhaps not surprising that there are significant and growing literatures on policy failure (for example, Bovens *et al.*, 2001; King and Crewe, 2013; Dunlop, 2017a and 2017b), and on policy success (for example, Bovens *et al.*, 2001; Prasser, 2006; McConnell, 2010), discussed further in the following section. However, it is also the case that many policies remain unevaluated, that much of the assessment of the extent of success or failure of policies remains anecdotal, and much of the policy evaluation that does take place stems from the initiatives of academics and pressure groups, rather than being systematic evaluation planned as part of the decision-making process by the organisations responsible for formulating and implementing policies, as implied by rational decision-making models. Because of this, the coverage of policy areas is inevitably haphazard.

The evaluation of policy inevitably involves a judgement on what has gone before or what is taking place, with a variety of approaches outlined later in this chapter. When rational decision making was becoming more common during the 1960s there was an increase in the attention paid to evaluation, although the emphasis tended to be on resource allocation and effectiveness, rather than on policy impact. For a period from 1979, it might be argued that the nature and emphasis of evaluation, at least by government, changed somewhat, with a greater focus on monitoring and measuring performance, and on efficiency, effectiveness and economy. Following their return to government in 1997, Labour ostensibly placed greater emphasis upon evidence, including the greater use of policy pilots (for example, Bochel and Duncan, 2007; Hudson and Lowe, 2009; see also Chapter 4), although they also maintained and developed the use of targets and performance measures, albeit largely as tools for directing the implementation of policy, as with attempts to measure the performance of schools, hospitals and councils, rather than for assessing the extent of success. From 2010, while the Coalition and Conservative governments continued to pay lip-service to the use of evidence, the extent of this varied across policy areas (Bochel, 2016), with evaluation largely being associated with measurement of performance; however, they did, for example, make use of policy pilots in a range of areas, as well as evaluating a number of behaviour change initiatives (as discussed in Chapter 4). Another way of considering change over time is posited by Howlett *et al.* (2009), who suggest that at one stage evaluation was grounded in positivist approaches, with a view that it could be systematic, objective, empirical and rational, but that it began to be recognised that policy evaluation is more contentious than such a picture suggests, so that there has been a move towards 'post-positivist policy evaluation' (p. 178), with the awareness that the same policy can be evaluated very differently by different people, and that the interpretation of the success of a policy depends on a range of political factors, so that it may be appropriate to view evaluation as part of a process of policy learning (Grin and Loeber, 2007), which may also have benefits in engaging policy makers and others, as with lesson-drawing (Rose, 1991).

One way of considering different types of evaluation is to begin with the evaluators, and for Howlett *et al.* (2009) this leads to the identification of three broad categories:

➤ *administrative evaluation* – normally undertaken within government or its agencies, or commissioned by them. This frequently focuses on efficiency and the achievement of value for money, and can take a variety of forms, with inspection having become a significant mechanism, along with attempts to encourage public participation in the evaluation process;

➤ *judicial evaluation* – concerned with the legal issues relating to the implementation of government policies, and whether they meet constitutional or other established standards of administrative conduct and individual rights, including judicial review (see Chapter 5);

➤ *political evaluation* – which according to Howlett *et al.* (2009) is 'usually neither systematic nor technically sophisticated …[. M]any are inherently partisan, one-sided and biased' (p. 189). It includes the work of many think tanks as well as consultations with members of relevant policy subsystems, such as special consultative committees and taskforces, and parliamentary oversight committees.

Palfrey *et al.* (2012) suggest that it is also worth considering what is being evaluated: a *project* – a particular activity designed to achieve particular goals within a given period; a *programme* – a set of separate planned activities brought together into a coherent group; or a *policy* – a broader statement of how a government or organisation would respond to particular eventualities; although this leads to questions about how each of those can be identified, and, as discussed elsewhere in this book, such distinctions are not always clear.

Policy failure and policy success

As noted above, the literature on policy success is relatively sparse compared with that on policy failure (McConnell, 2010). However, much of the work that has focused on failure has arguably been more concerned with examining established failures and why policies have failed, rather than considering how 'failure' might relate to the aims of a policy in the first place. In one of the best known and most substantial contributions, Bovens and 't Hart analysed 26 cases of what they believed were 'clear-cut policy fiascoes' (1996, p. ii) across a range of policy areas and liberal democracies. They sought to look empirically at inherent reasons why policies might fail, and that if the reasons were more case-specific than general, that might be used to support arguments for government actions in the face of neo-liberal critiques. They also pointed out that, over time, governments have implemented more and more policies, so that, almost inevitably, more policies would fail, and argued that failure was as much about social expectations and ideological interpretation as a result of substantive shortcomings in the delivery of public services. Given the focus of their research, Bovens and 't Hart were aware that policies were frequently being judged on criteria other than their original aims, and indeed on standards that might have changed considerably from when the policies were devised. It is perhaps unsurprising, therefore, that as their work progressed the focus moved away from an attempt to explain 'fiascoes' (in itself a potentially problematic label) and towards a concern to explain why policy episodes might be constructed as fiascos, which they note are different from failures.

More recently, King and Crewe (2013) have considered 'blunders' of governments in the United Kingdom over a period of 30 years. They differentiate 'blunders' from 'policy disappointments' and mistaken judgements, on the grounds that they completely fail to achieve the objectives, waste considerable sums of public money or cause widespread distress, are eventually abandoned or reversed, and were foreseeable and avoidable. They suggest that blunders occur in the UK for both structural reasons, such as a lack of deliberation and accountability, and behavioural reasons, including ministerial hyper-activity, cultural disconnect (a failure to recognise the values and assumptions of those affected by policies) and operational disconnect (a failure to take account of issues of implementation).

In relation to considerations of policy success and failure, McConnell (2010) has made a significant contribution (see also Marsh and McConnell, 2010), including by proposing a spectrum from 'complete success' to 'complete failure' and different dimensions of policy success. In relation to the latter, he identifies: process success, concerned with the process of policy formulation; programme success, involving assessments based on outcomes and evidence; and political success, including in relation to the capacity to govern. His spectrum from success to failure also includes a number of categories, such as the idea of 'durable' success (where policies more or less achieve what they set out to do and are quite resilient), 'conflicted' success (where the views of supporters and opponents vary considerably, either because there is a considerable departure from the original goals of the policy, or because the issue is intrinsically controversial) and 'precarious' success, where policies are on the edge of failure, deviate significantly from their original goals or display major shortfalls, and where there is conflict over the future of the policy. For McConnell, 'failure' occurs where a policy does not achieve its goals and no longer receives support from its proponents. He recognises that assessments of success and failure are challenging, and that there may be a variety of 'complicating factors', including: success for whom; partial achievement of goals; unintended consequences; difficulties in isolating the effect of one policy; the potential for a lack of evidence; the challenge of potentially multiple and even contradictory objectives; and short-term versus long-term assessments. It might also be argued that McConnell's continuum is actually measuring somewhat different characteristics, so that, for example, a policy that was wholly successful in achieving its intended aims might nevertheless be judged as having conflicted success if it does not become widely accepted.

The Institute for Government has also undertaken work on policy success and failure, drawing to a degree on McConnell's framework (Rutter *et al.*, 2012). It used a definition of success in relation to achieving or exceeding the original goals, becoming embedded and surviving a change of government, representing a starting point for subsequent development, or removing an issue from the agenda. It applied these to six case studies, moving towards a more rigorous application of ideas of success.

Regulation, audit and inspection

Although mechanisms of regulation, audit and inspection have long been among the instruments or tools of government (Lodge and Wegrich, 2012b), they have come to greater prominence in recent decades, not least as they have been used in response to reforms of the public sector that have changed traditional lines of accountability and required different methods of ensuring the quality and appropriateness (and sometimes the price) of provision. Hughes (2012) highlights a number of forms of regulation:

➤ *financial regulation* – including supervision of the banking and financial sector, interest rates, exchange rates and the registration of companies, so that information and standards are set out clearly. The challenges of such regulation became clear with the financial crisis of 2008–09, when inadequate regulation was seen as contributing to the failure of banks and the need for governments to step in and use taxpayers' money to address the crisis;

➤ *restriction on the supply of goods and services* – including allowing or prohibiting activities in the public sector, such as the licensing of broadcasters, regulations around gambling, and regulation of the railways;

➤ *occupational licensing* – as with medicine, dentistry and nursing, and other professions that require a licence to practice;

➤ *standards* – these may range from building standards to food regulation;

➤ *competition policy* – this aims to ensure competition in the private market, for example to prevent cartels and price-fixing, or the creation of monopolies;

➤ *environmental regulation* – from the 1960s, as concern for the environment has grown, so have attempts to regulate the impact of external effects, such as the creation of pollution, through both traditional and newer market-based mechanisms.

Typologies such as this can be helpful when examining the variety of regulatory mechanisms that is used in relation to public services. For example, the privatisation of many former public utilities saw the emergence of a number of regulators, including the Office of Communications (Ofcom), the Office of Gas and Electricity Markets (Ofgem) and the Office of Water Services (Ofwat), and a licensing regime that enables these bodies to set prices and performance standards, to collect financial and performance data, and to provide assurance on the probity and safety record of the companies involved (Burnham and Horton, 2013), as well as seeking to ensure some degree of competition. Such regulation in theory allows the public interest to be represented, in terms of prices and the quality of services, and for operators to make adequate profits, including for re-investment, while keeping the system at arm's length from political interference. However, as noted below, some critics have suggested that regulators can be 'captured', with the needs of the suppliers coming to dominate, so that they may come to see the world through their eyes, rather than from the perspective of consumers (for example, Stigler, 1975).

Away from the economic regulation of the public utilities, regulation, audit and inspection have also become commonplace, with a proliferation of bodies involved in the scrutiny of state, private and third sector organisations that deliver public services. Much of this is often traced back to the attempts by the Thatcher and Major governments in the 1980s and 1990s to reform public services, with government retaining regulatory oversight (Power, 1994), but with no clear rationale or consistency of practice, meaning that there was both complexity and a lack of coordination, although there was something of a trend towards greater prescription in terms of the standards expected (Burnham and Horton, 2013). Under the Labour governments from 1997 to 2010, further new regulatory bodies were created both in specific policy areas, such as health care and teaching, and more generally, as with Best Value reviews, which were applied to local government activities, although towards the end of their period in office there was a shift towards something of a lighter touch approach in some areas. The Coalition government that took office in 2010 sought to reduce some of this regulatory framework, including through a reduction in the use of performance indicators and a claimed 'bonfire of the quangos' (see Chapter 7), although at the same time it introduced policies, such as the spread of academy schools, that in turn required new regulators in the form of the National Schools Commissioner and regional schools commissioners. Despite some claims, it is questionable as to whether there was any significant reduction in the 'regulatory burden' for most providers of public services.

Audit and inspection

Both audit and inspection have a long history in the United Kingdom, with HM Inspectors of Constabulary being created in the 1850s in England and Scotland, and the Comptroller and Auditor General and the Public Accounts Committee in the House of Commons in the 1860s, with the latter having a responsibility for ensuring that government departments spend their money correctly as parliament has allocated it, and in 1983 the National Audit Office was created to support the Comptroller and Auditor General (see Chapter 5). Northern Ireland has had its own Audit Office since the 1920s, and following devolution to Scotland and Wales, they now have audit offices that cover all public bodies.

Another significant development under the Thatcher governments was the establishment of the Audit Commission in 1983 to encourage economic, efficient and effective public services, initially for local government, but from the 1990s its brief expanded to cover the NHS, social landlords and fire and rescue services. The Audit Commission's focus also changed somewhat, from a primary concern with economy and control to one with efficiency, effectiveness and value for money, and indeed performance assessment more broadly, with comprehensive performance assessments of local authorities being introduced in 2002 (Burnham and Horton, 2013). The Audit Commission was, however, abolished by the Coalition government and closed in 2015.

As discussed in greater depth elsewhere in this book, during the 1980s and 1990s there was a considerable degree of fragmentation of many public services, and this, together with resource constraints and high levels of demand in many areas, was accompanied by increased use of audit and inspection (Downe and Martin, 2007), in part because of the need to ensure standards, and in part because governments believed that such approaches could help improve the quality of provision. This was very obviously the case in education. While His Majesty's Inspectorate of Schools (HMIS) had existed from 1944, during this period every stage was subject to inspection, from pre-school, through primary and secondary education, to further (all by Ofsted, which replaced HMIS in England, and by devolved bodies in Northern Ireland, Scotland and Wales) and higher education (by the Quality Assurance Agency and the Higher Education Funding Councils). Roughly similar developments have occurred in other areas, such as social care. Following a series of scandals in the 1990s, in 2004 the Labour government created the Commission for Social Care Inspection, a single inspectorate for social care in England, including residential and nursing homes for adults and children, and fostering and adoption services, although Ofsted was briefly given responsibility for regulating children's social care from 2007, before another scandal (over the death of Baby P (Peter Connelly) in Haringey) and the establishment of a single body responsible for regulating both health and social care in 2009, the Care Quality Commission. As Flynn (2012) notes, prisons, too, have been subject to many regulatory mechanisms for a considerable period of time, but while several Chief Inspectors of Prisons have been very critical of the conditions and management of prisons (Flynn, 2012), relatively little has changed.

While the Thatcher and Major governments increased the use of measures such as 'league tables' of school performance, the Blair and Brown governments made much greater use of targets to measure performance, outputs and outcomes. The devolved administrations have also developed their own audit and measurement mechanisms (Figure 8.1 shows a summary of an Audit Scotland report on one local authority). Indeed, Burnham and Horton note that audit and inspection have changed markedly in recent decades, with the former becoming increasingly concerned with efficiency, value for money and improving management, and the latter with assessing whether national targets and standards are being met and the effectiveness of the leadership and management of public organisations, with both also being used to govern at a distance, rather than being undertaken by independent agencies acting as buffers between government and delivery organisations (Burnham and Horton, 2013). Governments have also increasingly used the judgements of audit and inspection bodies to criticise some providers, and to support their own policy proposals, with Labour identifying some schools as 'Beacon Schools', with good-quality education and high standards, and placing others, judged by Ofsted to be 'inadequate', in 'special measures' until they were no longer seen as 'failing', while some such schools were

Commission findings

1   The Commission accepts the Controller of Audit's report on Best Value in Falkirk Council.

2   In our findings in August 2015, we stated that the council needs to make a step-change in its pace of improvement. It is disappointing that we have not yet seen this.

3   While there has been much activity in the council in responding to our previous findings, we remain concerned that the scale of improvement required necessitates the council making more radical change. It urgently needs to agree its key priorities. These need to be supported by a more robust approach to financial planning for the medium and longer term and a more coordinated and streamlined approach to its improvement activity, showing how substantial change will be achieved. While a corporate workforce strategy is now in place, the council needs to show how this will drive and deliver change across services.

4   Increased collaboration among elected members in the budget process and in business transformation activity is encouraging. Scrutiny by elected members has also improved, but this could be more transparent. This needs to be supported by better reporting of performance by officers. The council also needs to demonstrate its change and improvement more effectively.

5   Strong and effective leadership by elected members and the corporate management team is critical for the council to address its challenges in coming years.

6   We continue to have a close interest in how the council is progressing. We require the Controller of Audit to update us by the end of 2017 through the annual audit and in our revised approach to auditing Best Value.

Figure 8.1   Summary findings from Audit Scotland's 2016 report on Falkirk Council

Source: Audit Scotland (2016) *Falkirk Council: Best Value Audit Report*, Edinburgh: Audit Scotland, p. 4 (reproduced under the Open Government Licence).

rebranded as 'academies', a policy then built upon by the Coalition and Conservative governments in their monitoring of schools and the expansion of academies (Figure 8.2 gives an example of an Ofsted report).

There is, inevitably, a variety of arguments about the merits, or otherwise, of different forms of regulation, as outlined above, and there remain significant criticisms of the spread of regulation, audit and inspection, including questions about whether they have resulted in improved services or better value for money (for example, Ashworth *et al.*, 2002; Davis and Martin, 2002; Downe and Martin, 2007), and the risks that a regulatory body may, over time, be 'captured' by the industry that it is supposed to be regulating, for example because of close links and career moves between regulator and industry employment (Stigler, 1975; Ashworth *et al.*, 2002). Other issues include the difficulties associated with stipulating measures (for example, what constitutes good-quality teaching in universities, and what outcomes might be associated with it), and the fact that measurements are frequently quantitative rather than qualitative (Dorey, 2014). There are also both financial and other costs associated with regulation: financial in terms of the running of the regulatory bodies, but also in relation to the work that has to be done within organisations that are audited and inspected; and non-financial in terms of staff morale, gaming and displaced activities.

The development and more widespread use of mechanisms of regulation, audit and inspection are not restricted to the United Kingdom, or even to other countries associated with being at the forefront of new public management techniques, although, equally, the rhetoric and reality vary considerably across states. While there may be something of a sense of crisis in regulation, due in part to the financial crisis and the questions that it raised about regulatory strategies, awareness of other regulatory failures (including food safety, with BSE in the 1990s and 2000s, oil platforms, such as Deepwater Horizon in 2010, and nuclear safety, with Fukushima in 2011), and some recognition that regulatory tools had not always had the desired effects (Lodge and Wegrich, 2012b), it remains central to the functions of modern states, so that Moran (2002) has suggested that while there may be particular episodes of deregulation, nevertheless complex social processes will continue to require regulation, and notes three broad approaches: 'self-regulation'; the 'European regulatory state', which seeks to remedy market failure; and the British regulatory state, which he sees as concerned with 'audit', 'trust' (actually, a lack of trust in existing regulatory processes and institutions) and 'risk' and its 'management'. Indeed, a number of writers have referred to the idea of the 'regulatory state' (Majone, 1994), which sees the state as focusing on regulatory activities, steering within a market society, rather than providing services itself, and enabling individuals and families to take responsibility for their lives, rather than the government (Moran, 2002 and 2003). From that perspective, the regulatory state therefore seeks to further embed the type of restructuring of state institutions that has taken place in the United Kingdom, and a number of other states, from the 1980s (Palumbo, 2015), although there is far from consensus on whether that is an appropriate direction for states to follow.

The need for policy evaluation

In order to know whether a policy is working, and the extent to which it is or is not successful, it needs to be monitored and evaluated. Despite this, evaluation is something which is not always automatically incorporated into the policy-making process, and it is often seen as taking place simply at the end of the policy-making cycle. However, this can relegate it to a minor and incomplete role, and thus undermine its importance and potential in the policy process. Above all, evaluation provides information:

> ➤ it can tell us whether a policy is working – it may expose failure of implementation strategies, under- or over-resourcing, or over-ambitious goals;

> ➤ it can provide feedback to improve future policy-making decisions (feeding into policy formulation);

> ➤ it can provide policies with credibility – without appropriate evaluation this may be brought into question – and influence resource allocation;

> ➤ it enables successful policies to be cited as examples of good practice and picked up and used by others;

> ➤ it may be able to indicate whether benefits exceed costs, according to different perspectives (such as users', government's and society's);

> ➤ and in doing these things, it can enhance both internal and public accountability.

To maximise its role and potential benefits, evaluation needs to be an integral part of the policy process. If approached in a considered manner, and fully integrated into the process, monitoring and evaluation may enable adjustments to policies, confirm that policies do (or do not) work well in practice, and serve as the foundation for new polices. Easton's systems model (see Chapter 1) illustrates the potential role of evaluation in policy making, as part of the policy-making cycle, which itself is a continuous process. This model is particularly useful as it sets the policy cycle in the context of the internal and external environment, and thus relates it to real-world events. Evaluation can also provide a valuable opportunity to improve future policy-making decisions. Yet much of the emphasis on policy making goes into the formulation and implementation processes; as a result, evaluation sometimes gets overlooked, and questions that need to be asked may not be raised. Such questions include: to what extent did the policy meet its stated objectives, and has the implementation of the policy raised other issues that need to be addressed? In the absence of policy evaluation we may have little idea whether the allocated budgets have been spent correctly, whether individuals have carried out their tasks as required, or whether rules and procedures have been applied in practice. Thus, without evaluation the credibility of the policy and the accountability of individuals and institutions responsible for its development are brought into question.

The primary concern of the remainder of this chapter can be related to Gerston's (1997) statement that '[s]imply defined, policy evaluation assesses the effectiveness of a public policy in terms of its perceived intentions and results' (p. 120), so that policy evaluation is a judgement on what has gone before or what is taking place, and it provides feedback on what has occurred and the extent to which ends have been achieved. Crucially, evaluation is concerned with how a policy is measured against the goals it was designed to achieve, and the actual impact of the policy.

However, whilst the principle of evaluation as part of the policy process is widely accepted, it is also the case that so much political capital and other attention tends to be directed to agenda setting, policy formulation, and to a lesser extent policy implementation, that basic questions, such as whether a policy achieved its stated objectives, or the level of satisfaction and dissatisfaction with it and its outcomes, are frequently neglected (Gerston, 1997). In addition, evaluation, as with other parts of the policy process, can itself be seen as an inherently political activity (Howlett *et al.*, 2009), and it is often possible to interpret the same evaluation in different ways. It is therefore important to recognise the ways in which politics, conflicts and compromises may shape both evaluations and their interpretation. One example of this was the Labour government's appointment of Professor David Nutt in 2008 as chair of the Advisory Council on the Misuse of Drugs, only to sack him in 2009 after he claimed that research showed that alcohol and tobacco were more harmful than many illegal drugs, such as cannabis, ecstasy and LSD.

Monitoring and evaluation can involve the full gamut of social science research techniques, including both qualitative and quantitative methods, such as case studies, field research, consumer surveys, ethnographic research, comparative research, experiments, primary and secondary data analysis. Since 1979 there has arguably been a series of relatively consistent attempts to incorporate some forms of monitoring and evaluation into parts of the policy process. The use of performance indicators, target setting, audit and inspection, quality management and efficiency scrutinies, for example, has effectively become accepted as one part of the policy process, while, since 2003, the Treasury's *Green Book* has set out guidance for the appraisal and evaluation of new policies and programmes (HM Treasury, 2013) and the *Magenta Book* has given more detailed advice on evaluation (HM Treasury, 2011). However, the extent to which these have been used, their quality (Hallsworth *et al.*, 2011) and their interpretations have perhaps owed as much to politics and ideology as to a concern with the desire to assess the degree of success or failure of policies themselves.

The very idea of evaluation, and related concepts such as evidence-based policy (see Chapter 4), appears to fit most closely with rational approaches to decision making. This is the idea that evaluation of policies can help improve both the policy process and potentially policy outcomes because decisions are based on research evidence, rather than ideology (Solesbury, 2001). Political leaders can therefore present themselves to the public as being 'post-ideological, and thus as pragmatists and technocrats concerned merely with finding the most effective and workable policy solutions to tackle problems, based on an objective evaluation of the evidence' (Dorey, 2014, p. 276). However, as discussed in Chapter 3, there are significant limitations to the utility of such models. In more incremental approaches, and those grounded in a more pluralistic process, evaluation and other forms of 'evidence' are more likely to be used as weapons by different sides in debates, with evidence being accepted when it fits with a political argument and rejected when it does not. Understanding the nature of evidence and what role it might play is therefore important. Hudson and Lowe (2009) draw attention to this, with the rational model fitting with a positivist view that emphasises the measurement of observable 'facts', and an alternative, formative model that seeks to guide policy utilising a wider evidence base, including more qualitative data and involving major stakeholders (Bate and Robert, 2003), which they see as fitting with a more constructivist approach. Essentially, this highlights different approaches to how we understand the social world and to research, with the former fitting more with the approach taken in the natural sciences and the latter with a greater emphasis on the interpretation of social phenomena. The approach taken to evaluation will generally reflect these differing perspectives.

Challenges in policy evaluation

Whilst the preceding sections have considered arguments for the inclusion of monitoring and evaluation as part of the policy process, including from the developmental stage of policies, it is nevertheless important to recognise that there is a variety of additional potential problems and difficulties (Anderson, 1997), including:

➤ uncertainty over policy goals – the goals of policy are often diffuse, unclear or diverse. This may be because the policy area itself may be amorphous, or governments may outline what is effectively a general strategy rather than setting specific targets, as, for example, with claims that encouraging schools to become academies would lead to improvements in educational performance. Policy makers may deliberately make policy goals obscure in an attempt to obtain the widest acceptance from the public and/or influential groups. The inclusion of vague or obscure aims, and the avoidance of specific objectives, also makes it difficult to measure success or failure, thereby making it harder to judge particular policies and enabling governments to avoid criticism of their policies. There are also times when the nature of policy formulation may mean that goals may not be clear, for example in incremental responses to short-term problems. In such instances, there is a danger that evaluation itself may be worthless because it is not possible to clearly identify the aims of policies, or because the outcomes may be too general to be of use;

➤ policy making often has to take into consideration many competing claims on resources. Consequently, the formulation and implementation of policy may be as concerned with achieving a balance between these competing claims as with ensuring effective policy;

➤ difficulties with implementation may mean that policies are not implemented as intended, and that, in turn, may impact on the results of any evaluation;

➤ a key challenge for many evaluations is the difficulty of devising a methodology that is capable of answering the research question;

➤ there are significant difficulties in determining causality – in public policy (indeed in social sciences generally) it is sometimes difficult to determine whether there is a cause and effect relationship. If action A is taken and condition B results, that does not necessarily mean that A causes B, as other influences may also have an impact; this is further complicated if the aim is to consider the extent to which a policy achieves an objective. Examples of this include the relationships between the levels of policing and crime, and the form and severity of punishment and crime. Where there is a range of initiatives, for example in seeking to improve public health, it will inevitably be hard to identify the effects of each;

➤ diffuse policy impacts – policy may affect groups other than those at whom the policy was directed; similarly the side-effects of policies may not be clear. The provision of benefits, such as housing benefit, will affect not only the recipients of those benefits, but also their families, taxpayers, the individuals or organisations that they rent from, and local and central government officials;

➤ there are often problems around acquiring accurate and up-to-date information. For many areas of public policy, little is known about the range of variables. For example, we may not have full knowledge of a particular target group, such as homeless people, or those vulnerable to radicalisation. Similarly, take-up of some benefits can only be estimated as we do not know the full extent of the population that might be eligible to receive them, while the extent of tax evasion, and the success of policies designed to reduce it can, understandably, only ever be estimated;

➤ resistance to policy evaluation – if the results of evaluations show that policies have not achieved their intended aims then there may be negative consequences for policy makers, those responsible for implementation, and others. This might affect the current programme being implemented, the influence of individuals or groups, or their careers. Some might seek to resist evaluations, or attempt to make it difficult for evaluations to proceed by, for example, making access to data difficult, possibly refusing or restricting access, or keeping incomplete records;

➤ limited time perspective – the time span of politicians, the media and the public is often short (it may, for example, frequently focus on the period until the next election). There may therefore be a demand to have the results from programmes quickly, despite the fact that good-quality results about the impact of a policy may take many years to achieve. If the time dimension is not taken into account, the results may be flawed and neglect important long-term effects. The pressure for rapid feedback may also be a dilemma for evaluators. Programmes with long-term aims, such as health promotion, and those that involve attempts to change behaviour, may find it difficult to illustrate real achievements over the short term, or alternatively may show short-term change that does not persist, whilst pilot projects may not have sufficient time to affect the full implementation of policies.

Overall, it is important to bear in mind the two main types of issue in evaluation: first, there are the methodological challenges; and second, there is the fact that evaluation is an inherently political activity and that there is inevitably a variety of interests and values involved in and affected by the process (Palfrey et al., 2012). These need to be taken into account in understanding the strengths and weaknesses of evaluations.

Approaches and methods

It is clearly possible to take a variety of perspectives on policy evaluation. For example, Pollitt *et al.* (1979) observe that it is possible to evaluate the quality of policy formulation, the quality and quantity of information used, the viability of a policy or set of policies, their appropriateness for the intended aims, or the policy outcome, whilst Parsons (1995) notes that evaluation has two interrelated aspects: the evaluation of policy and its constituent programmes, and the evaluation of people who work in the organisations which are responsible for implementing policy and programmes (see also the discussion of policy failure and policy success earlier in this chapter). Similarly, evaluation can be ongoing or retrospective, asking questions such as 'Has the policy worked?', which is perhaps the most common approach, or it may be prospective, looking to the future, perhaps asking 'What policy would work?'

Whilst monitoring and evaluation are sometimes treated interchangeably, and may frequently be part of the same process, Hogwood and Gunn (1984) identify a clear role for monitoring in the continuous appraisal of a programme. This can help reduce programme drift, where those responsible for implementation undertake different activities from those initially envisaged, or where a programme reaches clients other than those originally intended. Monitoring can therefore help to avoid, or at least mitigate, failures of implementation. For effective monitoring, they note that it is necessary to have an initial specification of what a policy aims to achieve, such as the numbers and types of people it aims to serve. Monitoring therefore requires the collection of information about the extent to which goals are being met; however, it should also involve decisions about what actions should be taken if the policy is not achieving its goals.

There is a very wide-variety range of methods and techniques that can contribute to policy evaluation. The choice will vary with the policy to be evaluated, the timescale, budget and other factors. Rossi (1999) suggests that evaluation can generally be structured around three issues: the questions the evaluation is to answer, with a clear need to identify the guiding purpose of the evaluation; the methods and procedures to be used to answer the questions; and the nature of the relationship between the evaluator and the stakeholders. As indicated above, the thinking behind the measures is important. For example, the increased use of audit and inspection, as discussed in greater depth earlier in this chapter, may have been seen by some as a way of ensuring that organisations were adhering to certain standards, but these tools are now perhaps more widely used in attempts to contribute to and demonstrate improved performance (or not). The selection of approaches set out below is not exhaustive, but is rather intended to be indicative of the variety of methods that are used, together with some assessment of their strengths and weaknesses.

Performance measurement

Targets, league tables, audit and inspection and similar mechanisms can all be seen as types of performance measurement; indeed, there may well be overlaps in the use of these. As noted in the discussion above, the culture of audit and inspection, and the use of performance indicators, targets and other measures by which public service organisations are judged on their performance, grew in part from the shift from government to governance in the late 1970s and early 1980s, with the spread of the new public management encouraging government to outsource many of its functions to other bodies, while emphasising efficiency and effectiveness and stronger management for those that remained; at the same time, developments in technology made it easier to collect and record such information (Royal Statistical Society, 2003). These were closely related to the emergence of the new public management, which took a more instrumental approach to management, placing considerable emphasis on performance appraisal, efficiency, target setting and the parsimonious use of resources (see Hood, 1991), so that by the 1990s Power (1994) was suggesting that Britain had become an 'audit society'. With the considerable emphasis on austerity since 2010, this agenda arguably became even more important.

Of course, many countries, particularly members of the OECD, have sought to measure performance as a driver for reform (Pollitt and Boukaert, 2011), although the focus of measurement and attempts to manage it have arguably changed somewhat over time, so that recently the decline in trust in public institutions has pushed performance measurement towards concerns with quality of life, trust and quality of governance (Bouckaert and van Dooren, 2016).

Performance indicators

Performance indicators are based on quantifiable measures and are frequently used for comparison, either over time or between organisations. They have, for example, been used in relation to levels of school truancy, road deaths, numbers of students achieving grades A to C in school examinations, and hospital waiting times. They are also widely used to construct 'league tables'. However, while they are intended to tell us how close a policy has come to achieving its objectives (Bouckaert and van Dooren, 2016), they rely upon the sources of data being reliable, and it is important to be aware of what they do and do not tell us, such as whether a school or university 'adds value' to its student intake. In the UK, performance measurement was to a considerable extent encouraged or imposed by Conservative governments from 1979 to 1997, including through attempts to reform the civil service. Under Labour governments from 1997 this emphasis continued (albeit with attempts, in at least some instances, to make performance indicators more useful, for example by adding data on 'contextual value', such as gender, special educational needs and levels of deprivation, to assessments of school performance), so that virtually all public services including the police, prison service and libraries, as well as health and social services, have seen the use of performance indicators in attempts to measure the quantity and quality of provision.

However, while performance measures and indicators, and their use as targets for services, may provide an indication of performance, and may highlight areas that need further consideration and evaluation, they are also underpinned by particular values and political positions, so that, as Parsons (1995) notes, it is important to consider questions such as '...who sets up the criteria for measurement, how is it calculated, who asks the questions and what time period is selected for assessment?' (p. 548). There are also a number of weaknesses with such approaches, including that they measure only what appears to be measurable, despite the complexity of outputs from many public policies, they encourage a focus on targets or whatever element is being measured rather than the broader possible outputs, and they are likely to result in 'gaming', with organisations seeking to manipulate their activities to give the best possible picture of their performance, or even to misrepresent data (Greener, 2013). Labour's extensive use of targets from 1997 was seen by Hood as leading to three main gaming responses: ratchet effects, with those who set targets increasing them gradually year by year, so that those trying to meet those targets responded by reining back on the current year's outputs; threshold effects, where there is no incentive to exceed targets; and output distortion, the deliberate misrepresentation of results (Hood, 2006). Another example of the potential for meeting targets in different ways can be seen with the element of the 'key information set' for higher education that is concerned with students' contact hours, where, for example, it is likely to be much cheaper for an institution to increase contact hours through a one-hour lecture to a group of 200 students, than 10 one-hour seminars for groups of 20 students.

Similarly, the use of particular measures may skew the activities of the organisations and individuals being measured. Remaining with higher education, the introduction of the measurement of 'research quality' in UK higher education with the Research Assessment Framework and then the Research Excellence Framework, for example, has been widely portrayed as encouraging institutions (and many of their staff) to focus on research (and, indeed, particular types of research) rather than teaching, with the Conservative government introducing a Teaching Excellence Framework from 2016, at least in part to seek to encourage what was seen by some to be a need for a greater concentration on teaching and learning.

Systematic review and meta-analysis

Systematic reviews and meta-analysis are often seen as being rigorous means of drawing together the findings of individual studies.

Systematic reviews

Systematic reviews are a form of literature review that can be characterised as having: a clearly stated set of objectives and pre-defined eligibility criteria for studies; an explicit, reproducible methodology; a systematic search that seeks to identify all studies that meet the eligibility criteria; a formal assessment of the validity of the studies that are included; and a systematic synthesis and presentation of the characteristics and findings of those studies (HM Treasury, 2011). They make clear what the search and eligibility criteria are, and how studies were selected for detailed review. Gough and Tripney (2016) outline 10 basic stages in the systematic review process:

1. developing the initial question, which is important in determining how the research is conceptualised and undertaken and which will affect the findings;
2. clarifying which studies are relevant, for example in terms of topic and methods;
3. identifying studies that might be included;
4. checking that the studies found meet the selection criteria;
5. 'mapping' how the studies relate to the research question, for example by sub-topic or research methods;
6. further coding of studies for synthesis;
7. quality and relevance appraisal of the studies, for example in terms of the methods and relevance;
8. synthesis, the bringing together of the results of the studies to answer the research question;
9. communication, or the reporting of the results to the desired audience;
10. recommendations and guidance.

Systematic reviews have been championed by the international Cochrane (around health care) and Campbell (around social change) collaborations as means of providing summaries of the best available research on a given issue or question. Gough and Tripney suggest that systematic reviews not only tell us what we know from existing research, but also help us see what we do not know, and what more we might want to learn from research.

However, while systematic reviews are intended, by their very nature, to be thorough and reliable, it is important to be aware that, clearly, they depend on the quality of the studies that they are reporting on, and in turn are dependent upon the reviewer identifying weaknesses in those studies and assessing the value that they bring to the subject under consideration (Palfrey *et al.*, 2012). In addition, although there is no consensus on this, and indeed it would be difficult, if not impossible to be sure, it has been suggested that in medical research, in particular, there has been a bias (see Gomm, 2008) towards publishing work that has produced positive results, while those studies with negative or neutral results are less likely to be published (for example, Needham, 2000; Dubben and Beck-Bornholdt, 2005), and similar claims have been made for the social sciences (Franco *et al.*, 2014), and this would clearly risk skewing the results of systematic reviews. Nutley *et al.* (2007) also point out that for some policy issues systematic reviews can conclude that it is not possible to draw firm conclusions because there are insufficient high-quality primary studies to enable synthesis, although they suggest that this may improve as the number of studies increases.

While systematic reviews are valuable, given that there is often a need for the provision of information in a short timescale, rapid review, or rapid evidence assessment, is a less comprehensive tool that is sometimes recommended (HM Treasury, 2011), although it can be argued that ideally these should be further developed into full systematic review (Walker and Duncan, 2007).

Meta-analysis

Meta-analysis is a form of review that aggregates the findings of comparable studies and seeks to 'pool' the observations to provide a statistical analysis of effects. It is perhaps used most commonly in relation to randomised controlled trials, but is also applied to other types of primary study (HM Treasury, 2011). However, it is not unproblematic. For example, it is rare to be able to pool data that is very similar (there may be differences in the populations, the interventions, etc.), studies may use different methods to calculate their results, so that there may be problems associated with analysing them together, and if the quality of one or more of the studies is poor it may affect the overall review.

Before and after studies

One obvious approach to evaluation is to compare the position after a policy has been implemented with the position before. From this, it may be possible to conclude whether the position has altered in line with the aims of the policy. However, this has a number of problems, in particular the difficulty of disentangling the impact of one policy from the general social and economic environment, including other policies that might also affect the outcome. Such arguments were, for example, sometimes applied to the 1997 Labour government's New Deal for Young People, where the apparent success of the programme coincided with falling unemployment generally, including amongst the programme's target group, making it difficult to make a clear judgement; similarly, attempts to attribute changing crime rates to particular policies are likely to be fraught with difficulty. Essentially, it is clearly important that before and after studies attempt to take account of the variety of possible influences on a policy's targets.

Audit and inspection

As highlighted earlier in this chapter, from the 1980s and 1990s there has been widespread use of audits of bodies providing public services. While these often draw upon measures such as targets and performance indicators, they frequently go beyond them, sometimes incorporating more qualitative data, as well as considering the processes by which organisations themselves seek to ensure quality, based upon the premise that if the correct mechanisms and procedures are in place and effectively managed, then appropriate performance, outputs and outcomes will follow (Dorey, 2014).

While there is no formal, agreed definition of these activities (see, however, Table 8.1 for a summary of audit and inspection bodies in the United Kingdom), Levitt *et al.* (2010) suggest that as working definitions 'audits' can be seen as involving the 'periodic external assessment of corporate governance and management systems, financial statements and underlying financial systems, and the performance, performance management and reporting of public bodies', and 'inspections' as 'periodic, targeted assessment of specific services, to check whether they are meeting national and local performance standards, legislative and professional requirements, and the needs of service users' (p. 4). Audits typically involve a combination of written documentation, such as self-evaluation reports, and on-site inspections, often with advance notice but sometimes with no notice, as with the Care Quality Commission's unannounced inspections. Inspections normally result in a report and some sort of grading, such as the CQC's 'Outstanding', 'Good', 'Requires improvement' and 'Inadequate', and Ofsted's 'Outstanding',

Table 8.1   Audit and inspection bodies, England, Northern Ireland, Scotland and Wales

	England	Northern Ireland	Scotland	Wales
Audit	National Audit Office	Northern Ireland Audit Office	Auditor General, Accounts Commission, Audit Scotland	Wales Audit Office
Children's Services	Ofsted	Regulation and Quality Improvement Authority	Care Inspectorate	Care and Social Services Inspectorate Wales
Criminal Justice	HM Inspectorates of Constabulary, Crown Prosecution Service, Court Administration, Probation, Prisons	Criminal Justice Inspection Northern Ireland	HM Inspectorates of Constabulary in Scotland, Prosecution in Scotland, Prisons in Scotland	As England
Education	Ofsted	Education and Training Inspectorate	Education Scotland	HM Inspectorate for Education and Training in Wales
Health	Care Quality Commission	Regulation and Quality Improvement Authority	Healthcare Improvement Scotland	Healthcare Inspectorate Wales
Housing	Homes and Communities Agency	Department for Communities	Scottish Housing Regulator	Wales Audit Office

Source: Adapted from Flynn, 2012, p. 169.

'Good', 'Requires improvement' and 'Inadequate' (see Figure 8.2). As with performance indicators, there are issues over what is and is not measurable, and the emphasis on what is (or at least appears to be) measurable may drive institutions and their staff to focus more on those areas, and less on those that are not measured, and therefore may in some respects drive how people do their jobs and what they do in them. Similarly, if the throughput of patients is measured in a hospital or GP practice, that says nothing about the quality of the experience of the patient or the relationship with the staff.

Palfrey *et al.* (2012) suggest that inspections can sometimes have a different underpinning ethos from audits, with the former being concerned with the accountability of public sector organisations to the public (although, they note that they also serve, less positively, as a 'wholly

School report

raising standards
improving lives

Lincoln Christ's Hospital School

Wragby Road, Lincoln, LN2 4PN

Inspection dates		25–26 June 2013	
Overall effectiveness	Previous inspection:	Not previously inspected	
	This inspection:	**Good**	**2**
Achievement of pupils		Good	2
Quality of teaching		Good	2
Behaviour and safety of pupils		Good	2
Leadership and management		Good	2

Summary of key findings for parents and pupils

This is a good school.

- The school is welcoming and has a strong sense of community spirit that is appreciated by students, staff, parents and visitors.
- School records and the lessons seen during the inspection show that the quality of teaching is mainly good, with some outstanding teaching.
- Students make good progress as they move through the school and, from low starting points, achieve results in line with most students of a similar age.
- In the core subjects students make the most rapid progress in English, although attainment in mathematics is rising.
- The sixth form is good. Sixth form students also make good progress from their various starting points, particularly in AS level courses.

- Students are friendly, polite and helpful. Behaviour in most classrooms and around the school site is consistently good.
- School records, confirmed by discussions with students, show that bullying is very rare, and is quickly dealt with. Students feel very safe in school.
- The school is led and managed well and self-evaluation is accurate and detailed. Senior members of staff are approachable and experienced.
- Teaching and learning are led well, and well-chosen staff training is further developing the amount of good and outstanding teaching.
- Governors know the school well and provide support and challenge where they are required.

It is not yet an outstanding school because

- Teaching in a minority of lessons is not good and not enough teaching is outstanding.
- Work is not always matched carefully enough to students' different needs, with the same tasks often given to all.

- Questioning is not always used well to encourage students to think more deeply or to check on what is being learned during a lesson.
- Expectations of students' behaviour are too low in a small minority of lessons, occasionally disrupting learning.

Information about this inspection

- The inspection team observed 49 lessons taught by 49 different teachers. They also made some shorter visits to some classrooms.
- The team observed tutor periods and visited many different areas of the school and the site during lessons and at break times.
- Meetings were held with three different groups of students, the Chair of the Governing Body with a governor colleague, senior staff and subject and year leaders.
- The inspection team examined a range of school documentation, including school development plans and policies, lesson plans, records of lesson monitoring and checks on students' work, and the minutes of meetings, including those of the governing body. Inspectors examined a range of data, both that available to the public and that used by the school to monitor current rates of students' progress and attendance.
- Only two responses had been made to Parent View by the end of the inspection, so no analysis of these results was available for consideration. Staff questionnaires were considered, alongside a survey of parents and carers carried out by the school earlier this year.

Figure 8.2   Ofsted's 2013 report on Lincoln Christ's Hospital School

pragmatic endeavour to secure the survival of a political entity' (p. 22), and the latter a more quality-oriented remit, and highlight also that inspections have increasingly sought to involve service users in the process, as well as management and staff of the providing agencies.

The range of organisations undertaking a scrutiny function has led to debates around whether there are too many mechanisms for holding organisations to account, but at the same time high-profile scandals, such as over child abuse, the Mid-Staffordshire NHS Trust, and Winterbourne View care home, may serve not only to illustrate the need for such mechanisms, but also to raise questions about whether existing safeguards are sufficient (Levitt *et al.*, 2010).

Levitt *et al.* (2010) have proposed eight principles and practices for the effective use of evidence in audit, inspection and scrutiny:

1. Be clear about what is expected of each audit, inspection and scrutiny project.

2. Consider the appropriateness and feasibility of different methods and ensure that you have the necessary skills.

3. Seek out a range of different kinds of evidence.

4. Test the quality of evidence.

5. Consider alternative interpretations of the evidence.

6. Tailor reporting to the needs of different audiences.

7. Check the implementation of findings and recommendations.

8. Reflect on the lessons for future projects.

While there may be differences of opinion on some of these, taken together they provide a useful guide to the type of thinking and the nature of activities required for audit and inspection processes.

Cost–benefit analysis

Seeking to assess the cost-effectiveness of public policies is frequently problematic, not least because seeking to apply monetary values to issues such as improved health, increased longevity, educational experience and environmental enhancement is clearly problematic. In the health sphere, Quality Adjusted Life Years (QALYs) have been used in many countries to measure the benefits, in terms of quality and length of life, following a particular treatment or intervention. However, given the difficulties associated with such approaches, other methods have also been used.

Perhaps the best known of these is cost–benefit analysis (CBA), a quantitative form of evaluation that sets out to identify the costs and benefits of a proposed or actual policy and to translate these into monetary values to enable comparison. It is recommended by the Treasury's *Green Book* (2013) for its ability to take account of wider social costs and benefits, and to provide outcome measures that are directly comparable with intervention costs, although it also recognises that the technique is not without its problems, and, for example, warns that '[i]t is important not to be spuriously accurate when concluding from, and presenting the results of, data generated by the appraisal' (p. 19). Whilst most widely used in policy formulation, it is sometimes applied to existing policies. The first stage is to identify the effects of a policy and to categorise them as costs or benefits for particular groups. Then monetary values are applied to the various costs and benefits. For some goods and services this may be relatively easy, but for things such as good health or clean air, this may be difficult. At this stage, it is necessary to take account of whether the effects will occur in the short or long term, and to make an appropriate adjustment to estimated costs and benefits for this. Finally, the costs and benefits, direct and indirect, current and future, of the policy can then be compared and a decision made on accepting or rejecting it. However, whilst in some respects apparently straightforward, there can be significant difficulties in the use of this approach. In particular, good-quality data may be unavailable and almost impossible to gather, and for many public policies there are enormous difficulties in trying to value costs and benefits, particularly when moral and ethical questions arise, as indeed occurred during attempts to develop QALYs during the 1980s and 1990s as a way of enabling judgements about the value of different forms of treatment, and potentially to provide a basis for decisions about rationing. In addition, those who bear costs, for example through income tax, may not be the same people as those who receive benefits, particularly directly, as some social policies aim to distribute benefits to the poor.

Experimentation

For those who aspire to follow the methods of the sciences, experimentation frequently appeals, for example through testing the impact of a new policy and comparing it with an established policy. Burch and Wood (1990) noted that effectiveness can sometimes be tested in advance through experimentation, giving the example of an experiment used in New Jersey and Pennsylvania in the United States from 1969 to 1972, which aimed to test the impact of a guaranteed annual income upon recipients' work effort, while Hudson and Lowe (2009) cite an example from Florida in the 1990s which suggested that the expectations of both the supporters and opponents of a policy intended to encourage welfare recipients into work were not met. The use of random allocation is often seen as being the 'gold standard' for this approach, together with the use of experimental and control groups, whereby one group receives inputs from the policy or programme whilst the other does not, as is often used in testing the effectiveness of new drugs. Such an approach means that both groups are also affected by all the other possible influences, thus making it possible to judge the impact of a policy. Under the Labour governments there were pilots in areas such as the introduction of Individual Budgets in Social Care and Partnerships for Older People Projects, while the Coalition used pilots (along with performance indicators) to try to improve the speed of handling of asylum cases. However, as Burch and Wood recognise, there are often very significant ethical problems as well as practical obstacles associated with such measures. Notably, it is arguably ethically wrong to withhold potential benefits such as higher income, better education or better health care from a 'control' group.

In addition, and despite some of the difficulties outlined above, governments have continued to use the introduction of policy in limited areas as a form of piloting or experimentation, with the Labour governments piloting initiatives such as Best Value in local government and elements of the New Deal. As Burch and Wood (1990) suggest, these indicate an approach to policy making 'which places an emphasis on "looking before you leap", but lacks the rigour needed for proper evaluation' (p. 213).

Sometimes 'natural' or 'quasi-experiments' may be used, where the assignment of subjects to experimental and control groups may be haphazard, but it may nevertheless be possible to infer causal links between a policy and what appear to be the outcomes, so that Green and South (2006) have noted that the use of 'naturally occurring units such as schools, hospitals or communities' (p. 22) might enable evidence of effectiveness to be produced. In the United Kingdom, the use of Community Development Projects in the 1970s was effectively a form of action research that was also in some senses experimental and was compared with control areas. However, the lack of clear objectives together with methodological problems meant that it was difficult to draw any firm conclusions from this initiative. Similarly, examining the effect of two separate initiatives on public health, Petticrew et al. (2005) highlight that many of the major social determinants of health and health inequalities were not amenable to randomisation, and while such challenges may not invalidate natural experiments, they do require caution in the interpretation of the results.

There can also be other challenges, such as the time frame allowed for an experiment, with the time for adequate testing being unlikely to meet the requirements of policy makers who want to introduce a particular policy. For example, changes to child care or school-age education, or public health measures, may take many years to yield results, but politicians are typically expected to respond quickly to problems and to present themselves for election every four or five years.

Despite these problems, many authors, such as Davies *et al.* (2000) and John (2016), argue that the need for good-quality evidence is such that there is a strong case for experimentation in some areas and that this may be particularly appropriate where a setting is relatively stable and where human intervention is likely to have a relatively small impact on the outcome.

Quality management

The idea and practice of quality management originated in the private sector, but have become more prominent in public services over time (Bovaird and Loeffler, 2016a), with a number of different methods being used, varying from relatively simple attempts to assess levels of satisfaction amongst the users of services to the use of recognised standards for quality assurance and other mechanisms designed to provide comprehensive approaches to achieving quality. However, as discussed elsewhere in this book (see Chapter 1), public services are likely to be very different from those in the private sector, including in relation to identifying what 'quality' might be (so that different stakeholders may have quite different perceptions), who users and customers are, and in terms of lines of accountability (see, for example, Bovaird and Loeffler, 2016a).

An early attempt to introduce a fairly comprehensive policy initiative in the United Kingdom came in the early 1990s with 'citizens' charters', under the premiership of John Major. These sought to establish basic principles and service standards (often identifying minimum standards), although they were grounded in the ideas of competition and choice through market-type mechanisms, at least as much as in the idea of rights for citizens (see also the discussion of some of the uses of open data in Chapter 4). While they were fairly widespread by the time of the 1997 general election, over time they largely faded away under the Labour government.

Alternative approaches have included the use of a variety of widely recognised quality assurance mechanisms, such as the International Organization for Standardization (ISO) standards, and the Common Assessment Framework (CAF) that public agencies, like private sector bodies, have sought to align with. Bovaird and Loeffler (2016b) note, however, that while the ISO 9000 series focuses on assuring processes (see also Schedler and Helmuth (2016) for a discussion of process management in public sector organisations) and is therefore helpful for notions of quality such as fitness for purpose or conforming to specifications, the CAF, and broadly similar models such as the EFQM Excellence Model, may be more useful in ensuring fit between the 'enablers' and the results of an organisation's activities.

There have also been some attempts to introduce ideas such as 'total quality management' (TQM) into public services. This involves the creation of an organisational culture that encourages quality services, including by emphasising employee involvement, empowering workers at all levels, and encouraging integrated strategies for planning and delivering services. However, the extent and success of such an approach is very dependent upon how TQM is interpreted, by whom, and for what purposes, and in practice there is frequently little consensus about how it should be carried out.

The commissioning and use of evaluations

The results of most evaluations are likely to be both political and contestable to varying extents, as they are frequently commissioned by individuals or organisations who may have a stake in their outcome, are undertaken by others who will also have an interest in the evaluation, and who will generally make some estimation of the extent of success or failure that may be used to argue for or against a policy or set of policies and those who instigated them. Evaluations may also feed back into the decision-making process either directly or indirectly.

While considerable amounts of evaluation are commissioned by different tiers of government, a substantial amount is also funded by other organisations, sometimes directly as evaluation, but more often under the broad heading of 'research', such as into economic, environmental or social issues. Such research can take the form of an evaluation of a policy, but, equally, may be concerned with the impact of part of a policy, or a set of policies, or even a perceived lack of policy. In addition, it may or may not be designed to evaluate the stated aims or objectives of a policy, but may instead be looking at the impact of a measure on one or more groups of people. It may not, therefore, always fall within a strict definition of 'evaluation', but nevertheless can still provide information relevant to the evaluation of a policy, particularly where evaluations are not built into the policy process itself. In the United Kingdom there are many organisations that fund such research, with some of the main ones including the Arts and Humanities Research Council, the Economic and Social Research Council (government-funded bodies responsible for funding research and training in their subject areas) and major charitable foundations such as the Joseph Rowntree Foundation, the Leverhulme Trust, the Nuffield Foundation and the Wellcome Trust, each of which may have their own interests and agendas. In addition, think tanks and pressure groups can undertake a considerable amount of work that can shed light on policy implementation, and which might be seen as falling under a general 'evaluation' umbrella, although, again, they are likely to have a particular underlying viewpoint. Finally, a considerable amount of unfunded work is undertaken, including by academics and others with interests in particular issues, policies or groups.

Palfrey *et al.* (2012) note the issues of power in relation to the commissioning of evaluations and identify a number of important questions:

1. What will be evaluated, and what will not be?

2. How will a policy or service be evaluated, and by whom?

3. What criteria will be used and how will they be weighted?

4. Who will collect and analyse the data and how?

5. To what extent and in what ways will the findings of the evaluation be implemented?

Clearly, for analysts of the policy process, as well as those involved in undertaking evaluations, such questions, along with the broader questions about the distribution and exercise of power and influence discussed throughout this book, raise questions about the nature and extent of evaluations, and their links with other parts of the policy process.

Who evaluates?

Gerston (1997) points out that almost everyone evaluates how they are affected by policies. When taxes fall or rise, individuals and businesses make judgements on that. Consumers of services such as education or health also consider how policies, and policy changes, affect them. However, in terms of the policy process, the choice of who undertakes an evaluation is important, affecting not just the quality of the work, but also potentially the credibility of the findings, although that is rarely the only factor. Evaluations are often undertaken by experts with familiarity with an issue or topic, although, of course, policy makers and others may decide to listen to alternative interpretations, and there are arguments that the views of those most immediately affected by a policy can sometimes be neglected, as in earlier parts of the policy process (Bochel and Evans, 2007).

At its most basic, it is possible to identify two types of evaluation. Internal evaluation is undertaken within an organisation or process. This has the advantage of ensuring familiarity with the main issues and the policy environment; however, it may make it harder to demonstrate independence from a particular policy authority. External evaluation is undertaken by independent organisations who nevertheless claim to have appropriate expertise. They are clearly more able to demonstrate independence, and potentially to bring a fresh perspective, but they may also be less aware of the context and environment within which policies operate. In the UK, a considerable amount of policy evaluation is undertaken by academics, funded either by bodies responsible for policy making and implementation, or by external bodies, including the research councils and charitable foundations, or unfunded. Think tanks and interest groups also sometimes present themselves as independent, external evaluators, and can often produce high-quality work, although at other times they are clearly affected by their aims and values. Finally, parliamentary committees, and in particular select committees (see also Chapter 5) and their equivalents in the devolved legislatures, can be involved in evaluating policies, with, at Westminster, the National Audit Office, working with the Public Accounts Committee, producing value-for-money reports, and they can frequently be critical of governments' approaches, although, again, the extent of their influence is sometimes unclear (see, for example, Norton, 2013; Russell and Benton, 2013).

'Evaluation', therefore, can arguably range from being a high-quality, largely independent and objective exercise to a much more political practice more concerned with the values that underpin policies than by any attempt to judge the extent of success and failure.

The use of evaluations

Hogwood and Gunn (1984) argued that in most cases no actions appear to result from policy evaluations, regardless of the quality of the methodology. They suggest that there is a variety of reasons for that, including that there are inevitably political judgements to be made about acceptable levels of effectiveness; the potential limitations of the findings; the lack of fit with the decision-making timetable; organisational resistance to findings; and the degree of acceptability to those who fund, deliver or receive the outputs of the policy. Palfrey *et al.* (2012) consider a variety of possible perspectives on the impacts of evaluations, including expanding upon Hogwood and Gunn's list, and conclude that it remains difficult to assess the impact of evaluations on policy. This reinforces further the point that most evaluations are likely to be essentially political and contestable. It also encourages us to examine the extent to which evaluations feed into policy succession (replacement by one or more new policies), maintenance (adjustments to policies), or termination (Hogwood and Peters, 1983).

However, as outlined in Chapter 4, Weiss (1979) pointed out that there are a number of different ways in which research might be used, and while examples of the more 'direct' models of knowledge-driven and problem-solving use may be relatively scarce, it may be that the more indirect and often longer-term influences that she identifies mean that evaluations can and do have impacts, although they may be harder to identify (see also Walker and Duncan, 2007).

Conclusion

Returning to the discussion at the start of this chapter, while evaluation might in some respects be expected to be a central part of the policy process in the United Kingdom, particularly where there are more 'rational' approaches to policy making, in practice its use is much more irregular. The lack of evaluation designed and built into policies and programmes by governments and by other organisations has meant that many policies have not been evaluated, and where evaluations have taken place they have frequently been dependent upon the work of those outside government, such as academics, pressure groups and think tanks, and that there have often been significant resource and time constraints.

From the 1980s, the Conservative governments made significant attempts to use performance measurement, in particular, along with other business performance tools, as a means of enhancing the management and efficiency of the delivery of many public services, although arguably underplaying possible measures of effectiveness, and drawing heavily on the belief that the private sector and its practices were more efficient than the public sector, which was seen as too bureaucratic and inherently inefficient. A similar pattern could be observed under the Labour governments of 1997 to 2010, including the widespread use of 'targets' for public services, while at the same time, for much of that period, monitoring and evaluation were sometimes linked to evidence-based policy and the idea of 'what works' (Davies *et al.*, 2000; Bochel and Duncan, 2007), although in some policy areas they were also used to identify organisations that might be seen as 'failing', and therefore to justify particular forms of government intervention. Under the Coalition and Conservative governments from 2010, monitoring and evaluation, while following broadly similar lines, tended to be overshadowed by the wider impacts of the governments' austerity policies, although in some areas, as noted earlier in this chapter, they continued to be developed, as with the use of pilots and experiments, while in others, assertion and values might be seen as having crowded out such evidence.

Almost two decades ago, Davies *et al.* (2000) noted that while there had been an increased emphasis on effectiveness, 'there is relatively little examination of the related questions of efficiency and cost-effectiveness', and that '[i]n part, this reflects the infancy of cost-effectiveness and cost-benefit analyses in the public sector, and the relative paucity of activity in this area' (p. 3). While the intervening years have arguably seen increased sophistication in the use of evaluation methods, and some greater attention to the use of evidence in policy making (see Chapter 4), it nevertheless remains the case that evaluation is rarely built into the policy process. Even when evaluation of various types does take place, as with research in general (see, for example, Nutley *et al.*, 2007), it may sometimes have an impact while sometimes it does not.

Finally, it is worth returning briefly to the idea of 'realistic evaluation', as noted in Chapter 4. This derives from Pawson and Tilley's work (1997). They have argued that much evaluation, especially that focusing on outcomes, has been superficial, and that rather than simply seeking to identify whether or not a particular outcome has been achieved, much greater consideration needs to be given to how and in what circumstances a particular programme or policy works, and for whom. It can perhaps be seen as a form of theory-driven evaluation, which looks at the intended (effectiveness) and unintended (perhaps why policies fail) outcomes and consequences of policy, with the evaluator generating a theory about why and how a policy or programme works. They summarise their approach as: context + mechanism = outcome. Context relates to 'the spatial and institutional locations of social situations together ... with the norms, values and interrelationships found in them' (1997, p. 216); 'mechanisms' refer to 'what it is about a programme that makes it work' (p.66); and they are clear that 'outcomes' should include not only intended consequences, but also those that are unintended and unwanted. It is therefore necessary to consider and test what combination of mechanisms and contexts might lead to the outcomes that are being sought (see also, Pawson, 2002).

Further reading

Comprehensive, if rather different, approaches are given in:

Nutley, S. M., Walter, I. and Davies, H. T. O. (2007) *Using Evidence: How Research Can Inform Public Services*, Bristol: Policy Press.

Palfrey, C., Thomas, P. and Phillips, C. (2012) *Evaluation for the Real World: The Impact of Evidence in Policy Making*, Bristol: Policy Press.

A governmental view is given in:

HM Treasury (2011) *The Green Book*, London: HM Treasury. Available at: http://www.hm-treasury.gov.uk/d/green_book_complete.pdf, accessed 27 June 2017.

Another, rather different but important take is provided in:

McConnell, A. (2010) *Understanding Policy Success: Rethinking Public Policy*, Basingstoke: Palgrave Macmillan.

A number of chapters relevant to the concerns of this chapter are in:

Bovaird, T. and Loeffler, E. (eds) (2016) *Public Management and Governance*, London: Routledge.

9

Conclusions

This book has set out a wide range of perspectives that can inform our understanding of the variety of influences on the processes of formulating, implementing and evaluating public policy and the exercise of power. Developments from the 1970s onwards have been examined and can be seen as reflecting many of these influences. This chapter outlines some of the lessons that can be learnt from a consideration of the policy process in the United Kingdom.

This book has introduced a wide range of theories, perspectives, models and approaches that can be applied to the policy process in order to enable us to better understand the making, implementation and evaluation of policy. As is apparent throughout the book, some of these conflict with each other, directly or indirectly, while others may serve to reinforce each other to varying extents; some may be descriptive, some analytical, and some prescriptive. However, they do have considerable value in offering a variety of lenses through which, singly or jointly, we can analyse the exercise of power in the public policy process.

A focus on the contemporary policy process is likely to emphasise the ongoing, complex and dynamic nature of policy making and implementation, and to require consideration of the wide variety of influences and the ways in which power is exercised and decisions are made. As is made clear throughout this book, it is not always easy to define and recognise the parameters of many of the ideas dealt with here, including the definitions of 'public policy' and the 'policy process'. It is also apparent that there are continual changes not only in the policies and practices that we study, but also in the tools that we can use to analyse them. For example, it is clear that the emergence of neo-liberal ideas in the 1980s and 1990s has not only influenced the nature of policies since then, but has also added to the tools that we can use to understand the policy process, as with the perspectives that they bring to the ways in which bureaucracies work (and indeed, through the critiques that those neo-liberal ideas have in turn been subject to). Similarly, debates over the value of institutional approaches, evidence-based policy and behaviour change and other ideas, as well as over multi-level governance (and Brexit) and globalisation, inform and can be applied to aid our comprehension of the policy process. Following 18 years of Conservative government from 1979 to 1997, 13 years of Labour governments led to further change in both policies and the policy context, to some extent reflecting continuing emphases, for example in relation to notions of choice, and the use of markets, performance measurement and regulatory mechanisms, but also differences, such as in devolution to Northern Ireland, Scotland and Wales, and greater emphases on partnerships, joined-up government and evidence-based policy. The Coalition government from 2010 to 2015 also reflected both continuity with and difference from its predecessors, with further use of markets, the impact of austerity, some devolution to (some) English regions, and attempts to encourage localism and the Big Society. The Conservative government from 2015 to 2017 was almost immediately notable for the referendum on leaving the European Union and the subsequent replacement of David Cameron as Prime Minister with Theresa May, while following the 2017 general election, Brexit, and its consequences, appeared likely to dominate the political and policy agenda for a considerable period of time.

Inevitably, new developments also lead to new concerns, such as over accountability (whether the European Union, directly elected mayors in English cities and regions, or the use of arm's-length bodies), the increasing use of markets and the private sector in the delivery of public services, or the development and use of performance measurement in attempts to improve efficiency and the implications for effectiveness and equity, while, in addition to the relationship with the EU, the election of President Trump in the United States provided another reminder of the potential impact of international change on the UK policy process.

It is also important to recognise that governments themselves frequently pay attention to the process of policy making and implementation, as well as to the development of policies, and, for example, that may be reflected in the instruments that they choose to utilise. The emphasis of the Conservatives on markets during the 1980s and 1990s derived from a perspective that viewed markets, rather than the state, as the best means of distributing goods and services, and that, inevitably, had significant implications for the making and delivery of public policies, including the need for regulatory, audit and inspection mechanisms. While in government, Labour continued to use some of the same approaches, including being willing to use the private sector where public sector bodies such as schools and hospitals were perceived to be 'failing'; it also placed much greater emphasis on the idea of partnerships, and devolved power to Northern Ireland, Scotland and Wales. The Coalition government's attempts to invoke localism and the idea of the Big Society were intended

:o encourage individuals and communities to replace the state in some areas of delivery. And, inevitably, the UK's departure from the EU will have an impact upon the policy process, for example in relation to regulation, a change in the number and nature of power centres at different levels of government, and accountability. The ideas and concepts discussed in Chapters 2 and 3, in particular, are designed to assist in our understanding of how policy is made and implemented in such changing circumstances, and the strengths and weaknesses of different approaches. They highlight the multi-faceted nature of 'power', but can also encourage us to consider the differences between how the world is and how we might like it to be, with some ideas being both normative and analytical, while others may contribute to understanding, for example, why inequalities might continue to exist.

In a complex society and political system, the policy process is also likely to be complicated and untidy, with a wide range of actors and other influences. Building upon such ideas, Chapter 4 identifies a number of additional trends that can be seen as influencing the policy process to greater or lesser extents. Some, such as the tensions between market and non-market mechanisms, may be seen as reflecting very long-term debates, with some degree of toing-and-froing in the acceptance of different perspectives; others, such as the emphasis on 'evidence-based' policy, may be seen as, at least in some respects, more time-specific, for example reflecting New Labour's modernising and Third Way agenda; while the shift to e-government clearly reflects and has been enabled by technological development, although it remains to be seen whether it transforms policy making and implementation to the extent that some advocates suggest it might.

Chapters 5 to 8 focus to a greater degree on the policy process in the United Kingdom, with Chapter 5 concentrating on central government and the resources and powers available to different actors and institutions. It again highlights the complex and fragmented nature of the policy process, including as a result of both internal and external changes in recent decades. It also highlights the apparent concentration of power in some areas among groups who often share a common socio-economic background. Building upon that, Chapter 6 reflects the changing distribution of power 'upwards', towards the EU from the 1970s, at least until the referendum decision that the United Kingdom should leave, and some of the impacts that has had on the policy process at EU and UK government levels. It also notes that, despite Brexit, supra-national organisations, including potentially the EU in some policy areas, will continue to influence the policy agenda and even policies themselves in the UK. At the same time, since 1997, the devolution of power 'downwards' to Northern Ireland, Scotland and Wales has seen responsibility for many policy areas shift from Westminster to Belfast, Edinburgh and Cardiff, and this is perhaps best seen as an ongoing process, rather than as fixed points.

The discussion in Chapter 7 of arm's-length government reflects the continuing significance of unelected bodies in the policy process in the United Kingdom. While principled arguments in favour of and against such organisations can be made, their usefulness to governments, and indeed in some respects to the public, means that they are likely to remain an important, albeit continually contested, part of the system. On broadly similar lines, while Chapter 8 makes clear that it can certainly be argued that evaluation should play a central part in the policy process, the challenges associated with integrating evaluation into policy making and implementation, and the political uses to which it will inevitably be put, mean that the incentives for governments to do so are, at best, mixed, and that they are likely to continue to be selective in those policies and programmes that are evaluated, and in their judgements about them.

Finally, this book has made clear that there are considerable inequalities in the abilities of different individuals and groups to influence and exercise power. That is perhaps not news, although the increasing inequality in terms of income and wealth in recent years, for example, has been greater than for most of the post-war period, and arguably is one obvious symptom (and indeed outcome) of inequalities of power. Wherever there is a struggle for resources that are not available in sufficient quantity or quality for those who need or desire them, there will be disputes. Similarly, there will be disagreements about the values that underpin the distribution of goods and services. Much of the study of the policy process is therefore concerned with the interaction between issues, actors, institutions and society. In addition, there is a wide variety of concepts, including democracy, participation and individual freedom, that might be seen as valuable in underpinning the policy process, and those, and the ways in which they are interpreted, are likely to have a significant impact on the selection, development, implementation and evaluation of policies, and thus on the outcomes experienced by individuals and society. However, given such imbalances of power, it may be argued that there is a need to consider the extent to which they are justifiable, and whether it is possible to rebalance power to some extent, for example by creating greater democratic control and additional opportunities for influence over the institutions and organisations that make decisions and provide services, and a greater emphasis on processes that allow for bottom-up and inclusive policy making, accountability and evaluation, with the concept of 'citizenship' including not just notions of rights and responsibilities, but also participation and the ability to be involved at all levels of decision making.

Bibliography

6, P. (2015) 'If governance is everything, maybe it's nothing', in Massey, A. and Johnston, K. (eds) *The International Handbook of Public Administration and Governance*, Cheltenham: Edward Elgar, 56–80.

Alaszewski, A. and Brown, P. (2012) *Making Health Policy: A Critical Introduction*, Cambridge: Polity.

Althusser, L. (1971) *Lenin and Philosophy and Other Essays*, London: New Left Books.

Amenta, E. and Skocpol, T. (1989) 'Taking exception: explaining the distinctiveness of American public policies in the last century', in Castles, F. G. (ed.) *The Comparative History of Public Policy*, Cambridge: Polity, 292–333.

Anderson, J. E. (1997) *Public Policymaking: An Introduction*, Boston: Houghton Mifflin.

Andrews, R. and Ashworth, R. (2013) 'Determinants of representation: an empirical assessment of the UK civil service', *Policy and Politics*, 43(3), 429–448.

Arnstein, S. R. (1969) 'A ladder of citizen participation', *Journal of the American Institute of Planners*, 35(4), 216–224.

Ashworth, R., Boyne, G. A. and Walker, R. M. (2002) 'Regulatory problems in the public sector: theories and cases', *Policy and Politics*, 30(2), 195–211.

Audit Scotland (2013) *Improving Community Planning in Scotland*, Edinburgh: Audit Scotland.

Bach, S. and Kessler, I. (2011) *The Modernisation of Public Services and Employment Relations*, Basingstoke: Palgrave.

Bachrach, P. and Baratz, M. (1963) 'Decisions and nondecisions: an analytical framework', *American Political Science Review*, 57(3), 641–651.

Bachrach, P. and Baratz, M. (1970) *Power and Poverty: Theory and Practice*, New York: Oxford University Press.

Baggott, R. (1995) *Pressure Groups Today*, Manchester: Manchester University Press.

Baggott, R. (2011) *Public Health: Policy and Politics*, Basingstoke: Palgrave Macmillan.

Baird, J., Issacs, T., Johnson, S., Stobart, G., Yu, G., Sprague, T. and Daugherty, R. (2011) *Policy Effects of PISA*, Oxford: Oxford University Centre for Educational Assessments.

Ball, S. J. (2008) 'New philanthropy, new networks and new governance in education', *Political Studies*, 56(4), 747–765.

Ball, S. J. (2009) 'Privatising education, privatising education policy, privatising educational research: network governance and the competition state', *Journal of Education Policy*, 42(1), 83–99.

Ball, S. J. and Junemann, C. (2012) *Networks, New Governance and Education*, Bristol: Policy Press.

Bannister, J. and O'Sullivan, A. (2014) 'Evidence and the antisocial behaviour cycle', *Evidence & Policy*, 10(1), 77–92.

Barber, A. (2015) *How to Run a Government: So that Citizens Benefit and Taxpayers Don't Go Crazy*, London: Allen Lane.

Barker, K. (2004) *Review of Housing Supply – Delivering Stability: Securing our Future Housing Needs*, London: The Stationery Office.

Barnett, M. (2016) 'Accountability and global governance: the view from paternalism', *Regulation and Governance*, 10(2), 134–148.

Barrett, S. and Fudge, C. (1981) *Policy and Action*, London: Methuen.

Bate, P. and Robert, G. (2003) 'Where next for policy evaluation? Insights from researching National Health Service modernisation', *Policy and Politics*, 31(2), 249–262.

Baumgartner, G. and Jones, B. (1993) *Agendas and Instability in American Politics*, Chicago: University of Chicago Press.

Baumgartner, G. and Jones, B. (2009) *Agendas and Instability in American Politics*, Chicago: University of Chicago Press.

BBC News (2016) 'In full: Iain Duncan Smith resignation letter', http://www.bbc.co.uk/news/uk-politics-35848891 [accessed 13 April 2016].

Beetham, D., Byrne, I., Ngan, P. and Weir, S. (2002) *Democracy Under Blair: A Democratic Audit of the United Kingdom*, London: Politico's.

Bellamy, C. A. (2009) 'Managing ICTs in public sector organizations', in Bovaird, T. and Loeffler, E. (eds) *Public Management and Governance*, London: Routledge, 135–149.

Bellamy, C. and Campbell, D. (2016) 'Digital technology, information policy and social media in public services', in Bovaird, T. and Loeffler, E. (eds) *Public Management and Government*, London: Routledge, 134–147.

Benn, T. (1988) *Office without Power: Diaries, 1968–72*, London: Hutchinson.

Bennett, C. (1991) 'What is policy convergence and what causes it?', *British Journal of Political Science*, 21(2), 215–233.

Benton, M. and Russell, M. (2013) 'Assessing the influence of parliamentary oversight committees: the select committees in the British House of Commons', *Parliamentary Affairs*, 66(4), 772–797.

Berman, S. (1998) *The Social Democratic Moment: Ideas and Politics in the Making of Interwar Europe*, Cambridge: Harvard University Press.

Berry, F. S. and Berry, W. D. (2014) 'Innovation and diffusion models in policy research', in Sabatier, P. A. and Weible, C. M. (eds) *Theories of the Policy Process*, Boulder: Westview, 307–359.

Billis, D. (1984) *Welfare Bureaucracies: Their Design and Change in Response to Social Problems*, London: Heinemann.

Birch, A. H. (1993) *The Concepts and Theories of Modern Democracy*, London: Routledge.

Birkland, T. A. (2011) *An Introduction to the Policy Process*, New York: M. E. Sharpe.

Birrell, D. and Gray, A. M. (2016) 'Social policy, the devolved administrations and the UK coalition government', in Bochel, H. and Powell, M. (eds) *The Coalition Government and Social Policy*, Bristol: Policy Press, 325–346.

Black Report (1980) *Inequalities in Health*, London: Department of Health and Social Security.

Bloch, A. and Solomos, J. (eds) (2010) *Race and Ethnicity in the 21st Century*, Basingstoke: Palgrave.

Block, F. (1987) *Revising State Theory: Essays in Politics and Postindustrialism*, Philadelphia: Temple University Press.

Blondel, J. (1987) *Political Leadership: Towards a General Analysis*, London: Sage.

Boaz, A. and Nutley, S. (2016) 'Evidence-based policy and practice', in Bovaird, T. and Loeffler, E. (eds) *Public Management and Governance*, London: Routledge, 376–392.

Bochel, C. (2006) 'New Labour: participation and the policy process', *Public Policy and Administration*, 21(4), 10–22.

Bochel, C. (2016) 'The changing governance of social policy', in Bochel, H. and Powell, M. (eds) *The Coalition Government and Social Policy*, Bristol: Policy Press, 53–77.

Bochel, C. and Bochel, H. (2010) 'Local political leadership and the modernisation of local government', *Local Government Studies*, 36(6), 723–737.

Bochel, C. and Bochel, H. (2016), '"Reaching in"? The potential for e-petitions in local government in the United Kingdom', *Information, Communication and Society*, 20(5), 683–699.

Bochel, C. and Evans, A. (2007) 'Inclusive policy making', in Bochel, H. and Duncan, S. (eds) *Making Policy in Theory and Practice*, Bristol: Policy Press, 105–123.

Bochel, C., Bochel, H., Somerville, P. and Worley, C. (2008) 'Marginalised or enabled voices? "User participation" in policy and practice', *Social Policy and Society*, 7(2), 201–210.

Bochel, H. (1992) *Parliament and Welfare Policy*, Aldershot: Ashgate.

Bochel, H. and Defty, A. (2010) 'A question of expertise: the House of Lords and welfare policy', *Parliamentary Affairs*, 63(1), 66–84.

Bochel, H. and Duncan, S. (eds) (2007) *Making Policy in Theory and Practice*, Bristol: Policy Press.

Bochel, H. and Powell, M. (eds) (2016) *The Coalition Government and Social Policy*, Bristol: Policy Press.

Booker, C. and North, R. (2007) *Scared to Death: From BSE to Global Warming: Why Scares Are Costing Us the Earth*, London: Continuum.

Boswell, C. and Rodriguez, E. (2016) 'Policies, politics and organisational problems: multiple streams and the implementations of targets in UK government', *Policy and Politics*, 44(4), 507–524.

Bouckaert, G. and van Dooren, W. (2016) 'Performance measurement and management in public sector organizations', in Bovaird, T. and Loeffler, E. (eds) *Public Management and Governance*, London: Routledge, 148–161.

Bovaird, T. and Klijn, E.-H. (2016) 'Partnership working across public and private sectors', in Bovaird, T. and Loeffler, E. (eds) *Public Management and Governance*, London: Routledge, 236–249.

Bovaird, T. and Loeffler, E (2016a) 'Quality management in public sector organizations', in Bovaird, T. and Loeffler, E. (eds) *Public management and governance*, London: Routledge, 162–177.

Bovaird, T. and Loeffler, E. (2016b) 'Understanding public management and governance', in Bovaird, T. and Loeffler, E. (eds) *Public Management and Governance*, London: Routledge, 3–13.

Bovens, M. and 't Hart, P. (1996) *Understanding Policy Fiascoes*, New Brunswick: Transaction.

Bovens, M. 't Hart, P., and Peters, B. G. (eds) (2001) *Success and Failure in Comparative Governance: A Comparative Analysis*, Cheltenham: Edward Elgar.

Boyle, D. (2013) *Good Choice, Bad Choice: The Barriers to Choice Review*, London: Cabinet Office.

Boyle, D. and Harris M. (2009) *The Challenge of Co-production*, London: NESTA.

Boyne, G. (2002) 'Public and private management: what's the difference?', *Journal of Management Studies*, 39(1), 97–122.

British Medical Association (2012) *Behaviour Change, Public Health and the Role of the State – BMA Position Statement*, London: British Medical Association.

Brodkin, E. Z. (2013a) 'Street-level organizations and the welfare state', in Brodkin, E. Z. and Martson, G. (eds) *Work and the Welfare State: Street-Level Organizations and Workfare Politics*, Washington, DC: Georgetown University Press, 17–34.

Brodkin, E. Z. (2013b) 'Work and the welfare state reconsidered: street-level organizations and the global workfare project', Brodkin, E. Z. and Martson, G. (eds) *Work and the Welfare State: Street-Level Organizations and Workfare Politics*, Washington, DC: Georgetown University Press, 271–281.

Brodkin, E. Z. and Marston, G. (2013) *Work and the Welfare State: Street-Level Organizations and Workfare Politics*, Washington, DC: Georgetown University Press.

Brown, C. (2007) 'Tragedy, tragic choices and contemporary international relations theory', *International Relations*, 21(1), 5–13.

Brown, R. G. S. (1971) *The Administrative Process in Britain*, London: Methuen.

Buchanan, J. (1986) *Liberty, Market and State: Political Economy in the 1980s*, Brighton: Wheatsheaf.

Buckingham, H. and Rees, J. (2016) 'The context for service delivery: third sector, state and market relationships 1997–2015', in Rees, J. and Mullins, D. (eds) *The Third Sector Delivering Public Services: Developments, Innovations and Challenges*, Bristol: Policy Press, 41–62.

Bullock, H., Mountford, J. and Stanley, R. (2001) *Better Policy Making*, London: Centre for Management and Policy Studies.

Bulmer, A. and Burch, M. (2009) *The Europeanisation of Whitehall: UK Central Government and the European Union*, Manchester: Manchester University Press.

Burch, M. and Holliday, I. (2005) 'The Blair government and the core executive', *Government and Opposition*, 39(1), 1–21.

Burch, M. and Wood, B. (1990) *Public Policy in Britain*, Oxford: Blackwell.

Burnham, J. and Horton, S. (2013) *Public Management in the United Kingdom: A New Introduction*, Basingstoke: Palgrave Macmillan.

Burnham, J. and Pyper, R. (2008) *Britain's Modernised Civil Service*, Basingstoke: Palgrave Macmillan.

Burns, J. M. (1978) *Leadership*, New York: Harper and Row.

Business, Innovation and Skills Committee (2016) *Employment Practices at Sports Direct*, London: The Stationery Office.

Cabinet Office (1996) *government.direct*, London: The Stationery Office.

Cabinet Office (1999) *Modernising Government*, London: The Stationery Office.

Cabinet Office (2002) *Viewfinder: A Policy Maker's Guide to Public Involvement*, London: Cabinet Office.

Cabinet Office (2008) *Promoting Equality, Valuing Diversity: A Strategy for the Civil Service*, London: Cabinet Office.

Cabinet Office (2009) *Public Bodies 2009*, London: Cabinet Office.

Cabinet Office (2011) *Applying Behavioural Insights to Reduce Fraud, Error and Debt*, London: Cabinet Office.

Cabinet Office (2012a) *Government's Nudge Unit Goes Global*, London: Cabinet Office.

Cabinet Office (2012b) *The Civil Service Reform Plan*, London: Cabinet Office.

Cabinet Office (2013) *What Works: Evidence Centres for Social Policy*, London: Cabinet Office.

Cabinet Office (2015) *Public Bodies 2015*, London: Cabinet Office.

Cabinet Office (2016) *List of Cabinet Committees and Their Members as at 11 April 2016*, London: Cabinet Office.

Cabinet Office Efficiency and Reform Group (2015) *Government Saves £18.6 Billion for Hard Working Taxpayers in 2014 to 2015*, August 13, London: Cabinet Office.

Cabinet Office Strategic Policy Making Team (1999) *Professional Policy Making for the Twenty First Century*, London: Cabinet Office.

Cairney, P. (2012) *Understanding Public Policy: Theories and Issues*, Basingstoke: Palgrave Macmillan.

Cairney, P. (2016) 'The "Scottish approach" to policy and policymaking: what issues are territorial and what are universal?', *Policy and Politics*, 44(3), 333–350.

Cameron, D. (2010) *Letter to Government Departments on Opening Up Data*, London: Cabinet Office.

Cawson, A. and Saunders, P. (1983) 'Corporatism, competitive politics and class struggle', in King, R. (ed.) *Capital and Politics*, London: Routledge and Kegan Paul, 8–27.

Challis, L., Fuller, S., Henwood, M., Klein, R., Plowden, W., Webb, A., Whittingham, P. and Wistow, G. (1988) *Joint Approaches to Social Policy*, Cambridge: Cambridge University Press.

Chester, N. (1979) 'Fringe bodies, quangos and all that', *Public Administration*, 57(1), 51–54.

Clark, A. (1993) *Diaries: In Power 1983–1992*, London: Weidenfeld and Nicholson.

Clarke, J., Gewirtz, S. and McLaughlin, E. (2002) 'Reinventing the welfare state', in Clarke, J., Gewirtz, S. and McLaughlin, E. (eds) *New Managerialism, New Welfare?*, London: Sage, 1–26.

Clarke, N. and Cochrane, A. (2013) 'Geographies and politics of localism: the localism of the United Kingdom's coalition government', *Political Geography*, 34, 10–23.

Cobb, R. W. and Elder, C. E. (1972) *Participation in American Politics: The Dynamics of Agenda-Building*, Baltimore: Johns Hopkins University Press.

Coen, D. and Richardson, J. (2009) *Lobbying the European Union: Institutions, Actors and Issues*, Oxford: Oxford University Press.

Cohen, A. I. (2015) *Philosophy, Ethics and Public Policy*, Abingdon: Routledge.

Cohen, M., March, J. and Olsen, J. (1972) 'A garbage can model of organizational choice', *Administrative Science Quarterly*, 17(1), 1–25.

Cole, A. and John, P. (2001) *Local Governance in England and France*, London: Routledge.

Colebatch, H. (2002) *Policy*, Basingstoke: Palgrave Macmillan.

Coleman, A., Segar, J. and Checkland, K. (2015) 'The devolution project in Greater Manchester: introduction to the special issue', *Representation*, 51(4), 377–384.

Collier, R. B. and Collier, D. (1991) *Shaping the Political Arena: Critical Junctures, the Labour Movement and Regime Dynamics in Latin America*, Princeton: Princeton University Press.

Colomer, J. (2001) *Political Institutions: Democracy and Social Choice*, Oxford: Oxford University Press.

Commission on Public Service Governance and Delivery (2014) *The report of the Commission on Public Service Governance and Delivery*, Cardiff: Commission on Public Service Governance and Delivery.

Commissioner for Public Appointments (2015) *Annual Report 2014–15*, London: Commissioner for Public Appointments.

Commissioner for Public Appointments (2016) *Annual Report 2015–16*, London: Commissioner for Public Appointments.

Committee on Standards in Public Life (1995), *First Report*, London: The Stationery Office.

Conservative Party (2015) *Strong Leadership, A Clear Economic Plan, A Brighter, More Secure Future*, London: Conservative Party.

Cooke, G. and Muir, R. (eds) (2012) *The Relational State*, London: Institute for Public Policy Research.

Copus, C. S. (2013) 'Repoliticising and redemocratising local democracy and the public realm: why we need councillors and councils', *Policy and Politics*, 43(3), 389–408.

Cowley, P. (2002) *Revolts and Rebellions: Parliamentary Voting under Blair*, London: Politico's.

Cowley, P. (2005) *The Rebels: How Blair Mislaid His Majority*, London: Politico's.

Coxall, B. (2001) *Pressure Groups in British Politics*, Harlow: Pearson.

Craig, G., Atkin, K., Chattoo, S. and Flynn, R. (eds) (2012) *Understanding 'Race' and Ethnicity*, Bristol: Policy Press.

Crawshaw, P. (2013) 'Public health policy and the behavioural turn: the case of social marketing', *Critical Social Policy*, 33(4), 616–637.

Crenson, M. A. (1971) *The Unpolitics of Air Pollution: A Study of Non-Decision Making in the Cities*, Baltimore: Johns Hopkins University Press.

Crerar Report (2007) *The Crerar Review: The Report of the Independent Review of Regulation, Audit, Inspection and Complaints Handling of Public Services in Scotland*, Edinburgh: Scottish Government.

Crossman, R. (1975) *The Diaries of a Cabinet Minister. Volume One: Minister of Housing 1964–66*, London: Hamilton and Cape.

Crossman, R. (1976) *The Diaries of a Cabinet Minister. Lord President of the Council, 1966–68 volume 2*, London: Hamish Hamilton.

Crossman, R. (1977) *The Diaries of a Cabinet Minister: Secretary of State for Social Services, 1968–70 volume 3*, London: Hamish Hamilton.

Crown Commercial Service (2015) *A Brief Guide to the EU Public Contracts Directive 2014*, London: Crown Commercial Services.

Culture, Media and Sport Committee (2012) *News International and Phone-hacking*, London: The Stationery Office.

Dahl, R. A. (1957) 'The concept of power', *Behavioral Science*, 2(3), 201–205.

Dahl, R. A. (1961) *Who Governs? Democracy and Power in an American City*, New Haven: Yale University Press.

Dahl, R. A. (1985) *A Preface to Economic Democracy*, Cambridge: Polity.

Dahl, R. A. (1986) 'Rethinking who governs? New Haven revisited', in Waste, R. J. (ed.) *Community Power: Directions for Future Research*, New Haven: Yale University Press, 179–196.

Daily Telegraph (2010) 'A healthy nudge', *The Daily Telegraph*, 1 December.

Davies, H. T. O., Nutley, S. M. and Smith, P. C. (2000a) 'Introducing evidence-based policy and practice in public services', in Davies, H. T. O., Nutley, S. M. and Smith, P. C. (eds) *What works? Evidence-based Policy and Practice in Public Services*, Bristol: Policy Press, 1–11.

Davies, H. T. O., Nutley, S. M. and Tilley, N. (2000b) 'Debates on the role of experimentation', in Davies, H. T. O., Nutley, S. M. and Smith, P. C. (eds) *What Works? Evidence-based Policy and Practice in Public Services*, Bristol: Policy Press, 251–275.

Davies, M. and Woodward, R. (2014) *International Organizations: A Companion*, Cheltenham: Edward Elgar.

Davies, P. (2004) 'Is evidence-based government possible?', Washington DC, Jerry Lee Lecture, 4th Annual Campbell Collaboration Colloquium.

Davis, H. and Martin, S. (2002) 'Evaluating the Best Value pilot programme: measuring "success" and "improvement"', *Local Government Studies*, 28(2), 301–322.

Deacon, B. (2007) *Global Social Policy and Governance*, London: Sage.

Deaner, B. and Phillips, D. (2013) *Government Spending on Public Services in Scotland: Current Patterns and Future Issues*, London: Institute for Fiscal Studies.

della Porta, D. and Dani, M. (2006) *Social Movements*, Oxford: Blackwell.

Department for Communities and Local Government (2015) *Local Authority Revenue Expenditure and Financing: 2015–16 Budget, England*, London: Department for Communities and Local Government.

Department of the Environment, Transport and the Regions (1998) *Modern Local Government: In Touch with the People*, London: The Stationery Office.

DiMaggio, P. J. and Powell, W. W. (1983) 'The iron cage re-visited: institutional isomorphism and collective rationality in organizational fields', *American Sociological Review*, 48(2), 147–160.

Dodds, A. (2013) *Comparative Public Policy*, Basingstoke: Palgrave Macmillan.

Doig, A. (1979) 'The machinery of government and the growth of governmental bodies', *Public Administration*, 57(3), 309–331.

Dolowitz, D. (2000) *Policy Transfer and British Social Policy*, Buckingham: Open University Press.

Dolowitz, D. and Marsh, D. (1996) 'Who learns what from whom: a review of the policy transfer literature', *Political Studies*, 44(2), 343–357.

Dolowitz, D. and Marsh, D. (2000) 'Learning from abroad: the role of policy transfer in contemporary policy making', *Governance*, 13(1), 5–24.

Dolowitz, D. and Marsh, D. (2012) 'The future of policy transfer research', *Political Studies Review*, 10(3), 339–345.

Dommett, K. and Flinders, M. (2015) 'The centre strikes back: meta-governance, delegation, and the core executive in the United Kingdom, 2010–14', *Public Administration*, 93(1), 1–16.

Dommett, K. and MacCarthaigh, M. (2016) 'Quango reform: the next steps?', *Public Money and Management*, 36(4), 249–256.

Dorey, P. (2014) *Policy Making In Britain*, London: Sage.

Dowding, K. (1995) 'Model or metaphor? A critical review of the policy network approach', *Political Studies*, 43(1), 136–158.

Downe, J. and Martin, S. (2007) 'Regulation inside government', *Policy and Politics*, 35(2), 215–232.

Downs, A. (1957) *An Economic Theory of Democracy*, New York: Harper and Row.

Downs, A. (1967) *Inside Bureaucracy*, Boston: Little, Brown and Company.

Downs, A. (1972) 'Up and down with ecology: the issue attention cycle', *Public Interest*, 28(1), 38–50.

Dror, Y. (1964) 'Muddling through – science or inertia?', *Public Administration Review*, 24(3), 153–157.

Dubben, H. and Beck-Bornholdt, S. (2005) 'Systematic review of publication bias in studies on publication bias', *British Medical Journal*, 331, 433.

Duncan, S. (2002) 'Policy discourses on "reconciling work and life" in the EU', *Social Policy and Society*, 1(4), 305–314.

Dunleavy, P. (1985) 'Bureaucrats, budgets and the growth of the state: reconstructing an incremental model', *British Journal of Political Science*, 15(3), 299–328.

Dunleavy, P. (1986) 'Explaining the privatization boom: public choice versus radical approaches', *Public Administration*, 64(1), 13–34.

Dunleavy, P. (1991) *Democracy, Bureaucracy and Public Choice: Economic Explanations in Political Science*, Hemel Hempstead: Harvester Wheatsheaf.

Dunleavy, P. (2016) '"Big data" and policy learning', in Stoker, G. and Evans, M. (eds) *Evidence-based Policymaking in the Social Sciences*, Bristol: Policy Press, 143–167.

Dunlop, C. (2017a) 'Policy learning and policy failure: definitions, dimensions and intersections', *Policy and Politics*, 45(1), 3–18.

Dunlop, C. (2017b) 'Pathologies of policy learning: what are they and how do they contribute to policy failure?', *Policy and Politics*, 45(1), 19–37.

Dunsire, A. (1999) 'Then and now: public administration, 1953–1999', *Political Studies*, 47(2), 360–378.

Durose, C., Justice, J. and Skelcher, C. (2015) 'Governing at arm's length: eroding of enhancing democracy?', *Policy and Politics*, 43(1), 137–153.

Dye, T. R. (1984) *Understanding Public Policy*, Englewood Cliffs: Prentice Hall.

Easton, D. (1953) *The Political System*, New York: Alfred A. Knopf.

Easton, D. (1965) *A Framework for Political Analysis*, Englewood Cliffs: Prentice Hall.

Edelman, M. (1977) *Political Language: Words that Succeed and Policies that Fail*, New York: Academic Press.

Ellis, K. (2015) 'Personalisation and adult social work: recasting professional discretion at the street level?', in Hupe, P., Hill, M. and Buffat, A. (eds) *Understanding Street-Level Bureaucracy*, Bristol: Policy Press, 187–202.

Ellison, N. (2006) *The Transformation of Welfare States?*, London: Routledge.

Elmore, R. (1980) 'Backward mapping: implementation research and policy decisions', *Political Science Quarterly*, 94(4), 601–616.

Engels, F. (1981) *The Origins of the Family, Private Property and the State*, London: Lawrence and Wishart.

Esping-Andersen, G. (1996) *Welfare States in Transition: National Adaptations in Global Economies*, London: Sage.

Etzioni, A. (1967) 'Mixed scanning: a "third" approach to decision making', *Public Administration Review*, 27(5), 385–392.

European Commission (2011) *Digital Agenda: Turning Government Data into Gold*, Brussels: European Commission.

Everett, M. and Falkner, E. (2015) *Special Advisers – House of Commons Library Briefing Paper Number 03813*, London: House of Commons Library.

Exley, S. and Ball, S. J. (2011) 'Something old, something new: understanding Conservative education policy', in Bochel, H. (ed.) *The Conservative Party and Social Policy*, Bristol: Policy Press, 97–117.

Farnham, D. and Horton, S. (1996) 'Managing public and private organisations', in Farnham, D. and Horton, S. (eds) *Managing the New Public Services*, London: Macmillan, 27–52.

Featherstone, D., Ince, A., Mackinnon, D., Strauss, K. and Cumbers, A. (2012) 'Progressive localism and the construction of political alternatives', *Transactions of the Institute of British Geographers*, 37(2), 56–80.

Fenwick, J. and Elcock, H. (2014) 'Elected mayors: leading locally?', *Local Government Studies*, 40(4), 581–599.

Field, F. (1982) *Poverty and Politics: The Inside Story of the CPAG Campaigns in the 1970s*, London: Heinemann.

Finer, S. (1997) *The History of Government*, Oxford: Oxford University Press.

Flinders, M. (2002) 'Governance in Whitehall', *Public Administration*, 80(1), 51–75.

Flinders, M., Dommett, K. and Tonkiss, K. (2014) 'Bonfires and barbecues: coalition governance and the politics of quango reform', *Contemporary British History*, 28(1), 56–80.

Flinders, M. and Geddes, M. (2014) 'The silent revolution: a political history of the politics of patronage and reform', *Contemporary British History*, 28(1), 24–55.

Flinders, M. and Kelso, A. (2011) 'Mind the gap: political analysis, public expectations and the parliamentary decline thesis', *British Journal of Politics and International Relations*, 13(2), 249–268.

Flinders, M. and Skelcher, C. (2012) 'Shrinking the quango state: five challenges in reforming quangos', *Public Money and Management*, 32(5), 327–334.

Flinders, M. and Tonkiss, K. (2015) 'From "poor parenting" to micro-management: coalition governance and the sponsorship of arm's-length bodies in the United Kingdom, 2010–13', *International Review of Administrative Sciences*, 82(3), 490–515.

Flinders, M. and Wood, M. (2015) 'Depoliticisation, governance and the state', in Flinders, M. and Wood, M. (eds) *Tracing the Political: Depoliticisation, Governance and the State*, Bristol: Policy Press, 1–19.

Flynn, N. (2012) *Public Sector Management*, London: Sage.

Forestier, K. and Crossley, M. (2015) 'International education policy transfer – borrowing both ways: the Hong Kong and England experience', *Compare: A Journal of Comparative and International Education*, 45(5), 664–685.

Foucault, M. (1977) *Discipline and Punish*, Harmondsworth: Penguin.

Franco, A., Malhotra, N. and Simonovits, G. (2014) 'Publication bias in the social sciences: unlocking the file drawer', *Science*, 345(6203), 1502–1505.

Franklin, M. and Norton, P. (1993) *Parliamentary Questions*, Oxford: Clarendon Press.

Freeguard, G. (2015) *A Sense of Direction: When Permanent Secretaries Object to Ministerial Decisions*, London: Institute for Government.

Freeguard, G., Andrews, E., Devine, D., Munro, R. and Randall, J. (2015) *Whitehall Monitor 2015: The Coalition in 163 Charts*, London: Institute for Government.

Fulton Committee (1968) *The Civil Service, Vol. 1, Report of the Committee 1966–68*, London: HMSO.

Gains, F. (2004) 'The local bureaucrat: a block to reform or a key to unblocking change', in Stoker, G. and Wilson, D. (eds) *British Local Government into the 21st Century*, Basingstoke: Palgrave Macmillan, 91–104.

Gains, F. (2015) 'Metro mayors: devolution, democracy and the importance of getting "Devo Manc" design right', *Representation*, 51(4), 425–437.

Gains, F. and Stoker, G. (2011) 'Special advisers and the transmission of ideas from the policy primeval soup', *Policy and Politics*, 39(4), 485–498.

Gains, F., Greasley, S., John, P. and Stoker, G. (2007) 'The impact of political leadership on organizational performance: evidence from English urban government', *Local Government Studies*, 35(1), 75–94.

Gamson, W. A. (2015) 'Defining movement "success"', in Goodwin, J. and Jasper, J. M. (eds) *The Social Movements Reader; Cases and Concepts*, Chichester: Wiley Blackwell, 383–433.

Gash, T., Magee, I., Rutter, J. and Smith, N. (2010) *Read Before Burning: Arm's Length Government for a New Administration*, London: Institute for Government.

Gash, T., Panchamia, N., Sims, S. and Hotson, L. (2013) *Making Public Service Markets Work: Professionalising Government's Approach to Commissioning and Market Stewardship*, London: Institute for Government.

Gaventa, J. (1980) *Power and Powerlessness, Quiesence and Rebellion in an Appalachian Valley*, Oxford: Clarendon Press.

Gerston, L. N. (1997) *Public Policy Making: Process and Principles*, New York: M. E. Sharpe.

Gerth, H. H. and Mills, C. W. (1970) *From Max Weber: Essays in Sociology*, London: Routledge and Kegan Paul.

Gibb, K. (2015) 'The multiple policy failures of the UK bedroom tax', *International Journal of Housing Policy*, 15(2), 148–166.

Giddens, A. (2008) *The Third Way: The Renewal of Social Democracy*, Oxford: Polity.

Goldacre, B. (2008) *Bad Science*, London: Fourth Estate.

Gomm, R. (2008) *Social Research Methodology: A Critical Introduction*, Basingstoke: Palgrave Macmillan.

Goodwin, J. and Jasper, J. M. (eds) (2015) *The Social Movements Reader; Cases and Concepts*, Chichester: Wiley Blackwell.

Gough, D. and Tripney, J. (2016) 'Systematic reviews for policy', in Stoker, G. and Evans, M. (eds) *Evidence-based Policy Making in the Social Sciences*, Bristol: Policy Press, 43–67.

Gramsci, A. (1971) *Selections from the Prison Notebooks*, New York: International Publishers.

Grant, W. (1995) *Pressure Groups, Politics and Democracy in Britain*, Hemel Hempstead: Harvester Wheatsheaf.

Grant, W. (2000) *Pressure Groups and British Politics*, Basingstoke: Palgrave Macmillan.

Gray, A. and Jenkins, W. (2002) 'Government and administration: reasserting public services and their consumers', *Parliamentary Affairs*, 55(2), 235–253.

Gray, A. M. and Birrell, D. (2012) 'Coalition government in Northern Ireland: social policy and the lowest common denominator thesis', *Social Policy and Society*, 11(1), 15–25.

Green, J. and South, J. (2006) *Evaluation*, Maidenhead: Open University Press.

Greener, I. (2005) 'The potential of path dependence in political studies', *Politics*, 25(1), 62–72.

Greener, I. (2013) *Public Management*, Basingstoke: Palgrave Macmillan.

Greenwood, J. and Wilson, D. (1989) *Public Administration in Britain Today*, London: Routledge.

Greer, S. L. (2007) 'The fragile divergence machine: citizenship, policy divergence and devolution', in Trench, A. (ed.) *Devolution and Power in the United Kingdom*, Manchester: Manchester University Press, 136–159.

Grin, J. and Loeber, A. (2007) 'Theories of policy learning: agency, structure and change', in Fischer, F., Miller, G. D. and Sidney, M. S. (eds) *Handbook of Public Policy Analysis*, London: Taylor & Francis, 201–219.

Gunn, L. (1978) 'Why is implementation so difficult?', *Management Services in Government*, 33(4), 169–176.

HM Treasury (1979) *The Government's Expenditure Plans 1980–81*, London: HMSO.

HM Treasury (2011) *The Magenta Book*, London: The Stationery Office.

HM Treasury (2013) *The Green Book: Appraisal and Evaluation in Central Government*, London: The Stationery Office.

Ha, E. (2008) 'Globalization, veto players, and welfare spending', *Comparative Political Studies*, 41(6), 783–812.

Habermas, J. (1984a) *The Theory of Communicative Action, Volume One: Reason and the Rationalization of Society*, Cambridge: Polity.

Habermas, J. (1984b) *The Theory of Communicative Action, Volume Two: The Critique of Functionalist Reason*, Cambridge: Polity.

Hall, P. A. (1986) *Governing the Economy: The Politics of State Intervention in Britain and France*, Cambridge: Polity.

Hall, P. A. (1993) 'Policy paradigms, social learning and the state', *Comparative Politics*, 25(3), 275–296.

Hall, W. and Weir, S. (1996) *The Untouchables: Power and Accountability in the Quango State*, London: Democratic Audit/Scarman Trust.

Hallsworth, S. with Parker, S. and Rutter, J. (2011) *Policy Making in the Real World: Evidence and Analysis*, London: Institute for Government.

Halpern, D., Bates, C., Mulgan, G. and Aldridge, S. with Beales, G. and Heathfield, A. (2004) *Personal Responsibility and Changing Behaviour: The State of Knowledge and Its Implications for Public Policy*, London: Prime Minister's Strategy Unit.

Ham C. and Hill, M. (1984) *The Policy Process in the Modern Capitalist State*, Brighton: Wheatsheaf.

Harrison, S. (2015) 'Street-level bureaucracy and professionalism in health services', in Hupe, P., Hill, M. and Buffat, A. (eds) *Understanding Street-Level Bureaucracy*, Bristol: Policy Press, 61–77.

Harrison, S., Hunter, D. J. and Pollitt, C. (1990) *The Dynamics of British Health Policy*, London: Unwin Hyman.

Harrison, S., Moran, M. and Wood, B. (2002) 'Policy emergence and policy convergence: the case of scientific-bureaucratic medicine in the USA and UK', *British Journal of Politics and International Relations*, 4(1), 1–24.

Hartley, J. and Benington, J. (2011) 'Political leadership', in Bryman, A., Collinson, D., Grint, K., Jackson, B. and Uhl-Bien, M. (eds) *The Sage Handbook of Leadership*, Los Angeles: Sage, 203–214.

Hathaway, T. (2016) 'Lukes reloaded: an actor-centred three-dimensional power framework', *Politics*, 36(2), 118–130.

Hawkins, B. and Holden, C. (2014) 'Water dripping on stone? Industry lobbying and UK alcohol policy', *Policy and Politics*, 42(1), 55–70.

Hay, C. (1999) 'Crisis and the structural transformation of the state: interrogating the process of change', *British Journal of Political Science and International Relations*, 1(3), 317–344.

Hay, C. (2002) *Political Analysis*, Basingstoke: Palgrave.

Hay, C. (2008) 'Globalization and public policy', in Goodin, R. R., Moran, M. and Rein, M. (eds) *The Oxford Handbook of Public Policy*, Oxford: Oxford University Press, 587–604.

Hayden, C. and Jenkins, C. (2014) '"Troubled families" programme in England: "wicked problems" and policy-based evidence', *Policy Studies*, 35(6), 631–649.

Head, B. W. (2008) 'Three lenses of evidence-based policy', *Australian Journal of Public Administration*, 67(1), 1–11.

Head, B. W. (2016) 'Toward more "evidence-informed" policy making?', *Public Administration Review*, 76(3), 472–484.

Health Committee (2011) *Public Health*, London: The Stationery Office.

Health Committee (2016) *Impact of the Spending Review on Health and Social Care*, London: The Stationery Office.

Heclo, H. (1974) *Modern Social Politics in Britain and Sweden*, New Haven: Yale University Press.

Held, D. M. (1999) *Global Transformations: Politics, Economics and Culture*, Cambridge: Polity Press.

Heffernan, R. (2002) '"The possible as the art of politics": understanding consensus politics', *Political Studies*, 50(4) 742–760.

Hellowell, M. and Pollock, A. (2009) 'Non-profit distribution: the Scottish approach to private finance in public services', *Social Policy and Society*, 8(3), 405–418.

Helms, L. (2012) 'Introduction: the importance of studying leadership comparatively', in Helms, L. (ed.) *Comparative Political Leadership*, Basingstoke: Palgrave Macmillan, 1–24.

Herman, E. and Chomsky, N. (1988) *Manufacturing Consent: The Political Economy of the Mass Media*, New York: Pantheon.

Hetherington, P. (2015) 'On social housing, Tory ideology trumps all evidence', *The Guardian*, 23 September, https://www.theguardian.com/society/2015/sep/23/social-housing-tory-ideology-trumps-evidence-housing-associations [accessed 16 October 2016].

Hickman, M. (2011) 'Nudge, nudge, wink wink... how the government wants to change the way we think', *The Independent*, 3 January, http://www.independent.co.uk/news/uk/politics/nudge-nudge-wink-wink-how-the-government-wants-to-change-the-way-we-think-2174655.html [accessed 4 May 2017].

Hill, M. (1997a) 'Implementation: introduction', in Hill, M. (ed.) *The Policy Process: A Reader*, Hemel Hempstead: Prentice Hall, 213–215.

Hill, M. (1997b) *The Policy Process in the Modern State*, Hemel Hempstead: Prentice Hall.

Hill, M. (2009) *The Public Policy Process*, Harlow: Longman.

Hill, M. and Bramley, G. (1986) *Analysing Social Policy*, Oxford: Blackwell.

Hill, M. and Hupe, P. (2002) *Implementing Public Policy*, London: Sage.

Hindmoor, A. L. (2006) 'Public choice' in Hay, C., Lister, M. and Marsh, D. (eds) *The State: Theories and Issues*, Basingstoke: Palgrave Macmillan, 79–97.

Hindmoor, A. L., Larkin, P. and Kennon, S. (2009) 'Assessing the influence of select committees in the UK: the Education and Skills Committee, 1997–2005', *Journal of Legislative Studies*, 15(1), 71–89.

Hirschman, A. O. (1970) *Exit, Voice and Loyalty: Responses to Decline in Firms, Organisations and States*, Cambridge: Harvard University Press.

Hirst, P. and Thompson, G. (1995) 'Globalization and the future of the nation state', *Economy and Society*, 24(3), 408–442.

Hirst, P. and Thompson, G. (1999) *Globalization in Question*, Cambridge: Polity.

Hirst, P., Thompson, G. and Bromley, S. (2009) *Globalization in Question*, Cambridge, Polity.

Hobbs, S. and Hamerton, C. (2014) *The Making of Criminal Justice Policy*, London: Routledge.

Hogwood, B. W. (1995) 'The "growth" of quangos', in Ridley, F. F. (ed.) *The Quango Debate*, Oxford: Oxford University Press, 29–47.

Hogwood, B. W. and Gunn, L. (1984) *Policy Analysis for the Real World*, Oxford: Oxford University Press.

Hogwood, B. and Peters, B. G. (1983) *Policy Dynamics*, Brighton: Wheatsheaf.

Holzinger, K. and Knill, C. (2005) 'Causes and conditions of cross-national policy convergence', *Journal of European Public Policy*, 12(5), 775–796.

Home Affairs Committee (2008) *A Surveillance Society?*, London: The Stationery Office.

Home Office (2004a) *Facilitating Community Involvement: Practical Guidance for Practitioners and Policy Makers*, London: Home Office.

Home Office (2004b) *The Government's Framework for Community Capacity Building*, London: Home Office.

Hood, C. (1976) *The Limits of Administration*, London: Wiley.

Hood, C. (1983) *The Tools of Government*, London: Macmillan.

Hood, C. (1991) 'A public management for all seasons', *Public Administration*, 69(1) 3–19.

Hood, C. (2006) 'Gaming in target world: the targets approach to managing British public services', *Public Administration Review*, 66(4), 515–521.

House of Commons Library (2010) *Key Issues for the New Parliament 2010*, London: House of Commons Library.

House of Commons Library (2014) *Privatisation: Research Paper 14/61, 20 November 2014*, London: House of Commons Library.

House of Commons Library (2016a) *Devolution to Local Government in England 2014–2016*, London: House of Commons.

House of Commons Library (2016b) *Social Background of MPs 1979–2015, Briefing Paper Number CBP 7483*, London: House of Commons.

House of Lords Science and Technology Select Committee (2011) *Behaviour Change*, London: The Stationery Office.

House of Lords Select Committee on the Constitution (2014) *Constitutional Implications of Coalition Government*, London: The Stationery Office.

Howlett, M. (2000) 'Managing the "hollow state": procedural policy instruments and modern governance', *Canadian Public Administration*, 3(4), 412–431.

Howlett, M. (2011) *Designing Public Policies: Principles and Instruments*, Abingdon: Routledge.

Howlett, M. Ramesh. M. and Perl, A. (2009) *Studying Public Policy: Policy Cycles and Policy Subsystems*, Don Mills: Oxford University Press.

Hudson, J. and Lowe, S. (2009) *Understanding the Policy Process: Analysing Welfare Policy and Practice*, Bristol: Policy Press.

Hughes, O. E. (2012) *Public Management and Administration*, Basingstoke: Palgrave Macmillan.

Hull, C. J. and Hjern, B. (1987) *Helping Small Firms Grow: An Implementation Perspective*, London: Croom Helm.

Hupe, P., Hill, M. and Buffat, A. (2015) 'Introduction: defining and understanding street-level bureaucracy', in Hupe, P., Hill, M. and Buffat, A. (eds) *Understanding Street-Level Bureaucracy*, Bristol: Policy Press, 3–24.

Ibbs, R. (1988) *Improving Management in Government: The Next Steps*, London: HMSO.

Immergut, E. M. (1990) 'Institutions, veto points and policy results: a comparative analysis of health care', *Journal of Public Policy*, 10(4), 391–416.

Immergut, E. M. (2008) 'Institutional constraints on policy', in Goodin, R. R., Moran, M. R. and Rein, M. (eds) *The Oxford Handbook of Public Policy*, Oxford: Oxford University Press, 557–571.

Ingold, J. and Monaghan, M. (2016) 'Evidence translation: an exploration of policy makers' use of evidence', *Policy and Politics*, 44(2), 171–190.

Institute for Government (2012) *The Development of Quasi-markets in Secondary Education*, London: Institute for Government.

Institute for Government (2015) *Whitehall Monitor 2015*, London: Institute for Government.

Jack, I. (2016) 'There are several metropolitan elites. But the same one still pulls the strings', *The Guardian*, 15 October.

James, O. and Lodge, M. (2003) 'The limitations of "policy transfer" and "lesson drawing" for public policy research', *Political Studies Review*, 1(2), 179–193.

James, O., Moseley, A., Petrovsky, N. and Boyne, G. (2011) 'United Kingdom', in Verhoest, K., van Thiel, S., Bouckaert, G. and Laegreid, P. (eds) *Government Agencies: Practices and Lessons from 30 Countries*, Basingstoke: Palgrave Macmillan, 57–68.

Jenkins, W. (1978) *Policy Analysis*, London: Martin Robertson.

Jenkins, W. (1982) 'The case of non-decisions', in McGrew, A. G. and Wilson, M. J. (eds) *Decision Making: Approaches and Analysis*, Manchester: Manchester University Press, 318–326.

Jenkins-Smith, H. C. and Sabatier, P. A. (1993) 'The study of public policy processes', in Sabatier, P. A. and Jenkins-Smith, H. C. (eds) *Policy Change and Learning: An Advocacy Coalition Approach*, Boulder: Westview Press, 1–9.

Jenkins-Smith, H. C., Nohrstedt, D., Weible, C. M. and Sabatier, P. A. (2014) 'The advocacy coalition framework: foundations, evolution and ongoing research', in Sabatier, P. A. and Weible, C. M. (eds) *Theories of the Policy Process*, Boulder: Westview Press, 183–223.

Jessop, B. (2007) *State Power: A Strategic-Relational Approach*, Cambridge: Polity.

John, P. (2009) 'Can citizen governance redress the representative bias of political participation?', *Public Administration Review*, 69(3), 494–503.

John, P. (2011) *Making Policy Work*, London: Routledge.

John, P. (2012) *Analyzing Public Policy*, London: Routledge.

John, P. (2014) 'The great survivor: the persistence and resilience of English local government', *Local Government Studies*, 40(5), 687–704.

John, P. (2016) 'Randomised controlled trials', in Stoker, G. and Evans, M. (eds) *Evidence-based Policy Making in the Social Sciences: Methods that Matter*, Bristol: Policy Press, 69–82.

John, P., Cotterill, S., Moseley, A., Richardson, L., Smith, G., Stoker, G. and Wales, C. (2013.) *Nudge, Nudge, Think, Think: Experimenting with Ways to Change Civic Behaviour*, London: Bloomsbury.

John, P. and Jennings, W. (2010) 'Punctuations and turning points in British politics: the policy agenda of the Queen's Speech', *British Journal of Political Science*, 40(3), 561–586.

Johnstone, D. (2013) *Squaring the Circle: Evidence at the Local Level*, London: Alliance for Useful Evidence.

Joint Committee on House of Lords Reform (2002) *House of Lords Reform: First Report*, London: The Stationery Office.

Jones, B., Kavanagh, D., Moran, M. and Norton, P. (2001) *Politics UK*, Harlow: Longman.

Jordan, A., Wurzel, R. and Zito, A. (2003) '"New" instruments of environmental governance: patterns and pathways of change', *Environmental Politics*, 12(1), 1–24.

Jordan, G. (1994) *The British Administrative System: Principles Versus Practice*, London: Routledge.

Jordan, W. (1985) *The State: Authority and Autonomy*, Oxford: Basil Blackwell.

Judge, D. (2005) *Political Institutions in the United Kingdom*, Oxford: Oxford University Press.

Kassim, H. (1994) 'Policy networks, networks, and European Union policy making: a sceptical view', *West European Politics*, 17(1), 15–27.

Kassim, H. and Le Galés, P. (2010) 'Exploring governance in a multi-level polity: a policy instruments approach', *West European Politics*, 33(1), 1–21.

Kemshall, H. and Wood, J. with Westwood, S., Stout, B., Wilkinson, B., Kelly, G. and Mackenzie, G. (2010) *Child Sex Offender Review (ICSOR) Public Disclosure Pilots: A Process Evaluation*, 2nd edition, Research Report 32, London: Home Office.

Keohane, R. O. and Nye, J. S. (1987) 'Power and interdependence revisited', *International Organization*, 41(4), 725–753.

Keohane, R. O. and Nye, J. S. (1997) *Power and Interdependence*, Boston: Little, Brown and Company.